The Fourth Gospel and the Manufacture of Minds in Ancient Historiography, Biography, Romance, and Drama

Biblical Interpretation Series

Editors-in-Chief

Paul Anderson (*George Fox University*)
Jennifer L. Koosed (*Albright College, Reading*)

Editorial Board

A. K. M. Adam (*University of Oxford*)
Colleen M. Conway (*Seton Hall University*)
Nijay Gupta (*Portland Seminary*)
Amy Kalmanofsky (*Jewish Theological Seminary*)
Vernon Robbins (*Emory University*)
Annette Schellenberg (*Universität Wien*)
Johanna Stiebert (*University of Leeds*)
Duane Watson (*Malone University*)
Christine Roy Yoder (*Columbia Theological Seminary*)
Ruben Zimmermann (*Johannes Gutenberg-Universität Mainz*)

VOLUME 173

The titles published in this series are listed at *brill.com/bins*

The Fourth Gospel and the Manufacture of Minds in Ancient Historiography, Biography, Romance, and Drama

By

Tyler Smith

BRILL

LEIDEN | BOSTON

Library of Congress Cataloging-in-Publication Data

Names: Smith, Tyler (Tyler James), author.
Title: The fourth Gospel and the manufacture of minds in ancient
    historiography, biography, romance, and drama / by Tyler Smith.
Description: Leiden ; Boston : Brill, [2019] | Series: Biblical
    interpretation series, ISSN 0928-0731 ; volume 173 | "This book is a
    revision of my 2016 PhD dissertation"—Author's acknowledgements. |
    Includes bibliographical references and index. |
Identifiers: LCCN 2019003770 (print) | LCCN 2019008298 (ebook) |
    ISBN 9789004396043 (E-book) | ISBN 9789004396036 (hardback : alk. paper) |
    ISBN 9789004396043 (ebk.)
Subjects: LCSH: Bible. John—Criticism, Form. | Bible. John—Criticism,
    interpretation, etc.
Classification: LCC BS2615.52 (ebook) | LCC BS2615.52 .S6555 2019 (print) |
    DDC 226.5/066—dc23
LC record available at https://lccn.loc.gov/2019003770

Typeface for the Latin, Greek, and Cyrillic scripts: "Brill". See and download: brill.com/brill-typeface.

ISSN 0928-0731
ISBN 978-90-04-39603-6 (hardback)
ISBN 978-90-04-39604-3 (e-book)

Copyright 2019 by Koninklijke Brill NV, Leiden, The Netherlands.
Koninklijke Brill NV incorporates the imprints Brill, Brill Hes & De Graaf, Brill Nijhoff, Brill Rodopi,
Brill Sense, Hotei Publishing, mentis Verlag, Verlag Ferdinand Schöningh and Wilhelm Fink Verlag.
All rights reserved. No part of this publication may be reproduced, translated, stored in a retrieval system,
or transmitted in any form or by any means, electronic, mechanical, photocopying, recording or otherwise,
without prior written permission from the publisher.
Authorization to photocopy items for internal or personal use is granted by Koninklijke Brill NV provided
that the appropriate fees are paid directly to The Copyright Clearance Center, 222 Rosewood Drive,
Suite 910, Danvers, MA 01923, USA. Fees are subject to change.

This book is printed on acid-free paper and produced in a sustainable manner.

Contents

Acknowledgements   VII
Abbreviations   VIII
Introduction   XIII

1 **Genre, Characterization, and Cognition**   1
   1 Genre Recognition and Character Cognition   1
   2 Real and Fictional Minds   3
   3 John, Genre, and Cognitive Narratology in Modern Literary Criticism   5
   4 Characterization and Cognition in Ancient Literary Criticism   14

2 **Historiography: Investigative Speculation and Cognitive Causation**   28
   1 John and Historiography   29
   2 Representing Minds in Greek and Roman Historiography   32
   3 Polybius's *Histories*   40
   4 Josephus's *Jewish Antiquities*   52
   5 Conclusion   69

3 **Βίος: Ethics and Mimesis**   71
   1 John and Βίος   71
   2 Conventions for Representing Minds in Βίοι   75
   3 Plutarch, the Parallel Lives, and the Conventions of a Genre   80
   4 Plutarch's *Life of Solon*   92
   5 Philo's *Life of Moses*   102
   6 Conclusion   114

4 **Romance: Thwarted Recognitions and the Πάθη Ποικίλα**   115
   1 John and Romance   116
   2 Conventions for Representing Minds in the Novels   120
   3 Chariton's *Callirhoe*   133
   4 *Aseneth*   153
   5 Conclusion   165

5 **Drama: Discrepant Awareness and Dramatic Irony**   166
   1 John and Drama   167
   2 Conventions for Representing Minds in Drama   179
   3 Euripides's *Hippolytus*   187
   4 Ezekiel the Tragedian's *Exagoge*   195
   5 Conclusion   206

6 Genre, Innovation, and Johannine Characterization 208

1 Historiography 208
2 Βίος 218
3 Romance 227
4 Drama 237
5 Conclusion 248

Epilogue 249

Bibliography 253
Index of Ancient Texts 280
Index of Modern Authors 296
Index of Subjects 301

Acknowledgements

This book is a revision of my 2016 PhD dissertation, completed under the auspices of Yale University's Department of Religious Studies. I am grateful for the opportunity here to publicly acknowledge some of the many debts I incurred in bringing this text to print.

For institutional and financial support, I would like to thank the Yale University Graduate School of Arts and Sciences, Yale Divinity School, Aarhus University School of Culture and Society, and the Social Sciences and Research Council of Canada.

For academic and professional development opportunities, I am grateful to Yale University's Department of Religious Studies, the Yale Center for Teaching and Learning, the Society of Biblical Literature, and the Canadian Society of Biblical Studies.

For stimulating conversations and kindnesses great and small, I thank Paul Anderson, Sonja Anderson, Sune Auken, Eve-Marie Becker, Christopher Beeley, Dylan Burns, John Collins, Matthew Croasmun, Kati Curts, Elizabeth Davidson, Stephen Davis, Michal Beth Dinkler, David Eastman, Mary Farag, Emily Greenwood, Judith Gundry, Christina Harker, Christine Hayes, Jeremy Hultin, Ryan Knowles, Paul Kolbet, Kasper Bro Larsen, Matthew Larsen, Richard Last, Bentley Layton, Pauline LeVen, Stéphanie Machabée, Dale Martin, Wayne Meeks, Hugo Mendez, Nick Meyer, Yoni Moss, Dan Nässelqvist, Hindy Najman, Chan Sok Park, Jonathan Pomeranz, Adele Reinhartz, Austin Rivera, Anders Runesson, Sara Ronis, Rachel Scheinerman, Tom Schmidt, Dan Schriever, Zachary Smith, Gregory Sterling, Olivia Stewart, Diana Swancutt, Heather Voorhees, Meredith Warren, and Adela Yarbro Collins. To Harold W. Attridge, who supervised the project from the beginning with grace, wisdom, and patience, I owe an incalculable debt of gratitude.

Last but not least, I am thankful for my family. Gabriella, Hugo, Eddie, and especially Krista have generously encouraged, supported, and indulged me as we have navigated the vicissitudes of real life and a life of the mind these past ten years. As a small token of gratitude, I dedicate this book to them.

Abbreviations

Abbreviations generally follow those recommended in the *SBL Handbook of Style*, 2nd ed. (Atlanta: SBL Press, 2014) and the *Internationales Abkürzungsverzeichnis für Theologie und Grenzgebiete* 3rd ed. (Berlin: De Gruyter, 2013). For titles not found in either guide, abbreviations have been created following the rules on pages xiv–xvi of the latter.

AAWG.PH	Abhandlungen der Akademie der Wissenschaften in Göttingen. Philologisch-historische Klasse
AB	Anchor Bible
ABR	*Australian Biblical Review*
AcBib	Academia Biblica
AGJU/AJEC	Arbeiten zur Geschichte des antiken Judentums und des Urchristentums/Ancient Judaism and Early Christianity
AJP	*American Journal of Philology*
ALGHJ	Arbeiten zur Literatur und Geschichte des hellenistischen Judentums
AmJT	*American Journal of Theology*
AN	*Ancient Narrative*
ANS	Ancient Narrative Supplementa
APACRS	American Philological Association Classical Resources Series
BAGB	*Bulletin de l'Association G. Budé*
BCAW	Blackwell Companions to the Ancient World
BCCS	Brill's Companions in Classical Studies
BGCL	Blackwell Guides to Classical Literature
BibInt	Biblical Interpretation Series
BICW	Blackwell Introductions to the Classical World
BJS	Brown Judaic Studies
BLE	*Bulletin de littérature ecclésiastique*
BMW	Bible in the Modern World
BNJ	*Brill's New Jacoby.* Edited by Felix Jacoby and Ian Worthington. Leiden: Brill, 2012–.
BPCrit	Biblical Performance Criticism
BSGRT	Bibliotheca scriptorum Graecorum et Romanorum Teubneriana
BSMEL	Brill Studies in Middle Eastern Literatures
Budé	Collection des universités de France, publiée sous le patronage de l'Association Guillaume Budé
BzAlt	Beiträge zur Altertumskunde
BZNW	Beihefte zur Zeitschrift für die neutestamentliche Wissenschaft

ABBREVIATIONS

CCSoc	Classical Culture and Society
CCSt	Cambridge Classical Studies
CCTC	Cambridge Classical Texts and Commentaries
CEA	Collection d'études anciennes
CGT	Complete Greek Tragedies
CJA	Christianity and Judaism in Antiquity
CJu	*Les Cahiers du Judaïsme*
ClA	*Classical Antiquity*
ClaHa	Classical Handbooks
ClQ	*The Classical Quarterly*
CLSoc	Classical Literature and Society
CogLin	*Cognitive Linguistics*
CP	*Classical Philology*
CRINT	Compendia rerum iudaicarum ad Novum Testamentum
CStG	Copenhagen Studies in Genre
CTJ	*Calvin Theological Journal*
DNP	*Der neue Pauly: Enzyklopädie der Antike.* Edited by H. Cancik and H. Schneider. Stuttgart: J.B. Metzler, 1996–2003
DRev	*Downside Review*
DSD	*Dead Sea Discoveries*
ECL	Early Christianity and its Literature
EJL	Early Judaism and its Literature
ERFC	*Evphrosyne: Revista de filología clássica*
ETL	*Ephemerides Theologicae Lovanienses*
Exp.	*The Expositor*
ExpTim	*The Expository Times*
FJTC	Flavius Josephus: Translation and Commentary
FN	Frontiers of Narrative
GApPs	Guides to Apocrypha and Pseudepigrapha
GCNov	*Groningen Colloquia on the Novel*
GCRW	Greek Culture in the Roman World
GR	*Greece & Rome*
GRBS	*Greek, Roman, and Byzantine Studies*
HCS	Hellenistic Culture and Society
Hist	*Historia: Zeitschrift für Alte Geschichte*
Hist.E	Historia. Einzelschriften
HSCP	*Harvard Studies in Classical Philology*
HTR	*Harvard Theological Review*
HUSLA	*Hebrew University Studies in Literature and the Arts*
Int	*Interpretation*

JAL	Jewish Apocryphal Literature Series
JBL	*Journal of Biblical Literature*
JH	*Jewish History*
JPICL	The Joan Palevsky Imprint in Classical Literature
JQR	*Jewish Quarterly Review*
JR	*Journal of Religion*
JSJ	*Journal for the Study of Judaism in the Persian, Hellenistic, and Roman Periods*
JSJS	Supplements to the Journal for the Study of Judaism
JSNT	*Journal for the Study of the New Testament*
JSNTSup	Supplements to the Journal for the Study of the New Testament
JSP	*Journal for the Study of the Pseudepigrapha*
JSPSup	Journal for the Study of the Pseudepigrapha: Supplement Series
JTSA	*Journal of Theology for Southern Africa*
LCL	Loeb Classical Library
LEC	Library of Early Christianity
LingBS	Linguistic Biblical Studies
LitTh	*Literature and Theology*
LNTS	Library of New Testament Studies
LXX	Alfred Rahlfs, ed. Septuaginta: Id est vetus testamentum graece iuxta lxx interpretes. 2 vols. Stuttgart: Priviligierte Württembergische Bibelanstalt, 1935
Mn.	*Mnemosyne*
MnS	Mnemosyne: Supplement
MPh	*Modern Philology*
MyPo	Myth and Poetics
NCLS	Nottingham Classical Literature Studies
Neot	*Neotestamentica*
NLitHist	*New Literary History*
NovT	*Novum Testamentum*
NovTSup	Supplements to Novum Testamentum
NPU	Neue philologische Untersuchungen
NSAA	Neue Studien zur Anglistik und Amerikanistik
NTGL	New Testament and Greek Literature
NTL	New Testament Library
NTMon	New Testament Monographs
NTRea	New Testament Readings
NTS	*New Testament Studies*
NTTS	New Testament tools and studies
OACL	Oxford Approaches to Classical Literature

ABBREVIATIONS

OCD	*Oxford Classical Dictionary*. Edited by Simon Hornblower and Antony Spawforth. 4th ed. Oxford: Oxford University Press, 2012.
OCG	The Oratory of Classical Greece
OCM	Oxford Classical Monographs
OED	*Oxford English Dictionary: The Definitive Record of the English Language.* Oxford: Oxford University Press.
ORCS	Oxford Readings in Classical Studies
OTP	*Old Testament Pseudepigrapha*. Edited by James H. Charlesworth. 2 vols. New York: Doubleday, 1983, 1985.
ÖZS	*Österreichische Zeitschrift für Soziologie*
Ph.	*Philologus*
PhAnt	Philosophia antiqua
PhMon	Philological Monographs
PMLA	*Publication of the Modern Language Association of America*
PSNBSF	Paul's Social Network: Brothers and Sisters in Faith
PVTG	Pseudepigrapha Veteris Testamenti Graece
PW	Pauly, A. F. *Paulys Realencyclopädie der classischen Altertumswissenschaft.* New edition G. Wissowa. 49 vols.
QJSp	Quarterly Journal of Speech
RCLec	Robson Classical Lectures
SAC	Studies in Antiquity and Christianity
SANt	Studia Aarhusiana Neotestamentica
SBB	Stutgarter biblische Beiträge
SBLDS	Society of Biblical Literature Dissertation Series
SBLSP	Society of Biblical Literature Seminar Papers
SBLSymS	Society of Biblical Literature Symposium Series
SBLTT	Society of Biblical Literature Texts and Translations
SBSt	Sources for Biblical Study
SBT	Studies in Biblical Theology
SCLec	Sather Classical Lectures
SCS	Septuagint and Cognate Studies
SJ	Studia Judaica
SJLA	Studies in Judaism in Late Antiquity
SNTSMS	Society for New Testament Monograph Series
SPEm	*Social Perspectives on Emotion*
SPhA	Studies in Philo of Alexandria
SPhAMA	Studies in Philo of Alexandria and Mediterranean Antiquity
SPNT	Studies on Personalities of the New Testament
StHell	Studia Hellenistica
StPB	Studia post Biblica

SUHei	Schriften der Universität Heidelberg
SVTP	Studia in Veteris Testamenti pseudepigrapha
SyFLL	Symbolae Facultatis Litterarum Lovaniensis
TANZ	Texte und Arbeiten zum neutestamentlichen Zeitalter
TAPA	*Transactions of the American Philological Association*
TED	Translations of Early Documents
Theol.	*Theology*
ThINS	The Theory and Interpretation of Narrative Series
THLit	Theory and History of Literature
ThResInt	*Theatre Research International*
TIN	Theory and Interpretation of Narrative
TynBul	*Tyndale Bulletin*
UALG	Untersuchungen zur antiken Literatur und Geschichte
UCPCS	University of California Publications in Classical Studies
UTPSS	University of Texas Press Slavic Series
WCl	The World's Classics
WGRW	Writings from the Greco-Roman World
WUNT	Wissenschaftliche Untersuchungen zum Neuen Testament
YCGL	*Yearbook of Comparative and General Literature*
YCS	Yale Classical Studies

Introduction

The proposition explored in this book is that genre associations and characters' minds are inextricably inter-implicated in readers' encounters with narrative. How readers imaginatively construct minds for characters they meet literarily or aurally is influenced by their assumptions about the genre of the narrative in which they find them. Furthermore, how a reader thinks about the essence of any given narrative genre is shaped in no small part by the representative narratives' representations of characters' cognitive lives. I will argue that narrative genres often develop characteristic ways of representing the cognition of the types of characters with which they are populated. These patterns and emphases both steer the reader's ability to associate a specific text with a more generalized genre category and also condition what cognitive-pertinent textual signals the reader subsequently notices in that text, following a tentative or dogmatic genre association.

This model has several consequences for thinking about the genre of the Fourth Gospel, not least that it suggests a novel account for the difficulty scholars have faced in trying to find "the" genre of the text. Or, to put it another way, this model accounts in part for the wide range of genres with which the Fourth Gospel has been connected. The Fourth Gospel's cognitive content is famously enigmatic. The narrative is full of tantalizing suggestions about the minds of its characters but short on definitive statements. Does Nicodemus ultimately come to believe in Jesus? What was it that allowed various characters in the text to recognize Jesus as the one sent by the Father? Does the Samaritan Woman understand the significance of what Jesus says to her? Do Jesus's various interlocutors fully appreciate the two or more levels on which their words register in the ears of the implied reader? How and why did Jesus love the beloved disciple? The evidence is maddeningly ambiguous. The questions are familiar to Johannine scholars, but how the gaps are filled is often entangled in unexplored or unacknowledged ways with what these scholars assume about the Fourth Gospel's genre.

After the first chapter, which offers a discussion of genre theory and characterization in connection to ancient literature generally and the Fourth Gospel in particular, this book looks at four different genres with which John has been affiliated—historiography, βίος, the romance novel, and tragic drama—exploring the kinds of cognitive activity characteristic in each as they developed in their ancient literary and historical contexts. Chapter 2 shows that a primary function of minds in ancient historiography is etiological; that is, they are one piece of a larger impulse to offer causal explanations for momentous deeds and events affecting groups of people. Chapter 3 contends that the preoccupation with ethical evaluation and imitation in ancient βίοι informs the representation of biographical subjects' minds. Chapter 4 explores techniques for creating and maintaining discrepant awareness and emotional activity in the Greek novel. Chapter 5 takes up classical drama, especially Euripidean tragedy, to show how discrepant awareness and represented "recognitions" are achieved without a narrator. The final chapter returns to the Fourth Gospel and a discussion of how genre affiliations shape the ways readers manufacture minds for the characters in the Johannine story of Jesus.

When we read, we find the kinds of mind we expect to find. Those expectations are conditioned by what we already think about our text's genre. Only, in the case of the Fourth Gospel, as with other disruptive and consequential narratives in the history of literature, we do the interpretive task a disservice if we attempt to force it into conformity with a single, abstractable genre tradition. For that reason, the present project builds towards a discussion of how these four genre traditions help us appreciate different dimensions of John's rich cognitive landscape. My hope is that this book models a methodologically rigorous, textually- and historically-grounded biblical interpretation where diverse perspectives and dynamic interpretation are integral to the interpretive process.

CHAPTER 1

Genre, Characterization, and Cognition

1 Genre Recognition and Character Cognition

How do you recognize a detective story when you see one? Is it a constellation of expected features? A list of necessary elements? A "family resemblance" with other detective stories? Do the author's intentions make it a detective story? Or is it a detective story for social and paratextual reasons—the publishing house, the jacket illustration, where it is shelved at a library or bookstore, the literary tastes of the friend who recommended it? Versions of all these approaches have been used to theorize genre, both at the abstract, universal level and also in connection to specific cultures, places, and times. The proposition explored in this book is that generic connections are forged by readers attending to what characters' minds are doing—what characters are represented as wanting, thinking, and otherwise cogitating.

Central to the detective story genre is a detective character that solves a mystery. Perhaps a corpse is discovered under suspicious circumstances; the authorities are engaged; the detective takes the case and works from hunches, inferences, and deduction to find and apprehend the culprit. The reader experiences the narrative by sharing in the initial confusion of the still-living characters, by following the detective's reasoning process as he or she solves the case, and then celebrating vicariously when the perpetrator is identified and apprehended.

My reader might now object that there are dozens of ways in which the schema just articulated fails to account for many detective stories. Potential variables are legion. On level of roles and identities: The detective might himself turn out to be the culprit. If the mystery to be solved is a crime, a murder, say, it could turn out that the victim and culprit are the same (e.g., in the event of suicide) or that the victim was killed accidentally, or that the victim is not really dead. Or on the script: The goal may be to solve something other than a crime (e.g., who sent these flowers?). Or an external culprit might be identified but not apprehended (e.g., because he died in the meantime, or escaped the detective's jurisdiction, or rigged the system in such a way as to escape conviction). Flouting a convention that bears on character types or script, however, is to acknowledge a convention. It is a means of participation in the genre with which that convention is associated. Innovations are not innovative without the precondition of expectations; they work in these cases because of the

© KONINKLIJKE BRILL NV, LEIDEN, 2019 | DOI:10.1163/9789004396043_002

expectation that culprits will be identified, apprehended, and held responsible for their crimes.

The conventions noted so far have had to do with character roles and plots, but they work on the level of characterization too. Take the culprit, for example, who often turns out to be the character least suspected by the audience. This in itself creates an opportunity for innovation. As the notion that the seemingly least suspicious character is probably the villain becomes conventionalized, new opportunities for innovation are created for subsequent texts participating in the genre.

Now take the conventional figure of the detective as a character. Audiences expect this person to have larger-than-life acumen, better-than-average powers of reasoning, and a keener insight into human nature than his peers. It is recognizable as a detective story as much because of what the protagonist's mind is doing as it is because of the plot, the mystery that needs to be solved. The plot may be only a pretext for putting the detective's mind to work. Episodes built into the early parts of detective stories often furnish opportunities to demonstrate the detective's exceptional powers of reasoning. This too is a convention with which storytellers can play, either by making the detective solve a mystery unwittingly, seemingly in spite of himself (à la Mr. Bean or Mr. Magoo), or the detective might be made to solve it using some kind of unconventional reasoning. In either case, audience expectations for these characters have to do with what we might broadly call their "minds": the detective story is a narrative about how this character's fictional mind perceives and processes his narrative world to arrive at a predictable outcome. Outcome, process, and character-drawing are all sites of potential innovation. Indeed, we expect texts to break conventions, and are pleased with ourselves for being able to understand how and when they do.

The attentive reader will have noted that what I am describing in connection to the conventions of genre sounds very close to structuralism, perhaps prompting the suspicion that what lies in ahead is an attempt to outline "the structures" that determine meaning in some or another genre with the idea that we can then see exactly how a given text conforms and/or innovates with respect to those structures. The suspicion is half right; I do intend to look at structures for representing the minds of characters in a range of ancient genres to which scholars have compared the Fourth Gospel. I do not think, however, that it will ever be possible to have said the last word about patterns or structures in these or any genres. The post-structuralist critique is well received. Derrida has helped us appreciate that centers shift; Foucault has helped us see that attempts to articulate structures are conditioned by our own episteme.

Nor do I think there is much to be gained by engaging in hyper-structuralist analysis of the mid-twentieth century variety, focusing on the level of phonemes and morphemes. My approach is indebted to the narrative grammar and discourse semiotics of Algirdas Julien Greimas, with a focus on narrative schemas and the semiotics of action and cognition. Especially significant for this project is his idea that cognitive states (including emotions, beliefs, and knowledge) bear on the capacity of actants to perform their narrative functions.

Genre-driven expectations, then, can exist in relation to many parts of narrative, including plot and character. These parts, moreover, can be broken into smaller parts. Plot expectations may have to do with beginnings, middles, and endings; with the kinds of circumstances that are necessary to launch a given story, to carry the story for a conventional number of pages, and to resolve the story; with the relationship of storytime to real time (i.e., the amount of time it takes to read the text); with the narrational strategy (whether a first- or third-person narrator is present, whether the narrator is reliable, whether the narrator is "omniscient"), and so on. Expectations having to do with characters in a given genre might concern the number of characters; the depth of their characterization (whether they are, to use terms made famous by E. M. Forster, "round" or "flat"); and with the kinds of stereotyped behaviors they are represented as performing and the kinds of mental experiences they are represented as having.

By walking through some conventions of a detective story above, we were able to see the broad spectrum of narrative "parts" that can be conventionalized and played with; we saw too that recognizing these conventions, even when they are absent or bent, is a default way of thinking about why we group certain texts together and call the group a genre; and finally that a necessary set of conventions will govern the work we expect characters' minds to do in narratives that are part of a given genre family. We will say more about this below. The assumption underlying this project is that other genres, both today and in antiquity, have conventions for representing the minds of characters and that these conventions merit investigation.

2 Real and Fictional Minds

The fact of genre conventionality means that no necessary, veridical link connects narratively-represented figures and their minds to real-world counterparts (where such counterparts exist). The mind of the protagonist in detective stories bears little resemblance to the minds of real-life detectives. Detectives in real life do not always solve their cases; the cases they do solve are not necessarily wrapped up in the periods of storytime that are conventional for detective stories; and the resolution of their cases is not necessarily due to the detective's superior powers of deduction. A study of real-life detectives could inform a literary analysis of detective stories, but the more important interpretive context is the set of patterns of representing the detective as a literary figure in the history of detective stories. If literary genres have conventions for how the minds of characters are typically represented and how they typically function in relation to the plot—in short, if we can speak in meaningful ways about cognitive narrative grammars—then studying these patterns helps us better understand both genres in general and the particular texts we associate with them.

The same point viewed from the opposite direction entails as a consequence that we keep separate the way characters are portrayed as thinking and acting in texts, on the one hand, from the ways that people exist in "real life," on the other. This is easily illustrated with recourse to another modern genre. The "Spaghetti Westerns" that flourished in the 1960s and '70s tell readers and viewers little about the experiences of the historical counterparts to the "Cowboys and Indians" featured in those spectacles. Less, at any rate, than they tell us about (1) the narrative conventions of an outmoded genre, (2) generic innovations made by Sergio Leone and other Italian directors to earlier models for "Westerns," and (3) the cultural values informing the problematic portrayals of the indigenous people purportedly represented in such narratives. By the same token, noticing patterns in the representation of minds and behaviors associated in ancient texts about sages, military commanders, lovers, and kings will tell us less about how their historical counterparts experienced the world, and more about the ways in which they were conventionally imagined in narrative traditions. And yet, a dialectic remains, in which narrative conventions inform the stylized selves of historical figures and in which historical people inform the activity of narrative producers. Those processes, however, lie beyond the scope of the current project.

This project operates, then, at the level of the text, focusing on genres and their conventions for representing the minds of the types of characters who typically feature in those genres. While I hope it is informed by historical awareness, I am not writing specifically about real people (e.g., the historical Jesus), real authors (e.g., the apostle John), or real readers (e.g., the so-called Johannine community). The more modest claim here concerning real-life people in antiquity is that they, like we, had conventional ways of representing the minds of characters, and that these conventions varied by genre.

3 John, Genre, and Cognitive Narratology in Modern Literary Criticism

Familiarity with the conventions of a genre is a necessary precondition for reading and interpreting texts affiliated with that genre. Readers familiar with those conventions—whether or not they are consciously aware of their knowledge—are able to select for those conventions when presented with texts deemed generically related.[1] Recent Johannine scholarship has benefited more than ever from the recognition that genre plays a controlling role in interpretation.[2] The genre(s) with which a text is linked create consequences for understanding the text's origins, its intended social functions, and the ways in which early readers might have filled in narrative gaps, formed expectations, and otherwise responded to it. It comes as no surprise, then, that the genre of the Fourth Gospel continues to attract attention and contestation.

As the introduction made clear, this book is not designed to identify "the" genre of the Fourth Gospel.[3] My goal, rather, is to explore the consequences of genre assignments on a central aspect of Johannine character- and plot-construction by juxtaposing the Fourth Gospel with conventions for representing minds in ancient historiography, βίος, the Greek novel, and classical tragedy. The conventions discussed under the label "mind" have to do especially with characters' represented thoughts, emotions, desires, and motivations. As Alan Palmer, George Butte, Lisa Zunshine, and others have shown, "theorizing the minds of others" is the activity that fundamentally undergirds our experience of narrative.[4]

---

1   On genre conventions as tacit knowledge in relation to the reader's "horizon of expectation," see Sune Auken, "Contemporary Genre Studies," in *The Gospel of John as Genre Mosaic*, ed. Kasper Bro Larsen, SANt 3 (Göttingen: Vandehoeck & Rupprecht, 2015), 53; Sune Auken, "Genre and Interpretation," in *Genre and...*, ed. Sune Auken, P. S. Lauridsen, and A. J. Rasmussen, CStG 2 (Copenhagen: Ekbátana, 2015), 158, 163–69. The idea of a "horizon of expectation" is derived from Hans Robert Jauss, "Theory of Genres and Medieval Literature," in *Toward an Aesthetic of Reception*, trans. Timothy Bahti, THLit 2 (Minneapolis: University of Minnesota Press, 1982), 76–109.

2   Kasper Bro Larsen, ed., *The Gospel of John as Genre Mosaic*, SANt 3 (Göttingen: Vandehoeck & Rupprecht, 2015); Harold W. Attridge, "Genre Bending in the Fourth Gospel," *JBL* 121 (2002): 3–21.

3   Cf. the goal of what has probably been the most influential book on the genre of the canonical gospels in recent decades: "it is of crucial importance that either the biographical hypothesis be given a proper scholarly footing or else exposed as a false trail." Richard A. Burridge, *What Are the Gospels?: A Comparison with Graeco-Roman Biography*, 2nd ed. (Grand Rapids: Eerdmans, 2004), 24.

4   Alan Palmer, *Fictional Minds*, FN (Lincoln: University of Nebraska Press, 2004); Alan Palmer, *Social Minds in the Novel*, TIN (Columbus: Ohio State University Press, 2010); George Butte,

6   CHAPTER 1

The term "mind" serves in this project as a placeholder for the seat of the intellect, the source of thoughts, intentions, and desires. It includes but is not limited to what an ancient Greek might call a person's γνώμη, διάνοια, νοῦς, φρήν, φρόνημα, or ψυχή. Without collapsing the English term "mind" and what an ancient Greek speaker could intend by the terms just listed, I operate from the basis that the linguistic concepts "to know," "to think," and "to want" are universal semantic primes.[5] That variety offers an invitation to explore the ways in which the activity or state of thinking is expressed in language, and to see how communication of those states is shaped by genre. The thesis advanced here is that fictional minds do different kinds of work depending on the conventions of the text and genre in which they participate. Furthermore, by taking the Fourth Gospel's representations of minds and reading them in dialogue with patterns of mind-representation in some of the ancient genres with which the gospel has been linked, readers will develop a more nuanced approach to interpreting Johannine characters.

Genres are artificial and dynamic phenomena. They are real, but always constructed and resistant to oversimplification.[6] Texts belong to genres, but modify or "bend" genres as new texts come into being, a fact of literary production that was as true in antiquity as it is today.[7] Genres are not especially useful for classifying texts. As Alastair Fowler argues in his groundbreaking book, *Kinds of Literature*, whenever pigeon-holing or classification is taken to be the function of genre *par excellence*, "the likely concomitants of such a view are puzzlement whenever a work does not fit, vexation when partitions can-

---

I Know That You Know That I Know: Narrating Subjects from Moll Flanders to Marnie, ThINS (Columbus: Ohio State University Press, 2004); Lisa Zunshine, *Why We Read Fiction: Theory of Mind and the Novel*, TIN (Columbus: Ohio State University Press, 2006); Lisa Zunshine, *Strange Concepts and the Stories They Make Possible: Cognition, Culture, Narrative* (Baltimore: Johns Hopkins University Press, 2008).

 The objection might be raised that it is anachronistic to speak of a private "mind" or an "inner life" in connection to the culture of the first century CE. This important question is discussed in chapter 3 with specific reference to Plutarch, but in terms that can be extended to the other texts considered in this book.

5 See, e.g., Michael Fortescue, "Thoughts about Thought," *CogLin* 12 (2001): 15–45; Cliff Goddard, "Thinking across Languages and Cultures: Six Dimensions of Variation," *CogLin* 14 (2003): 109–140.

6 The literature on genre is enormous. The idea that genres resist easy description is fundamental to the general shift from "list of features" approaches to genre to "family resemblance" and "prototype" theories of genre. Prototype theory has been more helpful to me, for reasons discussed in my "Characterization in John 4 and the Prototypical Type-Scene as a Generic Concept," in *The Gospel of John as Genre Mosaic*, ed. Kasper Bro Larsen, SANt 3 (Göttingen: Vandehoeck & Rupprecht, 2015), 233–47.

7 See Attridge, "Genre Bending in the Fourth Gospel"; Joseph Farrell, "Classical Genre in Theory and Practice," *NLitHist* 34 (2003): 383–408.

GENRE, CHARACTERIZATION, AND COGNITION

not be found, and despondency when the [pigeon] holes themselves shift."[8] To search for the definitive list of conventions, habits, or patterns of any given genre is a fool's errand, if taken as an end in itself. Take Arnaldo Momigliano's attempt to define biography: "an account of a man's life from birth to death."[9] This straightforward definition seems sufficiently flexible to account for most works we would want to call biographies, both in antiquity and today. Even this very encompassing definition, however, could break down with a little prodding, as Momigliano knew well. One ancient author, for example, wrote a *Life of Greece* (βίος Ἑλλάδος). Another wrote a *Life of the Roman People* (*vita populi romani*).[10] And many ancient biographies (including the Fourth Gospel, if we situate it here) gloss over the birth and/or death of their subjects. One no sooner discovers "the" necessary feature of a genre when one of its texts is found without that feature, or even counting on the expectation of finding the conventional feature in order to surprise the reader by its absence or mutation.[11] These subversions of expectations can apply to the patterns of representing minds discussed in the coming chapters.

Sometimes the innovation or bending visible in a genealogy of a genre is attributable to influence from other genres. No literary genre exists in isolation. It is easy enough to imagine a biographical mode of history, or a historicizing mode of tragedy, a novelistic mode of tragic biography, or any number of other combinations. Genre theorists talk about "genre sets" or "genre ecologies" or "genre repertoires" to describe such relationships; this is a helpful advance beyond the use of Wittgenstein's "family resemblance" idea as a paradigm for thinking about genres.[12] There is no theoretical difficulty posed, then, in having elements usually associated with one genre appearing in another. Those elements will include patterns of representing cognition.

---

8   Alastair Fowler, *Kinds of Literature: An Introduction to the Theory of Genres and Modes* (Cambridge: Harvard University Press, 1982), 37. Fowler's solution was to popularize Wittgenstein's "family resemblance theory" in connection to genre.

9   Arnaldo Momigliano, *The Development of Greek Biography*, Expanded ed. (Cambridge: Harvard University Press, 1993), 11.

10   Momigliano, *The Development of Greek Biography* 13.

11   But perhaps this way of thinking about genres undercuts itself twice; conspicuous absence is a kind of presence, providing some encouragement, then, for the ongoing exploration of habits, conventions, and persistent structures and motifs of narrative genres.

12   For genres forming larger patterns, see Auken, "Contemporary Genre Studies," 52. The trouble with the "family resemblance" theory, as John Swales points out, is that it "can make anything resemble anything." John M. Swales, *Genre Analysis: English in Academic and Research Settings* (Cambridge: Cambridge University Press, 1990), 51. Cf. Carol A. Newsom, "Spying out the Land: A Report from Genology," in *Seeking Out the Wisdom of the Ancients: Essays Offered to Honor Michael V. Fox on the Occasion of His Sixty-Fifth Birthday*, ed. Ronald L. Troxel, Kelvin G. Friebel, and Dennis Robert Magary (Winona Lake: Eisenbrauns, 2005), 441.

8 CHAPTER 1

Because genres interact and overlap, genre assignments are unstable and contestable. For illustration, one only has to look at the history of scholarship on the genre of the canonical gospels.[13] Faced with a contested genre assignment, the scholar of ancient texts might take one of several paths. One could advocate reading each ancient text "for its own sake" or "on its own grounds" or "in primary reference to itself," to paraphrase justifications sometimes offered for reading the Fourth Gospel without a named comparative apparatus. Such an approach is at best naïve and at worst disingenuous, since the mind of the reader instinctively fashions intertextual connections.[14] A text read without reference to other texts is meaningless.[15] A second strategy for responding to the difficulty of navigating genre assignments is to rely on "common sense" for categorizing gospels, but this falters if it turns out that "common sense" is socially constructed and ideologically inflected. Common sense either fails to translate universally or ends up translating by coercion.[16] A third strategy, which is really an inversion of the second, is to defer to another's common sense or to traditional categorizations when it comes to deciding which ancient texts belong together. Most contemporary scholars of early Christian literature choose this third option, identifying John as essentially a βίος or essentially a "gospel," although it is not always clear what they mean by these labels. But we are getting ahead of ourselves.

While forays have been made both into Johannine characterization and also into cognitive motifs of John,[17] the theoretical perspectives of cognitive

---

13 For an overview of the history of scholarship on the genre of the Gospels, albeit one that focuses on the relationship of the Gospels to βίος, see Burridge, *What Are the Gospels?*, 3–24, 252–88. To balance Burridge's account, see Adela Yarbro Collins, "Genre and the Gospels," *JR* 75 (1995): 239–46.

14 Julia Kristeva's work is foundational here. See "Word, Dialogue and Novel," in *The Kristeva Reader*, ed. Toril Moi (Oxford: Basil Blackwell, 1986), 35–61.

15 Jonathan Culler, "Presupposition and Intertextuality," *MLN* 91 (1976): 1380–96.

16 On the social construction of common sense, see especially Peter L. Berger and Thomas Luckmann, *The Social Construction of Reality: A Treatise in the Sociology of Knowledge* (Garden City: Doubleday, 1966).

17 Often focused on a particular pattern of repeating cognitive phenomena, such as the recurring scenes in the Fourth Gospel where Jesus is misunderstood by some other character. Some studies of John in connection to a cognitive theme are J. T. Nielsen, "The Lamb of God: The Cognitive Structure of a Johannine Metaphor," in *Imagery in the Gospel of John: Terms, Forms, Themes, and Theology of John*, ed. Jörg Frey, J. G. van der Watt, and Ruben Zimmermann, WUNT 200 (Tübingen: Mohr Siebeck, 2006), 217–56; Kasper Bro Larsen, *Recognizing the Stranger: Recognition Scenes in the Gospel of John*, BibInt 93 (Leiden: Brill, 2008); Kasper Bro Larsen, "Narrative Docetism: Christology and Storytelling in the Gospel

GENRE, CHARACTERIZATION, AND COGNITION

narratologists have not played a role in the study of Johannine characters.[18] Cognitive literary analysis is conceivable on at least three mutually implicated levels, which we might schematize like this:

TABLE 1.1

Mind(s) of author(s)/redactor(s)	Minds of characters	Minds of readers

This project is chiefly concerned with the minds of characters. Before coming to these minds, however, it may be helpful to describe what would be involved in speaking meaningfully about the minds of authors or readers. In a sense, most biblical scholars have taken the mind of an author as their default level of investigation: the meaning of the biblical text is coterminous with the intentions of the author.[19] What did the author *mean* by this? What did the author *hope* to achieve by putting it that way? Why did the author *think* it was necessary to include this bit of information? Did the author *forget* something here? When dealing with ancient literature, such questions can very rarely be answered with confidence. Among other challenges, (1) We cannot point to any one, definite, historical person as the author of many ancient documents, including the Fourth Gospel; (2) It is not clear whether an "author" in this context is the person holding the pen, someone giving dictation, someone credited for remembering and transmitting the traditions, or someone whose "authority" somehow validates the traditions; (3) The text's history of redaction adds a set of complications; as do (4) accidental changes introduced in the transmission

---

    of John," in *The Gospel of John and Christian Theology*, ed. Richard Bauckham and Carl Mosser (Grand Rapids: Eerdmans, 2008); Josaphat Chi-Chiu Tam, *Apprehension of Jesus in the Gospel of John*, WUNT 2/399 (Tübingen: Mohr Siebeck, 2015).

18   Nearly all theoretical work in cognitive narratology has unfolded in connection to modern literature, especially the Victorian novel. This has partly to do with the academic backgrounds of the theorists involved and partly because of the rich cognitive texture of the storyworlds created by modern writers. For cognitive narratology in connection to premodern corpora, see Mary Thomas Crane, *Shakespeare's Brain: Reading with Cognitive Theory* (Princeton: Princeton University Press, 2001); Jonas Grethlein, "Social Minds and Narrative Time: Collective Experience in Thucydides and Heliodorus," *Narrative* 23 (2015): 123–39.

19   A typical example of focusing on the mind of the author as a site of production is Tom Thatcher, *Why John Wrote a Gospel: Jesus, Memory, History* (Louisville: Westminster John Knox, 2006).

of the text. And finally, even if in the case of the Fourth Gospel we were able to identify a single author—call him John, if you like, or the beloved disciple—we would be no closer to getting inside his head. While living authors can be asked what they meant in this or that literary composition, no viable candidate for authorship of the Fourth Gospel would be available for interviews.[20]

So much for the mind of the author. A second level of potential cognitive analysis is the mind of the reader. This too is fraught with difficulties, including these: (1) Are we asking about real or ideal readers? If ideal, ideal in what sense? Perhaps something like Wolfgang Iser's "implied reader"?[21] Jonathan Culler's "competent reader"?[22] If real, then we would run into difficulties comparable to those outlined above in connection to a real author. (2) Bearing in mind that the most common way of encountering a text such as the Fourth Gospel would be by hearing short selections read aloud, is "auditor" the more important site of meaning-making?[23] What difference would it make?[24] (3) Modern scholars tend to discuss reading on the level of the individual, but how solitary

---

20   Even when living authors comment retrospectively on their intentions, there is a hobbling effect on the interpretation of a text, as Barthes famously argues in "The Death of the Author," in *Image, Music, Text*, trans. Stephen Heath (New York: Hill and Wang, 1977), 142–48. For discussion, see Seán Burke, *The Death and Return of the Author: Criticism and Subjectivity in Barthes, Foucault and Derrida*, 2nd ed. (Edinburgh: Edinburgh University Press, 1998); Seán Burke, *The Ethics of Writing: Authorship and Legacy in Plato and Nietzsche* (Edinburgh: Edinburgh University Press, 2008). "Outcomes become intentions, the name calling to a posthumous incarnation which will fill the inchoate space of the deontological realm with whatever retrospective coherence accrues from the future, the space of teleological judgement" (*Ethics of Writing*, 12).

21   "The concept of the implied reader is a transcendental model which makes it possible for the structured effects of literary texts to be described. It denotes the role of the reader, which is definable in terms of textual structure and structured acts." Wolfgang Iser, *The Act of Reading: A Theory of Aesthetic Response* (Baltimore: Johns Hopkins University Press, 1978), 38. Cf. Wolfgang Iser, *The Implied Reader: Patterns of Communication in Prose Fiction from Bunyan to Beckett* (Baltimore: Johns Hopkins University Press, 1978).

22   Jonathan Culler, *Structuralist Poetics: Structuralism, Linguistics and the Study of Literature* (London: Routledge, 1975), 131–52.

23   For aurality and reading with attention to the Fourth Gospel, see Dan Nässelqvist, *Public Reading in Early Christianity: Lectors, Manuscripts, and Sound in the Oral Delivery of John 1–4*, NovTSup 163 (Leiden: Brill, 2016); Dan Nässelqvist, "Translating the Aural Gospel: The Use of Sound Analysis in Performance-Oriented Translation," in *Translating Scripture for Sound and Performance: New Directions in Biblical Studies*, ed. James A. Maxey and Ernst R. Wendland, BPCrit 6 (Eugene: Cascade Books, 2012). Cf. William A. Johnson, *Readers and Reading Culture in the High Roman Empire: A Study of Elite Communities*, CCSoc (New York: Oxford University Press, 2010).

24   Recent studies suggest that human auditory memory operates at a disadvantage compared to retention and recall of visual and tactile stimuli. See James Bigelow and Amy Poremba, "Achilles' Ear? Inferior Human Short-Term and Recognition Memory in the Auditory Modality," *PLoS ONE* 9 (2014).

GENRE, CHARACTERIZATION, AND COGNITION

was the experience of reading in antiquity? Again, what difference would it make? Reader response criticism is a worthy undertaking, but a knottier business than its practitioners in biblical studies sometimes suppose.[25]

Certain functions of the reading mind in relation to narrative text are evident in antiquity as well as the present and can be described in comparable terms. Among these functions is the operation of a theory of mind: ancient and modern readers instinctively construct minds for literary characters comparable to the minds they theorize for people in real life.[26] Whatever differences in *content* there may be between modern and ancient readers theorizing text-bound minds, the physiological and mental *mechanisms* are the same in both instances.[27] A second-order goal of this project is to take stock of how some ancient readers contemporary to the Fourth Evangelist theorized the minds of characters in narratives they received: Plutarch reading Herodotus and constructing a mind for Solon, Josephus reading Nicolaus of Damascus and constructing a mind for Herod the Great, and so on. These explorations show only a filtered portion of the minds the Hellenistic authors mentally constructed while reading, hearing, and remembering ancient sources. That portion, however, will be sufficiently different from the source narratives (as far as we are able to see) to demonstrate that their theory of mind mechanism was alive and well. We will also see ancient critics working through comparable issues in more explicit terms, as when they note, for example, how a reader's διάνοια may be set in motion (κινεῖν) by a vivid (ἐναργής) description.[28] These forays may help us begin to appreciate how early readers of the Fourth Gospel understood its characters. Here again we will find that genre helps shape what readers see and expect in connection to characters' minds.

---

25 For a critical assessment of reader response criticism in biblical studies, see Stephen D. Moore and Yvonne Sherwood, *The Invention of the Biblical Scholar: A Critical Manifesto* (Minneapolis: Fortress, 2011), 101–5.

26 On theory of mind and literature, see Zunshine, *Why We Read Fiction*; Lisa Zunshine, "Theory of Mind and Experimental Representations of Fictional Consciousness," *Narrative* 11 (2003): 270–91.

27 Linguist and cognitive scientist Mark Turner, discussing "parable," writes that "cultural meanings peculiar to a society often fail to migrate intact across anthropological or historical boundaries, but the basic mental processes that make these meanings possible are universal" (*The Literary Mind*, 11).

28 See, e.g., schol. bT *Il.* 10.199c, schol. bT *Il.* 14.187. Both instances cited and discussed by René Nünlist, *The Ancient Critic at Work: Terms and Concepts of Literary Criticism in Greek Scholia* (Cambridge: Cambridge University Press, 2009), 139. The whole of his chapter 5, "Effects on the Reader," is magnificent in its coverage of ancient scholiasts finding ways to articulate the effects of literature on the reader's attention, emotions, expectations, and feeling of suspense.

The study of readers' minds is, then, more promising as a site of meaning-making than the study of authors' minds. The primary focus of this study, however, is not the right- and left-hand boxes of Table 1.1, but the center box, the representation of characters' minds. By virtue of existing in the text, characters are the only part of the three-part model above accessible today. This level of analysis has its own methodological obstacles, including the fact that we cannot access the text apart from our own status as readers.

The approach advocated here assumes a distinction between perceptible and non-perceptible parts of the world, where minds belong to the latter. Such a distinction allows real people to interact with other real people, always theorizing minds, comparable to their own, animating other bodies.[29] Those acts of theorization are instinctively extended to the minds of "paper people" in the texts encountered.[30] Readers know what we call characters are constellations of words rather than living people (even when the words on a page have referential relationships to real persons), and yet they nevertheless attribute minds to them. Signifiers for pieces of minds exist in the text like stars in the sky, but it takes a reader to turn the signifiers into a whole mind, just as it takes an act of imagination to see discrete stars as a constellation. Readers also expect characters in a narrative to interact with each other in a manner comparable to the ways in which we see people interact in the real world. But this is only true to a point, since represented minds vary according to the functions they characteristically perform in any given genre.[31]

---

29   The human ability to attribute and track the operations of "real" minds in other people is a bequest of our evolutionary history. For a general account, see William F. Allman, *The Stone Age Present: How Evolution Has Shaped Modern Life: From Sex, Violence, and Languages to Emotions, Morals, and Communities* (New York: Simon & Schuster, 1994). For the application to literature, see Zunshine, *Why We Read Fiction*, 7–17.

30   The language of "paper people" to describe literary characters is from Mieke Bal, *Narratology: Introduction to the Theory of Narrative*, 3rd ed. (Toronto: University of Toronto Press, 2009), 113.

31   Some of the foundational scholarship on our evolved cognitive ability to keep track of the sources of our representations (sometimes called "metarepresentations") was carried out by Leda Cosmides and John Tooby of the University of California, Santa Barbara, in the 1980s and 1990s. Their work (as well as that of others in the so-called "real mind sciences") has re-invigorated more than one stream of postclassical narrative criticism, with the realization that the same mechanisms we use to track real-world minds make possible our engagement with the minds of people in literature. See, e.g., H. Porter Abbott, "Unreadable Minds and the Captive Reader," *Style* 42 (2008): 448–67; Butte, *I Know That You Know That I Know*; David Herman, "Scripts, Sequences, and Stories: Elements of a Postclassical Narratology," *PMLA* 112 (1997): 1046–1059; Palmer, *Fictional Minds*; Palmer, *Social Minds in the Novel*; Gilles Fauconnier and Mark Turner, *The Way We Think: Conceptual Blending and the Mind's Hidden Complexities* (New York: BasicBooks, 2003); Zunshine, "Theory of Mind

Sometimes the patterns followed by literary minds depart in observable ways from default expectations for intermental interactions. Literary theorist Marie-Laure Ryan's "principle of minimal departure" is helpful here, holding that "whenever we interpret a message concerning an alternate world, we reconstrue this world as being the closest possible to the reality we know."[32] The principle, applied to patterns of character cognition, suggests that readers begin with a mind "like my own" or "typical for a certain type of person" to come up with default expectations for what a character's mind should be like. As experience accumulates, the default mind is modified to line up with the patterns one intuits for fictional minds in a given narrative genre. The reader may be (indeed, is likely to be) entirely unconscious of these processes as they transpire.

In addition to instinctively *attributing* minds to characters, readers instinctively *track* characters' minds as they change over the course of a narrative and as they relate to each other. What a character knows at any given point in the drama and what those characters think other characters know creates consequences for how they act. Readers of Sophocles understand that if Oedipus, Laius, and Jocasta knew what we know, they would have acted differently, and the tragedies of the Oedipus cycle might have been avoided.

Although Johannine characterization has been on the research agenda of New Testament scholars at least since R. Alan Culpepper's seminal *Anatomy of the Fourth Gospel* (1983) and is now a veritable cottage industry in its own right, Johannine characters' minds have not received sustained attention.[33] A focus

---

and Experimental Representations of Fictional Consciousness"; Zunshine, *Why We Read Fiction*; Zunshine, *Strange Concepts and the Stories They Make Possible*. Most of those writers, however, work chiefly with modern languages and texts. This project reaches further back, asking fresh questions in connection to a very familiar text and showcasing the possibilities and limitations of a cognitive approach for studies of other ancient texts.

32   Marie-Laure Ryan, "Fiction, Non-Factuals, and the Principle of Minimal Departure," *Poetics* 9 (1980): 403. See also Marie-Laure Ryan, *Possible Worlds, Artificial Intelligence, and Narrative Theory* (Bloomington: Indiana University Press, 1991).

33   Culpepper's book was the first widely-read, monograph-length discussion of John in narrative-critical terms. It was also largely responsible for introducing the vocabulary and categories of classical narratology and literary criticism to Johannine scholarship. Narrative-critical readings of the Fourth Gospel and other ancient Christian texts have multiplied in the three decades since. This past decade has seen a flurry of studies on John and characterization. Cornelis Bennema looks at all the characters in John and offers a classificatory system for them based primarily on how they encounter and respond to Jesus. Steven Hunt and his collaborators offer a wide-ranging collection of essays focusing on individual characters or character groups in the Fourth Gospel. Susan Hylen looks at eight of the most important Johannine characters and makes an argument for their relative complexity against the notion that John's characters merely stand as representative

14   CHAPTER 1

on the cognitive dimension of characterization promises to shed light on the Fourth Gospel's famously ambiguous cognitive motifs, including darkness and light; blindness and sight; madness and logos; and ignorance and recognition.[34] In their own, parallel ways, these epistemic motifs map onto the minds associated with the Gospel's characters. The genre-comparative cognitive approach advocated here supplies a language and a framework for drawing them into sharper relief. Before coming to genre-determined patterns for representing minds, however, it will prove instructive to look at how ancient theorists talked about minds and characterization.

4   Characterization and Cognition in Ancient Literary Criticism

Two perennial and pressing questions central to theories of characterization ask what "character" means and what relation holds between character and narrative action or plot. Some scholars attempt to answer those questions with frameworks provided by modern theory; others attempt to answer them using only categories theorized in antiquity, especially as reflected in ancient works

---

figures of belief and unbelief. Alicia Myers explores the Fourth Gospel's use of scripture to characterize Jesus in a way consonant with strategies articulated in the Greco-Roman rhetorical tradition. An edited volume by Christopher Skinner both attends to the theory of characterization and applies competing theories to figures in the Fourth Gospel. Cornelis Bennema, *Encountering Jesus: Character Studies in the Gospel of John* (Milton Keynes: Paternoster, 2009); Cornelis Bennema, *A Theory of Character in New Testament Narrative* (Minneapolis: Fortress, 2014); Steven A. Hunt, D. Francois Tolmie, and Ruben Zimmermann, eds., *Character Studies in the Fourth Gospel*, WUNT 314 (Tübingen: Mohr Siebeck, 2013); Susan Hylen, *Imperfect Believers: Ambiguous Characters in the Gospel of John* (Louisville: Westminster John Knox, 2009); Alicia D. Myers, *Characterizing Jesus: A Rhetorical Analysis on the Fourth Gospel's Use of Scripture in Its Presentation of Jesus*, LNTS 458 (London: T. & T. Clark, 2012); Christopher W. Skinner, ed., *Characters and Characterization in the Gospel of John*, LNTS 461 (London: Bloomsbury, 2013). Cf. the earlier interaction with Culpepper's chapter on characterization in J. A. du Rand, "The Characterization of Jesus as Depicted in the Narrative of the Fourth Gospel," *Neot* 19 (1985): 18–36. Hunt et al. and Skinner both offer detailed histories of research on characterization in connection to John.

34   See Craig S. Keener, *The Gospel of John: A Commentary*, 2 vols. (Peabody: Hendrickson, 2003), 1:233–51; Craig S. Keener, "Studies in the Knowledge of God in the Fourth Gospel in Light of Its Historical Context" (M.Div Thesis, Assemblies of God Theological Seminary, 1986). More recently and in connection to characterization, see Cornelis Bennema, "Christ, the Spirit and the Knowledge of God: A Study in Johannine Epistemology," in *The Bible and Epistemology*, ed. Mary Healy and Robin Parry (Milton Keynes: Paternoster, 2007), 107–33. In connection to the language of apprehension, see Tam, *Apprehension of Jesus in the Gospel of John*.

GENRE, CHARACTERIZATION, AND COGNITION

on rhetoric and literary criticism. This project belongs to the former group, insofar as the model it employs is premised on the modern idea that tracking characters' minds is a compelling way to discuss narrative structures and genre participation. Nevertheless, the questions pursued here intersect with questions that interested ancient theorists of rhetoric and literary criticism. Some evidence for that interest is collected here, beginning with classical scholiasts and Aristotle's *Poetics*, then moving into handbooks of rhetoric, including some of the *progymnasmata* of Theon and Hermogenes. The rhetorical handbooks illustrate how deeply attuned ancient discourse producers were to the idea that they were fashioning minds in their writing and speaking, and the literary theorists show how readers conceptualized the minds of authors, audiences, and characters in connection to the texts with which they dealt. The chief findings of this survey are (1) that ancient people were aware of the minds of others; (2) that they attributed minds to literary characters; and (3) that they had expectations about what those minds should be like. In connection to this last point, the principles of imitation (μίμησις) and "what is fitting" (τὸ πρέπον, οἰκεῖος) are of particular interest. Furthermore (4) ancient writers could be very attentive to the minds of their audiences, aiming at ἐναργεία in prose composition, the actualization of a scene in the reader's mind (one of Aristotle's three proposed aims for prose composition, along with appropriate use of metaphor and antithesis [*Rhet.* 1410b35–36]).[35]

Though others had already theorized literature as a τέχνη[36] (indeed, theories of characterization can readily be inferred from earlier writings, especially

---

35   Although this section highlights "emic" categories of ancient literary criticism, I am not suggesting that the Fourth Gospel can or should only be interpreted with the perspectives, tools, and vocabularies of its own time. George Kennedy rightly observes that "[modern] classical critics ... emphasise the timelessness and the continuing influence, though often with much misunderstanding or distortion, of the major texts.... This emphasis has, however, regularly been accompanied by historicism, the assumption that the ancient critics provide, or should provide, the best basis for the interpretation of the literature of their own time. Such a view led to a number of problems and in the twentieth century has been partially abandoned or at least practiced with restraint." George A. Kennedy, ed., *The Cambridge History of Literary Criticism: Volume 1: Classical Criticism* (Cambridge: Cambridge University Press, 1989), x.

36   No doubt much of Aristotle's thinking was prompted by engagement with Plato, whose *Republic* and *Ion* contain much that could be considered in connection to literary criticism. See, e.g., the selections in D. A. Russell and Michael Winterbottom, eds., *Classical Literary Criticism*, Rev. ed., OWC (Oxford: Oxford University Press, 1998), 1–50. What survives of Plato, however, has more to do with the value or disvalue of poetry as such to citizens of the Greek polis, and less to do with a theory of character(s) or characterization. Plato's Socrates criticizes Homer for trying to speak of matters (wars, governance, education) best left to the experts (generals, strategists, politicians, teachers) (*Resp.*

16   CHAPTER 1

of Plato), Aristotle's book-length discussion of epic and tragedy in the *Poetics* may safely be labeled the earliest surviving piece of literary theory in the Western tradition.[37] In it, Aristotle subordinates character to plot (or action): "Plot (μῦθος), then, is the first principle and, as it were, soul of tragedy, while character (ἦθος) is secondary.... Tragedy is mimesis of action (ἔστιν τε μίμησις πράξεως), and it is chiefly for the sake of the action that it represents the agents (καὶ διὰ ταύτην μάλιστα τῶν πραττόντων)" (*Poet.* 1450a–1450b).[38] This is often misunderstood. The Greek concept ἦθος is "moral character," not, as English speakers typically think of characters in narratives, "a personality invested with distinctive attributes and qualities, by a novelist or dramatist; also, the personality or 'part' assumed by an actor on the stage."[39] Aristotle's own definition of ἦθος is "that which reveals moral choice (προαίρεσις)—that is, when otherwise unclear, what kinds of thing an agent chooses or rejects" (*Poet.* 1450b).[40]

    10.599), for encouraging bad morals (by portraying gods engaged in warring, plotting, fighting with one another) (2.378), and for suggesting that gods could be the cause of evil to others (*Resp.* 2.380). Poetry arouses the passions, and so harms the aspirant to ἀπάθεια. According to Russell and Winterbottom, for Plato epic and tragedy are "based on a corrupting mythology, encourage feelings that we should strive to tame, and in any case give us only at second remove a world that is itself somehow inferior to the ultimate realities of the Forms." D. A. Russell and Michael Winterbottom, "Introduction," in *Classical Literary Criticism*, Rev. ed., OWC (Oxford: Oxford University Press, 1998), x.

37   Where "theory" is considered broadly. The work is "a series of working notes from which Aristotle would have lectured at far greater length and with far superior lucidity to his pupils, ... a work that does not so much describe the genres of tragedy and epic as analyse them to see what makes them what they are, with some admixture of historical information to show how they have developed. It gives not so much prescriptions as judgements." Nor was the work a set of "rules" for good poetry. "It was left to a much later and infinitely different world to try to use Aristotle's dicta as rules: though French neoclassicists and others tended to look for what they wanted there—and if they could not find it, to supply the deficiencies from Horace's *Art of Poetry*" (Russell and Winterbottom, "Introduction," xi).

38   Trans. LCL, modified.

39   *OED*, s.v., entry 17a.

40   Trans. LCL. A similar point is made in ch. 15: if what is said or done reveals a certain choice, character will be present—good character if the choice is good, etc. (*Poet.* 1454a17–19). In his commentary on the *Poetics*, O. B. Hardison, Jr., remarks, "Nothing could demonstrate more obviously the difference between modern 'character' and Aristotelian *ethos* than the fact that *ethos* is so emphatically distinguished from thought. In what sense are a person's thoughts distinct from his character? The answer is, 'In no sense,' if by 'character' we mean something like 'personality.' Aristotle's distinction is clear, on the other hand, if we think of character as related to moral type. O. B. Hardison, ed., *Aristotle's Poetics: A Translation and Commentary for Students of Literature*, trans. Leon Golden (Tallahassee: University Presses of Florida, 1981), 125.

The word that later Greeks would use to describe what is nearest the modern notion of a "character" (i.e., the participant in a storyworld) is πρόσωπον. Aristotle uses this term on several occasions (*Poet.* 1449a, 1449b, 1461a), but only in reference to the physical mask worn by an actor. Later critics would prefer this language for talking about the literary phenomena we are calling "characters." Scholiasts to Homer, for example, would distinguish between "major" and "minor" πρόσωπα (the former type is a συνεκτικὸν πρόσωπον, a "character who holds [the plot] together").[41]

Μῦθος, ἦθος, and διάνοια constitute for Aristotle three of the six "parts" (μέρη) of tragedy and together constitute the three *objects* of mimesis. The other three parts of tragedy are λέξις ("diction") and μελοποιία ("song"), constituting the *means* of mimesis, and ὄψις ("spectacle"), constituting its *manner*. Aristotle is more interested in the objects of mimesis than these latter three. He defines διάνοια and ἦθος in contrast to each other:

> Third in importance [after plot and character] is thought (ἡ διάνοια): that is, the capacity to say what is pertinent and apt (τὸ λέγειν δύνασθαι τὰ ἐνόντα καὶ τὰ ἁρμόττοντα), which in formal speeches is the task of politics and rhetoric. The earliest poets made people speak politically; present day poets make them speak rhetorically. Character is that which reveals moral choice (ἔστιν δὲ ἦθος μὲν τὸ τοιοῦτον ὃ δηλοῖ τὴν προαίρεσιν)—that is, when otherwise unclear, what kinds of things an agent chooses or rejects (which is why speeches in which there is nothing at all the speaker chooses or rejects contain no character); while thought covers the parts

---

41   See Nünlist, *The Ancient Critic at Work*, 244.

   Aristotle also talks about ὁ πράττων (the actor) and, in other contexts, ὁ χαρακτήρ. The word χαρακτήρ referred originally to a complex of activities involved in marking coinage, variously as the person doing the act, the tool employed, or the mark itself. As an extension of this, it could refer to a stamp, or even to a branding iron. In time it came to mean the coin type, as distinguished from other types. Once the notion of distinguishing one impression from another was introduced, it gained currency as a way of referring to figures and letters, which needed to be distinguished from one another, and from here to a metaphorical extension as indicative of what distinguishes one person or group of persons from others. Aristotle does not use the word χαρακτήρ in the *Poetics* (although he does use it elsewhere). Euripides's Medea compares the character of gold coins to the character of people: we have means of telling true from false in the former case, but no equivalent means of telling good from bad in the latter case (Euripides, *Med.* 516–9). On ὁ πράττων, note the etymological discussion in ch. 35, where Aristotle gives πράττειν as the Athenian word for acting (προσαγορεύειν), distinguishing it from the Dorian equivalent, δρᾶν.

18   CHAPTER 1

in which they demonstrate that something is or is not so, or declare a
general view.

Poet. 1450b[42]

Relative to his remarks on ἦθος and μῦθος, Aristotle says little about διάνοια because, he writes, "the discussion of διάνοια can be left to my discourses on rhetoric, for it is more integral to that enquiry" (*Poet.* 1456a).[43] As Stephen Halliwell
notes, it is unclear whether we are meant to take this as a direct reference to
Aristotle's extant *Rhetoric*.[44] In either case, Aristotle's discussion of διάνοια in
the *Rhetoric* (1403a35–36) is illuminating for the present project and will be
taken up below.

One of the cognitive topics addressed by Aristotle concerns whether a
speaker or actor operates "in knowledge" or "in ignorance." This is of obvious
interest for the study of John, where characters routinely speak "in ignorance,"
creating opportunities for dramatic irony. The early poets, Aristotle says,
"made the agents act in knowledge and cognizance (εἰδότας καὶ γιγνώσκοντας),"
while later poets have "the agents commit the terrible deed "in ignorance, then
subsequently recognize the relationship (ἀγνοοῦντας δὲ πρᾶξαι τὸ δεινόν, εἶθ᾽
ὕστερον ἀναγνωρίσαι τὴν φιλίαν), as with Sophocles' Oedipus" (*Poet.* 1453b).[45]
Aristotle also makes room for a "third possibility, when the person is on the
point of unwittingly committing something irremediable, but recognizes it
before doing so (τὸ μέλλοντα ποιεῖν τι τῶν ἀνηκέστων δι᾽ ἄγνοιαν ἀναγνωρίσαι
πρὶν ποιῆσαι)" (*Poet.* 1453b).[46] The pathos will be greatest, Aristotle writes, in
cases where the parties involved are closely related. Note that in the second
group what is recognized is "the relationship" (τὴν φιλίαν) itself. These observations are important to Aristotle as pieces of his theoretical discussion about
περιπέτειαι and ἀναγνωρίσεις, but it matters to the present study for its bearing
on the representation of characters' minds. It is up to the poet, Aristotle writes,
whether characters act in knowledge or in ignorance. Aristotle notices and tac-
itly endorses the notion that poets working with familiar tragic myths should
not change *actions*, such as who kills or begets whom, but they do (and should)
innovate in the cognitive domain.

The structures of narrative Aristotle discusses in the *Poetics* in connection
to tragedy and epic may be extended to the other genres considered in the

---

42   Trans. LCL, modified.
43   Trans. LCL.
44   LCL 199 *ad loc.*
45   Trans. LCL. Cf. Sophocles, *Oed. tyr.* 924–1085.
46   Trans. LCL.

GENRE, CHARACTERIZATION, AND COGNITION

following chapters, since each involves plot and characters acting with varying degrees of knowledge and ignorance. Although not all parts of tragedy considered in the *Poetics* translate easily to other genres,[47] ἦθος and διάνοια do, with the important difference that representing these parts outside of drama involves attending to what the narrator says about the contents of characters' minds.

Before turning to the rhetorical handbook tradition, we should take stock of a different type of literary critic. For every critic in the theoretical mode (Aristotle, Demetrius, Ps.Longinus, and others), there were dozens or hundreds of anonymous hands-on critics whose work is known to us in part from their scholia, most of which are attached to copies of Homer.[48] These critics commented on the intentions of the author, on the constructed minds of characters, and the effect of literary choices on the minds of readers. In other words, they attend to all three levels of the model in Table 1.1.

Plutarch, in a text that will receive more attention in chapter 3 below, observes that it is possible to discern a person's ἦθος from their actions. Ancient scholiasts do something comparable, but here it is easier to see the mechanics of the operation. The phenomenon, which might be called implicit characterization to distinguish it from direct claims made in a primary text about a person's ἦθος (explicit criticism), is visible in a Homeric scholion to *Iliad* 6. The ἦθος of Menelaus is inferred from his behavior towards a suppliant: "He [sc. Homer] shows the character of Menelaus to be moderate and not irascible (μέτριον καὶ ἀόργητον). For, though previously wronged [sc. by Paris] and then wounded [sc. by Pandarus in *Iliad* 4] on terms of a truce, he [sc. Menelaus] now refrains from striking the enemy [sc. Adrestus] and does not kill him,

---

47   The difference here can be described in terms of fixity and fluidity, with the characters in texts existing as relatively fixed entities and the characters in theatrical performances as relatively fluid, thanks to the variables introduced by directors, production teams, and individual actors. Aristotle writes of "spectacle" (ὄψις) as one of the qualitative components of tragedy. Of the components designed to give pleasure, "song-writing is the most important, while spectacle, though attractive, has least to do with art, with the art of poetry, that is; for a work is potentially a tragedy even without public performance and players, and the art of the stage designer contributes more to the perfection of spectacle than the poet's does" (*Poet.* 1450b).

48   For an introduction to the scholia, "commentary or notes written in the margins of a text," as opposed to ὑπόμνημα (self-standing commentary) and gloss (a short interlinear definition), see Eleanor Dickey, *Ancient Greek Scholarship: A Guide to Finding, Reading, and Understanding Scholia, Commentaries, Lexica, and Grammatical Treatises, from Their Beginnings to the Byzantine Period*, APACRS 7 (New York: Oxford University Press, 2007), 11.

because he is a suppliant (ὡς ἱκέτην οὐ φονεύει)" (schol. T *Il.* 6.62b1)."[49] This text is interesting both for the inference of disposition from Menelaus's behavior and for the process of causal reasoning used to draw the conclusion. Menelaus does not kill Adrestus because he was ὡς ἱκέτην. Menelaus's character is both revealed in the action and used to explain why he acted this way towards a suppliant. Scholia also comment on whether a character is characterized consistently (recognized as a sign of good composition) or inconsistently, whether a character is characterized in speech or through silence, whether a character is characterized succinctly or with special clarity (both of which are signs of good composition).[50]

The question of whether a character is characterized consistently is of special interest, showing as it does that ancient critics came to associate certain characteristic dispositions and consequent behaviors with individual characters. Thus it is ἀνάρμοστον (inconsistent) for Hector to mock Diomedes (see schol. A. *Il.* 8.164–6a *Ariston.*), and it is οὐκ οἰκεῖον (not fitting) for Medea to burst into tears, when she is about to kill her children (schol. E. *Med.* 922).[51] The sense that an action or speech was "not fitting" to a character could lead, in some scholiasts' hands at least, to the excision of a line from a manuscript.[52] These decisions were defended either on patterns observed more generally for the character, or on inference from what was perceived to be typical human behavior, or both. Many scholia comment on an action in the text and connect it to a given state of mind, appending a comment along the lines of, "because that is how people generally behave in such situations."[53] The ability to theorize the minds of people in general and specific characters in particular also informs the theory and curriculum of classical rhetoric, to which we now turn.

A famous section of book 2 of Aristotle's *Rhetoric* has been described as "the earliest systematic discussion of human psychology" (chs. 2–11).[54] Its discussion

---

49   Trans. Nünlist. For discussion and further examples, see Nünlist, *The Ancient Critic at Work*, 246–47.

50   For examples, see Nünlist, 248–51.

51   Nünlist, 250n45.

52   Nünlist, 251–52.

53   Examples at Nünlist, 253n55.

54   George A. Kennedy, *Aristotle: On Rhetoric: A Theory of Civic Discourse* (New York: Oxford University Press, 1991), 122. The text appears "to have originated in some other context and have been only partially adapted to the specific needs of a speaker."

      The *Rhetoric* poses some of the same challenges as the *Poetics*. It is elliptical and compressed, suggesting a *Sitz im Leben* in a school. It seems to combine several pieces of writing, unevenly revised, sometimes with tensions in the content. Scholarly opinion has it that books 1–2 formed the initial publication, with book 3 appended later. But tensions exist even in that initial pair of books, where book 1 advocates the use of rhetoric only

GENRE, CHARACTERIZATION, AND COGNITION

of how to arouse a range of πάθη in an audience paints a heuristically valuable context for the current project. Each of the πάθη can be theorized in terms of its definition, its representative causes, those at whom it is directed, and especially the "state of mind" (πῶς ἔχοντες) of those who possess it. The πάθη discussed are anger (ὀργή), calmness (πραότης), friendliness (φιλία), hostility (ἔχθρα), fear (φόβος), confidence (θάρσος), proper shame (αἰσχύνη), shameless-ness (ἀναισχυντία), goodwill or gratitude (χάρις), ingratitude (ἀχάριστία), pity (ἔλεος), being indignant (τὸ νεμεσᾶν), envy (φθόνος), and zeal (ζῆλος).[55] As πάθη, these can be distinguished from the more permanent ἕξεις that constitute the more static conditions of a person's ἦθος. These qualities are discussed in the second half of book 2, in chapters on the ἦθος of the young (2.12), the old (2.13), those in the prime of life (2.14), the wellborn (2.15), the wealthy (2.16), and the powerful (2.17). In each case, Aristotle reflects stereotypes of a sort that are commonly visible also in Roman comedy.[56] The particulars of the portraits are less significant at present than the fact that they bear out this tendency to psychologize.

The *Rhetoric* was flagged above for its potential to help explain διάνοια, dis-cussed only briefly in the *Poetics* as "the capacity to say what is pertinent and apt (τὸ λέγειν δύνασθαι τὰ ἐνόντα καὶ τὰ ἁρμόττοντα)" (*Poet.* 1450b), and subsum-ing "all effects which need to be created by speech: their elements are proof, refutation, the conveying of πάθη (pity, fear, anger, etc.) as well as enhance-ment and belittlement" (*Poet.* 1459b). The *Rhetoric* and the *Poetics* have differ-ent agendas: the *Rhetoric* explores λόγος, ἦθος, and πάθος as the three possible means of persuasion, while the *Poetics* looks at ἦθος and διάνοια as two "parts" (μέρη) of tragedy. Διάνοια and ἦθος in the *Rhetoric* are tools of persuasion rather than objects of mimesis. Correspondingly, the πάθη mentioned in the *Rhetoric* are tools the rhetorician might use when attempting persuasion by πάθος. More than πάθος or ἦθος, however, Aristotle attends to λόγος as a means of per-suasion, and it is under this heading that he discusses διάνοια.

Underlying Aristotle's discussion of mimesis is a cognitively-grounded proposal about why people enjoy contemplating (θεωροῦντας) images. His theory is that they enjoy achieving understanding: "Understanding gives great pleasure not only to philosophers but likewise to others too, though the

---

in pursuit of the good and book 2 presents rhetoric as a tool for winning any argument. Some passages may have been written for other projects, not directly concerned with rhetoric, and then loosely adapted to fit in the new work. These scholarly challenges affect the parts of *Rhetoric* that most interest us here, where most of the πάθη discussed are not linked to the practice of rhetoric.

55   Cf. the discussion of this passage in chapter 3, below.

56   Kennedy, *Aristotle: On Rhetoric*, 163.

22 CHAPTER 1

latter have a smaller share in it. This is why people enjoy looking at images, because through contemplating them it comes about that they understand and infer what each element means (ὅτι συμβαίνει θεωροῦντας μανθάνειν καὶ συλλογίζεσθαι τί ἕκαστον), for instance that 'this person is so-and-so'" (*Poet.* 1448b).[57] Understanding can take a variety of forms, but the example Aristotle provides is of recognizing a person in a work of art. That work could take the form of paint, print, sung words, or even the movements of dance. Whatever the medium of the mimetic work and its corresponding goodness or badness, its function (eliciting pleasure) can be explained by its capitalization on the human drive to understand.[58] Returning with this perspective to the construction of narratives, we see that in Aristotelian terms thoughts, emotions, and states of mind are mimetic objects susceptible to recognition and understanding on the part of the reader.

Plato anticipates Aristotle in theorizing audience psychology, dealing with the subject in several places, especially the *Phaedrus*. Although the *Phaedrus* is more interested in whether speech is detrimental or beneficial to the soul of the hearer than it is in the mechanics of persuasion, it nevertheless develops a psychological model that would prove profoundly significant in later antiquity. In the first part of the treatise, Plato distinguishes two sources of behavior: irrational desire and the rational desire for the good. In the second part, he develops a more complex psychology, dividing the soul into three parts. The irrational part has been divided into appetitive and spirited parts and famously likened to two unequal winged horses drawing along a chariot housing the third part, the driver representing the rational faculty (*Phaedrus* 246a). What is

---

57 Trans. LCL., modified.

58 Plato famously criticized art because of its mimetic nature, which is generally understood to be one of the factors motivating the composition of Aristotle's *Poetics* as a response. Aristotle frames his discussion of poetry in terms of μίμησις. And, he writes, "since mimetic artists represent people in action, and the latter should be either elevated or base (for characters almost always align with just these types, as it is through vice and virtue that the characters of all men vary), they can represent people better than our normal level, worse than it, or much the same" (*Poet.* 1447b–1448a). One can hear echoes of book 10 of the *Republic*, in which Plato's Socrates and Glaucon discuss what poetry is ("the business of imitation" and "the third stage from the truth") and his correlated rationale for excluding most poets and painters from his ideal city (that is, all but those who serve the republic by fostering good morals). The distinction sets up for Aristotle the basic difference between comedy and tragedy; the former shows people as worse than they really are, tragedy makes them appear better (*Poet.* 1448a). It has also been suggested that book 10 of the *Republic* was written as "a response to challenges from his young student." Thomas G. Rosenmeyer, "Ancient Literary Genres: A Mirage?," YCGL 34 (1985): 77. Cf. Gerald Frank Else, *The Structure and Date of Book 10 of Plato's Republic* (Heidelberg: Carl Winter, 1972).

GENRE, CHARACTERIZATION, AND COGNITION

important for us to notice is Plato's affirmation of the idea that rhetoricians are effective (not to say good) when they appeal to the corresponding appetitive, spirited, and rational parts of their audiences.[59]

Another approach to audience psychology is found in a Hellenistic-period work attributed to Hermogenes, which offers standardized instructions for bringing about states of mind in an audience.[60] Dealing with παράλειψις (where the speaker itemizes items he claims he is omitting) and ἀποσιώπησις (where the speaker breaks off after beginning to say something, when the audience already has some notion of what he wants to say), for example, the author writes that these figures are used when the speaker "wishes to implant greater suspicion about the subject in the mind of the hearers" (ὅταν βουληθῶμεν τὴν ὑπόνοιαν μείζονα καταστῆσαι τοῦ πράγματος ἐν τῇ γνώμῃ τῶν ἀκουόντων) ([Hermogenes], *On Forceful Speaking* 7.1–2).[61] Comparable recipes for bringing about particular states of mind can be found in the *Rhetoric for Alexander*; Demetrius's *On Style*; Cicero's *On Invention* and *On the Orator*; the *Rhetoric for Herennius*; and Quintilian's *Education of the Orator*.

Aristotle encourages the aspiring rhetorician to consider "what is fitting" (τὸ πρέπον) in a variety of contexts. For example, a fitting style (λέξις) should be clear, "and neither flat nor above the dignity of the subject, but appropriate (πρέπουσαν)" (*Rhet.* 1404b).[62] In the *Poetics*, the aspiring poet is encouraged to search for τὸ πρέπον with respect to plots (e.g., "One should construct plots, and work them out in diction, with the material as much as possible set before the eyes [μάλιστα πρὸ ὀμμάτων τιθέμενον]. In this way, by seeing things most vividly [ἐναργέστατα], as if present at the actual events, one will discover what is apposite [τὸ πρέπον] and not miss contradictions" [*Poet.* 1455a]),[63] but also

---

59   This tripartite model is developed in the *Timaeus* and the *Republic*. An enormous literature exists on Plato's psychology. For an anthology of some of the most important articles, see Ellen Wagner, ed., *Essays on Plato's Psychology* (New York: Lexington Books, 2001). See also T. M. Robinson, *Plato's Psychology* (Toronto: University of Toronto Press, 1970); Sabina Lovibond, "Plato's Theory of Mind," in *Psychology*, ed. Stephen Everson, Companions to Ancient Thought 2 (Cambridge: Cambridge University Press, 1991).

60   The author of the treatise *On Forceful Speaking* (Περὶ μεθόδου δεινότητος) is unknown, although the work has been attributed to Hermogenes and transmitted with the Hermogenic corpus. Discussion of the text's contents, history, and relation to Hermogenes and another Hermogenic work, *On Invention* (Περὶ εὑρέσεως), is discussed and a translation provided in George A. Kennedy, *Invention And Method: Two Rhetorical Treatises from the Hermogenic Corpus*, WGRW 15 (Atlanta: SBL, 2005), 201–3.

61   Trans. Kennedy, *Invention And Method*.

62   Trans. Kennedy, *Aristotle: On Rhetoric*.

63   Trans. LCL, modified. On making the reader a spectator, see Nünlist, *The Ancient Critic at Work*, 153–54.

24 CHAPTER 1

with respect to the conventions of writing epic or drama (*Poet.* 1456a). Style, plot, and genre, then, are three domains where τὸ πρέπον is encouraged, but the principle, as we saw above in the Homeric scholiasts, can be extended also to the "characters" in the text as well. Additional support for that application is found later in the third book of the *Rhetoric*, where Aristotle talks about tailoring one's λέξις to express πάθος and ἦθος proportional to the subject matter, meaning there is neither discussion of weighty matters in a casual way nor trivial matters solemnly (*Rhet.* 1408a–b; cf. *Poet.* 1456b–1459a). Readers operate with pre-fabricated constructions of how young people think, how old people think, how Achilles or Hector might think, and so on, and are alert to deviations from those expectations.

The background to understanding how a poet or prose composer would know what διάνοια would be fitting for a character lies in the classical education curriculum.[64] Our clearest picture of that curriculum comes in the *progymnasmata* ("preliminary exercises") studied from about the ages of twelve to fifteen, prior to one's rhetorical education, some of which survived antiquity for our examination.[65] The exercises would have been commenced after one learned to read and write, "and were continued in rhetorical schools as written exercises even after declamation had begun."[66] The rhetorical handbooks and the *progymnasmata* are as important for the study of literary compositions as they are for the study of speeches.[67] Rhetoric as an academic discipline shaped both the production and the reception of literary texts, and so deserves careful consideration in an analysis of characterization in ancient narratives.[68]

---

64   This curriculum remained remarkably stable from the Hellenistic period until early modern times. See, e.g., George A. Kennedy, *Progymnasmata: Greek Textbooks of Prose Composition and Rhetoric*, WGRW 10 (Atlanta: SBL, 2003), ix. The seminal treatment of classical education is Henri Irénée Marrou, *Histoire de l'éducation dans l'Antiquité* (Paris: Seuil, 1948). On classical education generally, see now Teresa Morgan, *Literate Education in the Hellenistic and Roman Worlds*, CCSt (Cambridge: Cambridge University Press, 1998); Raffaella Cribiore, *Gymnastics of the Mind: Greek Education in Hellenistic and Roman Egypt* (Princeton: Princeton University Press, 2005).

65   Kennedy, *Progymnasmata*; Craig A. Gibson, *Libanius's Progymnasmata: Model Exercises in Greek Prose Composition and Rhetoric*, WGRW 27 (Atlanta: SBL, 2008); Ronald F. Hock, *The Chreia and Ancient Rhetoric: Commentaries on Aphthonius's Progymnasmata*, WGRW 31 (Atlanta: SBL, 2012).

66   Kennedy, *Progymnasmata*, x.

67   Heinrich Lausberg, *Handbook of Literary Rhetoric: A Foundation for Literary Study*, ed. David E. Orton and R. Dean Anderson (Boston: Brill, 1998). For a range of applications outside of oratory, see Theon 60.

68   One of the earliest adopters in connection to New Testament texts is Hans Dieter Betz, with his *Galatians: A Commentary on Paul's Letter to the Churches in Galatia*, Hermeneia

The exercises called ἠθοποιία and προσωποποιία both have to do with composing speeches "in character."[69] These are the means by which a character's διάνοια is expressed. Such speeches can be external or represent a character's internal monologue. Aelius Theon, author of the earliest surviving book of *progymnasmata*, defines προσωποποιία as "the introduction of a person (προσώπου) to whom words are attributed that are suitable to the speaker and have an indisputable application to the subject discussed" (Theon 115).[70] The exercise is not only used in historical writings, Theon writes, referring to the tradition in historiography of speech-writing (on which, see the discussion in chapter 2 below), "but applicable also to oratory and dialogue and poetry" (Theon 60), that is, in every genre in which characters are imagined as speaking.[71] Theon encourages his student to consider the personality of the speaker (τό τε τοῦ λέγοντος πρόσωπον ὁποῖόν ἐστι) as well as that of the speech's addressees. "Then one is ready to try to say appropriate words (λόγους ἁρμόττοντας)" (Theon 115).[72] This recalls what we noticed above about striving for what is "appropriate" or "fitting" in literary ποίησις. It sets up Theon to underscore for his readers that "different ways of speaking would also be fitting by nature for a woman and for a man, and by status for a slave and a free man, and by activities for a soldier and a farmer, and by state of mind for a lover and a temperate man, and by their origin the words of a Laconian, sparse and clear, differ from those of a man of Attica, which are voluble" (Theon 116). Readers are sensitive to how well authors attribute speeches to characters, and this is why "we praise Homer first because of his ability to attribute the right words to each of the characters he introduces, but we find fault with Euripides because his Hecuba philosophizes inopportunely" (Theon 60).[73] That persons can have set, predictable characters explains also why we have a handbook from Aristotle's student Theophrastus, describing stock figures like "the flatterer" and "the coward."[74]

This compact, selective survey of ancient literary criticism (both at the theoretical level and in practice) and ancient rhetorical theory and training argues for a principle that undergirds the following study, namely, that ancient

---

(Philadelphia: Fortress, 1979). For attention to the rhetorical curriculum in a study of Johannine characterization, see Myers, *Characterizing Jesus*.

69 See Theon 6; Hermogenes 9; Aphthonius 11; Nicolaus 9. Cf. Kennedy, *Progymnasmata*, 13.

70 Trans. Kennedy, *Progymnasmata*. Cf. text and translation in James R. Butts, "The Progymnasmata of Theon: A New Text with Translation and Commentary" (PhD diss, The Claremont Graduate School, 1986).

71 Kennedy, *Progymnasmata*, 4n13.

72 Trans. Kennedy, *Progymnasmata*.

73 Trans. Kennedy, *Progymnasmata*.

74 Text and commentary in James Diggle, ed., *Theophrastus: Characters*, CCTC 43 (Cambridge: Cambridge University Press, 2004).

readers and writers were attentive to the minds of characters in narrative. En route, we looked at evidence of interest in the separate but related issue of access to the minds of readers, spectators, and auditors. Characterization in classical terms had to do chiefly with the stereotyped ethical status of individuals as revealed by their choices; characterization in this project includes moral evaluation but extends to encompass also the broader domain ancient theorists labeled διάνοια.

We turn now to an exploration of techniques by which minds were constructed in genres with which John has been linked. The goal, it bears repeating, is not to identify "the" genre of the Fourth Gospel or the genre traditions that "influenced" it.[75] I propose that the Fourth Gospel is best appreciated when we allow that ancient audiences will plausibly have related it to different genres depending on the context in which they read, and so with different sets of generic expectations in mind. I would go further and agree with Joseph Farrell and others that the essentializing idea of a fixed, classificatory system of genres is itself an inheritance from classical genre theory (in contrast to classical literary production), which potentially obscures more than it reveals.[76] The arrangement of this study in what appears to be a four-part taxonomy is intended as a heuristic strategy for constructive analysis, not an attempt to reinscribe a classificatory approach to genre negotiation. The project could easily be expanded to consider more genres or sub-genres, and the texts studied here could find homes under other labels in other classificatory schemas. The rationale for choosing *these* four genres and not others is that they are those with which the Fourth Gospel is most commonly associated. The rationale for choosing these *four* is that the task would become unwieldy if I attempted to expand the book to look at other generic contexts like the philosophical dialogue, New Comedy, the courtroom speech, testament literature, rabbinic

---

75   On the contrary, I contend that the more dogmatically one attempts to stabilize a genre, the more one reveals one's own political fantasies. Neither authors nor readers are able to determine finally the genre of a work. Problems arise when readers co-opt the voice of the author to articulate their own vision of a text's genre and meaning, usually by reference to intentions. Such a discursive move simultaneously erases the past and suppresses the readings of others. To the first point, it is better to admit that an author's voice cannot be recovered than to presume to speak for the author. To the second point, while interpreters are obliged to present their readings in the best possible light, it is an act of conservative hubris to presume to rule out the possibility of good readings by others.

76   Genres exist, but ancient texts (especially, Farrell says, in the Hellenistic period) are constantly innovating. Classical texts are often intergenetic in relation to what came before themselves, and are sometimes generically ambiguous. Farrell, "Classical Genre in Theory and Practice," 384–96, 402–3.

midrash, and so on.[77] The exemplars chosen for close readings in each chapter below include a more prototypical and a less prototypical instance of the genre, for reasons explained as each text is introduced.[78] The more prototypical texts are well known from the classical Greek tradition; the less prototypical texts are Jewish Greek participants in those same genres.[79]

---

[77] All viable options. For John and philosophy, see George H. van Kooten, "The 'True Light Which Enlightens Everyone' (John 1:9): John, Genesis, The Platonic Notion of the 'True, Noetic Light', and the Allegory of the Cave in Plato's Republic," in *The Creation of Heaven and Earth: Re-Interpretations of Genesis in the Context of Judaism, Ancient Philosophy, Christianity, and Modern Physics*, ed. George H. van Kooten (Leiden: Brill, 2005), 149–94. For the courtroom, see Andrew T. Lincoln, *Truth on Trial: The Lawsuit Motif in the Fourth Gospel* (Peabody: Hendrickson, 2000); George L. Parsenios, *Rhetoric and Drama in the Johannine Lawsuit Motif*, WUNT 258 (Tübingen: Mohr Siebeck, 2010). For testament literature, see George L. Parsenios, *Departure and Consolation: The Johannine Farewell Discourses in Light of Greco-Roman Literature*, NovTSup 117 (Leiden: Brill, 2005). For midrash, see Peder Borgen, *Bread from Heaven: An Exegetical Study of the Concept of Manna in the Gospel of John and the Writings of Philo*, NovTSup 10 (Leiden: Brill, 1965).

[78] For prototypical genre theory, see Daniel Chandler, "Schema Theory and the Interpretation of Television Programmes," April 1997, http://users.aber.ac.uk/dgc/Documents/short/schematv.html; Michael Sinding, "After Definitions: Genre, Categories, and Cognitive Science," *Genre* 35 (2002): 181–219; Newsom, "Spying out the Land: A Report from Genology"; Benjamin G. Wright, "Joining the Club: A Suggestion about Genre in Early Jewish Texts," *DSD* 17 (2010): 289–314. For an attempt to put prototypical genre theory in conversation with the Fourth Gospel, see my "Characterization in John 4 and the Prototypical Type-Scene as a Generic Concept."

[79] In setting up the project this way, I was inspired by a question posed by Hindy Najman: "Are Jewish Greek traditions trying to conform to rules of the Greek literature? This has to be considered case by case, for another day." She posed the question in relation to drama, which had institutionalized rules for participation in the genre (on which, see chapter 5 below). The other Greek genres considered in this project, however, did not have as clearly defined rules. Hindy Najman, "The Idea of Biblical Genre: From Discourse to Constellation," in *Prayer and Poetry in the Dead Sea Scrolls and Related Literature: Essays in Honor of Eileen Schuller on the Occasion of Her 65th Birthday*, ed. Jeremy Penner, Ken M. Penner, and Cecilia Wassen, STDJ 98 (Leiden: Brill, 2012), 311.

CHAPTER 2

Historiography: Investigative Speculation and Cognitive Causation

In connection to ancient genre categorization, historiography refers broadly to writings narrating past events, usually with an emphasis on the work of ἱστορία ("investigation") that went into these productions. Although this description fits many ancient texts, it has become customary to distinguish within that broad collection a narrower historiographical tradition connected to Herodotus, Thucydides, and their Greek and Roman successors.[1] Hellenistic Jewish historiographers like Eupolemus, Demetrius, Artapanus, and Josephus participated in the "narrow" tradition of historiography too, but their projects were also informed by a largely separate historiographical tradition as found

---

1   The classic modern attempt to categorize "historiography" into sub-genres was undertaken by Felix Jacoby in *Fragmente der griechischen Historiker*. The sub-genres are arranged in the order in which he believes they developed: mythography, ethnography, chronography, contemporary history (*Zeitgeschichte*), and horography (or local history). This model has been criticized as overdetermined and teleologically-constructed to culminate in Herodotus and Thucydides as the apex of the genre, after which the genre fell into decline. The model also includes several categories (notably Zeitgeschichte and ethnography) which are never labeled in antiquity. For discussion, see John Marincola, ed., *A Companion to Greek and Roman Historiography*, BCAW (Oxford: Blackwell, 2007), 4–6. Jacoby's work has since been revised, expanded, and moved online: http://referenceworks.brillonline.com/browse/brill-s-new -jacoby. The process is ongoing, with an expected completion in 2019.

   An ancient attempt to subdivide "history" into subgenres worth comparing with Jacoby's can be found in Theon's *Progymnasmata* 16, where six genres are proposed, each with representative figures: (1) genealogical history (Apollodorus of Athens, Acusilaus of Argos, and Hecataeus of Miletus); (2) political history (Thucydides and Philistus); (3) mythical history (Asclepiades); (4) memory of fine sayings (Xenophon's *Memorabilia*) and biographical writing (Aristoxenus, Satyrus); (5) "general" histories about countries, towns, rivers, situations, nature, etc. (Cimnus, Philias, Philostephanus, or Istrus) and descriptions of constitutions (Aristotle); and (6) "the more highly developed form of history" (Herodotus and "many other historians"). Note, however, that Theon's object in this section is training in elocution, not genre or literary theory per se. Dionysius of Halicarnassus shows a familiarity with such ways of distinguishing subgenres within history, though he makes it clear that not all are equally good, and that his own contribution is best because "it is a combination of every kind, forensic, speculative and narrative, to the intent that it may afford satisfaction both to those who occupy themselves with political debates and to those who are devoted to philosophical speculations, as well as to any who may desire mere undisturbed entertainment in their reading of history" (*Ant. Rom.* 1.8.3). Trans. LCL.

© KONINKLIJKE BRILL NV, LEIDEN, 2019 | DOI:10.1163/9789004396043_003

in the Hebrew Bible.[2] In this chapter, I begin by discussing how Johannine scholars have talked about the relationship between the Fourth Gospel and the narrow tradition of ancient historiography. In the main part of the chapter, I start a new conversation by describing the conventions in that narrow historiographical tradition for representing minds, illustrating the analysis with a pair of case studies drawn from Polybius's *Histories* and Josephus's *Jewish Antiquities*. I argue that individual thinking actors are ubiquitous in the historiographical tradition represented by these authors, but that they are largely overshadowed by narrative descriptions of events (πράξεις, πράγματα, γεγενημένα) connected to larger social groups, and by inquiry into the causes (αἰτίαι) for those events. The result is that in cases where individual thoughts are signaled or (more rarely) narrated in detail, the thoughts offer aetiological explanations for events.

1   John and Historiography

The Fourth Gospel has been compared to historiography in both broad and narrow conceptions of the genre, often by readers more concerned with the historicity of the Gospels than questions about genre. One might plot the modern conversation using C. H. Dodd's second major book on John as a point of departure.[3] The consensus Dodd rejects, represented by predecessors like Baur, Strauss, and Schweitzer, held that John was the least historical of the canonical Gospels, that its reflection of Jesus's life and ministry was fainter, less accurate, than its canonical counterparts. Dodd's counterthesis holds that John was written without knowledge of the Synoptics and is therefore significant as an independent and historically-valuable tradition. The view has been adopted by many subsequent New Testament scholars, including Raymond Brown in his landmark Anchor Bible commentary on the Fourth Gospel.[4] The most

---

2   On this tradition, see John Van Seters, *In Search of History: Historiography in the Ancient World and the Origins of Biblical History* (Winona Lake: Eisenbrauns, 1997).

3   C. H. Dodd, *Historical Tradition in the Fourth Gospel* (Cambridge: Cambridge University Press, 1963).

4   The perspective taken in the commentary is described as "a moderately critical theory of the composition of the Gospel, combined with the conviction that the Gospel is rooted in historical tradition about Jesus of Nazareth." Brown credits Dodd's *Historical Tradition* for shaping his view of the value of the Gospel for historical work. Raymond E. Brown, *The Gospel According to John I–XII: A New Translation with Introduction and Commentary*, AB 29 (Garden City: Doubleday, 1966), v–vi.

exhaustive exploration of John and history is to be found in the proceedings of the "John, Jesus and History" program unit of the Society of Biblical Literature.[5]

On the other hand, "the Fourth Gospel is not history but theology" was and remains a truism for many biblical scholars. The sentiment may be as old as Clement of Alexandria, who famously distinguished John from the Synoptics as the "spiritual gospel" (apud Eusebius, *Hist. eccl.* 6.14.5–6).[6]

By far the most common position one encounters in recent Johannine scholarship, however, is one which raises the history-versus-theology perspective only to dismiss it as a false choice, as when Marianne Meye Thompson asks rhetorically, "In what sense does the fact that it [the Johannine account of Jesus's death] is theological interpretation rule out its 'historical' character?"[7]

Few scholars, even in the "John, Jesus, and History" group, have attempted to look at the Fourth Gospel in a sustained way in connection to the conventions of historiography in the narrow sense. Richard Bauckham addresses this relative void in the published version of a 2005 lecture, prefacing his own contribution by indicating that Craig S. Keener was the only prior scholar to discuss John in connection with "the features characteristic of Greco-Roman historiography."[8] The possibility of a connection between a gospel and historiography has been

---

5 The group has produced a substantial body of work in three large volumes comprising over eighty essays. For an annotated bibliography, see http://johannine.org/JJH.html; Paul N. Anderson, Felix Just, S.J., and Tom Thatcher, eds., *John, Jesus, and History, Volume 1: Critical Appraisals of Critical Views*, SBLSymS 44 (Brill: Leiden, 2007); Paul N. Anderson, Felix Just, S.J., and Tom Thatcher, eds., *John, Jesus, and History, Volume 2: Aspects of Historicity in the Fourth Gospel*, ECL 2 (Atlanta: SBL, 2009); Paul N. Anderson, Felix Just, S.J., and Tom Thatcher, eds., *John, Jesus, and History, Volume 3: Glimpses of Jesus through the Johannine Lens*, ECL 18 (Atlanta: SBL, 2016).

Whether or not John belongs to "historiography" as a genre is a very different question than whether or not and in what sense historiographical works furnish reliable historical data. The present chapter is concerned only with the first of those two questions. For the latter, the critique of Robinson in connection to scholarship on Mark is still useful: James McConkey Robinson, *The Problem of History in Mark*, SBT 21 (London: SCM Press, 1957).

6 Typical 19th-century language: "the fourth gospel is not an historical work; on the contrary, it is a dogmatic, mystical, speculative production probably of some theologian of the Alexandrian school." Henry Truro Bray, *Essays on God and Man: Or A Philosophical Inquiry Into the Principles of Religion* (St. Louis: Nixon-Jones Printing, 1888), 62.

7 Marianne Meye Thompson, "The 'Spiritual Gospel': How John the Theologian Writes History," in *John, Jesus, and History*, ed. Paul N. Anderson, Felix Just, and Tom Thatcher, ECL 2 (Atlanta: SBL, 2009), 106.

8 Bauckham, "Historiographical Characteristics," 19. Cf. Craig S. Keener, *The Gospel of John: A Commentary* (Peabody: Hendrickson, 2003), 12–51. The lecture anticipated his then-in-progress book on the testimony motif in John and ancient historiography. See Richard Bauckham, *The Testimony of the Beloved Disciple: Narrative, History, and Theology in the Gospel of John* (Grand Rapids: Baker Academic, 2007).

treated more fully in connection to Luke, and more recently in connection to Mark and Matthew.[9]

Though Keener and Bauckham find "historiographical features" in John (i.e., hallmark features of the genre historiography), both emphasize that what they find is not sufficient to assign the Fourth Gospel to historiography in a narrow sense.[10] No modern scholar, as far as I know, has tried to make such a case.

We turn now to the narrow historiographic tradition and its conventions for representing minds. After setting the stage here, we will return in chapter 6 to the Fourth Gospel and compare its patterns of cognitive representations. This

---

9 For Luke-Acts, see Martin Dibelius, "Der erste christliche Historiker," in *Aus der Arbeit der Universität 1946/47*, ed. Hans Freiherr von Campenhausen, SUHei 3 (Berlin: Springer, 1948), 112–25. See also Gregory E. Sterling, *Historiography and Self-Definition: Josephos, Luke-Acts, and Apologetic Historiography*, NovTSup 64 (Leiden: Brill, 1992), 311–89; Hubert Cancik, "The History of Culture, Religion, and Institutions in Ancient Historiography: Philological Observations Concerning Luke's History," *JBL* 116 (1997): 673–95; Daniel Marguerat, *The First Christian Historian: Writing the "Acts of the Apostles,"* SNTSMS 121 (Cambridge: Cambridge University Press, 2002). More recently, see especially Molthagen's essay in Jörg Frey, Clare K. Rothschild, and Jens Schröter, eds., *Die Apostelgeschichte im Kontext antiker und frühchristlicher Historiographie*, BZNW 162 (Berlin: de Gruyter, 2009). Keener, in making "lives" the natural category ancient readers would have assigned the Gospels, makes room for a possible exception in Luke's case, as possibly constituting a "historical monograph" because of its pairing with Acts. Keener, *The Gospel of John*, 1:11. A recent addition to the list of works connecting Luke with historiography is Andrew Pitts, "Greco-Roman Historiography and Luke's Use of Scripture" (PhD diss, McMaster Divinity School, 2014).

For Mark, see Eve-Marie Becker, *Das Markus-Evangelium im Rahmen antiker Historiographie*, WUNT 194 (Tübingen: Mohr Siebeck, 2006); Eve-Marie Becker, "Patterns of Early Christian Thinking and Writing of History: Paul—Mark—Acts," in *Thinking, Recording, and Writing History in the Ancient World*, ed. Kurt A. Raaflaub (Chichester: Wiley Blackwell, 2014), 276–313. Adela Yarbro Collins describes Mark as an "eschatological historical monograph," after demonstrating some of the ways it fails to fit neatly into either biography or historiography. See Adela Yarbro Collins, *Mark: A Commentary*, Hermeneia (Minneapolis: Fortress, 2007), 18, 42–44. For the social networks of Gospel writers as comparable to those of historiographers, see Richard Last, "The Social Relationships of Gospel Writers: New Insights from Inscriptions Commending Greek Historiographers," *JSNT* 37 (2015): 223–52.

10 The underlying assumption seems to be that genre identifications are made by comparing a given text to a list of features. For more nuanced alternatives to the "list of features" approach, see Carol A. Newsom, "Spying out the Land: A Report from Genology," in *Seeking Out the Wisdom of the Ancients: Essays Offered to Honor Michael V. Fox on the Occasion of His Sixty-Fifth Birthday*, ed. Ronald L. Troxel, Kelvin G. Friebel, and Dennis Robert Magary (Winona Lake: Eisenbrauns, 2005), 437–50; Benjamin G. Wright, "Joining the Club: A Suggestion about Genre in Early Jewish Texts," *DSD* 17 (2010): 289–314. Also some of the papers in Kasper Bro Larsen, ed., *The Gospel of John as Genre Mosaic*, SANt 3 (Göttingen: Vandehoeck & Rupprecht, 2015).

32   CHAPTER 2

undertaking is not to rule John in or out of historiography as a genre, but rather
to illustrate how framing our expectations with data from the historiographical tradition affects what we see in John.

2   **Representing Minds in Greek and Roman Historiography**[11]

A genre-defining point of departure for Greek and Roman historiography lies
with Herodotus (ca. 484–425 BCE), who at least since Cicero has been called
the *pater historiae* (Cicero, *On the Laws* 1.5).[12] We cannot know if his fifth-
century contemporaries recognized in his work the origins of a new genre;
what is clear, however, is that his *Histories* would retroactively be constituted
as the prototype of a prominent literary genre. Among the features of the work
marked by later readers as distinctive was the impulse to render accounts of
specific periods, peoples, and events, selectively sifting documentary sources

---

11   Translations of Herodotus, Polybius, and Josephus follow the LCL, unless noted otherwise.
12   This chapter focuses on Hellenistic historiography, which is impossible to describe with-
      out reference to Herodotus and Thucydides in the fifth century. It largely brackets out
      Roman and Hebrew traditions of historiography. Fragments of other Hellenistic Jewish
      historiographers also survive. Among these, alongside and antecedent to Josephus, note
      especially 2 Maccabees (and the five-volume work by Jason of Cyrene of which it is an
      epitome; cf. 2 Macc 2.24). Both Josephus's corpus and 2 Maccabees were written and are
      extant in Greek, though Josephus may have penned an earlier version of *Jewish War* in
      Hebrew or Aramaic, depending on what one makes of his claim at *J. W.* 1.3. Other works
      from that period, including 1 Maccabees and Pseudo-Philo's *Liber antiquitatum biblicarum*
      were likely written in Hebrew, though both were translated into Greek at an early date.
      1 Maccabees survives in Greek; its Hebrew original is lost. Pseudo-Philo's *LAB* survives only
      in a Latin translation of the Greek; both the Hebrew and the Greek versions are non-extant.
      Whatever their original language of composition, all these historiographers had imbibed
      from the Greek tradition already mentioned and a precedent set by Jewish historiographi-
      cal writings including (but not limited to) those in the Hebrew Bible. Other Jewish histo-
      rians (depending on how expansive a definition one wishes to set on that label) from the
      Hellenistic period survive in fragments, via Eusebius (whose main source is Alexander
      Polyhistor) and other late Christian writers: Demetrius, Eupolemus, Artapanus (*On the
      Jews*), Cleodamus Malchus, Ps.Eupolemus, Aristeas (*On the Jews*), Ps.Hecataeus (*On the
      Jews*), Thallus (*Histories*), Justus of Tiberias (*A Chronicle of the Jewish Kings*, and *Jewish
      War*). Scholars label some of these works "historical fiction" or "historical novels" rather
      than "historiography," but this is a modern distinction seemingly motivated by the same
      kinds of historiographic anxieties that govern questions about the Gospels and "what re-
      ally happened." See further Gregory E. Sterling, "The Jewish Appropriation of Hellenistic
      Historiography," in *Greek and Roman Historiography*, ed. John Marincola, ORCS (Oxford:
      Oxford University Press, 2011), 231–43; Harold W. Attridge, "Historiography," in *Jewish
      Writings of the Second Temple Period: Apocrypha, Pseudepigrapha, Qumran, Sectarian
      Writings, Philo, Josephus*, ed. Michael E. Stone, CRINT 2 (Assen: Van Gorcum, 1984), 157–83.

(such as personal letters), material culture (such as monuments and statuary), and eyewitness testimonies.[13] Texts in this Herodotean tradition, moreover, would be marked by insistence on "truthfulness" and "accuracy" (though it would be a mistake to conflate these values with the positivist ideals of the nineteenth century, the uninflected transmission of pure information).[14] Some of these values come together in Herodotus's critique of Homer, which is on display, for example, in what he writes about Helen (*Hist.* 2.112–120).[15]

Herodotus claims to have discovered from investigation in Egypt that Helen had been detained for the ten years of the Trojan War by King Proteus at Memphis, rather than (as one reads in the *Iliad*) by Alexander at Troy. The shift from straightforward narrative to narrative based on investigation (ἱστορία, Ionic ἱστορίη) will become a hallmark of the emerging genre. Herodotus thinks he can show that Homer, despite knowing the truth about Helen's whereabouts, used the Helen-in-Troy version because the true account was not fitting for epic poetry (οὐ γὰρ ὁμοίως ἐς τὴν ἐποποιίην εὐπρεπὴς ἦν). Here, we see something like the beginnings of a consciousness of historiography as a genre distinct from poetry, with ideas about what was "fitting" in each.[16]

Herodotus believes Homer was right that the Greeks and the Trojans fought and that the Greeks eventually took the city. He names as the cause for this war

---

13   T. James Luce, *The Greek Historians* (London: Routledge, 1997), 1–2.

14   On the historical method of Herodotus, see Catherine Darbo-Peschanski, *Le discours du particulier: essai sur l'enquête hérodotéenne* (Paris: Seuil, 1987); Donald Lateiner, *The Historical Method of Herodotus* (Toronto: University of Toronto Press, 1989).

15   Homer, from the earliest stratum of surviving Greek literature (ca. seventh c. BCE), has what would appear to later readers as a historical consciousness. Many Hellenistic and Roman imperial readers viewed Homer as the author of historical accounts in the *Iliad* and *Odyssey*. The emergence of writers like Herodotus and Thucydides, moreover, did not stop readers from reading the *Iliad* and *Odyssey* and other texts in the mythopoetic tradition as historical. On the contrary, an industry emerged the chief function of which was to rationalize aspects of the mythos that strained credulity. Homer, moreover, was largely to thank for the subject matter and form taken up by antiquity's authors remembered as historians: the Trojan War of the *Iliad* gave way to the Persian Wars in Herodotus and the Peloponnesian War in Thucydides; the wanderings of Odysseus in the *Odyssey* informed the ethnographic and geographic content which formed so great a part of later histories. For some aspects of the reception of Homer in Herodotus, Thucydides, Strabo, Dio Chrysostom, Lucian, and Philostratus, see the discussion in Lawrence Young Kim, *Homer between History and Fiction in Imperial Greek Literature*, GCRW (Cambridge: Cambridge University Press, 2010).

16   Despite Herodotus's attempts to distance himself from Homer, the latter's influence on the *Histories* is a favorite subject of Herodotean scholarship. See, e.g., "The Homeric Background," in Emily Baragwanath, *Motivation and Narrative in Herodotus*, OCM (Oxford: Oxford University Press, 2008), 35–54.

the Greeks' mistaken evaluation of what the Trojans told them, namely, that Helen was with Proteus in Egypt:

> On coming within the city walls, they demanded restitution of Helen and the possessions which Alexander had stolen from Menelaus and carried off, and reparation besides for the wrong done; but the Teucrians then and ever afterwards declared, with oaths and without, that neither Helen nor the goods claimed were with them, she and they being in Egypt; nor could they (so they said) justly make reparation for what was in the hands of the Egyptian king Proteus. But the Greeks thought that the Trojans mocked them (οἱ δὲ Ἕλληνες καταγελᾶσθαι δοκέοντες ὑπ' αὐτῶν), and therewith besieged the city, till they took it; and it was not till they took the fortress and found no Helen there, and heard the same declaration as before, that they gave credence to the Trojans' first word.
>
> *Hist.* 2.118[17]

Although he does not use the language of αἰτίαι here, Herodotus here and throughout the work is pursuing the etiological agenda he announces in his preface: "so that time may not blot out the memory of the past from human reckoning, and that great and marvelous deeds (ἔργα μεγάλα τε καὶ θωμαστά) done by Greeks and foreigners and *especially the reason* why they warred against each other (τά τε ἄλλα καὶ δι' ἣν αἰτίην ἐπολέμησαν ἀλλήλοισι) may not lack renown" (*Hist.* 1.1).[18] His method allows him to identify the cause of the Greek assault on Troy as a cognitive failure.

Herodotus credits his account to the investigative efforts undertaken by his sources: "the priests told me that they had learnt some of this tale by inquiry (ἱστορίῃσι)" (*Hist.* 2.119). Of course, Herodotus's readers would not know about the priests' investigative labors were it not for Herodotus's own inquiries. Furthermore, Herodotus does not simply relay the investigative work of others; he adds his own speculative considerations. In favor of the Egyptian priests' alternative account of the causes for the Trojan War, Herodotus theorizes Priam's mind: "I reason thus (τάδε ἐπιλεγόμενος)," he writes, "that had Helen been in Ilion, then with or without the will of Alexander she would have been given back to the Greeks." Herodotus defends his proposition by exploring the rationality of Priam and his fellow decision-makers: "for surely neither was Priam so mad (φρενοβλαβής), nor those nearest to him, as to consent to risk their own persons and their children and their city, that Alexander might

---

17   Trans. LCL, modified.
18   Trans. LCL, modified.

take Helen as a wife." This is a mode of discourse production we might call, for our purposes, "investigative speculation." Herodotus reinforces his speculation by considering the counterargument and rejecting it:

> Even be it granted that they were so minded (ταῦτα ἐγίνωσκον) in the first days, yet when not only many of the Trojans were slain in fighting against the Greeks, but Priam himself lost by death two or three or even more of his sons in every battle (if the poets are to be trusted), in this turn of affairs, had Helen been Priam's own wife, I cannot but think (for myself) that he would have restored her to the Greeks, if by so doing he could escape from the present evil plight.
>
> *Hist.* 2.120

The impulse to explain historical events in causal terms persists into the Hellenistic period and becomes a hallmark of the genre. Dionysius of Halicarnassus, the Hellenistic historiographer active in the first century BCE and responsible for the twenty-volume *Roman Antiquities*, describes his task as relating "all the foreign wars that the city waged during that period and all the internal seditions with which she was agitated, showing from what causes (αἰτιῶν) they sprang and by what methods and by what arguments they were brought to an end" (*Ant. Rom.* 1.8.2).[19] His duty involves relaying not only the "bare outcome of events," but also causes, since "everyone demands that the causes of events be investigated (τὰς αἰτίας ἱστορῆσαι τῶν γενομένων), as well as the ways in which things were done, the motives of those who did them (τὰς διανοίας τῶν πραξάντων), and the instances of divine intervention, and that they be left uninformed of none of the circumstances that naturally attend those events" (*Ant. Rom.* 5.56.1).[20] Sometimes this investigation into causes involved traveling and questioning (as Herodotus claims to have done in Egypt), sometimes it seems to have been sufficient merely to use his rational faculties to theorize the mind of a subject (as Herodotus does with Priam).

While the seminal work of Herodotus cast a long shadow over that of future historiographers, it was his younger contemporary Thucydides (ca. 460–395 BCE) whose unfinished *History of the Peloponnesian War* would be more prototypical for political historiography in later antiquity. The structures and organizing concerns of Thucydides are palpable in the works of both Polybius and

---

19   Trans. LCL.
20   Trans. LCL, modified.

36   CHAPTER 2

Josephus, the Hellenistic historiographers whose work will be examined more minutely below, justifying careful attention here to etiology in Thucydides.[21]

While appreciation for the methods and historical value of Herodotus has waxed and waned over the centuries, Thucydides has enjoyed a relatively positive and stable reputation.[22] Thucydides likely knew Herodotus's work and offers occasional, implicit critiques of his methodology.[23] Like Herodotus,

---

21 Readers have viewed Polybius as the most Thucydidean of all ancient historians. Frank Walbank remarks that "for all his own occasional lapses, Polybius stands for a return to the aims and methods of Thucydides." F. W. Walbank, *Polybius*, SCLec 42 (Berkeley: University of California Press, 1972), 40. On Polybius's relationships to these genre-defining historians, see the essays by McGing ("Polybius and Herodotus"), Rood ("Polybius, Thucydides, and the First Punic War"), and Longley ("Thucydides, Polybius, and Human Nature") in Christopher Smith and Liv Mariah Yarrow, eds., *Imperialism, Cultural Politics, and Polybius* (Oxford: Oxford University Press, 2012).

     Josephus read Thucydides and assimilated features of his style, but is more eclectic in method. For a negative assessment of Josephus in comparison to Thucydides, see H. St. J. Thackeray, *Josephus, the Man and the Historian* (New York: Ktav, 1968). "If we ask what use our historian made of these ample and firsthand materials and turn to consider his motives and personality, it must be confessed that his work cannot stand the test of comparison with that highest of standards, the History of the Peloponnesian War. Josephus lacks the sober impartiality of Thucydides and, with all his reiterated protestations of his zeal for the truth, shows from time to time, when his statements are subject to control, a lax sense of the full meaning of that word" (46).

22 For the reception of Thucydides, see Christine Lee and Neville Morley, eds., *A Handbook to the Reception of Thucydides* (Oxford: John Wiley & Sons, 2015). N.B. Valérie Fromentin and Sophie Gotteland, "Thucydides' Ancient Reputation," on pages 13–25.

     Although Thucydides remains a darling of modern historians for his ostensibly objective pursuit of the facts of history, he is also a skilled literary artist. The classic treatment is Francis M. Cornford, *Thucydides Mythistoricus* (London: Edward Arnold, 1907). See also Kieran Egan, "Thucydides, Tragedian," in *The Writing of History: Literary Form and Historical Understanding*, ed. Robert H. Canary and Henry Kozicki (Madison: University of Wisconsin Press, 1978), 63–92.

     Thucydides would have the historian verify his sources before including an encountered tradition in his work. This does not mean, however, transcribing the full process of one's investigation. Herodotus likes to report on a wide variety of the traditions he encounters; Thucydides almost never does. Modern historians set out the facts, propose an interpretation, and leave it to the reader to decide if the interpretation fits the evidence. Ancient historians, after Thucydides, tend to take this responsibility on themselves. Paul Veyne, *Did the Greeks Believe in Their Myths?: An Essay on the Constitutive Imagination*, trans. Paula Wissing (Chicago: University of Chicago Press, 1988), 10.

23 On Thucydides's relationship to Herodotus, see the essays in Edith Foster and Donald Lateiner, eds., *Thucydides and Herodotus* (Oxford: Oxford University Press, 2012). Note especially the article by Philip A. Stadter, "Thucydides as a 'Reader' of Herodotus" (39–66). Also useful are Zacharias Rogkotis, "Thucydides and Herodotus: Aspects of Their Intertextual Relationship," in *Brill's Companion to Thucydides*, ed. Antonios Rengakos and

Thucydides owes a debt to Homer,[24] he casts his own work as a monument for the ages (Thuc. 1.22; cf. Herodotus, *Hist.* 1.1), and he tells much of his story with the device of reported speeches.[25] These speeches are a primary access point for character cognition. Some regular features of Herodotus, however, are abandoned or minimized in Thucydides, including geographic and ethnographic digressions, or stories about Greek and oriental despots.[26] After Thucydides, history becomes chiefly about events, πράξεις, *res gestae* in the sphere of "politics" broadly conceived, encompassing wars, diplomacy, and statecraft.[27] Such events occasion myriad opportunities for humans to desire, strategize, and react, all of which can happen in the perceptible field of narrative or be limited to the non-perceptible domain.

The reader who moves from Herodotus to Thucydides may be struck by the reduced prominence of individuals and, correspondingly, reduced access to individual minds. Like Herodotus, Thucydides attends to the fortunes of groups, especially groups constituted of men from a given πόλις involved in the Peloponnesian War. Unlike Herodotus, the intrigues of individual despots play less of a role in Thucydides. Many named individuals figure in Thucydides's narrative, and like his Herodotean counterpart, the Thucydidean narrator generally enjoys unobstructed speculative access to those individual minds.[28] Neither Herodotus nor Thucydides is shy about describing the motivations of historical actors, a fact which has troubled some of his modern interpreters. Lionel Pearson describes Thucydides's treatment of individuals and their thoughts as "arbitrary," and A. G. Woodhead wryly remarks that in connection to the figure Cleon, Thucydides is a "remarkable thought reader."[29] Cognitive narratologists more familiar with modern literature sometimes make "access

---

Antonis Tsakmakis, BCCS (Leiden: Brill, 2006), 57–86; Tim Rood, "Thucydides and His Predecessors," *Histos* 2 (1998): 230–67.

24   Kim, *Homer between History and Fiction in Imperial Greek Literature*, 38–46.

25   Christopher Pelling, "Thucydides' Speeches," in *Thucydides*, ed. Jeffrey S. Rusten (Oxford: Oxford University Press, 2009), 176–90.

26   Philip A Stadter, "Thucydides as 'Reader' of Herodotus," 39.

27   See Charles W. Fornara, *The Nature of History in Ancient Greece and Rome* (Berkeley: University of California Press, 1983), 3.

28   Rogkotis, "Thucydides and Herodotus: Aspects of Their Intertextual Relationship"; Mabel L. Lang, "Participial Motivation in Thucydides," *Mn.* 48 (1995): 48–65; A. G. Woodhead, "Thucydides' Portrait of Cleon," *Mn.* 13 (1960): 289–317; Lionel Pearson, "Thucydides as Reporter and Critic," *TAPA* 78 (1947): 37–60.

29   Woodhead, "Thucydides' Portrait of Cleon," 313; Pearson, "Thucydides as Reporter and Critic," 56. Both cited in Lang, "Participial Motivation in Thucydides," 48.

to minds" a quality exclusively characteristic of fiction or the novel; such a distinction, however, does not hold up in ancient literary contexts.[30] The Lacedaemonians' decision to go to war, as Thucydides represents it in narrator speech, is explained with causal language and with reference to their fear: "the vote of the Lacedaemonians that the treaty had been broken and that they must go to war was determined, not so much by the influence of the speeches of their allies, as by fear of the Athenians, lest they become too powerful (οὐ τοσοῦτον τῶν ξυμμάχων πεισθέντες τοῖς λόγοις ὅσον φοβούμενοι τοὺς Ἀθηναίους μὴ ἐπὶ μεῖζον δυνηθῶσιν), seeing that the greater part of Hellas was already subject to them" (Thuc. 1.88).[31] Thucydides's most striking vehicle for providing access to the minds of individual and group characters in his narrative, however, is not the narrator but reported speeches.[32]

Thucydides functions stylistically and methodologically as a benchmark for subsequent generations of historians in antiquity. Despite occupying a stylistically- and methodologically-prototypical position in ancient historiography, many of the historians who succeeded him—even some, like Xenophon, who conspicuously resumed their histories from where he had left off (ca. 411 BCE)—departed from the Thucydidean model in various ways.[33] The fact of divergences does not come as a surprise, given the inherent instability of genres. Some ancient theorists like Dionysius and Lucian lament the divergences of post-Thucydidean historians as degenerative.[34] Generic innovation, however, was a regular feature of the Hellenistic period, as we saw already in

---

30   See Jonas Grethlein, "Social Minds and Narrative Time: Collective Experience in Thucydides and Heliodorus," *Narrative* 23 (2015): 123–39.

31   Trans. LCL.

32   On the speeches in Thucydides, see Pelling, "Thucydides' Speeches." On speeches as a sub-genre within historiography, see Fornara, *The Nature of History in Ancient Greece and Rome*, 142–68. For motives articulated in character speech, see, e.g., Thuc. 1.73, 76, 86. For the narrator's access to characters' minds, see, e.g., 1.88, 90, 91.

33   E.g., Xenophon in his *Hellenica* or Theopompus in his *Philippica*. Cf. BNJ 115. Polybius noticed this about the relationship between Theopompus and Thucydides (*Hist.* 8.11.3). Other historians who mention Thucydides are the so-called Oxyrhynchus historian and Ephorus (BNJ 70), who uses Thucydides almost exclusively as his source for events of the fifth century. See Roberto Nicolai, "Thucydides Continued," in *Brill's Companion to Thucydides*, ed. Antonios Rengakos and Antonis Tsakmakis, BCCS (Leiden: Brill, 2006), 691–719.

34   Dionysius of Halicarnassus complains about degeneration. See his critical essays collected in LCL 465 and 466, especially *On Thucydides* and *Letter to Gnaeus Pompeius*. Cf. Lucian of Samosata, who frames his cynical pamphlet *How to Write History* (ca. 166 CE) with accusations of incompetence directed at his contemporary historians.

the previous chapter.[35] What is more interesting, at least for our purposes, is how changes at one level of the genre structure play off against and thus reinforce genre conventions at a deeper level.

One departure from the Thucydidean model noted by ancient theorists has to do with the tendency of the fourth-century historian Theopompus "not only to see and to state what is obvious to most people (μὴ μόνον τὰ φανερὰ τοῖς πολλοῖς ὁρᾶν καὶ λέγειν), but to examine even the hidden reasons for actions and the motives of their agents (ἀλλ᾽ ἐξετάζειν καὶ τὰς ἀφανεῖς αἰτίας τῶν πράξεων καὶ τῶν πραξάντων αὐτάς), and the feelings in their hearts (καὶ τὰ πάθη τῆς ψυχῆς)" (Dionysius of Halicarnassus, *Pomp.* 6).[36] Although Dionysius presents this as a service rendered to the reader and a mark of Theopompus's skill as a historian, other ancient theorists treat it as problematic.[37] In a discussion about the teacher's duty to attend to the temperaments of his students, Cicero attributes to Isocrates a remark about Theopompus and another fourth-century historian, Ephorus: "Isocrates used to say that he made a practice of employing the spur with Ephorus and the bridle with Theopompus—meaning that he used to check the one's exuberance and boldness of style and spur on the hesitation and diffidence of the other" (Cicero, *Or. Brut.* 204).[38] Although it has become conventional in scholarship to speak of these divergences from a Thucydidean precedent in terms of difference, it is important for our purposes to notice that at least in Theopompus's case the novel attention to "hidden reasons for actions" and "motives of agents" and "feelings in hearts"—all features of the nonperceptible cognitive realm—are in continuity with the Herodotean and Thucydidean concern for the causes of events.

The Greek model of historiography rooted in Thucydides would directly or indirectly shape virtually all subsequent historiographical paradigms in the

---

35   Cf. Joseph Farrell, "Classical Genre in Theory and Practice," *NLitHist* 34 (July 1, 2003): 383–408. One way of thinking about the changes as innovation is, in Eve-Marie Becker's perspective, to see a general move towards "person-centered" historiography in the Hellenistic period. Becker, *Das Markus-Evangelium im Rahmen antiker Historiographie*, 16–20; Becker, "Patterns of Early Christian Thinking and Writing of History: Paul—Mark—Acts," 282.

36   Trans. LCL. On the psychological method of Theopompus, see Michael A. Flower, *Theopompus of Chios: History and Rhetoric in the Fourth Century BC* (Oxford: Oxford University Press, 1994), 169–83.

37   Cf. Plutarch's remarks about Theopompus in *On the Malice of Herodotus*, discussed below in chapter 3. Cf. Lucian's characterization of Theopompus as a prosecutor "who impeached nearly everybody in a quarrelsome spirit and made a business of it" (*How to Write History* 59 [trans. LCL]).

38   Trans. LCL. Historians today reject the claim that Theopompus and Ephorus were students of Isocrates. See Flower, *Theopompus of Chios*, 42–62.

Western tradition, including Eusebius's *Ecclesiastical History*, the first Christian text to belong clearly to the narrow tradition of historiography. It is nevertheless fair to wonder whether some of its conventions in a broad sense are detectable in the Gospels. The author of the Fourth Gospel—indeed, the authors of all the documents in the New Testament—wrote in Greek about "Jewish" matters. This was true of Josephus too, a Jewish writer roughly contemporary with the Fourth Evangelist, who explicitly wrote in the historiographic tradition. Before turning to Josephus, however, we will look at patterns for representing thought in Polybius, one of Thucydides's most devoted students and (along with Thucydides) a generic model used by Josephus.

3   Polybius's *Histories*

Polybius of Megalopolis (ca. 200–118 BCE) began his career as a politician in the Achaean League, but the experience was cut short in 168 with the Roman victory over Macedon and the dissolution of the League. He spent the next seventeen years as a political prisoner in Rome, where he befriended Scipio Aemilianus and accompanied him to the destruction of Carthage in 146. He wrote on many topics, but his chief work was a 40-volume history of Rome's rise to hegemony, beginning in 220 and concluding with the destruction of Carthage in 146, titled simply *The Histories*. Most of that work is lost, although books 1–5 and substantial excerpts from book 6 (on the Roman constitution) and book 12 (on how to write history) survive. Fragments from most books are preserved in quotations by other authors, especially Livy, whose account of 220–146 BCE relies mainly on Polybius. The excerpts from book 12 are significant to the present context, insofar as they offer theoretical guidelines for representing figures in this genre.

Polybius is a detail-oriented writer and conscious of using a specific methodology.[39] His interest in best practices for historiography is evident in occasional programmatic comments and more often in his critiques of other historians.[40] He emphasizes that history should be useful (χρήσιμον) as a practical corrective to behavior (*Hist.* 1.1–2), an end he frequently contrasts with

---

39   Polybius makes several comments suggesting that he is intentionally dull. For general accounts of Polybius's historiographical method, see Paul Pédech, *La méthode historique de Polybe*, CEA (Paris: Société d'édition "Les Belles Lettres," 1964); Kenneth Sacks, *Polybius on the Writing of History*, UCPCS 24 (Berkeley: University of California Press, 1981).

40   Especially in book 12, which, along with book 6 on the Roman constitution, Brian McGing writes, has "perversely if understandably" attracted disproportionate scholarly attention. Brian C. McGing, *Polybius' Histories*, OACL (New York: Oxford University Press, 2010), 12.

pleasure (τερπνόν);[41] and that universal history is superior to the historical monograph (*Hist.* 29.12). "Universal" here has a spatial, not chronological, referent; it points to the οἰκουμένη gathered and mastered first by Rome. Accordingly, Polybius believed, universal history could not have been written prior to Roman domination (*Hist.* 1.3–4).[42] The role of Fortune in "guiding almost all the affairs of the world in one direction" is a key element of Polybius's view of history, but an ambiguous one.[43] He claims that it is the historian's task to "bring before his readers under one synoptical view the operations by which Fortune has accomplished her general purpose" (*Hist.* 1.4.1–2).[44] The emphasis on Fortune and the superiority of the universal are ways in which Polybius departs from Thucydides, but in many other respects he is Thucydides's best student: he insists that the historiographer's style should be ἀκριβολογία (*Hist.* 2.14.16), a technical term adopted from professional rhetoricians to signify straightforward accuracy in contrast to an ornate style, and he excoriates other historians for departing from the truth by exaggeration, dramatization, or sensationalism (τερατεία; *Hist.* 2.59.3; 2.17.6; 2.58.12), and by employing the ἐναργεία through which "the speaker places himself and his audience in the position of the eyewitnesses" to arouse their πάθη.[45] Here we are less concerned with whether Polybius's use of Fortune is artificial or organic, unifying

---

41   See F. W. Walbank, "Profit or Amusement: Some Thoughts on the Motives of Hellenistic Historians," in *Polybius, Rome, and the Hellenistic World: Essays and Reflections* (Cambridge: Cambridge University Press, 2002), 231–41; v. D'Huys, "XRHSIMON KAI TERPNON in Polybios' Schlachtschilderungen. Einige literarische Topoi in seiner Darstellung der Schlacht bei Zama (xv 9–16)," in *Purposes of History: Studies in Greek Historiography from the 4th to the 2nd Centuries B.C.: Proceedings of the International Colloquium, Leuven, 24–26 May 1988*, ed. H. Verdin, G. Schepens, and E. De Keyser, StHell 30 (Leuven, 1990), 267–88.

42   This informs his critique against Ephorus, who had attempted a universal history in the fourth century (cf. *Hist.* 5.33.2 for Polybius's knowledge of Ephorus); it also explains why Thucydides can still be Polybius's methodological hero. The *History of the Peloponnesian War* was a historical monograph, not a universal history, but it was written before Fortune had brought the οἰκουμένη into a single entity under Rome.

43   See Walbank, *Polybius*, 58–65; Pédech, *La méthode historique de Polybe*, 331–54; McGing, *Polybius' Histories*, 195–201.

44   Trans. LCL, modified.

45   John Thornton, "Oratory in Polybius' Histories," in *Hellenistic Oratory: Continuity and Change*, ed. Christos Kremmydas and Kathryn Tempest (Oxford: Oxford University Press, 2013), 35. Quoting Heinrich Lausberg, *Handbook of Literary Rhetoric: A Foundation for Literary Study*, ed. David E. Orton and R. Dean Anderson (Boston: Brill, 1998), 359. Cf. the discussion of ἐναργεία in chapter 1's discussion of ancient literary and rhetorical criticism. Lucian, however, suggests that the historian should make his account of events as vivid as possible (εἰς δύναμιν ἐναργέστατα ἐπιδεῖξαι αὐτά), within the constraints of a truthful account of events (*How to Write History* 51).

or extraneous, like or unlike Thucydides; what is notable about Fortune in the present context is its function in the discourse of causality.

Like Thucydides, Polybius sets "the political" as the agenda of history-writing: wars, political formation and reformation, and especially the causes underlying these events.[46] Polybius provides a rationale for why analysis of causes must accompany narration, since without it one is left with "a clever essay (ἀγώνισμα) but not a lesson (μάθημα)," a result which would be, in Thucydidean terms, "pleasing for the moment [but] of no possible benefit for the future" (Thuc. 3.31.13).[47] Polybius takes the first Roman military crossing from Italy as a natural starting point for his narrative but uses the first two books to set the context, "in order to leave no possible obscurity in my explanations of the causes (τὰς αἰτίας)" (*Hist.* 1.12.6). This focus on causes, theorized further at *Histories* 3.6–7, recalls a distinction made by Thucydides between the "reasons publicly alleged" (αἱ δ᾽ ἐς τὸ φανερὸν λεγόμεναι αἰτίαι) and the "truest explanation" (ἀληθεστάτην πρόφασιν) for the Peloponnesian War, Athenian growth and Sparta's fear of Athens (Thuc. 1.23.5–6).[48] Many of the causes Polybius explores, like the Spartans' fear, also belong to the cognitive domain.

A primary device Polybius employs to communicate states of mind is the constructed speech. This is a point of continuity with Thucydides, who tells readers he composed speeches "in the language in which, as it seemed to me, the several speakers would express, on the subjects under consideration, the sentiments most befitting the occasion" (Thuc. 1.22).[49] The problem, which Thucydides notes in that same passage, is the difficulty of recalling exactly

---

46   The main subject of Polybius's work is the Punic Wars, and the first two books deal primarily with causes. "From the events of that period [e.g., the battle between the Carthaginians and their mercenaries] one can get an idea of the causes of the Hannibalic war between the Romans and the Carthaginians" (τὸ δὲ μέγιστον τὰς αἰτίας ἐκ τῶν ἐν ἐκείνοις τοῖς καιροῖς πεπραγμένων κατανοήσειε, δι᾽ ἃς ὁ κατ᾽ Ἀννίβαν συνέστη Ῥωμαίοις καὶ Καρχηδονίοις πόλεμος). In this attention to the conflicts which preceded and occasioned the conflicts constituting the heart of his work, Polybius follows the examples set by Herodotus and Thucydides in their openings. On causation in Greek historiography generally, see P. S. Derow, "Historical Explanation: Polybius and His Predecessors," in *Greek Historiography*, ed. Simon Hornblower (Oxford: Clarendon, 1994), 73–90.

47   Polybius's language of ἀγώνισμα may allude to a famous passage in which Thucydides explains that his work "has been composed, not as a prize-essay (ἀγώνισμα) to be heard for the moment, but as a possession for all time" (Thuc. 1.22.4). Trans. LCL. Cf. Polybius's use of the characteristically Thucydidean contrast between what is "pleasing for the moment" and what is useful in perpetuity (e.g., *Hist.* 38.4.8).

48   For a general discussion of Polybius's debt to Thucydides, see McGing, *Polybius' Histories*, 58–60. In other ways, and perhaps to a lesser extent, Polybius is stylistically influenced by Herodotus and Xenophon (McGing, *Polybius' Histories*, 52–66).

49   Trans. LCL.

HISTORIOGRAPHY: INVESTIGATIVE SPECULATION & COGNITIVE CAUSATION   43

what was said in a given speech. A fair assumption, he claims, is that in every case the speakers would want to persuade listeners to do what the speaker wanted, and so this can be a guide in constructing appropriate speeches.[50] As with Thucydides, it is a disputed point in each case whether and to what extent Polybius's speeches correspond to historical speeches, and what his methods were for constructing speeches when they appear in his narrative.[51] On one occasion Polybius criticizes another historian, Timaeus, for inventing speeches, in particular for

> not setting down the words spoken nor the sense of what was really said, but having made up his mind as to what ought to have been said (ἀλλὰ προθέμενος ὡς δεῖ ῥηθῆναι) he recounts these speeches and all else that follows upon events like a man in a school of rhetoric attempting to speak on a given subject, and shows off his oratorical power, but gives no report of what was actually spoken (ἀλλ᾽ οὐκ ἐξήγησιν τῶν κατ᾽ ἀλήθειαν εἰρημένων).
>
> *Hist.* 12.25a.5

This critique needs to be read in light of Polybius's general animosity towards Timaeus as a rival historian and in particular his critique of Timaeus as what people today might call an "armchair historian."[52] Polybius took pride in conducting interviews, weighing the findings, and including only what was necessary for explaining the causes of events in his narrative. Only the speeches or parts of speeches that had historical consequences need to be included (*Hist.* 12.25i.5; cf. 36.1.7).[53] Polybius's speeches, then, are important for the present

---

50   Thucydides's psychologizing activity and his extrapolation of individual to crowd psychology are discussed by Antonis Tsakmakis, "Leaders, Crowds, and the Power of the Image: Political Communication in Thucydides," in *Brill's Companion to Thucydides*, ed. Antonios Rengakos and Antonis Tsakmakis, BCCS (Leiden: Brill, 2006), 161–87. Thucydides's theorizing about "human nature" and Polybius's ability to do the same in their respective constructions of speeches are discussed in Georgina Longley, "Thucydides, Polybius, and Human Nature," in *Imperialism, Cultural Politics, and Polybius*, ed. Christopher Smith and Liv Mariah Yarrow (Oxford: Oxford University Press, 2012), 68–84.

51   Even Thucydides muddles his method, after the remarks discussed above, saying, "I have adhered as closely as possible to the general sense of what was actually said [τῶν ἀληθῶς λεχθέντων]." Cf., e.g., Polybius, *Hist.* 5.53; 60.3.

52   Timaeus, as an established authority on Greek affairs in the West, represented Polybius's greatest challenger for authority in that domain, supplying Polybius with a motive to discredit Timaeus. Christopher A. Baron, *Timaeus of Tauromenium and Hellenistic Historiography* (Cambridge: Cambridge University Press, 2012).

53   This squares well with Lucian's criticism of writers "who leave out or skate over the important and interesting events, and from lack of education, taste, and knowledge of what

project in two respects: they provide windows into the minds Polybius and other historians constructed for their speakers, and they fit into the scheme of causality that is central to Polybius's historiographical method insofar as they can function as the proximate cause of whatever their listeners are persuaded to do.

Polybius's narrator freely enters the minds of his subjects when they are strategizing, as can be seen in this typical example:

> Hannibal, seeing that Fabius, while obviously wishing to avoid a battle (ὁρῶν τὸν Φάβιον φυγομαχοῦντα μὲν προδήλως), had no intention at all of withdrawing altogether from the open country, made a bold dash at Falernum in the plain of Capua, counting with certainty (πεπεισμένος) on one of two alternatives: either he would compel the enemy to fight or make it plain to everybody that he was winning and that the Romans were abandoning the country to him. Upon this happening he hoped (ἤλπιζε) that the towns would be much impressed and hasten to throw off their allegiance to Rome.
>
> *Hist.* 3.90

Like Thucydides, Polybius tends to give more attention to the minds of groups than individuals.[54] He infers states of mind like "fear" and "respect" from the actions of groups, and even foregrounds the fact that he is reasoning it out: "For up to now, although the Romans had been beaten in two battles, not a single Italian city had revolted to the Carthaginians, but all remained loyal, although some suffered much. From which one may estimate the awe and respect (τὴν κατάπληξιν καὶ καταξίωσιν) that the allies felt for the Roman state" (*Hist.* 3.90).

Polybius often criticizes his historiographical predecessors on methodological grounds. History-writing may need to have a lesson, but that fact does not rule out its status as an ἀγώνισμα.[55] Directing criticism at fellow historians is a standard feature of the genre and a mechanism for self-definition, prominent

---

to mention and what to ignore dwell very fully and laboriously on the most insignificant happenings" (*How to Write History* 27). For more on Polybius's speeches, see McGing, *Polybius' Histories*, 86–91.

54 On the individual (leader) and the masses in Polybius, see Frank Walbank's essay "Polybius' Perception of the One and the Many," in *Polybius, Rome, and the Hellenistic World: Essays and Reflections* (Cambridge: Cambridge University Press, 2002), 212–30. On the minds of groups in Thucydides with reference to cognitive narratology, see Grethlein, "Social Minds and Narrative Time."

55 Polybius's use of this term at *Histories* 3.31.12–13 is one of the clearest indications of his debt to Thucydides, who had famously hoped that his work would be "a possession forever, not a prize essay (ἀγώνισμα) written for present gratification" (Thuc. 1.22.4).

HISTORIOGRAPHY: INVESTIGATIVE SPECULATION & COGNITIVE CAUSATION   45

in both Polybius's and Josephus's historiographical works.[56] Although we may pass over most of those who find themselves in Polybius's crosshairs (e.g., Calisthenes, Theopompus, Ephorus, and especially Timaeus; targets concentrated in book 12), the case of Phylarchus is instructive here. Polybius criticizes Phylarchus for writing like one of the τραγῳδιογράφοι, infusing his narrative with sensationalism (τερατεία) (*Hist.* 2.56; cf. 2.58.12), a mode of writing that is in contrast with his own πραγματικὴ ἱστορία.[57] The criterion by which he distinguishes the two is truthfulness (τἀληθές).

The context of the key passage is Polybius's discussion of the Cleomenean War, where he informs the reader that he will be following the *Memoirs* of Aratus.[58] He anticipates the reader's surprise on three counts: Phylarchus had covered this war; Phylarchus was in many points "at variance and in contradiction" with Aratus's work; and some had received Phylarchus's narrative as worthy of acceptance. Polybius justifies his own venture by drawing attention to what he perceives to be Phylarchus's shortcomings. Four purportedly typical instances of Phylarchus's coverage are advanced, each with a commentary detailing Phylarchus's methodological failing.[59] Whether or not Polybius consistently meets his own ideals is less important than that he is able to articulate them and that he expects them to resonate with his readers' expectations.

---

56   See John Marincola, *Authority and Tradition in Ancient Historiography* (Cambridge: Cambridge University Press, 1997), 225–36.

57   Practical or pragmatic history, for Polybius, means *inter alia* that the historian has experience in the matters he is discussing and that the text produced will benefit readers who might find themselves needing to know, e.g., how to make smoke signals, the uses of the lotus shrub and its fruit, what goes into a general's training, or how to conduct oneself as a statesman. Cf. *Histories* 10.45.6; 9.12–20; 12.2; 20.4. Further examples are collected and discussed in Walbank, *Polybius*, 87–89.

58   Aratus's memoirs (*BNJ* 231) in forty books covered the period up to 220, and are Polybius's primary source of information for Peloponnesian affairs during that period. Cf. *Histories* 1.3.2; 2.47.11, 56.2; 4.2.1.

59   Although there is no doubt that Polybius was critical of Phylarchus, scholars are divided on whether or not the methodological grounds of the critique are sincerely felt or merely a mask for Polybius's class-based and politically-motivated antagonism towards Phylarchus. Aratus, whose *Memoirs* Polybius prefers, had acted in such a way as to protect Polybius's personal interests against the threat of Spartan intervention. Phylarchus would have advocated for Spartan intervention. See Thomas W. Africa, *Phylarchus and the Spartan Revolution* (Berkeley: University of California Press, 1961), 31, 33. Note also the bibliography in Arthur M. Eckstein, "Polybius, Phylarchus, and Historiographical Criticism," *CP* 108 (2013): 315n4. Eckstein's article, the latest and most extensive contribution to the question, dismantles the cynical view persuasively.

Attending to them sheds light on the kinds of claims that made sense within the genre.[60]

The first of the four Phylarchan episodes concerns the sufferings of the Mantineans following their surrender to Aratus and the Achaeans, supported by Antigonus and the Macedonians. In question are Phylarchus's claims that "the Mantineans, when they surrendered, were exposed to terrible sufferings and that such were the misfortunes that overtook this, the most ancient and greatest city in Arcadia, as to impress deeply and move to tears all the Greeks (ὥστε πάντας εἰς ἐπίστασιν καὶ δάκρυα τοὺς Ἕλληνας ἀγαγεῖν)" (*Hist.* 2.56.6). Polybius goes on to theorize Phylarchus's motives: "in his eagerness to arouse the pity and attention of his readers (σπουδάζων δ᾽ εἰς ἔλεον ἐκκαλεῖσθαι τοὺς ἀναγινώσκοντας καὶ συμπαθεῖς ποιεῖν τοῖς λεγομένοις) he treats us to a picture of clinging women with their hair disheveled and their breasts bare, or again of crowds of both sexes together with their children and aged parents weeping and lamenting as they are led away to slavery" (*Hist.* 2.56.6). This kind of writing, Polybius claims, is typical of the whole work: he is "always trying to bring horrors vividly before our eyes (ἑκάστοις ἀεὶ πρὸ ὀφθαλμῶν τιθέναι τὰ δεινά)" (*Hist.* 2.56.9).[61] This prompts Polybius to ask about the nature of history:

> A historical author should not try to thrill his readers by such exaggerated pictures, nor should he, like a tragic poet, try to imagine the probable utterances (τοὺς ἐνδεχομένους λόγους) of his characters or reckon up all the consequences probably incidental to the occurrences with which he deals, but simply record what really happened and what really was said (τῶν δὲ πραχθέντων καὶ ῥηθέντων κατ᾽ ἀλήθειαν αὐτῶν μνημονεύειν πάμπαν), however commonplace.
>
> *Hist.* 2.56.10

The charge of exaggeration directed at Phylarchus alongside Polybius's recommended alternative (simply recording what was really said and done) implies that Polybius would describe his own work in the second sense. Plutarch, both in his *Life of Aratus* and in his *Life of Themistocles*, accuses Phylarchus of pedaling falsehoods, and particularly of desiring to stir up emotion in his readers (*Arat.* 28.8; *Them.* 32.4), supporting Polybius's assessment of Phylarchus's

---

60   It may also be instructive to look at postures of self-definition like this as a possible model for understanding the relationship of later gospels to earlier ones. A major difference would be that criticism of one's predecessors is often explicit in the historiographical tradition but implicit in the gospel tradition.

61   On Polybius's awareness of his audience and attention to how things would appear in their minds, see James Davidson, "The Gaze in Polybius' Histories," *JRS* 81 (1991): 10–24.

shortcomings as a historiographer. His shortcoming, according to Polybius (and Plutarch), was not in painting the minds of the Mantineans with a pathetic brush, but in exaggerating the extent and the severity of the events they experienced, a practice deemed inappropriate for what it does to the mind of the reader.[62]

The alternative account to the Mantinean crisis that Polybius prefers, taken from Aratus (the victor in this recorded conflict), is that the Mantineans had their property pillaged and their citizens enslaved (Polybius, *Hist.* 2.58.12). Expanding on the Mantineans' crimes, Polybius concludes that even if they had suffered what Phylarchus said they suffered (and they did not), they would have deserved it (*Hist.* 2.58.11–12).[63]

Polybius's primary criticism of Phylarchus here is couched in terms of truth and falsehood, not the intrusion of "tragic" elements into Phylarchus's history per se, as John Marincola has demonstrated.[64] This insight corrects over-hasty connections between Phylarchus's project and tragedy as a formal genre.[65] A common result of making such a connection is to say that Polybius was against tragic history because it puts the historian in a position of trying to stir up emotion. This is a mistake, Marincola notes, when what really is at stake is the historian's primary duty to the truth and eschewal of all falsehoods.[66] After all, Polybius himself has room for appropriate displays of emotion, as in Scipio's response to the fall of Carthage, and for discussions of tragic phenomena like περιπέτεια (reversals of fortune). Marincola corrects one over-determined

---

62 Polybius constantly performs anxiety about the consequences of inferior historiographies on the minds of readers. See also his comments about Fabius at *Histories* 3.9.3–4: "What I wish is to warn those who consult his book not to pay attention to the author's name, but to facts. For there are some people who pay regard not to what he writes but to the writer himself and, taking into consideration that he was a contemporary and a Roman senator, at once accept all he says as worthy of credit."

63 Polybius deals with the subsequent three Phylarchan episodes in a similar fashion. For close readings, showing subtle variations in Polybius's strategy in each case, see Eckstein, "Polybius, Phylarchus, and Historiographical Criticism."

64 John Marincola, "Polybius, Phylarchus, and 'Tragic History': A Reconsideration," in *Polybius and His World: Essays in Memory of F. W. Walbank*, ed. Bruce Gibson and Thomas Harrison (Oxford: Oxford University Press, 2013), 73–90.

65 For the argument that Polybius did not have first-hand acquaintance with such rare works as Aristotle's *Poetics*, as earlier scholars had assumed or argued, see F. W. Walbank, *A Historical Commentary on Polybius*, vol. 1 (Oxford: Clarendon, 1957), 2; Konrat Ziegler, "Polybios," *PW*, 1952, col. 1470.

66 The point could be made even more strongly by considering Polybius's critiques of other historians, especially Timaeus in book 12, in connection to willfully distorting the truth. See *Histories* 12.3, 4d, 11. *Histories* 12.12 distinguishes between (forgivable) falsehoods based on ignorance and (unforgivable) deliberate deceit.

48   CHAPTER 2

reading of Polybius, but forces a false choice. The fact that Polybius's critiques
are couched chiefly in terms of truth-telling does not rule out that Polybius is
upset at Phylarchus for shifting into a tragic register in a bid to make his history transcend the commonplace, even at the risk of bending or disregarding
the strict truth.[67] Both are problematic, and both are present in Poybius's criticisms. To exaggerate the pathetic is to pedal in falsehood.

After associating Phylarchus with tragedy, where the aims are to "amaze and
lead along his audience for the moment,"[68] Polybius criticizes him for neglecting causes: "Phylarchus simply narrates most of such catastrophes and does
not even suggest why things are done or to what end (οὐχ ὑποτιθεὶς αἰτίαν καὶ
τρόπον τοῖς γινομένοις), without which it is impossible in any case to feel either
legitimate pity or proper anger" (*Hist.* 2.56.13). The historian has a mandate
to attend to causes, some of which are cognitive.[69] Understanding causes,
Polybius explains, instructs the reader in the appropriate response to a work.
Pity (ἐλεεῖν) and anger (ὀργίζεσθαι), the responses he gives as examples, are
cognitive in a way that squares well with Aristotle's remarks on the function
of tragedy.[70]

Polybius criticizes his historiographical predecessors not only for neglecting causes (as in Phylarchus's case), but also for confusing causes (αἰτίαι), pretexts (προφάσεις), and beginnings (ἀρχαί).[71] Introducing the First Punic War,

---

67   Polybius does not always follow the methodological best practices he advocates. This
      might help explain why he includes displays of emotion and rhetorically constructs tragic
      περιπέτειαι. The sharp distinction between tragedy and history is itself a rhetorical con-
      struction more often found in invective against one's competitors than used as a rule in
      one's own writing.
           The gendered inflection of methodological comments by historians about tragedy
      would make a fascinating study. Cf. Lucian's discussion of the inappropriateness of bring-
      ing "poetry's embellishments" into history: "It is as if you were to dress one of our tough,
      rugged athletes in a purple dress and the rest of the paraphernalia of a pretty light-o'-love
      and daub and paint his face. Heavens! how ridiculous you would make him look, shaming
      him with all that decoration" (*How to Write History* 8; cf. 13).
68   ἐκπλῆξαι καὶ ψυχαγωγῆσαι κατὰ τὸ παρὸν τοὺς ἀκούοντας (*Hist.* 2.56.11). Recall the
      Thucydidean hope that his work would be "a possession forever, not a prize essay written
      for present gratification" (Thuc. 1.22.4).
69   Jonas Grethlein rightly observes that ancient historians in general had no problem theo-
      rizing the minds of their subjects in constructing causation, a discursive move often
      encountered in modern novels but (rarely) in modern histories. See Grethlein, "Social
      Minds and Narrative Time," 124. Cf. Dorrit Cohn, *The Distinction of Fiction* (Baltimore:
      Johns Hopkins University Press, 1999), 16–17.
70   This need not entail that Polybius had a direct acquaintance with the *Poetics*; only that
      the terms it uses to theorize tragedy would have made sense to him.
71   On this tripartite distinction, see Pédech, *La méthode historique de Polybe*, 78–93, 123–40.
      The language of προφάσεις occasions some difficulty, since Thucydides's distinction noted

he writes, "some of those authors who have dealt with Hannibal and his times, wishing to indicate the causes (τὰς αἰτίας ἡμῖν ὑποδεικνύναι) that led to the above war between Rome and Carthage, allege as its first [cause] the siege of Saguntum by the Carthaginians and as its second their crossing, contrary to treaty, the river whose native name is the Iber" (*Hist.* 3.6.1). This is to mistake causes (αἰτίαι) with beginnings (ἀρχαί). If an event has preparations standing behind it, as was evidently the case with the siege and the crossing of the Iber, then it cannot be called a cause (*Hist.* 3.6.5; cf. 22.18.6). Beginnings, then, are a first attempt to put into practice what has already been decided; causes are "what is leading up to decisions and judgments (τὰς προκαθηγουμένας τῶν κρίσεων καὶ διαλήψεων), that is to say our notions of things, our state of mind, our reasoning about these (ἐπινοίας καὶ διαθέσεις καὶ τοὺς περὶ ταῦτα συλλογισμοὺς), and everything through which we reach decisions and projects" (*Hist.* 3.6.7). The true causes of the war against Persia, then, are "easy for anyone to see": Philip's perception of Persian cowardice, visible in their failure to act when Xenophon's Greek troops passed through or when the Spartan king Agesilaus trespassed in their country.

> From both of these facts Philip perceived and reckoned (κατανοήσας καὶ συλλογισάμενος) on the cowardice and indolence of the Persians as compared with the military efficiency of himself and his Macedonians, and further fixing his eyes on the splendor of the great prize which the war promised, he lost no time, once he had secured the avowed goodwill of the Greeks, but seizing on the pretext (προφάσει χρώμενος) that he was eager to take vengeance on the Persians for their injurious treatment of the Greeks, he bestirred himself and decided to go to war (ὁρμὴν ἔσχε καὶ προέθετο πολεμεῖν), beginning to make every preparation for this purpose.
>
> *Hist.* 3.6.12–14

The true cause, as we can see from this explanation, lies in Philip's κατανόησις and συλλογισμός. The passage also introduces another key term in Polybius's theory of history-writing: the πρόφασις ("pretext") is a regular feature in accounts of war, involving the misrepresentation of motives. Here, the pretext is Philip's eagerness to take vengeance on the Persians. The historian's task is to help readers distinguish between causes and pretexts. Later, Polybius identifies

---

above was between the "reasons publicly alleged" (αἱ δ' ἐς τὸ φανερὸν λεγόμεναι αἰτίαι) and the "truest explanation" (ἀληθεστάτην πρόφασιν). For a discussion of the semantic range of the terms separately and in relation to each other, see Lionel Pearson, "Prophasis and Aitia," *TAPA* 83 (1952): 205–23.

50   CHAPTER 2

the cause of the war between the Anatolians and the Romans as ὀργή (*Hist.*
7.1.1) and distinguishes this cause from the pretext of desiring to free Greece
from Roman rule (*Hist.* 7.1.3). The chief cause of the war between Rome and
Carthage, Polybius's main subject for the *Histories*, is the θυμός of Hamilcar and
his son Hannibal (*Hist.* 3.9.6).[72]

Sometimes Polybius's search for causes attracts criticisms from later authors. Christian Habicht, introducing the revised Loeb translation, comments
on Polybius's method: "his way of thinking leads him to construct causali-
ties of doubtful validity." To illustrate, Habicht points to Polybius's naming as
causes for the Third Macedonian War Philip's bitterness after defeat in 197 and
the abuse he subsequently suffered from the Romans in the 180s, a feeling he
passed on to his successor Perseus (*Hist.* 22.18.1–11).[73] Habicht counters, however, that "it is nevertheless quite clear that the Senate wanted this war and not
Perseus, who did his utmost to avoid it."[74] A similar observation can be made
in connection to Hannibal's invasion of Italy. This was not, as Polybius suggests in the previous paragraph's example, a long-germinating plan explained
by a bitterness he inherited from his father Hamilcar; it rather appears to have
been an improvisation made when Hannibal heard of Rome declaring war
on Carthage.[75]

In Polybius's analysis of causes, he sometimes looks to character or disposition for the explanation of an action. This is true both at the level of the
individual and the level of the group. Importantly, however, the character of individuals is bound up with the imagined character of the larger ethnic groups
to which they belong. Thus Hannibal's individual ἦθος, with θυμός motivating
his war against the Romans, can be read as representative of Carthaginians in
general.

Dispositions, which serve in Polybius as causal explanations for events—
as when Hannibal's disposition leads to war with the Romans—can also be

---

72   Secondary causes are apparently the loss of Sardinia (*Hist.* 3.10.3) and Carthage's success
      in Spain (*Hist.* 3.10.6). Both involve an event with an attendant cognitive consequence:
      Carthage's loss of Sardinia to Rome obviously instigates a rankling in the Carthaginian
      spirit; Carthage's successes in Spain obviously involve the production of anxiety on the
      Roman side and an emboldening of ambition on the Carthaginian side.

73   Christian Habicht, "Introduction," in *Polybius: The Histories, Books I and II*, ed. F. W.
      Walbank and Christian Habicht, LCL 128 (Cambridge: Harvard University Press, 2010),
      xix–xx. For a historical reconstructive account supporting Habicht's remark, see N. G.
      L. Hammond and F. W. Walbank, *A History of Macedonia: 336–167 B.C.*, vol. 1 (Oxford:
      Clarendon, 1972), 505–31.

74   Habicht, "Introduction," xix–xx.

75   Habicht, xix–xx.

explained in causal terms. The construction of dispositions is informed by the Greek intellectual tradition in which observable differences between individuals or groups can be causally explained by reference to nature (φύσις), climate and environment, or state organization.[76] This is why πολιτεῖαι are so important in Polybius's view of cultures and history, and why he devotes nearly an entire book to discussing the Roman constitution and the life cycle of πολιτεῖαι (book 6). In *Histories* 5, Polybius asks why the Peloponnesians have found it so difficult to lead a tranquil life, despite having ideal conditions to do so. His answer: "It seems to me to be an inevitable consequence of the Peloponnesian character. They like to lead and they do not like to be answerable to anyone" (*Hist.* 5.106). Their character is explained by reference to their πολιτεία.

Several conclusions may be drawn from this probe into Polybius's historiographical theory and praxis. Investigation and articulation of events' causes, properly distinguished from events' pretexts and beginnings, is a key task of the historian. These often involve a cognitive component. The Polybian narrator, like those of Herodotus and Thucydides, enjoys unrestricted access to the minds of characters in his narrative. Sometimes he narrates their dispositions, motivations, and thought processes in third person narrative; at other times he constructs speeches in which they report their own thoughts and seek to persuade other characters to act in certain ways. The dispositions and motivations of individuals and groups in *The Histories* can themselves be explained in causal terms, often in a circularly causal relationship. The majority of internal glimpses in Polybius have to do with military strategizing of the sort exemplified by Hannibal and Fabius in the examples given above. This emphasis on military strategizing is explicable in terms of Polybius's expressed position that the best historiographer is he who has experience in statecraft and military affairs.[77] One cannot write history merely from studying the written records of others (cf. Polybius's excoriation of Timaeus in book 12); one must combine library research with what one learns by interrogating eyewitnesses and what one learns by walking the places where one's narrative unfolds, and draw on one's political and military experience to reconstruct what must have

---

76 For an illuminating discussion with reference to Polybius, see Craige B. Champion, *Cultural Politics in Polybius' Histories*, JPICL (Berkeley: University of California Press, 2004), 75–84.

77 This, along with personal experience of the geographical and topographical knowledge. Cf. Lucian (*How to Write History* 34), whose criteria for the historian are political understanding and power of expression (σύνεσίν τε πολιτικὴν καὶ δύναμιν ἑρμηνευτικήν). Lucian's political understanding cannot be taught, he tells us; this seems to stand in tension with Polybius's view of political and military experience, which one *can* acquire.

52   CHAPTER 2

transpired in the heads of the great men whose decisions determined the outcome of the battles explained by the historian.

4   Josephus's *Jewish Antiquities*

Very similar historiographical criteria may be seen in the works of Josephus.
Josephus (ca. 37–100 CE) fought in the Jewish War against Rome (66–70 CE),
was captured by Vespasian, and managed to secure the patronage of his Flavian
captors. After the war, he took up an imperial residence in Rome, where he
composed at least four works: *Jewish War, Jewish Antiquities, The Life*, and
Against Apion. Our focus here is his twenty-volume *Antiquities* (completed ca.
94 CE), a work of universal history beginning with creation and concluding
in his own lifetime. The first half follows the contours of historical material
familiar to us from the Hebrew Bible; the second half unfolds in the Hellenistic
and Roman periods, and gives an account of Jewish political history based on
the books of the Maccabees, Nicolaus of Damascus's *Historia universalis*, and
Josephus's own experiences. This second half revisits events Josephus had previously covered in *War* (completed ca. 75 CE).

Looking at Josephus's historiographical works in the context of a tradition
shaped by figures such as Thucydides and Polybius,[78] one is struck by what we
might call a biographical impulse, a move towards narrating history by means of
a succession of portraits of outstanding men.[79] Similar observations might also
apply in cases like Arrian's *Anabasis of Alexander*, Dionysius of Halicarnassus's

---

78   Momigliano observed that neither of these fifth century figures pays much attention to
      "individuals," in contrast to historiography from the ancient Orient, where the "deeds of
      kings" are a persistent feature. Arnaldo Momigliano, *The Development of Greek Biography*,
      Expanded ed. (Cambridge: Harvard University Press, 1993), 35. It has also been sug-
      gested that Herodotus is at his most "biographical" in those parts of his narrative deal-
      ing with Persians or other eastern non-Greeks (Cyrus, Xerxes, Croesus). Albrecht Dihle,
      "The Gospels and Greek Biography," in *The Gospel and the Gospels*, ed. Peter Stuhlmacher
      (Grand Rapids: Eerdmans, 1991), 361–86.

79   Feldman connects this to Josephus's concern to refute a charge made by Apion (among
      others) that the Jews had not produced eminent sages or inventors in the arts. Feldman
      also makes this a characteristic feature of Peripatetic biography. This is of interest insofar
      as one of Josephus's major sources, Nicolaus of Damascus, was a practicing Peripatetic.
      Louis H. Feldman, "Josephus' Portrait of Moses," *JQR* 82 (1992): 290–91. But to tie the bio-
      graphical impulse too tightly to a particular school or tradition is to oversimplify matters.
      See also George W. E. Nickelsburg, "Good and Bad Leaders," in *Ideal Figures in Ancient
      Judaism: Profiles and Paradigms*, ed. John Joseph Collins and George W. E. Nickelsburg,
      SCS 12 (Chico: Scholars, 1980), 49–65; Louis H. Feldman, *Josephus's Interpretation of the
      Bible*, HCS 27 (Berkeley: University of California Press, 1998), 74–75.

Roman Antiquities, Appian of Alexandria's *Roman History*, and Cassius Dio's *Roman History*,[80] a trend that has led some scholars to describe Hellenistic historiography as moving towards a "person-centered" model.[81] Dionysius in particular has attracted attention in connection to Josephus as a generic parallel and precedent.[82] Josephus's biographical impulse is thrown into sharper relief if his *Antiquities* is compared with the Hebrew Bible. The work as a whole, however, remains unified by the larger theme of Jewish antiquity, understood in terms of political and social events affecting the whole people.

To appreciate the relative importance of nation-shaping events over the experiences of private individuals in Josephus's *Antiquities*, we can look at the functions played by the named individuals who feature in its prologue. Like Polybius, Josephus presents himself within the text in his persona as a historian alongside other historians, discussing the motives of historians in general, and theorizing his own noble motives and qualifications in contrast to those of others. This is a discursive strategy woven into the body of the work too, where he occasionally interrupts the narrative to highlight his motives

---

80   Arrian focuses on Alexander the Great. Dionysius writes novelistically, focusing on great figures in the history of Rome from its mythical origins to the beginning of the First Punic War. Appian focuses on individuals active in the century commencing with the reforms of Tiberius Gracchus in 133 BCE. Dio focuses on the leading characters in the transition from Republic to Empire.

81   Becker, *Das Markus-Evangelium im Rahmen antiker Historiographie*, 16–20; Becker, "Patterns of Early Christian Thinking and Writing of History: Paul—Mark—Acts."

Similar observations might be made for contemporary Latin historiography: Caesar's *Bellum gallicum* offers a justification for the author's activities in battles against the Gauls and a self-portrait of a military hero and political leader; Sallust's *Bellum catilinae* centers on the conspiracy of the patrician Catiline, and his *Bellum jugurthinum* is structured around the activities of individuals; and Livy's *Ab urbe condita* includes extended character portraits, such as that of Hannibal in book 21.

The relationship of Greek to Latin historiography is not straightforward. Most scholars seem to see a difference of emphasis, a new and distinctly Roman attention to praise and blame in the latter camp not present (to the same extent) in earlier or even contemporary Greek historiography. See the measured assessment in John Marincola, "Introduction," in *Greek and Roman Historiography*, ORCS (Oxford: Oxford University Press, 2011), 1–10.

82   Both produced ἀρχαιολογίαι that traced the fortunes of a people group from a distant origin (the earliest inhabitants of Italy, the ancestors of the Jews); both conclude with a nation-defining war (the First Punic War, the Jewish War); both discuss matters ranging from constitution and laws to social life and customs; both compose set speeches for their often dramatic or even novelistic narratives; both represent the investment of a nonRoman elite in a Roman system. Both the title of Josephus's work and its division into 20 books seem to be modeled on the precedent of Dionysius. Cf. also the Dionysian words and phrases in Josephus's *Antiquities* collected in R. J. H. Shutt, *Studies in Josephus* (London: SPCK, 1961), 97–101.

for including some material.[83] He describes the process by which he came to write *War* first and *Antiquities* later, which involved encouragement from his patron Epaphroditus (*Ant.* 1.8). Considering whether the work he wanted to write would have a ready audience, Josephus describes his pleasure at noticing Ptolemy II Philadelphus's engagement of the high priest Eleazar to translate the Jewish Law and political constitution into Greek. These individuals are mentioned in the context of Josephus's justification of his decision to write the *Antiquities*; they are precedents, not the subject of his work. In the comments he makes regarding the content and scope of the project, he mentions "the lawgiver" Moses as a subject (*Ant.* 1.1, 15) and a source (*Ant.* 1.18–24) of his history.[84] "The poets" show up in the proem, but are unnamed (*Ant.* 1.16). Their function is to fail at what the Jewish scriptures are able to do. Josephus also notes that the 5000 years of history covered in the Jewish scriptures include "all sorts of surprising reverses, many fortunes of war, heroic exploits of generals, and political revolutions" (*Ant.* 1.13). Though στρατηγοί are mentioned, Josephus is not concerned with these men as individuals; his attention is directed at the heroic deeds (ἀνδραγαθίαι) they brought about. Josephus uses his own experience as a στρατηγός to authorize his speculations on the causal strategizing that prefaced their great deeds. God functions in Josephus's proem in a way comparable to Polybius's Fortune, though in Josephus's moral vision a greater role is assigned to human agency:

> The main lesson to be learnt from this history by any who care to peruse it is that men who conform to the will of God, and do not venture to transgress laws that have been excellently laid down, prosper in all things beyond belief, and for their reward are offered by God felicity; whereas, in proportion as they depart from the strict observance of these laws, things

---

83   E.g., three motives are given for including the ten plagues of Exod 7–12 (cf. *Ant.* 2.294–313). He recounts the dreadful sufferings which overtook the Egyptians, he tells us, "first because no such plagues as the Egyptians then experienced ever befell any nation before, next from a desire to show that Moses in not one of his predictions to them was mistaken, and further because it behoves mankind to learn to restrict themselves to such action as shall not offend the Deity nor provoke Him in wrath to punish them for their iniquities" (*Ant.* 2.293).

84   This section of the prologue is rich in imputed motives, dispositions, and knowledge: "the sage deemed it necessary" to make study of God and his works the foundation of an education; the lawgiver attained to a νοῦν ἀγαθόν; Moses desired to instill in his readers the lesson that the all-seeing God "grants to such as follow Him a life of bliss, but involves in dire calamities those who step outside the path of virtue"; Moses leads upwards the thoughts of his readers (τὰς γνώμας αὐτῶν ἀναγαγὼν) and persuades them (πείσας) that humans are the fairest of God's works and other such doctrines.

HISTORIOGRAPHY: INVESTIGATIVE SPECULATION & COGNITIVE CAUSATION   55

otherwise practicable become impracticable, and whatever imaginary good thing they strive to do ends in irretrievable disasters.

Ant. 1.14–15[85]

This purpose recalls Polybius's insistence that good historiography contain a μάθημα of use to future generations of readers. If there is a biographical impulse in his *Antiquities*, it is in service of the larger, unified story he is writing about the whole people in relation to other whole peoples. What he says about the minds of those great individuals is important both for how it reflects on the nation of Israel and how the decisions of individuals could be used to explain events that affected the whole people.

Josephus's *Antiquities* is massive in scope. For the first twelve books, Josephus relies primarily on Greek translations of the Hebrew Bible.[86] For books 13–17, Josephus draws heavily on Nicolaus, and in the final books, he draws on his own experience and more or less directly on *War*, completed shortly after his arrival in Rome in the 70s. Because Nicolaus was the primary source for the relevant books of *War*, it is unclear whether Josephus has one or both of the *War* and Nicolaus at hand when composing the corresponding books in *Antiquities*. In looking at the *Antiquities*, it is worth asking at each step how Josephus was using his sources (to the extent that this is possible).

If in a given passage Josephus was working closely with his sources (e.g., by having a copy open beside him as he composed the parallel section in *Antiquities*, or by having recently read the source), then differences between source texts and the *Antiquities* may be made to bear more weight in our attempts to come to grips with his aims and ideology. In the many cases where we cannot know how Josephus uses his sources, and in those cases where he appears not to have been working closely with them, differences in content, focus, or framing might be chalked up to something less intentional, like imperfect recollection. In either event, the usual caveats about differences between Josephus's sources and our versions of those source texts apply. In particular,

---

85   Trans. LCL, modified.

86   Whether and to what extent he employs multiple Greek versions of biblical texts and/or Hebrew copies is unclear. He claims in the prologue to *Antiquities* (1.5) to have "translated" (μεθηρμηνευμένην) from the Hebrew Scriptures (cf. *Ag. Ap.* 1.54). Later he characterizes his use of those sources differently when he claims to have paraphrased (μεταφράζειν) the Scriptures (10.218). For discussion of Josephus's knowledge of textual variants, concluding that Josephus knew and used multiple forms of given passages, including those with definite differences in "sense contours," see Jonathan Norton-Piliavsky, *Contours in the Text: Textual Variation in the Writings of Paul, Josephus and the Yaḥad*, LNTS 430 (London: T. & T. Clark, 2011), 57–81.

not every difference is indicative of authorial intent.[87] This is especially important to remember for Josephus, where so many of his academic readers obsess about his apologetic anxieties and self-presentation towards a Roman audience. Without neglecting that dimension of his identity, it should be emphasized that many differences can be explained as paraphrastic accidents, particularly in a literary tradition that disparaged verbatim copying. Not every difference between text and hypotext is equally significant for understanding the rewriter's intentions.

Whatever we make of his use of sources, Josephus's characterization involves the attribution of minds, expansion, contraction, and revision in both the biblical part of the narrative and its sequel.[88] If Josephus wants his work to be read as Hellenistic historiography, we would expect that some of his changes to the cognitive domain bring his representations of minds into line with the conventions of the genre as he understood it. Josephus need not have been self-conscious of his facility with those conventions, which are often invisible to those who use them most.[89] The remainder of this section takes

---

87   "Reconstruction of authorial intent," even more so than the trope of the "reconstruction of the past," is a red herring. All that exist are more and less convincing constructions of authorial intent (or, for that matter, constructions of the past). See the methodological discussion of the mind of the author in chapter 1, above.

88   Although I remain open to the possibility that Josephus's historiographical praxis looked different when applied to "biblical" figures than "post-biblical" or "non-biblical" figures, these labels are not the best way to capture the difference. To do so is to map an anachronistic canonical consciousness onto Josephus. Even if "our" canon looked much the same as his, the category "canon" does not have the same meaning in both cases. A more promising way of constructing internal historiographical differences is to point to standard practices appropriate to "ancient" and "contemporary" history. On early Jewish understandings of sacred texts prior to the emergence of the concepts "Bible" and "book," see Eva Mroczek, *The Literary Imagination in Jewish Antiquity* (Oxford: Oxford University Press, 2016).

89   See note 1 in chapter 1 above and Auken, "Contemporary Genre Studies," 53–54. Auken offers an illustrative anecdote: "Paré, Starke-Meyerring, and McAlpine describe how even highly experienced PhD supervisors are unable to explicate the generic norms of good scholarship they are trying to teach their PhD students: 'Much of the advice offered by supervisors comes from a deep discipline-specific, but inexpressible discourse knowledge. Although we are attempting to get colleagues to articulate the standards to which they hold their doctoral students, even the most experienced supervisors seem uncertain.' This does not mean that they do not understand or master these norms, but merely that they have acquired them through exposure to the practice of other genre users, and from practicing them themselves, not by way of explicit genre teaching. So most of our understanding of genres is learned through practice, and is tacit, even unrecognised, as genre knowledge." Cf. Anthony Paré, Doreen Starke-Meyerring, and Lynn McAlpine, "The Dissertation as Multi-Genre: Many Readers, Many Readings," in *Genre in a Changing*

up Josephus's representation of minds in the parts of his *Antiquities* that deal with Moses and Herod the Great. In both cases, the bulk of Josephus's information will have been anchored to a written text or set of texts. For Moses, Josephus's narrative reflects what he knew from biblical books, especially Exodus and Deuteronomy. For Herod, Josephus's narrative is derived mainly from the *Historia universalis* by Herod's friend and court historian, Nicolaus of Damascus.[90] The point of this exercise is to see what patterns emerge in the representation of minds in the *Antiquities*. Where comparisons or contrasts are drawn to his source texts (especially Exod 1–14 [LXX]), the goal is to show that Josephus's cognitive representations are not merely echoes or artifacts transposed from a source. Rather, Josephus is actively shaping the cognitive profiles of the actors in *Antiquities* to bring them into line with the genre conventions of Greek historiography.[91]

Moses plays several roles in the *Antiquities*. Like Nicolaus, he has a function as author (so Josephus believed) of what would become Josephus's main source for a large part of the narrative and he is also an actor in the narrative.[92] If Josephus is generally generous towards both Nicolaus and Moses as historical actors, a difference emerges in his attitude towards them as fellow historiographers. The critical scrutiny to which Josephus subjects Nicolaus is

---

World, ed. Charles Bazerman, Adair Bonini, and Débora de Carvalho Figueiredo (Fort Collins: Parlor, 2009), 179–93.

90 The nature of use in both cases is difficult to decide with confidence. Had he just recently read the source? Was he working from notes? Was he working with texts of one or more of these sources open beside him? These are process questions, with a bearing on authorial motivation and intention. At one level, they do not matter if we are chiefly interested in the result. At another level, our reading of that final product becomes more textured if we can see and say why it turned out this way rather than that. Some of these questions will resurface in the section below on Herod.

91 A major difference between Josephus's narrative and the biblical "source" is that Josephus's account is a unified composition. The biblical exodus account has inconsistencies, e.g., the idea that there were only two midwives (Exod 1.15) for a population of Hebrews numbering 600,000 (Exod 12.37), prompting Josephus to leave unspecified the number of midwives tasked with disposing of Hebrew baby boys (*Ant.* 2.206). Another is that Moses says to Pharaoh, "I will not see your face again!" (Exod 10.29), but then meets with Pharaoh in the next chapter (cf. Exod 11.10). Josephus drops the initial promise. The discrepancies and tensions in the biblical account might well be explained by different assumptions in the documentary sources E and J about the size of the Hebrew population, on the one hand, and the timeline of Moses's interactions with Pharaoh, on the other. See F. C. Conybeare and St. George William Joseph Stock, *A Grammar of Septuagint Greek* (Grand Rapids: Zondervan, 1980), 152.

92 For a look at Nicolaus in these two different roles (author-historian and actor), see Sarah Christine Teets, "ΧΑΡΙΖΟΜΕΝΟΣ ΗΡΩΔΗΙ: Josephus' Nicolaus of Damascus in the Judaean Antiquities," *Histos* 7 (2013): 88–127.

58   CHAPTER 2

not extended to Moses.[93] Josephus's Moses is first a lawgiver, a status which seems to exempt him from criticism.[94] Our interest, however, is Josephus's handling of the thoughts, feelings, and motivations of Moses the character whose birth is first predicted in *Antiquities* 2.205 and whose eulogy is sung in *Antiquities* 4.326–31.

A reader familiar with Exodus might be struck by how tightly Josephus's version is cast around the figure of Moses. If the Pentateuchal narrative tends to cast God as a direct actor, Josephus's Moses narrative tends to reassign agency for God's decisions and actions to Moses. Where the Exodus narrative casts Moses and Aaron as partners in confronting Pharaoh and leading the Hebrews out of Egypt, Josephus minimizes the role of Aaron. For example, signs performed by Aaron in Exodus are performed by Moses in *Antiquities*, and where the Hebrews murmur against both brothers in Exodus 16.2–3, Moses is the sole target in *Antiquities* 3.11.[95]

With the shift in Josephus's narrative to focus on Moses, one might expect this section of *Antiquities* to be focalized through Moses, thickly populated with Moses's thoughts and feelings in response to outside events. And yet, while Moses's mind is accessible to the narrator, the narrative is not focalized through it. For instance, although ὑπολαμβάνω appears thirty times in *Antiquities* 2–4, usually with the sense "to suppose" or "to think,"[96] only one of these is in reference to Moses (*Ant.* 4.167). Often the subject of a verb of thinking is a group. In that same range of text, the Ethiopians (*Ant.* 2.240), the Egyptians (*Ant.* 2.321, 324, 334), the Amalekites (*Ant.* 3.45), the Hebrews (*Ant.* 3.98, 306), and the Amorites (*Ant.* 4.89) all do collective thinking (with ὑπολαμβάνω). This reinforces the point made above that a convention of the genre in which Josephus's *Antiquities* participates is the focus on groups and their fortunes.[97]

Josephus's narrator characteristically articulates characters' thoughts and perceptions, especially when they are mistaken. This may help explain why

---

93   Josephus nevertheless anticipates reservations about Moses as a source and addresses them, a process which involves his capacity to reflect on how others would treat Moses as a fallible source like a Xenophon or a Theopompus.

94   On the polemical self-definition of historians vis-à-vis other historians, see Marincola, *Authority and Tradition in Ancient Historiography*, 225–36.

95   Aaron is named 29 times in *Antiquities* 2–4, compared with 116 times in Exodus (119 in LXX Exod).

96   The verb does not appear in LXX Exodus.

97   Cf. the introduction to Josephus's *Jewish War*, where he describes the focus of the work as an event (i.e., τὸν Ἰουδαίων πρὸς Ῥωμαίους πόλεμον [*J. W.* 1.1–2]), not the participants in that event.

reports about Moses's thinking are overshadowed by those around him. Moses sees things as they are; those around him often do not. The Egyptians pursuing the Hebrews into the path through the Red Sea, for example, "did not realize (ἐλάνθανον) that it was a road reserved for the Hebrews" (*Ant.* 2.342), a failure of cognition with disastrous consequences for them.[98]

In terms of character and disposition, Josephus's Moses outshines his biblical counterpart.[99] In the biblical account, Moses is timorous, prone to anger, self-serving, and given to arguing with God. Josephus, however, omits incidents like the fear (φοβέω / ירא) felt by the biblical Moses when an Israelite mentions his attack on the Egyptian and his flight from the staff-turned-serpent (cf. Exod 2.14; 4.3). Josephus seems to limit Moses's experience of fear and anger to situations where it reflects favorably on his justice and piety. Moses is frightened (ἔδεισε) at the sight of the burning bush, and still more confounded (κατεπλάγη δ' ἔτι μᾶλλον) at the emanation of a voice from the flame.[100] Receiving a commission "to take courage and return to Egypt to be general and leader of the multitude of the Hebrews and to liberate his kinsmen from the insolence there" with God's help (*Ant.* 2.268), Moses responds with astonishment (ἐκπεπληγμένος, in *Ant.* 2.270) at what he sees and hears, and later with marveling (θαυμάζοντα, in *Ant.* 2.274), but cannot help but trust in the Deity's promise (*Ant.* 2.275).[101] Josephus has reshaped the commissioning scene to emphasize this trust. Moses's inability to distrust is made explicit on several occasions (*Ant.* 2.270; cf. 275, 276). Josephus has dropped the biblical Moses's objection on account of a speech impediment, the divine reassurances that Aaron will speak for Moses (Exod 4.10, 14–16), and Moses's running from the staff-turned-serpent (Exod 4.3). In Exodus, Moses asks for God's name because he worries that the Israelites will want to know it when he gets to Egypt; in Josephus, he asks in order to offer appropriate sacrifices (*Ant.* 2.275), never troubling himself about what the Hebrews will think.

Josephus's Moses is not immune to fear, but his fear figures only when it does not reflect poorly on his character. Moses is afraid (δείδω) at the sight of the

---

98   Trans. LCL, modified. Cf. the strategy of theorizing the Egyptians' minds in Ezekiel's *Exagoge* with a messenger speech. See chapter 5 below on drama for discussion.

99   This is generally true of Josephus's biblical heroes. For comparisons of biblical portrayals to Josephan portrayals, see the studies produced by Christopher Begg and especially Louis Feldman. Bibliographic information is readily available *ad loc.* in the FJTC series.

100   Cf. Moses's reaction in Exodus 3.6: Moses hid his face, for he was afraid (ירא / εὐλαβεῖτο) to look at God. Plato also uses εὐλαβέομαι in connection to the deity (e.g., *Leg.* 879e), as does Plutarch in connection to the δῆμος (e.g., *Per.* 7).

101   Trans. Louis H. Feldman, *Josephus: Judean Antiquities, Books 1–4*, ed. Steve Mason, FJTC 3 (Leiden: Brill, 1999).

burning bush,[102] and astounded (καταπλήσσω) at the sound of the voice coming forth (*Ant.* 2.267).[103] When the Hebrews are angry and threaten to stone him, Moses claims to be afraid (δείδω) not for his own safety but for theirs (*Ant.* 3.21). Similarly, at *Antiquities* 4.63, Moses is afraid (δείδω) for the people, that they would attempt a second sedition (following the sedition of Korah and his followers). Moses's response to the assignations of the Israelite men and the Moabite women in *Antiquities* 4.141–44 is also worth comparing with the biblical hypotext. And again at *Antiquities* 4.9, fearing (φοβέω) that the enemies of the Hebrews might grow insolent at their first victory, Moses withdraws his people into the desert. Then at *Antiquities* 4.326, fear is involved in Moses's reasoning about why he chose to write about his own death: "because he was afraid (δείσας) that they might dare to say that because of the abundance of the virtue surrounding him he had gone up to the Divinity."[104] The obvious pattern in Josephus's mentions of Moses's fear is that they showcase his concern for God and his people, not his own person or wellbeing. Furthermore, many of them figure in causal explanations for events involving larger groups of people.

Anger in Josephus's portrait of Moses follows a similar pattern. Sometimes Josephus simply omits any mention of anger in his retellings of biblical scenes where the anger of a character is highlighted, as in the account of Moses's). Where the biblical Moses is angry or embittered or indignant on a handful of occasions, the character who is angry most in the biblical account is the LORD.[105] Josephus's God is hardly ever angry, and his Moses is angry only when it is justifiable and/or redounds to his credit (*Ant.* 4.169; cf. Josephus's omission of Moses's anger in other episodes, as in the confrontation described in Lev 10.16 with Eleazar and Ithamar over an improper sacrifice). In *Antiquities*, the Egyptians and their king are angry (*Ant.* 2.219, 239, 310, 336), the Hebrew multitude in the wilderness is angry (*Ant.* 3.12, 33, 310, 315–16), and the anger of God is in reserve for those who disobey (*Ant.* 2.293; 3.321). Interestingly, the ability to pacify angry people becomes a hallmark of Josephus's Moses (*Ant.* 3.315–6; cf. 3.13–14, 33–38, 310). Exodus 11.8 has Moses leave Pharaoh's presence in hot

---

102 Many of Josephus's heroes experience this emotion, including Noah, Abraham, Joseph, Isaac, Judah, Joseph, Amram. Villains and antagonists experience it as well (e.g., Laban, Pharaoh, the Egyptians).

103 Neither verb appears in LXX Pentateuch.

104 Trans. Feldman, *Josephus: Judean Antiquities, Books 1–4.*

105 Moses angry: Exod 11.8; 16.20; 32.19; Lev 10.16; Num 16.15; 31.14 (LXX). God angry: Exod 14.4; 15.7, 32.10–12; Num 11.1, 10, 33; 14.34; 16.22; 25.4; 32.14; Deut 1.37; 4.21; 6.15; 9.8, 19–20; 11.17; 13.18; 29.19, 23–24 (22–23), 28 (27); 32.19; 33.10 (LXX).

anger (θυμός / בחרי־אף). The parallel scene in Josephus transfers the anger to Pharaoh: "infuriated by this speech, the king threatened to behead him" (*Ant.* 2.310). The change contributes to a shift in characterization between the two men as Josephus absorbs them into his historiographical account. The shift also conforms to the pattern identified for historiography insofar as Moses's anger in the biblical account did not explain an event (it simply characterizes the manner of Moses's exit), whereas in *Antiquities* Pharaoh's anger explains why he would threaten to cut off Moses's head.

Tracking Josephus's use of the verb θέλω in the Moses narratives offers a sketch of the narratological strategies he uses to write about minds. It illustrates, for example, how Josephus narrates the cognitive dispositions of characters both from the perspective of the narrator and from the perspective of other characters. We see examples of the narrator-facilitated glimpses into desiring minds where Pharaoh was "no longer willing to be wise"; when Moses wished to invade Canaan through the desert; or when the Hebrews wished to stone Moses (*Ant.* 2.296, 323, 327). Usually these appear in narrating the narrative present, but sometimes they refer to the narrative past, as when God wished to destroy the rule of the Persians or when God wished to help the Hebrews by employing Moses as a subordinate (*Ant.* 2.348; 4.317). Examples of dispositions narrated through the perspective of other characters are when the people see that Moses is unwilling to increase Zimri's foolishness by outright controversy and when Moses infers that the tribes of Gad and Reuben are unwilling to participate in remaining struggles (*Ant.* 3.150; 4.168).

Potential dispositional or cognitive states are described by narrator and characters alike in Josephus's historiography. Continuing to look at θέλω in *Antiquities* 2–4, we find that one of Moses's reasons for leading the Hebrews by an indirect route to Palestine is that *if* the Egyptians, experiencing a change of mind, should wish to pursue (εἰ μετανοήσαντες οἱ Αἰγύπτιοι διώκειν ἐθέλοιεν) the Hebrews, they would suffer punishment for their wickedness (*Ant.* 2.322). On another occasion, Moses remarks that mountains would be leveled and land would become sea, if God willed it (τοῦ θεοῦ θελήσαντος; *Ant.* 2.333). At *Antiquities* 2.342, the Egyptians fail to realize (ἐλάνθανον) that the path through the sea is dangerous to those who wish to use it for destructive ends. This cognitive failure is noted directly by the narrator, a straightforward instance of the kind of cognitive reporting noted in the previous paragraph. What is remarkable here is that their cognitive disposition as they take that fateful step determines what happens next: *if* they walk in willing destruction, they will be destroyed; conversely, *if* seeking safety, they will be fine. In either case, it conforms to the general principle in historiography: by articulating the Egyptians' intentions, Josephus gives an etiological account of their destruction.

In these observations of Josephus's handling of the Exodus narrative, we have seen that the focus is on groups rather than individuals. While the minds of individuals are by no means off limits, the focus is on how the content of those minds bears on the fortunes of the larger groups for which their decisions and actions are representative, have consequences, or both. Moses as an individual hero is used as an organizing device around which the fortunes of Israel are narrated. His thought process is important for when it bears on the whole people, either directly, by functioning as a cause in the Polybian sense, or indirectly, by counting for or against the group's reputation in later ages. Moses's character is elevated and sanitized, compared with his biblical counterpart. Almost paradoxically, the idealization of Moses in Josephus scrubs away much of what gave an impression of individuality to the flawed Moses of the biblical text.

If Moses dominates the first part of *Antiquities*, Herod dominates the second. This is due to the central role played by Herod in creating the conditions for the Jewish-Roman War, a climactic event around which both the *War* and the second half of the *Antiquities* are organized. It is also due to the fact that Josephus had access to a wealth of literary sources for the Herodian period in Nicolaus's *Historia universalis* and in Herod's own *Memoirs*.[106]

Josephus's attitude towards Herod has occasioned controversy in the mutually imbricated fields of Josephan scholarship and Second Temple Jewish history. The portraits of Herod vary between the *War* and the *Antiquities*, and while most scholars agree that the latter is more negative, as it contains critical remarks not found at their parallel passages in *War*, one can also find favorable comments about Herod in the later work that are missing from parallel passages in *War*.[107] If one maintains, however, that the *Antiquities* offers a

---

106 Nicolaus's *Historia universalis* is universally agreed to be the main source for Josephus's account of Herod in *Ant.* 14–17. Herod's ὑπομνήματα were certainly available to Nicolaus. It is unclear whether Josephus had independent access to them. On the historiographical questions involving the Herod-Nicolaus-Josephus triangle, many of them insoluble, see Mark Toher, "Nicolaus and Herod in the 'Antiquitates Judaicae,'" *HSCP* 101 (2003): 427–47; Joseph Sievers, "Herod, Josephus, and Laqueur: A Reconsideration," in *Herod and Augustus: Papers Presented at the IJS Conference, 21st–23rd June 2005*, ed. David M. Jacobson and Nikos Kokkinos (Leiden: Brill, 2009), 83–112; Teets, "ΧΑΡΙΖΟΜΕΝΟΣ ΗΡΩΔΗΙ: Josephus' Nicolaus of Damascus in the Judaean Antiquities."

107 E.g., Herod is praised for the famine relief he orchestrates at *Antiquities* 15.305–16. It is difficult to say whether positive remarks like this are the result of borrowing from the pro-Herod Nicolaus, or if they represent a nuancing of Josephus's evaluation. The frequent positive evaluative remarks about Herod in *War* are often assumed to be from Nicolaus (e.g., the encomium at *J.W.* 1.429–30). On the face of it, this conclusion seems plausible. But Nicolaus was also able on occasion to criticize Herod, as recognized by Toher

HISTORIOGRAPHY: INVESTIGATIVE SPECULATION & COGNITIVE CAUSATION   63

more negative portrait of Herod, several interpretive possibilities compete to explain the discrepancy. Josephus may have changed his mind, may have envisioned different audiences for the two works (perhaps a Jewish audience in the first case and Greek-literate Romans in the second), improved as a scholar-writer, or lost his edge.[108]

As a result of his centrality in Josephus, his function as a cipher for a certain posture of Judaism (or anti-Judaism) in dialogue with empire, or the ability of his story to capture the imagination, Herod has become the subject of many studies, from Abraham Schalit's magisterial *König Herodes: der Mann und sein Werk* to the popular treatments that continue to appear.[109] Our task in this

---

and already by Destiton in the nineteenth century. Toher, "Nicolaus and Herod in the 'Antiquitates Judaicae,'" 434; Justus von Destinon, *Die Quellen des Flavius Josephus* (Kiel: Lipsius & Tischer, 1882), 95–100.

The classic discussion of Josephus's shifting portraits of Herod from *War* to *Antiquities*, originally published in 1920, is Richard Laqueur, *Der jüdische Historiker Flavius Josephus; ein biographischer Versuch auf neuer quellenkritischer Grundlage*, 2nd ed. (Darmstadt: Wissenschaftliche Buchgesellschaft, 1970). Cf. Jan Willem van Henten, "Constructing Herod as a Tyrant: Assessing Josephus' Parallel Passages," in *Flavius Josephus: Interpretation and History*, ed. Jack Pastor, Pnina Stern, and Menahem Mor, JSJS 146 (Leiden: Brill, 2011); Jan Willem van Henten, *Josephus: Judean Antiquities, Book 15*, ed. Steve Mason, FJTC 7b (Leiden: Brill, 2014), xiii.

108 Some combination of the four is possible although the last two possibilities are probably incompatible. Landau takes an optimistic view: "treating the same material twice, and in two different ways, allows a modern reader to follow the growth of authorial confidence in writing history." Tamar Landau, *Out-Heroding Herod: Josephus, Rhetoric, and the Herod Narratives*, AGJU/AJEC 63 (Leiden: Brill, 2006), 188. Thackeray's theory of Sophoclean and Thucydidean assistants is premised on the idea that Josephus grew fatigued around the end of book 14.

A variation on the fourth possibility is that Josephus was only ever a second-rate historian unable to master his sources—some of which were likely disparaging of Herod, while others (including Nicolaus) undoubtedly encomiastic. How one answers this question is potentially revealing of one's biases with respect to Josephus (traitor or patriot?) and Herod (Machiavellian psychopath or a maker of royal lemonade from life's proverbial lemons?). A substantial body of Jewish scholarship on Herod, the Romans, and Josephus was produced in the twentieth century and continues to be produced, sensitive to questions of Jewish autonomy and imperial powers. See both Daniel Schwartz's article on Schalit and Feldman's bibliographic survey of Josephus as a historian of the postbiblical period for two valuable perspectives on the conversation, summarizing in English a great deal of the relevant Hebrew scholarship. Daniel R. Schwartz, "On Abraham Schalit, Herod, Josephus, the Holocaust, Horst R. Moehring, and the Study of Ancient Jewish History," *JH* 2 (1987): 9–28; Feldman, *Josephus's Interpretation of the Bible*, 367ff.

109 Schalit's work first appeared in Hebrew in 1960 and in German translation with updated content in 1969. A second edition was published in 2001 with a foreword by Daniel R. Schwartz: Abraham Schalit, *König Herodes: der Mann und sein Werk*, 2nd ed., SJ 4 (Berlin: De Gruyter, 2001). Popular treatments include: Stewart Perowne, *The Life and Times of*

section is explore how Josephus represents minds in his accounts of Herod. Two factors make this task particularly interesting.

The first is the existence of these two diverging portraits in the *War* and in the *Antiquities* (*J.W.* 1.201–673; *Ant.* 14.156–17.200). The differences are worth exploring, not just for what they reveal about Josephus's sources and his academic ability to sift them critically and marshal their data (a chief concern of scholars who have attended to the discrepancies), but also because they may reveal developments in Josephus's conscious or unconscious thinking about how portraits of minds could be put to work in the service of historiographical aims.

The second factor is that the life of Herod as told by Josephus is rich with cognitive detail. This abundance of material has encouraged many attempts to nail down just what was going on in the minds of Herod and those connected to him. Such attempts tend to focus on the mind of the historical Herod and not Josephus's construction of Herod's mind in prose, meaning that the mental states Josephus attributes to Herod need to be sifted for the truth. Such scholars are typically sensitive to Josephus's navigation of biased sources and his own biases. That they do not address Josephus's mind-building in light of historiographic trends is less an oversight on their part than it is an unintended consequence of a dominant trajectory in Josephan scholarship, which privileges assessments of the author's fraught personal history as a (reluctant?) ally of the Romans and his social-political position in relation to a recently beaten people. Still, it is the fact of this abundance of cognitive material—more for Herod than most ancient figures in any historiographical text—that explains the proliferation of forays into Herodian psychological territory.[110]

Herod the Great (London: Hodder and Stoughton, 1957); Samuel Sandmel, *Herod: Profile of a Tyrant* (Philadelphia: Lippincott, 1967); Michael Grant, *Herod the Great* (New York: American Heritage Press, 1971); Peter Richardson, *Herod: King of the Jews and Friend of the Romans*, SPNT (Columbia: University of South Carolina Press, 1996); Géza Vermes, *The True Herod* (London: Bloomsbury, 2014); Adam Kolman Marshak, *The Many Faces of Herod the Great* (Grand Rapids: Eerdmans, 2015).

110   One remarkable contribution to this literature attempts to "delve into Herod's past from childhood onward and to trace the tortuous path of his life, exploring his emotional state at each and every stage until his death." Aryeh Kasher, *King Herod: A Persecuted Persecutor: A Case Study in Psychohistory and Psychobiography*, trans. Karen Gold, SJ 36 (Berlin: De Gruyter, 2007), 14. Kasher recognizes as an important forerunner Richard K. Fenn, *The Death of Herod: An Essay in the Sociology of Religion* (Cambridge: Cambridge University Press, 1992). Fenn takes inspiration from the "psychoanalytic tradition within sociology" (101) and combines "psychoanalytic insights with social anthropology in a disciplined approach towards limited generalizations" (31). Both Kasher and Fenn explicitly draw on Freudian categories to guide their interpretations.

Josephus comments on the motives of other historians in a way that parallels Polybius's polemics against Timaeus and Phylarchus.[111] Josephus wants his reader to understand that where he reports the tradition differently from a source, it is because the source was biased in a way that made it disregard the truth. Introducing Herod's father Antipater, for example, he identifies the family as Idumean (*Ant.* 14.8) and immediately goes on to note that Nicolaus attaches Antipater to the leading Jews returning to Judea from Babylon, "but he says this in order to please Antipater's son Herod" (*Ant.* 14.9).[112] Josephus does not here explain the relationship between Herod and Nicolaus, or why Nicolaus would write to please Herod. As we saw earlier in this chapter with Polybius, Timaeus, and Phylarchus, accusing a source of bias was a regular feature of Greek historiography.

Josephus does not restrict his comments on motives to human actors. God is an actor in the narrative, and human impropriety can motivate God to take punish evildoers. Antipater is introduced to the narrative in the context of the power struggle between the Hasmonean brothers Hyrcanus and Aristobulus. Antipater attaches himself to Hyrcanus's cause at a moment when Hyrcanus had abdicated the throne to Aristobulus, and he persuades Hyrcanus to enlist the Arab king Aretas in an effort to reclaim the throne. After Antipater brokers the arrangement, Aretas and Hyrcanus's faction launches an attack on Aristobulus in Jerusalem at Passover. Aristobulus shelters in the temple and the people of Jerusalem rally to Hyrcanus. These people, in the course of pressing their siege, seize a priest named Onias, whose prayers for rain God had once answered. The Jerusalemites now want him "to place a curse on Aristobulus and his fellow-rebels, just as he had, by his prayers, put an end to the rainless period" (*Ant.* 14.22). He refuses and instead prays for the safety of the priests besieged in the temple. The response of "the villains among the Jews" is to stone Onias to death. "But," Josephus continues, "God straightway punished them for this savagery, and exacted satisfaction for the murder" (*Ant.* 14.25). The account that follows offers further proof of the villainy of the nameless

---

111 Josephus's primary source for Herod is Nicolaus of Damascus's *Historia universalis*, perhaps one of antiquity's most ambitious historiographical projects in its original 144 books, beginning from the dawn of time and carrying on until the death of Herod. Josephus's *Antiquities* 14–17 is largely drawn from *Historia universalis* 123–4. See Athenaeus (*Deipn.* 6) for the figure 144 books. The Suda puts it at 80 books, but this can be shown false on the basis of the fragments that have survived. Cf. Shutt, *Studies in Josephus*, 82.

112 It is this statement above all which has led scholars (perhaps unfairly) to criticize Nicolaus as a fawning sycophant and to praise Josephus's critical acumen. These are separate but related conclusions, and both are too simple. Nicolaus could write about his patron in a critical way, and Josephus's criticism of other historians is standard for the genre.

Jews in Hyrcanus's party, and a resulting prayer from the besieged priests that God would "exact satisfaction on their behalf on their countrymen." God "did not delay their punishment" and sends a violent wind to destroy their crops (*Ant.* 14.28). Both this episode (set in the narrative present) and Onias's backstory (set in the narrative past) represent God as a historical actor, responsive to human entreaties. There are no reservations of the kind that often accompany descriptions of divine activity in Greek historiography.[113] The emphasis, which comes through even in this short summary, is on actions. God's motivations, like human motivations, are visible and inferable from sequences of events.

Much of the latter part of the account of Herod in *Antiquities* revolves around his domestic difficulties. To tell the story, Josephus needs to help the reader track (1) the dispositions of those involved; (2) what each knows and wants; and (3) whether in each case the "knowledge" held by a given party is true. If the biographical material in an author like Plutarch focuses on the disposition and knowledge of the protagonist (see chapter 3), Josephus's cognitive searchlight casts about more freely in the minds of Herod's friends and family. This is consistent with the pattern in his account of the Exodus narrative, where Josephus ventured freely into the minds of Moses and other characters around him.

Herod unravels in the wake of his wife Mariamme's execution. His failure of mind is on spectacular display when, afterwards, Mariamme's sons Alexander and Aristobulus return to Herod's house from Rome (*Ant.* 16.7). To make sense of what happens next, Josephus's narrator needs access to the minds of Herod, Alexander, Aristobulus, Antipater (Herod's son by Doris of Jerusalem), and Herod's siblings Salome and Pheroras. In the previous book, Josephus had narrated the plot against Mariamme, in which Salome was a chief actor. Mariamme, Salome thought, because of her royal, Hasmonean lineage, treated Herod and his Idumean family with contempt. Thus provoked, Salome began looking for opportunities to do Mariamme harm, then leveraged an opportunity to make Herod believe that Mariamme had been unfaithful, resulting in Mariamme's execution and Herod's great, consequent distress. Now, with the return of Mariamme's sons, Salome redirects her hatred at the sons, "as if it were a legacy, and she was trying everything that had succeeded against their mother in a desperate and reckless way so as not to leave alive any of her offspring who would be able to avenge the death of the woman who had been destroyed by her" (*Ant.* 16.66). The reader is thus furnished with an idea of

---

113   But observe that God's interventions here unfold by proxy (God does not get directly involved) and involve natural phenomena beyond human control (the rain, the wind).

Salome's disposition (hateful, reckless) and its motivation (continued antipathy towards Mariamme, wanting to avoid future retribution). Next, Josephus paints a picture of the sons' disposition—"The youths too, on their part, were rather reckless and were hostile to their father"—and their reasons—"both because of their remembrance of their mother's undeserved fate and also because of their desire to rule." Josephus has the youths take an open posture in expressing their feelings (cf. *Ant.* 16.84), and infers the belief he thinks they must have held for them to proceed this way ("believing, in their inexperience, that it was noble to let their anger be unrestrained"), while Salome and Pheroras, on the other hand, plot against the youths (εἰς τὰ μειράκια καὶ μετὰ πραγματείας ἐπιβουλή), making use of "slander, in a calculatedly malicious way" (πραγματικῶς καὶ κακοήθως ἐχρῶντο ταῖς διαβολαῖς). Josephus creates the impression that as tension mounted between these two parties, the Jerusalemites took notice and pitied the youths because of their inexperience (*Ant.* 16.71). Salome's strategy was to fan the youths' moral outrage over their mother's death and simultaneously to report to Herod "that he was in great danger from the youths, who were openly threatening that they would not leave the murder of their mother unavenged" and adding that they were seeking to enlist Archelaeus, king of neighboring Cappadocia, in a bid to turn Caesar against Herod (*Ant.* 16.73). The result was that Herod was immediately disturbed (ἐτετάρακτο), perplexed (ἐξεπέπληκτο), "in a confused state of mind (ἐν συγχύσει τῆς ψυχῆς)," and "disturbed, in this disposition (ταρασσόμενος δὲ καὶ διακείμενος τὸν τρόπον τοῦτον)" (*Ant.* 16.75, 76, 78). Other characters in Josephus's account of Herod do not waver in their dispositions. They do not become confused or perplexed, even where they hold a belief the reader knows to be false.

Even at the scenes busiest with cognitive activity, Josephus rarely presents διανοία in characters' speech. The most common way of handling thoughts and motives is in narrator speech with a participle-facilitated indication of the actor's state of mind (hostile, perplexed, avaricious, fearful). These indications are almost always presented in the context of something that the associated characters have just done or experienced, or to explain what they are about to do. Another common technique of the Josephan narrator is to trace characters' reasoning processes. These processes rarely go beyond a single consideration and the action-related conclusion drawn from it, but they can sometimes extend to three- or four-step processes. The reader frequently has special knowledge not available to the reasoning character (e.g., the future, or a missing piece of key information), which creates discrepant awareness.[114] This is comparable

---

114   This concept will be discussed at greater length in chapters 4 and 5.

68   CHAPTER 2

to Polybius's constructions of the strategizing of military and political actors like Hannibal and Fabius in the *Histories*. A third technique for representing characters' thoughts is the monologue. The Herod narrative in *War* has ten such speeches in a variety of contexts: seven attributed to Herod and three to other actors. There are more in the parallel chapters of *Antiquities*, occurring infrequently in books 14 and 15 and becoming much more prominent in books 16 and 17.[115] Direct speech was the primary vehicle used in Thucydides for representing individual minds. But where Thucydides often lets characters "show" their states of mind in speeches rather than "telling" the reader via a narrator, Josephus is more direct in announcing characters' true thoughts and motives via his narrator. The speeches thus offer opportunities to see Josephus's view of Herod's attempts to control the perceptions of those around him while disguising his true motives. For example, in the prelude to the renovation and expansion of the Jerusalem temple, where Josephus observes that Herod's true motivations were love of honor (φιλοτιμία in *Ant.* 15.194, 271, 303, 328; φιλοτιμούμενος in 15.330), Herod's speech conspicuously omits these motives. Instead, his motives are couched in terms of what the Jerusalemites stand to gain by the undertaking. One can imagine the two sets of motives coexisting, but the way they are presented in *Antiquities* is illuminating for what it says about Josephus's sense of his duties as a historiographer. Josephus, like Thucydides (Thuc. 1.23) and Polybius (*Hist.* 3.6), distinguishes between real motives and pretexts.

Josephus's attention to the cognitive plane in his account of Herod's career can best be understood by the historiographical principle of working backwards from events to their causes.[116] While he does not formally adopt

---

115   *Ant.* 14.165–67 (Jewish leaders appeal to Hyrcanus, warning about giving power to Antipater and his sons); 14.172–75 (Samias to the Sanhedrin, a prediction that Herod will one day punish Hyrcanus and the Sanhedrin); 15.127–47 (Herod's exhortation to his soldiers, on why fight the Arabs; cf. *J.W.* 1.373–79); 15.382–87 (Herod to the people, on why rebuild the temple; cf. the parallel passage *J.W.* 5.184–237, where no speech is offered); 16.31–57 (Nicolaus to Marcus Agrippa, intercession on behalf of the Ionian Jews); 16.90–99 (Herod to Augustus, indirect speech with his concerns about hostility and possible conspiracy hatched by Alexander and Aristobulus); 16.105–20 (Alexander's reply to Herod's accusation); 16.209–16 (exchange between Herod, Pheroras, and Salome, on (dis)loyalty and slander); 16.339–50 (Nicolaus to Caesar, reconciling Herod and Caesar and attacking the Arabs); 16.375–76, 379–83 (two speeches by Tiro to the court, accusing Herod of unlawfulness and unreason); 17.96–120 (speeches given by Herod, Antipater, and Nicolaus in Antipater's trial; cf. *J.W.* 1.630–6). For discussion of the speeches, see Landau, *Out-Heroding Herod*, 134–56.

116   That ancient historiographers understood the elucidation of causes (αἰτίαι) as central to their project is illustrated in an aside in the preface to Polybius's *Histories* 1.5.3, where Polybius has been justifying his decision to start his history in the 260s BCE, with the

Polybius's distinctions between causes, pretexts, and beginnings, all of these concepts—especially causes and pretexts—play important roles in his *Antiquities*. Herod, son of a mid-level Idumean advisor to Hyrcanus, eventually becomes king of the Jews. One way of explaining this is by reference to Herod's aggressive, ambitious, impulsive character, congenitally determined by his father's political advancements and opportunism, and foreshadowed in his administration of Galilee, his suppression of brigandage, and his negotiation of the legal obstacles that followed. Similar explanations could be offered for the events of Herod's later life. The actions taken by Herod are important because of the consequences they had for the Jewish people in Josephus's grand narrative. Those individual actions can be explained in many cases by reference to the state of Herod's mind when he carried them out. To understand why Herod's mind was confused, troubled, and perplexed, one needs to understand what information was being presented to him and the forms of delivery in which it arrived. To understand why these contradictory messages arrive to Herod in the forms they take, one needs to appreciate what motives were driving the message producers and bearers. The resulting account of the cognitive domain is unusually textured for a work of history, and yet that texture remains explicable by reference to conventional mandates of the genre, especially the attention to actions and their causes.

5 Conclusion

A major concern of historians in the narrow tradition of ancient historiography was to provide an account of political history, broadly construed, including especially the events that were consequential on national scales. Individuals, especially political figures like lawmakers, kings, and generals, naturally play important roles in those accounts. Compared to their modern counterparts, however, ancient historiographers showed a greater willingness to enter their subjects' minds and offer, with varying degrees of confidence, what they reasoned must have been the desire, the emotion, the disposition, or the strategy that explains an event. They saw, further, that it would be silly

---

crossing of the Romans from Italy. "The actual cause (αἰτίαν) of their crossing must be stated without comment; for if I were to seek the cause of the cause and so on, my whole work would have no clear starting point and principle (ἵνα μὴ τῆς αἰτίας αἰτίαν ἐπιζητούσης ἀνυπόστατος ἡ τῆς ὅλης ὑποθέσεως ἀρχὴ γένηται καὶ θεωρία). The starting point must be a date generally agreed upon and recognized, and one self-apparent from the events, even if this involves my going back a little in point of date and giving a summary of intervening occurrences."

to take a speaker's articulation of his own motives at face value. Such articulations could be explained as pretexts—necessary pretexts, sometimes, if the speaker was going to be effective in winning over the people he needed to act, but pretexts nevertheless and not to be confused with real causes. Because the group's fortunes are more central to the concerns of the genre than those of the individual, it comes as no surprise that a great deal of the attention to desires, passions, and thoughts in historiography are in connection to groups: the Romans, the Hebrews, the Egyptians, and so on. These references to states of mind held by a group are also used to explain actions taken by the larger group, as for example when the Egyptians were made to follow the Hebrews into the path in the Red Sea because they did not know what lay in store for those who set foot on the path willing harm. The historiographer can assume that his reader's interest is to know the causes of major historical events (cf. Polybius, *Hist.* 7.66.2–3), and position himself as a privileged purveyor of access to those causes. The most frequent causal factor in the genre, on display for example in the desire of Herod's sons to rule as the cause for their behavior, is the will—an object to which ancient historiographers presume what is, from a modern perspective, startling access. In the next chapter we take up a major off-shoot of historiography, the βίος or "Life" of an individual to find that the biographer's project overlaps in many respects with the historiographer's, including access to characters' motivating thoughts and desires, but also that those minds become ethically charged in ways that go beyond what we have seen in this chapter.

CHAPTER 3

Βίος: Ethics and Mimesis

Most contemporary Gospels scholars identify the genre of their subject as biography, often with the caveat that Greco-Roman biographies should not be conflated with the modern genre biography. Many prefer a term like βίος or Life to underscore the distance between "our" biographies and "their" βίοι or Lives.[1] While recognizing the danger of overstressing the differences between modern biographies and ancient βίοι, I use separate terms in this book for the sake of clarity. After surveying John-as-βίος scholarship, I look at the βίος tradition broadly and then at particular texts by Plutarch of Chaeronea and Philo of Alexandria. The argument advanced is that the works discussed in this chapter belonged to a generic tradition that coalesced around ethical interests: biographical characters in the Greek tradition functioned as moral exemplars or object lessons.[2] Ethics in this context has to do with assessing characters' permanent and temporary dispositions as motivating factors in their actions, as well as their function as exemplars for readers' moral formation. In the case studies of Plutarch's *Solon* and Philo's *Moses* that make up the second half of the chapter, we will see that represented thoughts both inform and are themselves the product of attention to ethical concerns. Βίος is a complicated and wide-ranging genre. No doubt one could produce βίοι where ethics and thought representations are less tightly intertwined. For Johannine scholars, the advantage of heuristic comparison with these texts is that they are roughly contemporary with the Fourth Gospel.

1   John and Βίος

The prevailing view among New Testament scholars at the end of the 1970s was that the Gospels were *sui generis*. Mark was thought to have inaugurated a new

---

1   The first attested use of the term βιογραφία occurs in a fragment of the *Life of Isidore* by the Neoplatonist Damascius (ca. 458–538 CE), preserved by Photius (ninth c. CE) in the *Bibliotheca* (181, 242). Cf. Arnaldo Momigliano, *The Development of Greek Biography*, Expanded ed. (Cambridge: Harvard University Press, 1993), 12.

2   For the ethical in βίοι, see in general Tomas Hägg, *The Art of Biography in Antiquity* (Cambridge: Cambridge University Press, 2012), 282, 387; Tim Duff, *Plutarch's Lives: Exploring Virtue and Vice* (Oxford: Clarendon, 1999).

genre subsequently adopted by Matthew, Luke, and John. Some understood *sui generis* in terms of literary genre, but most scholars followed Rudolf Bultmann and Karl Ludwig Schmidt in viewing the Gospels as sub-literary accumulations of oral traditions reflecting the kerygma of the early church. "Biography" was thought to be too elevated a term for the Gospels on the assumption that the label was appropriate only to a few ancient works by named, independent, and motivated intellectuals like Suetonius and Plutarch. The view was eventually recognized as problematic because neither quality nor composite authorship nor anonymous authorship can exclude a text from participating in almost any literary genre. The *sui generis* thesis in its strong form also fails to account for how the Gospels could have communicated without some kind of relationship to existing forms of communication, which would necessarily have been subject to generic constraints.

Charles Talbert was one of the first post-Bultmannian scholars to revive a pre-Bultmannian link between the Gospels and Greco-Roman biography.[3] Readers in the nineteenth and early twentieth centuries had instinctively linked the Gospels with biography; what was new with Talbert and his contemporaries was a better appreciation of the distance separating the conventions of ancient biographies from modern biographies, especially with respect to differences in how far psychological exploration would play a necessary component of the genre.[4] In fact, the Gospels' apparent indifference to the psychological profile and development of their protagonist was one of the factors behind the general exclusion of the Gospels from the category "biography" for the greater part of the twentieth century. As form- and source-criticism fragmented the Gospels, as scholars focused on recovering *Urliteratur* behind canonical pastiches, the Gospels grew to look less and less like biographies in

---

3 Charles H. Talbert, *What Is a Gospel?: The Genre of the Canonical Gospels* (Philadelphia: Fortress, 1977). The book was widely reviewed. Many readers were sympathetic to Talbert's conclusions but were confounded by the routes by which he arrived at them and his idiosyncratic readings of ancient biographies without reference to classical scholarship. The book's strength was the challenge it posed to the *sui generis* hypothesis, not necessarily the positive case it made for situating the Gospels among Greco-Roman biographies.

  Contemporaries of Talbert were developing similar positions. Cf. Graham Stanton, *Jesus of Nazareth in New Testament Preaching*, SNTSMS 27 (London: Cambridge University Press, 1974); Philip L. Shuler, *A Genre for the Gospels: The Biographical Character of Matthew* (Philadelphia: Fortress, 1982). Cf. Richard A. Burridge, *What Are the Gospels?: A Comparison with Graeco-Roman Biography*, 2nd ed. (Grand Rapids: Eerdmans, 2004), 78–101.

4 The most detailed studies of the Gospels as biographies from the pre-Bultmannian period were Clyde Weber Votaw, "The Gospels and Contemporary Biographies," *AmJT* 19 (1915): 45–73; Clyde Weber Votaw, "The Gospels and Contemporary Biographies: Concluded," *AmJT* 19 (1915): 217–49. Reprinted as Clyde Weber Votaw, *The Gospels and Contemporary Biographies in the Greco-Roman World* (Philadelphia: Fortress, 1970).

ΒΙΟΣ: ETHICS AND MIMESIS

the modern sense. The rise of redaction criticism in the mid-twentieth century led to a renewed interest in the figure of the author—no longer as an independent genius producing a text *de novo* but rather as the redactor revealing a distinctive theological *Tendenz* in managing traditional materials. Talbert and others were part of a move to reconsider ancient biography as a possible context for the Gospels, not least because they recognized that genre associations have exegetical and hermeneutical consequences. One of the ways in which they accomplished this was to show that ancient biographies need to be analyzed apart from the expectations of modern biography. This view gathered momentum through the 1980s and culminated with the publication of Richard Burridge's *What are the Gospels? A Comparison with Graeco-Roman Biography* in 1992.

It would be difficult to overstate the impact of Burridge's work on subsequent gospel genre scholarship.[5] Burridge explains that he embarked on his study in the late 1980s because he was skeptical about the links others had drawn between the Gospels and βίοι, only to change his mind as he carried out his research. The book that resulted is a carefully articulated case for the genre of the Gospels as βίοι, beginning with a history of scholarship, then moving into a discussion of literary and genre theory,[6] then an analysis of formal internal and external features of ten ancient βίοι, then returning to the Gospels to show how the Synoptics and John share those features. His interaction with genre theory and his attention to internal and external features of typical

---

5   The second edition (2004) contains a new foreword by Graham Stanton and an added chapter on "Reactions and Developments." These, in combination with the history of scholarship in the book's first chapter, offer a fine account of the history of scholarship connecting the Gospels to βίοι. The book and the conversation predicated on it have shaped the scholarly consensus in the field. Some recent attempts to challenge or complicate Burridge's thesis in connection to Mark and Luke, respectively, are Eve-Marie Becker, *Das Markus-Evangelium im Rahmen antiker Historiographie*, WUNT 194 (Tübingen: Mohr Siebeck, 2006); Andrew Pitts, "The Genre of the Third Gospel and Greco-Roman Historiography: A Reconsideration" (Society of Biblical Studies Annual Meeting, Atlanta, 2015).

6   Burridge interacts especially but not only with Jonathan Culler, *Structuralist Poetics: Structuralism, Linguistics and the Study of Literature* (London: Routledge, 1975); Heather Dubrow, *Genre* (London: Methuen, 1982); Alastair Fowler, "The Life and Death of Literary Forms," *NLitHist* 2 (1971): 199–216; Alastair Fowler, *Kinds of Literature: An Introduction to the Theory of Genres and Modes* (Cambridge: Harvard University Press, 1982); Northrop Frye, *Anatomy of Criticism; Four Essays* (Princeton: Princeton University Press, 1957); E. D. Hirsch, *Validity in Interpretation* (New Haven: Yale University Press, 1967); E. D. Hirsch, *The Aims of Interpretation* (Chicago: University of Chicago Press, 1976); René Wellek and Austin Warren, *Theory of Literature*, 3rd ed. (Harmondsworth: Penguin, Pelican, 1982). Burridge claims that this careful interaction with genre criticism and literary theory is an advance on previous scholarship.

74   CHAPTER 3

works in the genre are largely responsible for the book's impact on the subsequent conversation.[7]

Burridge discusses the genre of John in a chapter apart from his discussion of the Synoptics, although in both cases he arrives at the same conclusion, namely, that an ancient person would identify the text as a βίος. Despite noting the exemplary function of ancient βίοι and their attention to the subject's ἦθος,[8] Burridge gives no sustained account of this dimension of characterization in his two chapters on the Gospels. The chapter on John emphasizes that "with respect to external features, the Fourth Gospel shares a similar mode of representation, size, structure and scale to those of the synoptic gospels and βίοι, and makes use of similar literary units, drawn from oral and written sources to display the character of Jesus by means of his deeds, words and sayings in a manner typical of βίοι."[9] In other words, Burridge identifies the Gospels as βίοι on other grounds than shared conventions in their ethical agendas.

An important critique registered by Adela Yarbro Collins in response to the first edition of *What are the Gospels?* is that Burridge fails to consider the Gospels in connection to genres other than βίος.[10] That critique is one of the reasons the present study looks at John in dialogue with a larger genre set. At the same time, I adopt here what I take to be a strength of Burridge's project in his attention to the conventions (what he calls internal and external features) of John in relation to the conventions of a sample group of texts representing a given genre.

---

7   It is curious, though, that someone who has evidently read carefully in genre theory should conceive of his project as putting the Gospels-as-βίοι theory "on a sound scholarly footing or exposed as a false trail" (Burridge, *What Are the Gospels?*, 78), as if genre participation were best addressed in binary terms.

8   E.g., in connection to Plutarch, "βίος is interested in men's character" (61); following Brenk, "[Plutarch's] major interest is in illuminating the virtues or vices of a hero through the type of 'insignificant' detail which he felt was often overlooked by the major historians" (65; cf. Frederick E. Brenk, *In Mist Apparelled: Religious Themes in Plutarch's Moralia and Lives*, MnS 48 [Leiden: Brill, 1977], 184); following J. K. Anderson, noting that over a third of Xenophon's *Agesilaus* deals with a single campaign, perhaps "because Xenophon considers this campaign to show Agesilaus' character best" (132; cf. J. K. Anderson, *Xenophon* [London: Duckworth, 1974], 146–71). On Xenophon's *Agesilaus*, he notes that a third of the work analyzes Agesilaus's "piety, justice, self-control, courage, wisdom, patriotism, graciousness, foresight and simplicity of life" (132). In the chapter added to the second edition, he writes, "Many [ancient biographies] were written explicitly to give an example to others to emulate: Xenophon composed his *Agesilaus* to provide an example (παράδειγμα) for others to follow to become better people (ἀνδραγαθίαν ἀσκεῖν, x.2). Equally, Plutarch aims to provide examples so that by immitation (μίμησις) of the virtues and avoidance of the vices described, the reader can improve his own moral character (*Pericles* 1; *Aem. Paul.* 1)." Burridge, *What Are the Gospels?*, 305.

9   Burridge, *What Are the Gospels?*, 232.

10   Adela Yarbro Collins, "Genre and the Gospels," *JR* 75 (1995): 241.

BIOΣ: ETHICS AND MIMESIS

Burridge's work has spurred a wealth of scholarship on the Gospels and genre, much of it supportive of his thesis. Especially notable are studies by Dirk Frickenschmidt, who looks at narrative conventions in 142 ancient biographical texts with the aim of demonstrating that the Gospels *eindeutig* belong to the literary family of ancient biographies; Albrecht Dihle, who uses Plutarchan moral βίος as a model; and Detlev Dormeyer, who describes the Gospels as redactionally-shaped "ideal biographies" insofar as they emphasize the "typical" (in contrast to modern biographies, which emphasize the psychological and individual).[11] Although more space could be devoted these and other contributions to Gospels-as-βίοι scholarship, not to mention the arguments that have been made about the purposes and functions of the Gospels predicated on their classification as βίοι, I turn now to consider what can be said in general about the contours of the βίος tradition and its cognition-representing tendencies.

2   Conventions for Representing Minds in Βίοι

Any account of the origins of βίος as a genre entails discussion of its genealogical ties to historiography, often beginning with the observation that major sections of classic historiographical works focus on individuals, including Cyrus and Cambyses in Herodotus, or Themistocles in Thucydides. As noted in chapter 2, texts like Theopompus's *Philippica* have suggested to some that "person-centered historiography" was gaining ascendancy in the fourth century. The earliest surviving βίοι, most agree, are fourth-century works of Xenophon (some or all of the *Cyropaedia*, the *Memorabilia*, and the *Agesilaus*) and Isocrates (especially the *Evagoras*). Not everyone is content to label these works βίοι without qualification, however. The most important qualification is that they are at least as close to encomium as they are to historiography. Encomium was an originally rhetorical-poetical genre with its own conventions. It was not subsumed entire into the βίος tradition but continued as to flourish alongside it.[12] Genres, however, as we saw in chapter 1, exist not in isolation but in genre sets or ecologies. One of the features shared between βίοι and encomia,

---

11   Dirk Frickenschmidt, *Evangelium als Biographie: die vier Evangelien im Rahmen antiker Erzählkunst*, TANZ 22 (Tübingen: Francke, 1997), 2; Albrecht Dihle, "The Gospels and Greek Biography," in *The Gospel and the Gospels*, ed. Peter Stuhlmacher (Grand Rapids: Eerdmans, 1991), 361–86; Detlev Dormeyer, *Das Markusevangelium als Idealbiographie von Jesus Christus, dem Nazarener*, SBB 43 (Stuttgart: Verlag Katholisches Bibelwerk, 1999).

12   Cf. the remark of Isocrates, "I am fully aware that what I propose to do is difficult—to offer an encomium in prose of a man's virtue (ἀνδρὸς ἀρετὴν διὰ λόγων ἐγκωμιάζειν)" (*Evag.* 1.8 [trans. LCL, modified]).

for example, is a focus on αἱ τοῦ βίου κατασκευαί, the principles of a subject's life (Isocrates, *Evag.* 1.44). Other scholars have located the origins of βίος in a philosophical context, perhaps especially with the Peripatetics. Here we think of the *Cyropaedia*, and ways in which Socrates is memorialized by Plato and Xenophon.[13] One account of the origins of βίος has it that Aristoxenus, upset at being passed over in favor of Theophrastus as the successor to Aristotle, decided to write a βίος of Aristotle attacking his character.[14] He also wrote lives of Socrates, Plato, and Pythagoras.[15] Although the story should be taken with a healthy dose of skepticism, we should not fail to note that ἦθος is centrally at issue, albeit in negative terms rather than with the positive exemplars that would come to dominate the form in later years.

Confusion over the origins of βίος extends into attempts to categorize various trajectories within the tradition. Friedrich Leo, in his seminal *Die griechisch-romische Biographie nach ihrer literarischen Form* (1901), divides the tradition into three streams: one encomiastic, in the tradition of Isocrates's *Evagoras* and Xenophon's *Agesilaus*; one "Alexandrian," associated with Suetonius and privileging chronology over character; and one "Peripatetic," associated with Plutarch and centrally concerned with virtue and the provision of models for imitation. This schema, adopted in whole or in part by many subsequent scholars, has been critiqued for failing to do justice to Plutarch and Suetonius, the

---

13   Some have read Plato's Socratic dialogues as βίοι in dialogic form. The *Apology*, for example, "is biographical in the sense that its prime intention is to transmit Plato's picture of Socrates' personality by displaying and interpreting his *life* seen as an ethical unity. That unity is more important to the author than chronological succession. While the outer facts are comparatively few and scattered, the inner life is constantly in focus, through the simple expedient of making Socrates himself the speaker." Hägg, *The Art of Biography in Antiquity*, 19–30; quotation from p. 20. Cf. Albrecht Dihle, *Studien zur griechischen Biographie*, 2nd ed. (Göttingen: Vandenhoeck & Ruprecht, 1970).

14   Friedrich Leo, *Die griechisch-römische Biographie nach ihrer litterarischen Form* (Leipzig: Teubner, 1901), 102. Cf. Burridge, *What are the Gospels?*, 69–79. But note that Burridge here confuses Theopompus and Theophrastus.

15   Fragments of those on Socrates and Plato survive and are characterized by one of his readers as "scurrilous and vituperative." Andrew Barker, "Aristoxenus," in *OCD*, ed. Simon Hornblower, Antony Spawforth, and Esther Eidinow, 4th ed. (Oxford: Oxford University Press, 2012). But Hägg rightly notes in connection to the now-lost whole works that "if they were as idiosyncratic and mean as some modern critics conclude from what is left, Aristoxenus' honored position in the ancient biographical tradition would be difficult to explain." Hägg, *The Art of Biography in Antiquity*, 76–77. For the fragments, see Fritz Wehrli, *Die Schule des Aristoteles: Aristoxenus*, 2nd ed., vol. 2, 10 vols. (Basel: Schwabe, 1967).

BIOΣ: ETHICS AND MIMESIS

supposed archetypes of the two chief strands, let alone the variety of other Hellenistic βίοι.[16]

Where Leo proposed three strands, Talbert adds a fourth: "popular" biographies like *The Life of Aesop* or *Secundus the Silent Philosopher*, and offers a new model in which βίοι can initially be sorted into two categories (didactic or nondidactic), and subsequently the didactic lives can be sorted into five types by attending to the supposed social functions of the texts treated.[17] The five are (1) those providing readers with a model to imitate; (2) those dispelling a false image of the teacher or ruler and providing a model to imitate; (3) those discrediting a given teacher or ruler; (4) those pointing readers to the site of the "living voice" in the period after the death of the founder; and (5) those validating the teacher's doctrine. Talbert puts Mark and John in the second category, Luke in the fourth, and Matthew in the fifth. Talbert sees these five as accommodating all didactic lives of philosophers from antiquity. With the exception of the fourth, all have parallels in biographies of rulers.

The βίοι examined at length in this chapter fall under Leo's "Peripatetic" category or Talbert's first (Plutarch's *Solon*) and fifth (Philo's *Moses*) didactic types, but that matters only if the categories stand up to scrutiny. One could easily make Philo's *Moses* a part of Leo's "encomium" category—already in the first line, Philo describes Moses as the greatest and most perfect of men (*Moses* 1.1)—or put it in the Alexandrian category, on the grounds that the first book is chronologically-arranged and Philo is a native Alexandrian. Similarly, one could put Plutarch's *Solon* in any of Talbert's first, second, fourth, or fifth categories, depending on what one chose to emphasize. Whatever position they occupy within the general category βίος, however, the participation of both the *Solon* and the *Moses* in that larger genre is uncontested. Moreover, the hypothesis to be tested—that a bendable convention of the genre is the exposition of a famous man's ἦθος as a model for imitation or avoidance—at first blush accords well with nearly all of Leo or Talbert's subcategories.

Plutarch's surviving βίοι have exercised an outsized role in shaping academic discussions about βίος as a genre, but they did not occupy the same prototypical position for the genre in antiquity that Herodotus and Thucydides held for ancient historiography.[18] In addition to coming relatively late in the history of βίος, Plutarch had his own idiosyncrasies, including Platonist philosophical

---

16   Momigliano, *The Development of Greek Biography*, 19–21, 45–46.

17   Talbert, *What Is a Gospel?*, 93–98.

18   For the reception of Plutarch and Suetonius in the early modern period and their respective influences on the development of modern biography, see G. W. Bowersock, "Suetonius in the Eighteenth Century," in *From Gibbon to Auden: Essays on the Classical Tradition* (Oxford: Oxford University Press, 2009), 52–65.

78   CHAPTER 3

commitments and his unprecedented decision to compose βίοι in pairs of Greek and Roman men.[19] So although this chapter is like earlier scholarship in granting Plutarch a prominent role in teaching us the conventions of βίος, his idiosyncrasies and inconsistencies need to be kept in mind.[20]

Readily apparent in many ancient biographers, including Plutarch, is an emphasis on character (τρόπος, ἦθος), though in Plutarch's case direct description is rare apart from explicit comparison with others.[21] Plutarch prefers to show character than tell about it. Character-investigation is not a unique feature of βίος, but it is a central feature. Even in non-prototypical βίοι, ἦθος plays a vital role. This is why the Socratic material, including Xenophon's *Memorabilia* and Plato's dialogues, are often seen as participating in the genre. Encomium is also obviously implicated in this conversation.

Isocrates's *Evagoras* describes itself as an encomium. This could be taken as a primary genre identifier, on the same level as βίος, or it could be taken as a secondary identifier, allowing it to become a particular mode of βίος. Momigliano defines ἔπαινος or encomium as "an appreciation of the virtues and glory of a dead king," and sums up Isocrates's accomplishment: "Isocrates combines rather ineffectually a static description of Euagoras' character with a

---

19   Dihle, who has been criticized for overreliance on Plutarch for describing the history of biography, might respond that any given genre takes time to achieve a standard form and Plutarch is that moment of arrival for ancient biography. Cf. Dihle, "The Gospels and Greek Biography," 362.

      For Plutarch's complicated relationship to Rome as a Greek intellectual figure, see Simon Swain, *Hellenism and Empire: Language, Classicism, and Power in the Greek World, AD 50–250* (Oxford: Clarendon, 1996), 135–186; Philip A. Stadter and L. Van der Stockt, eds., *Sage and Emperor: Plutarch, Greek Intellectuals, and Roman Power in the Time of Trajan (98–117 A.D.)*, SyFLL A29 (Leuven: Leuven University Press, 2002); Philip A. Stadter, "Plutarch and Rome," in *A Companion to Plutarch*, ed. Mark Beck, BCAW (Oxford: Blackwell, 2014), 13–31.

20   Plutarch, after all, likely had different aims for different βίοι and his goals for the larger project may also have shifted over the years he worked on it. On Plutarch's flexibility, see Christopher Pelling, "Plutarch and Roman Politics," in *Past Perspectives: Studies in Greek and Roman Historical Writing: Papers Presented at a Conference in Leeds, 6–8 April 1983*, ed. I. S. Moxon, J. D. Smart, and A. J. Woodman (Cambridge: Cambridge University Press, 1986), 159–87. "Plutarch's biography is a very flexible genre, and his interest in historical background is one of the things which vary" (159). Geiger seems to think that genre-distinguishing remarks such as one finds at the outset of the *Alexander* are only a feature of "political" biographies, because there was a clear danger of "slipping into history." Joseph Geiger, *Cornelius Nepos and Ancient Political Biography*, Hist.E 47 (Stuttgart: Steiner Verlag Wiesbaden, 1985), 114.

21   On Plutarch's comparisons, see Christopher Pelling, "Synkrisis in Plutarch's Lives," in *Miscelanea Plutarchea*, ed. Frederick E. Brenk (Ferrara: Giornale filologico ferrarese, 1986), 83–96.

BIOΣ: ETHICS AND MIMESIS

chronological account of what other people did to Euagoras."[22] The comments on the dead man's virtues are concentrated in *Evagoras* 25–40. In her introduction to a recent translation of the *Evagoras*, Yun Lee Too suggests that Isocrates is implicitly "making the case for a new post-epic heroism, in which the fourth-century nonmaterial virtues, such as those celebrated in 25–40 of the speech, are privileged over and above the physical qualities, for example, strength and speed."[23] This corresponds with the shift away from the model of Pindar, who approached encomium in verse and dealing with physical excellences. Like Isocrates, Plutarch shifts away from physical and historical accomplishments to emphasize inner virtues in his βίοι.[24]

Though some scholars have been content to treat encomium as a genre separate from βίος,[25] it is worth asking what is gained by such a distinction. Isocrates writes that he is not afraid of appearing to exaggerate the qualities of Evagoras so much as he fears failing to do justice to his deeds (ὥστ' οὐ δέδοικα μὴ φανῶ μείζω λέγων τῶν ἐκείνῳ προσόντων, ἀλλὰ μὴ πολὺ λίαν ἀπολειφθῶ τῶν πεπραγμένων αὐτῷ [*Evag.* 1.48–49]), which may be read as a tacit admission of deliberate exaggeration.[26] Exaggeration, however, is present in every genre, including βίος. In a programmatic comment, Polybius writes that encomia demand a summary and somewhat exaggerated account of the subject's achievements.[27] Perhaps βίοι are more useful to modern scholars (including both conservative scholars of Christian origins and positivist historians of ancient Greece and Rome) if they can be read as "historical," cocooned safely away from the presumed anti-historicism of "encomium." Insisting on a sharp distinction between encomium and βίος, and subsequently assigning works to one or the other category, may say more about the classificant's ideology than about the

---

22   Momigliano, *The Development of Greek Biography*, 50.

23   David C. Mirhady and Yun Lee Too, *Isocrates I*, OCG 4 (University of Texas Press, 2000), 140.

24   Plutarch also notes physical characteristics, but these observations are often in support of his discussion of character. Cf. Plutarch's *Sulla* (2.1) and *Pericles* (3.2–4), where he buttresses character analysis with reference to physical features (a blotchy face and an oversized head, respectively).

25   Burridge sometimes speaks of the *Evagoras* as an example of Greco-Roman βίος (e.g., Burridge, *What Are the Gospels?*, 124) but at other times distances it from the genre: "*Evagoras* may be seen as a crossing over from rhetoric to βίος: it takes the form of a funeral eulogy praising the king, rather than a full biography." Burridge, 125.

26   At least, this is how it is often read. But note Isocrates's regular protests throughout the text to the effect that he is telling the whole truth (e.g., *Evag.* 1.5, 39, 66).

27   Although best known for his *Histories*, Polybius also authored a now-lost encomium of Philopoemen. Cf. Polybius, *Histories* 10.21 (= BNJ 173 T1); 21.8. Plutarch, who used it as a source, preserves some of its content and flavor in his *Philopoemen*. Cf. Momigliano, *The Development of Greek Biography*, 82.

80   CHAPTER 3

nature of the works in question. Most scholars who work on βίοι are content to see fuzzy boundaries between βίος, historiography, and encomium,[28] but in practice it seems that works they want to use for historicizing projects tend to be labeled βίοι or biography. Such a practice risks overlooking two principles developed above in chapter 1, namely, that genres interact and that genres have conventional ways of presenting plots and characters with the result that the path from text to real history is difficult to trace.

In sum, βίος is a flexible genre, interacting with history, encomium, rhetoric, and moral philosophy. It does not develop linearly, and the works associated with the genre are cross-fertilized with other genres in its genre set. This flexibility notwithstanding, a regular feature of the genre is an expressed interest in ἦθος—that of the subject, that of subject's contemporaries, and that of the reader. The subject's ἦθος can be inferred both from what they say and do. These observations are borne out in the following case studies of Plutarch and Philo.

3   Plutarch, the Parallel Lives, and the Conventions of a Genre[29]

Plutarch of Chaeronea (ca. 45–120 CE) was a Greek intellectual, philosopher, politician, and writer remembered especially for his paired βίοι of Greek and Roman statesmen. Most pairs include an introduction justifying the selection and a concluding comparison (σύγκρισις). Twenty-two of these pairs survive.[30] Plutarch regularly reminds readers that his chief concern is not to record the events of the past but to explore the moral character (ἦθος) of famous men as models for imitation (see, e.g., *Cim.* 5; *Nic.* 1; *Dem.* 11.7, *Alex.* 1.1–2).[31] His

---

28   "The gap between this type of historical encomium and a full biography of a king or of a general is so narrow that any neat separation is impossible." Momigliano, 83.

29   Translations in this chapter of Plutarch and Philo follow the LCL, unless otherwise noted.

30   One of these pairs involves four subjects: Agis and Cleomenes on the Greek side, and the Gracchi on the Roman side. In addition to the 22 surviving pairs, we know of a *Scipio-Epaminondas*, originally the first book in the series, which has been lost. Four other βίοι by Plutarch not written as part of the series of *Parallel Lives* have survived: the *Galba*, the *Otho*, the *Aratus*, and the *Artaxerxes*. The first two belonged to a series of emperors; the latter two were independent compositions. See Philip A. Stadter, "Introduction," in *Plutarch: Greek Lives*, OWC (Oxford: Oxford University Press, 1998), ix. Συγκρίσεις (Comparisons) are extant for all but four of the surviving pairs.

31   Plutarch's rationale for exploring the character of the men who figure in his *Parallel Lives* is to give examples for imitation. The theme of mimesis becomes explicit in the *Comparison* that follows the *Solon-Publicola* pair, when Plutarch claims that the second has become an imitator of the first (τὸν ἕτερον γεγονέναι μιμητὴν τοῦ ἑτέρου) (*Comp. Sol. Publ.* 1.1). Publicola, therefore, models for the reader what it is to imitate the virtues of a celebrated predecessor.

ΒΙΟΣ: ETHICS AND MIMESIS

emphasis on character allows him to compare figures that otherwise have little in common. For example, Pericles and Lucullus strike Plutarch as alike in their mildness (πραότης) and their ability to endure the follies of their colleagues and the masses, despite living in different eras and playing different roles in their respective polities.[32]

In spite of the common scholarly trope that ancient societies were collectivist and anti-introspective, so that what moderns might call the "interior" or "private self" was unknown to ancient biographers, Plutarch theorizes interiority as a necessary part of the human subject.[33] He tells readers that the interior reality of character is accessible by observation of external actions and deeds (πράξεις and ἔργα; *Alex.* 1.1–2), focal points of the historiographic tradition discussed in chapter 2. The trope surfaces in discussions of "character" in Plutarch and his context, where it is taken for granted that Plutarch's writing is motivated by his desire to understand and illustrate character. Tim Duff, for example, in an important recent book on Plutarch's aims in the *Parallel Lives*, describes ancient Greek views of character as "less about what somebody was like, more about recognizing right and wrong deeds; its consequence was a desire to judge and evaluate."[34] This is surely right, if "what somebody was like" refers to the developmental distinctiveness of a person, an essentializing

---

32   The one was "a leading statesman in a democracy when Athenian imperialism was at its height," and the other was "one member of a senatorial oligarchy during Rome's greatest crisis." On these and other differences, and on shared possession of πραότης as the great point of similarity, see Philip A Stadter, *A Commentary on Plutarch's Pericles* (Chapel Hill: University of North Carolina Press, 1989), xxx–xxxii.

     Note that although shared character qualities are often the link Plutarch makes in a pair of βίοι, he will sometimes make the connection on the basis of circumstantial evidence. For discussion of the processes by which Plutarch made the matches, see D. A. Russell, *Plutarch*, 2nd ed. (Bristol: Bristol Classical, 2001), 113–16. See also the comments below on Demosthenes and Cicero.

33   On the trope: Krister Stendahl's famous 1976 article "The Apostle Paul and the Introspective Conscience of the West," made an important intervention in scholarship, particularly scholarship on Paul. Some New Testament scholars have embraced a flatter version of Stendahl's proposal, when they force an either-or choice: ancient people were either like us in every way or they were totally different. This is the impression one is left with when reading, e.g., Bruce Malina's statements that all "persons in antiquity were anti-introspective and not psychologically minded at all. What counted was what went on outside of a person." Bruce J. Malina, *Timothy: Paul's Closest Associate*, PSNBSF (Collegeville: Liturgical, 2008), xv. François Bovon helpfully suggests that the pendulum has swung too far away from soul to emphasize body. See "The Soul's Comeback: Immortality and Resurrection in Early Christianity," *HTR* 103 (2010): 387–406. This line of thinking is developed further in Michal Beth Dinkler, "'The Thoughts of Many Hearts Shall Be Revealed': Listening in on Lukan Interior Monologues," *JBL* 134 (2015): 373–99.

34   Duff, *Plutarch's Lives*, 14.

distinctiveness built up so to foster an appreciation of how the subject of the βίος is different from oneself. Plutarch attends more to the generalizable human propensity for rational (and by extension virtuous) action. Pericles's mildness can be the reader's mildness, Cimon's generosity can be the reader's generosity, Alexander's ambition can be the reader's ambition, and so on. But when Duff elaborates the language of "more" and "less," he seems particularly keen to de-center the interior in connection to ancient conceptions of character. Duff makes it "less" about "the private, inner world of the individual" and "more" about actions and the evaluation of those actions.[35] Such a statement may hold for ancient discussions of ἦθος in the abstract, but by embarking on the project of the *Parallel Lives*, Plutarch deliberately moves away from abstractions to explore particularized moral characters in action. This is a crucial point. Plutarch is not here looking for clinical definitions of the virtues, but for real-life illustrations of the virtues in practice. Duff's language of "less" and "more" does not rule out the possibility of Plutarch's interest in the "private, inner world of the individual," but it would be easy to infer (wrongly) from Duff's language that if Plutarch was interested in actions and evaluation of actions, *ipso facto* the individuality of the subject must be unimportant. There is, however, no need to pull these apart; character can have to do both with the "private inner world of the individual" and the ways in which that inner reality shapes the observable actions that allow the biographer and his readers to assess that inner world. Plutarch's language for that inner reality is "soul."

What is not in question is that the two wheels driving Plutarch's character-discerning vehicle in the *Parallel Lives* are πράξεις and ἔργα. These are external, visible, and documentable. But actions and deeds are not all equal witnesses to a subject's character, as Plutarch makes clear in introducing the *Alexander*:

> It is the life (βίος) of Alexander the king, and of Caesar, who overthrew Pompey, that I am writing in this book, and the multitude of the actions (πράξεις) to be treated is so great that I shall make no other preface than to entreat my readers, in case I do not tell of all the famous actions of these men, nor even speak exhaustively at all in each particular case, but in epitome for the most part, not to complain. For it is not Histories that I am writing, but Lives (οὔτε γὰρ ἱστορίας γράφομεν, ἀλλὰ βίους); and in the most illustrious deeds (πράξεις) there is not always a manifestation of virtue or vice (δήλωσις ἀρετῆς ἢ κακίας), nay, a slight thing like a phrase or a jest often makes a greater revelation of character (ἔμφασιν ἤθους) than battles when thousands fall, or the greatest armaments, or sieges of cities.
>
> *Alex.* 1.1–2

---

35   Duff, *Plutarch's Lives*, 13.

BIOΣ: ETHICS AND MIMESIS   83

A strictly externalist approach would take the sum of deeds and actions as the measure of a man, or of what matters for the historical record. Plutarch's internalist approach is to mention only actions that shed light on character, regardless of the scale of their geo-political consequences, which may mean bypassing deeds that would be significant in a grand narrative of history.[36] Plutarch's frequently articulated rationale for showcasing character is what is also a primary function of narratives in this genre: to provide models for emulation or avoidance.

Plutarch's psychological sketch of the human being involves a mimetic impulse in the form of a drive to imitate virtuous behavior: "actions arising out of virtue immediately put one in a frame of mind such that one simultaneously admires the acts and desires to emulate the agents (ἅμα θαυμάζεσθαι τὰ ἔργα καὶ ζηλοῦσθαι τοὺς εἰργασμένους)" (Per. 2.2).[37] For Plutarch this is only true of works springing from virtue (τὰ ἀπ' ἀρετῆς ἔργα [Per. 1.4]), not other deeds. He assumes that people are motivated by desire for happiness (εὐδαιμονία) and that this is achieved by virtuous living. From these two assumptions follows the conclusion that everyone naturally wants to be virtuous.[38] Merely seeing virtue represented is not enough; the spectator acquires purpose through an account of the deed (Per. 1.4).[39] Plutarch's commitment to this mimetic drive (its existence and operation) is held out as justification for the labor invested in his Parallel Lives project.

A central concern of the Parallel Lives, then, is to attend to psychological matters in general, and to ἦθος in particular.[40] Rather than compete with other writers who have already covered Nicias's actions, Plutarch writes in the preface to the Nicias, he will review the πράξεις, but only briefly, since he "cannot entirely pass them by, indicating as they do the nature (τὸν τρόπον) of my hero and the disposition (τὴν διάθεσιν) which lay hidden beneath his many great sufferings" (Nic. 1.5). He has collected various sources of information, including "those details which have escaped most writers, and which others have mentioned casually, or which are found on ancient votive offerings or in public decrees," not because he wants "to mass together meaningless historical data, but

---

36 Such, at least, was the goal. He may be forgiven, however, if in practice he sometimes forgets to employ this sorting principle.

37 Trans. Robin Waterfield, Plutarch: Greek Lives, OWC (Oxford: Oxford University Press, 1998).

38 This assumption was shared among the various Hellenistic schools, though they diverged on what virtue entailed. The idea that everyone naturally wants to be virtuous is a premise of Plato's Protagoras and book 6 of the Republic.

39 For Plutarch's theory of mimesis, see Alan Wardman, Plutarch's Lives (Berkeley: University of California Press, 1974), 21–25.

40 "Psychological" in the sense of matters with a bearing on the ψυχή.

84   CHAPTER 3

to record data which promote the appreciation of character and temperament (τὴν πρὸς κατανόησιν ἤθους καὶ τρόπου)" (*Nic.* 1.5). This paragraph is remarkable for several reasons, not least of which is Plutarch's professed reluctance to compete with others (he names historians—Thucydides and Philistus—in the immediate context). In his desire to contribute something worthwhile and to justify his own composition alongside those of his predecessors, he proposes (1) to gather fresh data (instead of simply rewriting an earlier account in new language, which is what he accuses Philistus of doing to Thucydides); and (2) to shine his light on ἦθος and τροπός rather than πράξεις.

Focusing on character lets Plutarch bring together for comparison figures based on their virtues.[41] Neither Plutarch nor the majority of his readers will find themselves in exactly the same circumstances as his illustrious subjects, but the virtues propelling their great deeds may be cultivated by anyone.[42] By using βίοι as vehicles to present these virtues, Plutarch shows how a given characteristic can manifest with subtle and intriguing differences corresponding to its possessor and the circumstances of his formation and context. As he writes in *The Virtues of Women*,

> For the fact is that the virtues acquire certain other diversities, their own coloring as it were, due to varying natures, and they take on the likeness of the customs on which they are founded, and of the temperament of persons and their nurture and mode of living. For example, Achilles was brave in one way and Ajax in another; and the wisdom of Odysseus was not like that of Nestor, nor was Cato a just man in exactly the same way as Agesilaus, nor Eirene fond of her husband in the manner of Alcestis, nor Cornelia high-minded in the manner of Olympias.
>
> *Mulier. virt.* 243c–d[43]

---

41   E.g., in introducing the Pericles-Fabius Maxmius pair: "I decided to carry on writing βίοι and have composed this book.... There are a number of similarities between the two men in respect of their virtues, but the most important traits they shared were self-possession and integrity, and their ability to endure the foolishness of the populace and their colleagues (μάλιστα δὲ πρᾳότητα καὶ δικαιοσύνην, καὶ τῷ δύνασθαι φέρειν δήμων καὶ συναρχόντων ἀγνωμοσύνας)" (*Per.* 2). Trans. Waterfield, *Plutarch: Greek Lives*.

42   In his *On the Divine Vengeance* 550dff, Plutarch follows Plato in presenting the view that "god offers himself *to all* as a pattern of every excellence, thus rendering human virtue, which is in some sort an assimilation to himself, accessible *to all* who can 'follow god'" (trans. de Lacy and Einarson, LCL 405). The practice of virtue and its correlative assimilation to the divine are processes accessible to "all." This "all," however, should probably be interpreted in a limited sense, excluding most women, children, barbarians, and others not socially situated to enact the virtues with which Plutarch is concerned.

43   Trans. LCL, modified.

This does not mean that there are multiple justices or intelligences or braveries, Plutarch goes on to say, just that there are many ways of enacting these various virtues (*Mulier. virt.* 243d). The advantage of an exemplar-based approach over a definition-based approach is that the observer will achieve a more nuanced understanding of the virtue or vice as a whole, and the reader will be better equipped to choose the virtuous option in a wider variety of situations. Plutarch's decision to present βίοι in pairs on the basis of the virtues exemplified in each is an innovative move that promotes his goal of stimulating character recognition and appropriate response.

Plutarch's *Parallel Lives* differ from modern biography with respect to the sense of the self with which he works. In Plutarch's work, the self is not a unique genius transcending or standing apart from the rest of society as an autonomous spirit, but the actor remarkable for his rationality and well-ordered life. Croesus, in the story discussed below, furnishes an example of an ill-ordered life, as evidenced by his surprise that Solon "did not make an abundance of gold and silver his measure of happiness (τῆς εὐδαιμονίας [οὐκ] ποιεῖται τὴν ἀναμέτρησιν), but admired the life and death of an ordinary private man more than all this display of power and sovereignty" (*Sol.* 27). Solon, though strange (ἀλλόκοτος) and uncouth (ἄγροικος) to Croesus's eyes, is for Plutarch the measure of rational response. This rationality is accessible to himself and his readers, and he assumes that readers will want to order their lives to conform to it. What Solon said to Croesus is what anyone should say to a disordered individual.

Plutarch's programmatic statement to the *Alexander*, introduced above, draws a theoretical distinction between historian and biographer. While both draw on the same pool of raw materials, writers of history will focus on external acts (πράξεις) and Plutarch will take the interior road, building βίοι to illuminate moral character. Historical writers also wrote about interior realities, especially the motivations of individuals and groups resulting in πράξεις. What distinguishes Plutarch's work here from the historians discussed in the previous chapter is his frequent recourse to ἦθος as permitting or ruling out attributed motives.

In introduction to the *Alexander*, Plutarch likens himself to a painter. The connection to painting is made in the *Cimon* too, and the analogy is developed further. Plutarch considers "a portrait which displays a person's character and personality (τὸ ἦθος καὶ τὸν τρόπον) as far more beautiful than one which reproduces his body and face" (*Cim.* 2). The added dimension is this preference for the showcasing of ἦθος. The inner reality is more important than the outer, though Plutarch recognizes that the inner must be mediated by exterior signs.

In some cases, Plutarch makes use of a statue or portrait to describe the physical appearance of his subject, and he readily connects physical appearances (whether or not derived from artistic representation) to his literary portrait of the man's ἦθος and τρόπος. The *Themistocles* offers a good example: "a portrait statue of Themistocles stood in this temple of *Aristoboulé* down to my time, from which he appears to have been a man not only of heroic ψυχή, but also of heroic ὄψις" (*Them.* 22.2).[44] This portrait statue would have received a passing grade in Plutarch's book, insofar as it displayed what was ἡρωικός about his subject's ψυχή. The analogy in the *Cimon* is extended further:

> When painters are faced with a slight blemish of some kind on the beautiful and pleasing figures they portray, we do not expect them either to omit it altogether (which would stop their portraits being true likenesses) or to stress it (which would make them ugly to look at). By the same token, since it is difficult—or, more probably, impossible—to represent a man's life as entirely free from shortcomings and blemishes, we should supply the truth, confident in its verisimilitude, when dealing with the good aspects of our subject's life. However, the flaws and defects which, prompted by emotion or political necessity, taint his actions we should regard as lapses from a virtue rather than as manifestations of vice. We should not, then, be particularly eager to overemphasize these flaws in our account, but should write instead as if we felt ashamed of the fact that human nature fails to produce any character which is absolutely good or unequivocally virtuous.
>
> *Cim.* 2.4–5[45]

Those portrayed in the *Parallel Lives* are not airbrushed, ideal types. Even the best of Plutarch's illustrious men have lapses from virtue. The biographer has a choice in how to represent these lapses, and Plutarch's rule seems to be that the biographer ought not draw unnecessary attention to them. Plutarch does not consistently obey this rule;[46] again, that is less important than that he articulates it as a rule of the game. The "rule" also dovetails neatly with the

---

44   Trans. LCL, modified.

45   Trans. Waterfield, *Plutarch: Greek Lives.*

46   The tension between what Plutarch prescribes and what Plutarch practices could be compared to the tension between what Horace prescribes (to avoid the mixing of genres) and what Horace practices in the *Ars poetica*, which is itself a kind of hybrid text. Farrell calls it a "didactic poem," and possibly "verse epistles." Joseph Farrell, "Classical Genre in Theory and Practice," *NLitHist* 34 (2003): 394–95.

BIOΣ: ETHICS AND MIMESIS

implied prescriptions Plutarch offers historians in a polemical essay about the character of Herodotus.

Plutarch's treatise *On the Malice of Herodotus* begins with what some scholars have described as rules, canons, or "standards for what a historian ought to be about."[47] But Plutarch does not call them rules; they are "indications and means of determining (ἴχνη καὶ γνωρίσματα) whether a narrative is written with malice (κακοηθεία)" (*Her. mal.* 855b).[48] To make them rules, one would need to convert them from descriptions of problems into prohibitions of those problems. The problems include (1) the use of harsh terms when gentler alternatives would do; (2) the inclusion of unnecessary and discreditable details; (3) the omission of what is noble and good (καλοῦ τινος κἀγαθοῦ παράλειψίς); (4) the choice of a less-credible version when a more-credible version exists (τὸ δυοῖν ἢ πλειόνων περὶ ταὐτοῦ λόγων ὄντων τῷ χείρονι προστίθεσθαι); (5) the choice of the less credible cause (τὴν δ' αἰτίαν ἀφ' ἧς πέπρακται) or motivation (τὴν διάνοιαν ἐχόντων) for an agreed-upon deed; (6) detracting from the virtue or greatness of deeds by denying "that they were done in a noble spirit or by hard work or by the valor of a man's own effort"; (7) to lay out a slanderous suggestion and then deny it, once the devious seed has been planted; and (8) to qualify a slander with some token item of praise. The list, Plutarch says, could be expanded (*Her. mal.* 856d). Plutarch does not offer any examples in this catalogue from Herodotus. He illustrates the fifth, sixth, and eighth signs of malice using excerpts from other writers. For the first, second, and fourth items, he offers examples of how historians (mainly Thucydides) write without these signs of malice. No examples positive or negative are offered for the third and seventh items, though it is likely that Plutarch would have expected a reader familiar with Herodotus to supply his own examples for all eight. Lionel Pearson, translator of the treatise for the Loeb series, notes in connection to the seventh technique, for example, that Plutarch must have been thinking of the story that the Corinthian admiral took flight at Salamis (*Hist.* 8.94). Furthermore, Herodotean examples of each indication can be found in the main part of Plutarch's treatise, although they are not indexed back to this initial list. For example, when Plutarch notes that Herodotus calls the Greek withdrawal from battle (ἀπόπλουν) a "running away (δρασμόν)" (*Her. mal.* 868a), the reader might readily connect this to the first of the eight explicit indications.

---

47 So described by C. B. R. Pelling in "Truth and Fiction in Plutarch's Lives," in *Plutarch and History: Eighteen Studies* (Swansea: Classical Press of Wales, 2002), 143–70. Cf. Philip A. Stadter, *A Commentary on Plutarch's Pericles* (Chapel Hill: University of North Carolina Press, 1989), li.

48 Plutarch also describes them later as σημεία (*Her. mal.* 855e).

88   CHAPTER 3

The converse of several items on Plutarch's list are central to understanding his practices in the *Parallel Lives* for representing ἦθος and motivation. That they can be flipped and endorsed is evident in that he points to Thucydides's ability to avoid these problems in the first, second, and fourth items in his list. Evidence of Plutarch's own record of putting into practice his anti-malice principles can be found in Plutarch's interactions with literary sources.

Plutarch seems to have made use of an unprecedented number of written, oral, and visual sources.[49] Sometimes he seems to expect his audience to recognize the unnamed source (esp. Homer, Plato, Thucydides, and Herodotus); an example of this was suggested above. Plutarch never copies a source without attribution, preferring either (more often) to recast what he views as reliable content in his own words or (less often) to quote a named source.[50] The first of these two practices creates opportunities for readers familiar with his sources to see his mind at work psychologizing historical figures, as he digests information and recasts it in his own words.[51] Unfortunately, we can never be certain that the surplus of meaning in Plutarch's text is from Plutarch rather than another source. Plutarch's ability to handle a large number of sources has impressed many scholars, so it is often conceivable that what looks like

---

49   Cf. the comment in *Nicias* 1, discussed above, where Plutarch presents himself as different from (and, implied: better than) other writers by virtue of his industry in bringing new data and new kinds of data to bear on his accounts. See also the conclusion to the *Demosthenes*: "And so, Sosius, thou hast the promised βίος of Demosthenes, drawn from such written or oral sources as I could find" (*Dem.* 31).

50   Although most modern readers and writers would consider this a form of plagiarism, it would be anachronistic to charge Plutarch with that offence. Literary crimes related to our notion of "plagiarism" were live opportunities for Plutarch (e.g., copying somebody else's words without attribution, or trying to pass off his own work under somebody else's name), but whether Plutarch is guilty of these sorts of crimes is tangential to the present discussion. At any rate, Plutarch was sufficiently skilled and established as writer that it would difficult to find a motivation for such misbehavior. On plagiarism in antiquity, see Bernard Legras, "La sanction du plagiat littéraire en droit grec et hellénistique," in *Symposion 1999: vorträge zur griechischen und hellenistischen Rechtsgeschichte*, ed. Gerhard Thür and F. Javier Fernández Nieto (Pazo de Mariñàn: La Coruña, 2003), 443–61; Bart D. Ehrman, *Forgery and Counterforgery: The Use of Literary Deceit in Early Christian Polemics* (Oxford: Oxford University Press, 2013), 29–68. For comment on Plutarch's concern "de refaire chaque détail du contenu afin de ne pas laisser les traces d'une copie mal faite," see Mónica Durán Mañas, "Hérodote et Plutarque: l'histoire d'Arion," *Ploutarchos* 8 (2011): 67–79.

51   Plutarch regularly quotes other authors (more or less) exactly. But these quotations are marked in the text. See the collection in W. C. Helmbold and Edward N. O'Neil, *Plutarch's Quotations*, PhMon 19 (Baltimore: American Philological Association, 1959).

BIOΣ: ETHICS AND MIMESIS

theorization of a character's mind is actually Plutarch's skillful incorporation of an unacknowledged source.[52]

It is not uncommon for Plutarch to disagree with his source outright. In considering why Lycurgus expelled foreigners from Sparta, Plutarch writes:

> Thucydides is wrong to suggest that he did this because he was afraid that they would copy his political system and learn some valuable moral lessons; no, he was more afraid of the corrupting influence these foreigners might exert.... So to Lycurgus's mind it was more important to protect the state from infection by pestilential customs than it was to keep people from abroad bringing in disease with them (διὸ μᾶλλον ᾤετο χρῆναι φυλάττειν τὴν πόλιν ὅπως ἠθῶν οὐκ ἀναπλησθήσεται πονηρῶν ἢ σωμάτων νοσερῶν ἔξωθεν ἐπεισιόντων).
>
> Lyc. 27.3–4[53]

Here we have a case of Plutarch and Thucydides agreeing on the πρᾶξις but disagreeing about the motive. By registering his disagreement with Thucydides, Plutarch accomplishes two things. First, he signals independence from a well known writer he himself revered.[54] Second, he puts into practice one of his rules—that when the motives of a figure are in doubt, the writer should assume the best of his subject. Here that means casting Lycurgus as desirous to protect his city, rather than as fearful of having others copy his political ideas.

---

52   If this apparent ability has impressed some, it has inspired skepticism in others, who argue that he must have taken some kind of scholarly shortcut. A prevailing view is that of Luc Van der Stockt, who in several articles has developed the thesis that Plutarch's use of clusters of heterogenous materials repeated in the same order in different contexts is proof of Plutarch's use of personal notebooks. See his "A Plutarchan Hypomnema on Self-Love," *AJP* 120 (1999): 575–99; "Plutarch in Plutarch: The Problem of the Hypomnemata," in *La biblioteca di Plutarco: atti del IX Convegno plutarcheo, Pavia, 13-15 giugno 2002*, ed. Italo Gallo, Collectanea 23 (Napoli: M. D'Auria, 2004), 331–40.

   Still a valuable discussion of Plutarch's use of sources is C. B. R. Pelling, "Plutarch's Adaptation of His Source-material," in *Plutarch and History: Eighteen Studies* (Swansea: Classical Press of Wales, 2002), 91–115. First published in 1980 (*Journal of Hellenic Studies* 100 (1980): 127–40), this article marks a shift away from the "mining for earlier voices" perspective on Plutarch to a new perspective characterized by investigation of the "literary devices which Plutarch employed in streamlining his material: conflation of similar items, chronological compression and dislocation, fabrication of circumstantial material, and the like" (91).

53   Trans. Waterfield, *Plutarch: Greek Lives*. The material elided from the quotation is an excursus on customs foreigners bring. Cf. Thuc. 2.39.

54   Cf. the discussion of *Nicias* 1 above, in which Plutarch signals his reluctance to compete with Thucydides.

The reframing of the issue on customs (ἤθη) is important too. Plutarch shapes his narrative to represent the ethical orientation of his subject's mind in a more favorable light.

Plutarch's alleged rationale for writing these βίοι is the reader's moral formation. These βίοι are designed to bring readers (and ultimately Plutarch himself) to imitate the virtues embodied by their protagonists (cf. *Per.* 1.4; 2.2). But there is—after Plutarch, Plutarch's readers, and Plutarch's subjects—a fourth group with whose character Plutarch busies himself: that of other writers covering the same persons and subjects. The technique of setting his own work in a positive light by sniping at his peers is analogous to the agonistic nature of self-definition in historiography, discussed in the previous chapter. Earlier in this section, we noted Plutarch's criticism of Herotodus, and now we see Plutarch taking aim at Thucydides on the question of Lycurgus's motives for expelling foreigners from Sparta.[55] Near the end of the *Themistocles*, Plutarch turns his attention to the writers Andocides and Phylarchus. Andocides, in a work entitled *To My Companions*, claims that the Athenians stole Themistocles's remains and scattered them. Plutarch urges his readers to see that "these lies of his are motivated by a desire to inflame the oligarchs against the people of Athens (ψεύδεται γὰρ ἐπὶ τὸν δῆμον παροξύνων τοὺς ὀλιγαρχικούς)" (*Them.* 32.3).[56] Phylarchus's account of Themistocles's end apparently introduces two sons of Themistocles: Neocles and Demopolis. According to Plutarch, in doing so Phylarchus is behaving "like the composer of a tragedy [who] all but hoists up stage machinery for his account," and his motive for this theatrical fabrication is that "he is only wanting to stir up conflict and emotion in his audience (ἀγῶνα βούλεται κινεῖν καὶ πάθος), and it must be obvious to everyone that he has made the story up" (*Them.* 32.3).[57] As noted in chapter 2 in connection to "tragic history," two issues are involved: falsehood and the excitement of emotions, both of which are problematic according to ancient historiographical theory. In both cases, Plutarch theorizes the minds and the ignoble, malicious intentions of his peers.

---

55   On Plutarch's use of Thucydides in general, see Jacqueline de Romilly, "Plutarch and Thucydides or the Free Use of Quotations," *Phoenix* 42 (1988): 22–34. But note that this is especially concerned with Plutarch's "free use" of his source, and is mostly calculated to demonstrate how wonderful and exquisite Thucydides was. "Poor Plutarch used what he could," she writes, and, invoking the image of Plutarch as a muddler, "the difference in date or literary aim introduces into the text some remarkable distortions." For a perspective that is kinder to Plutarch, see C. B. R. Pelling, "Plutarch and Thucydides," in *Plutarch and History: Eighteen Studies* (Swansea: Classical Press of Wales, 2002), 117–41.

56   Trans. Waterfield, *Plutarch: Greek Lives*. Andocides's oration does not survive.

57   Trans. Waterfield, *Plutarch: Greek Lives*, modified.

BIOΣ: ETHICS AND MIMESIS

Some of Plutarch's peers are invoked regularly in his writings, only to be rejected as foils to Plutarch's better interpretations, as we saw just now with his use of Andocides and Phylarchus.[58] A favorite punching bag of Plutarch's is Idomeneus, author of a book on demagogues.[59] In the *Pericles*, for example, Plutarch asks:

> How, then, can we believe Idomeneus when he accuses Pericles of being so jealous and envious of the reputation (διὰ ζηλοτυπίαν καὶ φθόνον τῆς δόξης) of the popular leader Ephialtes that he assassinated him, although he was a friend and a colleague of the same political persuasion? No, he has raked up this charge from somewhere or other, as if he were gathering bile, and hurled it at Pericles. It may well be true that Pericles is not entirely without fault, but he had a noble pride and an ambitious mind, and these can harbor no such fierce and savage emotions (φρόνημα δ᾽ εὐγενὲς ἔχοντι καὶ ψυχὴν φιλότιμον, οἷς οὐδὲν ἐμφύεται πάθος ὠμὸν οὕτω καὶ θηριῶδες).
>
> *Per.* 10.7[60]

Plutarch takes issue primarily with the charge that Pericles was somehow responsible for Ephialtes's assassination. More important in the present context is that he rejects Idomeneus's theorization of Pericles's mind. Pericles could not have been motivated by ζηλοτυπία and φθόνος for two reasons. First, there is the lengthy account Plutarch has just given of Pericles's calculated attention to the people as a shrewd political tactic to create an advantage against Cimon (a pretense dropped once Cimon was ostracized and Pericles's power secure).

---

58 It is not uncommon for Plutarch to use a source to make a point that is very much in contrast to the point made by his source. Russell illustrates this pattern in connection to Plutarch's use of Dionysius of Halicarnassus in the *Coriolanus*. See D. A. Russell, "Plutarch's Life of Coriolanus," *The Journal of Roman Studies* 53 (1963): 21–28. See also the story, mentioned above, of Demosthenes appearing "in a splendid robe and wearing a garland on his head, although his daughter had died only six days before" (*Dem.* 22). Plutarch announces that he has taken this story from Aeschines, but the two differ markedly in their assessment. Aeschines told the story and "railed at him for this and denounced him as an unnatural father," where for Plutarch Demosthenes is to be praised for putting his civic duties ahead of his personal loss.

59 Plutarch cites the work in the *Aristides* (10.7–9), the *Pericles* (10.7), the *Demosthenes* (15.5; 23.4), and the *Phocion* (4.2). Philip Stadter notes this pattern in Plutarch's use of Idomeneus, and (apparently persuaded by Plutarch's characterization) describes him as "something of a scandalmonger, whom Plutarch uses for variants that he will reject." Stadter, *A Commentary on Plutarch's Pericles*, lxxxi.

60 Trans. Waterfield, *Plutarch: Greek Lives*, modified.

92   CHAPTER 3

The second and more concise reason, however, is that those emotions cannot
exist in a man with noble pride and an ambitious mind, conclusions Plutarch
has already demonstrated in building up his portrait of Pericles's character. This
is comparable to the reception of the historiographer Theopompus, discussed
above in chapter 2, but where the vicious motives imputed by Theopompus
to Philip were generally panned for being inappropriate to the genre, here the
bad motives are rejected because they do not fit with the ἦθος Plutarch has
constructed for Pericles. As an ethics-oriented biographer, Plutarch is more
likely than a historian to use ἦθος to decide arguments concerning motivation.

So far we have been speaking in general terms and illustrating the points
made from a wide range of Plutarch's writings. The next section explores in
more detail the manipulation of the ethical-cognitive domain in Plutarch's
Solon.

4   Plutarch's *Life of Solon*[61]

Plutarch had many more sources at his disposal in writing the *Parallel Lives*
than have survived him intact. For the Greek figures, his primary sources are
often Herodotus and Thucydides, supplemented by playwrights (especially
Aristophanes), philosophers (especially Aristotle), other historians (especially
Xenophon, Ephorus, and Theopompus), and in many cases documents produced by his biographical subject (e.g., the *Epistles* of Solon or the decrees of
Pericles). He also draws upon inscriptions, art, and architecture he has seen
himself.

Plutarch usually leaves his sources unnamed, apparently assuming his
reader's familiarity with standard histories of the periods in which his subjects
are set. A. Blamire lists as exceptions those occasions when his sources disagree (e.g., *Cim.* 12.5–6; 13.4–5), when a source provides him with an especially
memorable phrase or quotation (e.g., *Cim.* 10.4–5; 16.9–10), or when Plutarch is
keen to demonstrate his own erudition (cf. *Sol.* 1; *Arist.* 1).[62] Even where he does
not name his source for a passage in a βίος, however, it is often possible to identify it. This is true of *Solon* 27–29, which recounts a famous encounter between
the Athenian sage and the Lydian king Croesus. Plutarch may have known this

---

61   Studies of this encounter with wider ranging foci include Israel Muñoz Gallarte, "Hérodote
        et Plutarque: à propos de la rencontre entre Solon et Crésus, roi de Lydie," *Ploutarchos* 8
        (2011): 117–32; Constantine T. Hadavas, "The Structure, Form, and Meaning of Plutarch's
        'Life of Solon'" (PhD diss, University of North Carolina at Chapel Hill, 1995).

62   A. Blamire, *Plutarch: Life of Kimon*, ClaHa 2 (London: Institute of Classical Studies,
        University of London, 1989), 1.

BIOΣ: ETHICS AND MIMESIS 93

story from various accounts, but his foundational text would have been the one found in the first book of Herodotus's *Histories*.[63] As noted in chapter 2, the *Histories* contains biographical components, especially in connection to eastern despots, including the use of Croesus as an organizing figure in its first book. When Plutarch narrates the meeting and its aftermath in the *Solon*, the focalizing positions are reversed so that Croesus becomes the secondary figure in Solon's story. Since it is likely that Herodotus is Plutarch's main source for this part of the *Solon*, the shift in focalizing position highlights Plutarch's ability to theorize minds.[64]

The outline of the account in both Herodotus and Plutarch's *Solon* is as follows: Solon arrives at Croesus's court, is hospitably received, is sent on a tour of the treasuries, and is asked if he has ever known a happier man. Solon does not give the hoped-for answer, explains the folly of pronouncing someone happy before he has died well, and leaves empty-handed. Years later, Croesus is conquered by Cyrus the Persian. Cyrus hears Croesus crying out Solon's name from the pyre, where he is about to be executed. Interest piqued, Cyrus questions Croesus and calls off the execution. Croesus is subsequently held in lifelong honor among the Persians. The result, as Plutarch sums it up, is that "Solon had the reputation of saving one king and instructing another by means of a single saying" (*Sol.* 28.4).

---

63   In Plutarch's opening remark, he mentions that the story is "famous and well-attested" (ἔνδοξον οὕτω καὶ τοσούτους μάρτυρας ἔχοντα). It is unclear whether τοσοῦτος here has the sense of "so great a quantity" or "of so great a quality." Plutarch refers to Herodotus's version of this story explicitly in *On the Malice of Herodotus* 858d–f.

        In any event, Plutarch would have had additional versions of the legend available to him in Diodorus Siculus (first c. BCE), and several of his contemporaries and members of his personal literary circle also have versions of the encounter: Lucian of Samosata, Favorinus, Arrian, and later Diogenes Laertius. Gallarte, "Hérodote et Plutarque," 118.

64   For a discussion of focalization in connection to ancient literary criticism, see René Nünlist, "The Homeric Scholia on Focalization," *Mn.* 56 (2003): 61–71. Plutarch focalizes his *Parralel Lives* through the protagonist of each, tending to present the protagonist more positively than other characters. This is presumably because the general purpose of his βίοι is to give readers models for imitation; there is none of the modern biographical interest in "warts and all" sketches for sheer human interest. An illuminating activity is to look at cases where the protagonist of one text shows up as a secondary character in another, in which case he might not receive as charitable an interpretation. Sometimes this is due to his being focalized through the eyes of a hostile protagonist. E.g., Cimon in the *Pericles* and Pericles in the *Cimon*.

94   CHAPTER 3

The rest of this section is concerned mainly with commenting on Plutarch's version of the encounter, in dialogue with his Herodotean hypotext, attending particularly to changes Plutarch introduces to the cognitive domain.[65]

> As for his interview with Croesus, some think to prove by chronology that it is fictitious. But when a story is so famous and so well-attested, and, what is more to the point, when it fits so well with Solon's character (πρέποντα τῷ Σόλωνος ἤθει), and is so worthy of his magnanimity and wisdom, I do not propose to reject it out of deference to any chronological canons, so called, which thousands are to this day revising, without being able to bring their contradictions into any general agreement.
>
> *Sol.* 27.1[66]

This prefatory note justifying the inclusion of the interview describes how "some (ἔνιοι) think to prove by chronology that [the meeting] is fictitious" and Plutarch's reluctance to throw it out on the grounds that it (1) is famous and well-attested; (2) comports well with Solon's character (πρέποντα τῷ Σόλωνος ἤθει); and (3) is "worthy of his magnanimity and wisdom." This comment illuminates a key to Plutarch's project, namely that whether or not an episode "really happened" may be ignored if it fits his subject's ἦθος.[67] The language used is that of "what is fitting" (τὸ πρέπον), which was discussed in the first chapter. This is not to say that Plutarch is unconcerned with historicity, but rather that he sometimes allows his conception of a person's character to determine whether or not to pass along a story.[68]

---

65   For a broader treatment of Plutarch's adaptation of Herodotus's account, with a focus on Plutarch's elimination of the Herodotean motif of jealous divinities, see Gallarte, "Hérodote et Plutarque."

66   Trans. LCL, modified.

67   Invoking this story as an example of how Plutarch's scholarly criteria differs from modern sensibilities, Russell comments: "as Croesus came to the throne nearly thirty-five years after Solon's archonship, the story conflicts with the accepted chronology of the period, and Plutarch knew it did." Russell, *Plutarch*, 57. For arguments in favor of Plutarch's skill as a historian and his abiding interest in historicity, see Maria Teresa Schettino, "The Use of Historical Sources," in *A Companion to Plutarch*, ed. Mark Beck, trans. Pia Bertucci, BCAW (Oxford: Blackwell, 2014), 417–36. See also Pelling, who shows that Plutarch had the data to draw this conclusion himself, and that he would have, if it had suited his purposes. Christopher Pelling, "Truth and Fiction in Plutarch's Lives," in *Plutarch and History: Eighteen Studies* (Swansea: Classical Press of Wales, 2002), 162n2.

68   For an example of this tendency working in the opposite direction, consider Plutarch's disassociation of the Lacedaemonian κρυπτεία (the Spartan "secret police" infamous for terrorizing the Helots) from the protagonist in the *Lycurgus*.

ΒΙΟΣ: ETHICS AND MIMESIS

They say that Solon, on visiting Sardis at the invitation of Croesus, had much the same experience as an inland man who goes down for the first time to the sea. For just as such a man thinks each successive river that he sees to be the sea, so Solon, as he passed through the court and beheld many of the king's retainers in costly apparel and moving proudly amid a throng of couriers and armed guards, thought each in turn to be Croesus, until he was brought to the king himself, who was decked out with everything in the way of precious stones, [...] in order that he might present a most august and gorgeous spectacle.

Sol. 27.2–3[69]

The whole account of Solon's approach to the Lydian king with his series of misidentifications is not found in the Herodotean version of the story, suggesting that Plutarch adds it to foreground the theme of Solon and wealth. In Herodotus it is not clear that Solon has been invited to visit Croesus.[70] We read there only that Solon has left Athens for a period of ten years after enacting his laws, to "see the world" and "lest he be compelled to repeal any of the laws he had made, since the Athenians themselves could not repeal them, for they were bound by solemn oaths to abide for ten years by such laws as Solon should make" (*Hist.* 1.29). The opening of the narrative, then, already has Plutarch psychologizing Solon in terms of this text's ethical leitmotif, a theme that continues to be foregrounded as Solon enters into conversation with the king:

But when Solon, in this presence, neither showed any astonishment at what he saw, nor made any such comments upon it as Croesus had expected (οὔτ' ἔπαθεν οὐδὲν οὔτ' εἶπε πρὸς τὴν ὄψιν ὧν ὁ Κροῖσος προσεδόκησεν), but actually made it clear to all discerning eyes that he despised such vulgarity and pettiness (ἀλλὰ καὶ δῆλος ἦν τοῖς εὖ φρονοῦσι τῆς ἀπειροκαλίας καὶ μικροπρεπείας καταφρονῶν), the king ordered his treasure chambers to be thrown open for the guest, and that he should be led about to behold the rest of his sumptuous equipments.

Sol. 27.3

It may be that Plutarch is less particular about historicity in βίοι which treat individuals of the distant past, and is more careful in the βίοι for figures of the more recent past. But the case has also been made that Plutarch "historicizes" mythical and semi-mythical figures by including them in the *Parallel Lives* project. See Pascal Payen, "Plutarch the Antiquarian," in *A Companion to Plutarch*, ed. Mark Beck, BCAW (Oxford: Blackwell, 2014), 239.

69 Trans. LCL, modified. The text elided catalogues further fineries.

70 Plutarch shares this detail with Diodorus Siculus (*Lib. hist.* 9.2.1).

96   CHAPTER 3

This next part of the narrative offers further divergences from the Herodotean hypotext in both the pragmatic and the cognitive domains. Herodotus has Croesus entertain Solon for some three or four days before initiating the tour of the treasury, and to this point says nothing about either figure's state of mind. In fact, Herodotus says little about Croesus's thought processes in general.[71] In Plutarch's account, by contrast, the cognitive representations are articulated from the moment the two men meet. Coming into the presence of Croesus, Plutarch's Solon "neither showed any astonishment at what he saw, nor made any such comments upon it as Croesus had expected, but actually made it clear to all discerning eyes that he despised such vulgarity and pettiness." Cognitive states are described for both actors: Croesus's expectations, and Solon's self-control. The Plutarchan Croesus's subsequent command to take Solon on a tour of the treasury is what follows from his disappointed expectation. The provision of a motive is an obvious addition to Herodotus, who specifies no motive for Croesus's order that the servants take Solon for his tour. The implied motive in Herodotus might be extension of hospitality. Plutarch has likely inferred the motive from what he knows about Croesus's un-Solonic character, which comes out more clearly in the subsequent interview.

> Of this [visit to the treasury] there was no need, for the man himself sufficed to give Solon an understanding of his character (ἤρκει γὰρ αὐτὸς ἐν ἑαυτῷ τοῦ τρόπου κατανόησιν παρασχεῖν).
>
> *Sol.* 27.3

If Plutarch can read Croesus's τρόπος, so does the Plutarchan Solon. Plutarch distinguishes his narrative from Herodotus's account (where nothing is said explicitly about Croesus's character) by having the Greek sage channel a diagnosis of the king's character. Herodotus, whose guiding interest in a story like this is its narrative arrangement of a Greek in a position of ideological

---

71   This episode, though, is one of several in which the Herodotean Croesus's expectations will be upset. See also his expectation that his son Atys would be safe on a boar hunt, despite being warned in a dream that he would be killed with a javelin (*Hist.* 1.34), and his expectation of victory against Cyrus, based on a misunderstanding of the oracle that proclaimed "Croesus will destroy a great army" if he goes up against the Persians (*Hist.* 1.53, 73–79). These represented thoughts anticipate and explain Croesus's downfall. As we would expect in a historiographical work, the downfall has less to do with Croesus's personal fortunes and more to do with the concomitant end of Lydian hegemony.

BIOΣ: ETHICS AND MIMESIS

superiority to a Lydian king (and later a Persian one), does not share the biographer's concerns.[72]

> However, when Solon had seen everything and had been conducted back again, Croesus asked him if he had ever known a happier man than he. Solon said he had, and that the man was Tellus, a fellow-citizen of his own; Tellus, he went on to say, had proved himself an honest man, had left reputable sons behind him, and had closed a life which knew no serious want with a glorious display of valor in behalf of his country. Croesus at once judged Solon to be a strange and uncouth fellow, since he did not make an abundance of gold and silver his measure of happiness, but admired the life and death of an ordinary private man more than all this display of power and sovereignty.
>
> *Sol.* 27.4[73]

In the interview after the tour of the treasury, Herodotus makes his first comment about the mind of the king. "Croesus made his inquiry, supposing himself to be blessed beyond all men ('Ο μὲν ἐλπίζων εἶναι ἀνθρώπων ὀλβιώτατος ταῦτα ἐπειρώτα)" (*Hist.* 1.30.13–14).[74] Plutarch omits this insight into Croesus's suppositions, perhaps seeing it as latent in Croesus's question and therefore redundant. This would be in step with Plutarch's tendency to streamline his source material.[75]

After Solon answers, naming Tellus as the "more blessed," Herodotus writes that "Croesus wondered (ἀποθωμάσας) at this" and "sharply asked" for explanation. At the conclusion of Solon's explanation for why Tellus is the ὀλβιώτατος (Plutarch has αὐτοῦ μακαριώτερον), Herotodus segues: "now when Solon had roused the curiosity (προετρέψατο) of Croesus by recounting the many ways in which Tellus was blessed, the king further asked him whom he placed second after Tellus, thinking that assuredly the second prize at least would be his (δοκέων πάγχυ δευτερεῖα γῶν οἴσεσθαι)" (*Hist.* 1.31).[76] Plutarch's Croesus, by contrast, reveals his character when he "at once judged Solon to be strange and uncouth, since he did not make an abundance of gold and silver his measure of

---

72 For Herotodus's reasons for including this story, see Susan O. Shapiro, "Herodotus and Solon," *ClA* 15 (1996): 348–64.

73 Trans. LCL, modified.

74 Trans. LCL, modified.

75 For a discussion of some of the different ways in which he streamlines his sources, with an emphasis on Roman βίοι, see Pelling, "Plutarch's Adaptation of His Source-Material," 91–92.

76 Trans. LCL, modified.

98   CHAPTER 3

happiness."[77] To the reader familiar with Plutarch's philosophically-considered position on wealth and happiness, Croesus's judgment—an element added by Plutarch to the cognitive dimension of the narrative—communicates the king's moral shortfall.

> Notwithstanding, he asked him again whether, next to Tellus, he knew any other man more fortunate (εὐδαιμονέστερον) than he. Again Solon said he did, naming Cleobis and Bito, men surpassing all others in brotherly love and in dutiful affection towards their mother; for once, he said, when the car in which she was riding was delayed by the oxen, they took the yoke upon their own shoulders and brought their mother to the temple of Hera, where her countrymen called her a happy woman and her heart was rejoiced; then, after sacrifice and feasting, they laid themselves to rest, and never rose again, but were found to have died a painless and tranquil death with so great honor fresh upon them. "What!" said Croesus, who by this time was angered, "do you not count us among the fortunate at all?"
>
> *Sol.* 27.5–6[78]

The Plutarchan Croesus's self-incriminating judgment of Solon after the first part of the interview creates an obstacle in transitioning to Solon's second example. Plutarch has to have Croesus "ask him again, all the same" (οὐ μὴν ἀλλὰ πάλιν ἠρώτησεν αὐτόν) if he knows any other man more fortunate than he.[79] Herodotus does not have this problem, since his Croesus has not yet cast a judgment on Solon. Herodotus's Croesus still expects that the second place will fall to him, while Plutarch's Croesus cannot harbor that hope. Notice that the clear emphasis falls on the virtuous ἦθος telegraphed by Cleobis and Bito's πρᾶξις. For Plutarch, happiness is measured in terms of virtuous living, and his task in the βίοι is to illustrate that kind of life.

The two narratives come back together at the conclusion of Solon's account of Cleobis and Bito. Both narrators draw attention to Croesus's anger. Herototus: "But Croesus said in anger (σπερχθείς, perhaps "in haste"), 'Guest from Athens! Do you hold our prosperity so worthless that you match us not

---

77   Trans. LCL, modified.

78   Trans. LCL, modified.

79   The word choice here (εὐδαιμονέστερον, translated above as "fortunate") is significant, since εὐδαιμονία was the highest aim of practical and ethical philosophy and therefore discussions concerning its definition and the link(s) between ἦθος and εὐδαιμονία were the bread and butter of Greek philosophy after Aristotle.

BIOΣ: ETHICS AND MIMESIS

even with common men?'" (*Hist.* 1.32).[80] Plutarch's Croesus "by this time was already in a rage (ἤδη πρὸς ὀργὴν ὁ Κροῖσος)," and asks, "Do you not count us among the fortunate at all?" It is telling that Plutarch has introduced ὀργή into his characterization of Croesus. In another treatise he advocates extirpating (rather than merely controlling) ὀργή, and he attacks the Peripatetic position that would describe the passion as "righteous indignation" or "greatness of soul."[81] Plutarch has also muted the element of guest-friendship explicit in Herodotus.

> Then Solon, who was unwilling to flatter him and did not wish to exasperate him further (οὔτε κολακεύειν βουλόμενος αὐτὸν οὔτε περαιτέρω παροξύνειν), said: "O king of Lydia, as the Deity has given us Greeks all other blessings in moderation, so our moderation gives us a kind of wisdom which is timid, in all likelihood, and fit for common people, not one which is kingly and splendid. This wisdom, such as it is, observing that human life is ever subject to all sorts of vicissitudes, forbids us to be puffed up by the good things we have, or to admire a man's felicity while there is still time for it to change. For the future which is advancing upon every one is varied and uncertain, but when the Deity bestows prosperity on a man up to the end, that man we consider happy; to pronounce any one happy, however, while he is still living and running the risks of life, is like proclaiming an athlete victorious and crowning him while he is still contending for the prize; the verdict is insecure and without authority."
>
> *Sol.* 27.6–7

Before Solon's reply, Plutarch inserts a comment highlighting Solon's character by reference to his thought process. "Solon, who was unwilling to flatter him and did not wish to exasperate him further, [...]." Herodotus starts directly into Solon's reply without such an aside. There is no indication that the Herodotean Solon is concerned to spare the Lydian king exasperation, launching his reply with a lengthy excursus on calculating the duration of human life and some comments about calendars. After approximately fifty lines, he comes to the point: "we must look to the conclusion of every matter, and see how it shall end, for there are many to whom god has given a vision of blessedness, and yet

---

80   Trans. LCL, modified.

81   *On Freedom from Anger* 456f. For the likelihood that he is not consistent in this view of anger, sometimes making it an "ally of virtue," see John Dillon, *The Middle Platonists: 80 BC to AD 220*, Rev. ed. (Ithaca: Cornell University Press, 1996), 189.

100   CHAPTER 3

afterwards brought them to utter ruin" (*Hist.* 1.32).[82] The lesson of Herodotus's Solon for Croesus is one of divine unpredictability. While Plutarch is as interested as Herodotus in the gods, such questions are not central to this context.[83]

> When he had said this, Solon departed, leaving Croesus vexed, but none the wiser for it (ταῦτ᾽ εἰπὼν ὁ Σόλων ἀπηλλάττετο, λυπήσας μέν, οὐ νουθετήσας δὲ τὸν Κροῖσον).
>
> *Sol.* 27.9

The conclusion to the meeting, after Solon's lesson about dying well, is close in pragmatic terms (Solon is sent away in Herodotus, whereas he seems to leave of his own accord in Plutarch), and with little difference on the cognitive plane. Herodotus's Croesus acted this way "because he thought that man to be very foolish who disregarded present prosperity and bade him look rather to the end of every matter (κάρτα δόξας ἀμαθέα εἶναι, ὃς τὰ παρεόντα ἀγαθὰ μετεὶς τὴν τελευτὴν παντὸς χρήματος ὁρᾶν ἐκέλευε)" (*Hist.* 1.33).[84] Plutarch's Solon departs, "leaving Croesus vexed, but none the wiser for it." Compared to his source, Plutarch's conclusion is characteristically shorter and more tightly focused on ethics.

There is a great deal more one could say about the ethical motifs developed in the *Solon*, not least of which would address the rationale for the laws promulgated by Solon (at *Sol.* 5.2, to stop the ἀδικίας and πλεονεξίας of the citizens by means of written laws) and Solon's rejection of an offer to be tyrant (*Sol.* 14.3–6). Furthermore, it is evident that the theme of Solon's desire to avoid ἀδικία guides Plutarch when he makes selections from Solon's writings to incorporate into the βίος (*Sol.* 2.3; cf. 3.2).

In discussing a "surprising" law, Plutarch guesses that Solon "wishes, probably (βούλεται δ᾽, ὡς ἔοικε), that a man should not be insensible or indifferent to the common weal, arranging his private affairs securely and glorying in the fact that he has no share in the distempers and distresses of his country, but should rather espouse promptly the better and more righteous cause, share its perils and give it his aid, instead of waiting in safety to see which cause prevails" (*Sol.* 20.1). Explaining a law prohibiting gifts given under compulsion or impairment, Plutarch comments: "he thought, very rightly and properly, that

---

82   Trans. LCL.

83   See Gallarte, "Hérodote et Plutarque," 129–30. For Plutarch's interest in the gods, see e.g., his treatises *On the E at Delphi*; *Isis and Osiris*; and *On the Obsolescence of Oracles*.

84   Trans. LCL.

being persuaded into wrong was no better than being forced into it (εὖ πάνυ καὶ προσηκόντως τὸ πεισθῆναι παρὰ τὸ βέλτιστον οὐδὲν ἡγούμενος τοῦ βιασθῆναι διαφέρειν), and he placed deceit and compulsion, gratification and affliction, in one and the same category, believing that both were alike able to pervert a man's reason" (*Sol.* 21.3). In both cases, Plutarch gives the reader no suggestion that he has a source for this explanation beyond his own confidence in theorizing Solon's thought process.

In explaining Solon's decision to go abroad, Plutarch reasons that Solon, beset by people either praising, censuring, or questioning his laws, saw that it would be impossible to handle all the questions and odious to avoid them, and desired to be free of "the captiousness and censoriousness of the citizens" (ὁρῶν ὅτι ταῦτα καὶ τὸ πράττειν ἄτοπον καὶ τὸ μὴ πράττειν ἐπίφθονον, ὅλως δὲ ταῖς ἀπορίαις ὑπεκστῆναι βουλόμενος καὶ διαφυγεῖν τὸ δυσάρεστον καὶ φιλαίτιον τῶν πολιτῶν). He gained leave from the Athenians to go abroad for ten years, for "he hoped (ἤλπιζε) they would be accustomed to his laws after such time" (*Sol.* 25.5).[85] Once again, Plutarch has reasoned from what Solon did (go abroad for ten years) to a theorization of his motives, and the motivation is cast in terms of Solon's desire to act rightly and for justice to prevail in Athens.

The goodness of Solon's motives is set in relief against the supposed badness Plutarch theorizes in the lesser minds of Solon's unnamed contemporaries. While Solon was away, Plutarch writes, factions formed and "though the city still observed the new laws, yet all were already expecting a revolution and desirous of a different form of government, not in hopes of an equality, but each party thinking to be bettered by the change, and to get the entire mastery of its opponents (ἤδη δὲ πράγματα νεώτερα προσδοκᾶν καὶ ποθεῖν ἅπαντας ἑτέραν κατάστασιν, οὐκ ἴσον ἐλπίζοντας, ἀλλὰ πλέον ἕξειν ἐν τῇ μεταβολῇ καὶ κρατήσειν παντάπασι τῶν διαφερομένων)" (*Sol.* 29.1).

What Solon does with Croesus foreshadows Solon's interaction on his return with Peisistratus, leader of one of the lately-emerged factions and (though Solon alone can see it) the future tyrant of Athens: Although Peisistratus "completely deceived most people, ... Solon quickly detected his real character (τὸ ἦθος ἐφώρασεν αὐτοῦ), and was the first to perceive his secret designs. He did not, however, treat him as an enemy, but tried to soften and mold him by his instructions" (*Sol.* 29.3).[86] Although Solon failed, as he had also originally failed to bring Croesus round, the important observation is that Plutarch attributes to Solon the ability to detect a man's ἦθος and attempt to instruct him in virtue.

---

85   Trans. LCL, modified.
86   Trans. LCL, modified.

Plutarch both assigns motives to characters and disagrees with motives assigned to historical figures by other writers, as shown above. Plutarch's attribution of motives is notable for the self-reflexivity that often characterizes the deliberation and assignment of a motive. He knows that historical actors had motives, that discovering these motives is a separate task from determining the facts of the actions to which they are attached, that other writers can accurately report an action but misconstrue the motive, that motives are not in every case recoverable, and that motives can sometimes be difficult to capture in words. Many modern historians would agree with him thus far. Ancient historiographers also wrote frequently about the motives of their subjects, as we saw in chapter 2.[87] What is most Plutarchan about the discourse of motives here, however, are his further convictions that motives can be explained by reference to character, that a person's character is a relative constant, and that when the facts are murky, the biographer ought to err on the side of benevolence (as discussed above in connection to the *Her. mal.*). This leaves little room for good characters to have bad motives. The points made in our discussion of the *Solon* could be reinforced by lingering with Plutarch. A better-rounded picture would include attention to what Plutarch saw as Publicola's character and motives in the paired Life. An exhaustive treatment would need also to consider other "kinds" of βίοι from the larger corpus of *Parallel Lives*.[88] A full enough picture has emerged, however, to allow us to turn now to another βίος produced in another part of the empire by a rough contemporary of both Plutarch and the Fourth Evangelist: Philo of Alexandria. With fewer programmatic statements reinforcing the effect, and with less interaction with other writers, we will see in his *Moses* an even sharper distinction between virtuous and vicious characters with correspondingly noble and wicked motives.

5   Philo's *Life of Moses*

Philo was an Alexandrian Jewish philosopher and writer active in the first half of the first century CE. Little is known about his life apart from what can be inferred from his own writings; among his near contemporaries only Josephus mentions him by name (*Ant.* 18.259–60). His role in an embassy to Gaius

---

87   Cf. Emily Baragwanath, *Motivation and Narrative in Herodotus*, OCM (Oxford: Oxford University Press, 2008).

88   This adaptation of the Croesus meeting (a Herodotean story) might be compared with an adaptation of a Thucydidean story or, having looked at a positive exemplar, with an apotreptic case (e.g., the *Alcibiades* or the *Coriolanus*).

BIOΣ: ETHICS AND MIMESIS

Caligula in 39/40 CE is the one major political event with which he is associated, an event we know about chiefly from Philo's own treatise *Embassy to Gaius*. He counts himself among the aged (ἡμεῖς οἱ γέροντες) when he writes the treatise, which is the chief clue for dating his birth and death to the vicinity of 20 BCE and 50 CE, respectively (Note that Gaius ruled from 37 to 41 CE). His family was wealthy and several of his relatives played official roles in politics.[89] His brother Alexander, described by Josephus as wellborn and wealthy, was Alabarch in Alexandria.[90] Alexander's son Tiberius Julius Alexander served as procurator of Judea and later as prefect of Egypt. He may be the Alexander who figures in Philo's dialogues *On Providence* 1 and 2 and *Whether Animals Have Reason*.[91] These are among the few of Philo's few surviving works with virtually no interaction with the Bible; others in this category include *That Every Good Person is Free* and *On the Eternity of the World*. Philo also wrote historical-apologetic works, including the aforementioned *Embassy* and a related work titled *Against Flaccus*, as well as a treatise *On the Contemplative Life*, and a treatise called the *Hypothetica*.[92]

Approximately three-quarters of Philo's surviving writings interact with the Pentateuch. They are typically divided into three series: the Allegorical Commentary, the Exposition of the Law, and *The Questions and Answers on Genesis and Exodus*. The Allegorical Commentary includes the treatises *Allegorical Interpretation* 1–3, *On the Cherubim*, *On the Sacrifices of Cain and Abel*, *That the Worse Attacks the Better*, *On the Posterity of Cain*, *On Giants*, *That God is Unchangeable*, *On Agriculture*, *On Planting*, *On Drunkenness*, *On Sobriety*, *On the Confusion of Tongues*, *On the Migration of Abraham*, *Who is the Heir?*, *On the Preliminary Studies*, *On Flight and Finding*, *On the Change of Names*, and *On Dreams* 1–2. These treatises taken in this order offer a running allegorical commentary on Genesis, and have traditionally been understood as

---

89   For Philo's family in general terms, see Daniel R. Schwartz, "Philo: His Family and His Times," in *The Cambridge Companion to Philo*, ed. Adam Kamesar (Cambridge: Cambridge University Press, 2009), 9–31.

90   For a collection of the evidence about Philo's brother, Gaius Julius Alexander, see Katherine G. Evans, "Alexander the Alabarch: Roman and Jew," in *Society of Biblical Literature 1995 Seminar Papers*, ed. Eugene H. Lowering, SBLSP 34 (Atlanta: Scholars, 1995), 576–94.

91   This last treatise is sometimes alternatively titled the *Alexander*. Even if the identification is correct, it would not follow that the opinions expressed by the Alexander of the dialogue correspond with the positions held by Philo's historical nephew. Both treatises survive only in Armenian translation, except for brief Greek fragments of *On Providence* in Eusebius.

92   The most recent detailed discussion of Philo's literary production and its categorization is James R. Royse, "The Works of Philo," in *The Cambridge Companion to Philo*, ed. Adam Kamesar (Cambridge: Cambridge University Press, 2009), 32–64.

104   CHAPTER 3

written for a Jewish audience familiar with the Pentateuch and advanced philosophy. The allegorical readings offered are frequently presented as superior to literal readings.

The works traditionally assigned to the Exposition of the Law are *On the Creation of the World, On the Life of Abraham, On the Life of Joseph, On the Life of Moses* 1–2, *On the Decalogue, On the Special Laws* 1–4, *On the Virtues*, and *On Rewards and Punishments*. These works discuss the contents of Genesis and Exodus, largely without allegory, and are usually understood to have been written primarily for novices in philosophy and Judaism, perhaps especially inquisitive Gentiles.[93]

The third division, *Questions and Answers on Genesis and Exodus*, is distinguished from the Allegorical Commentary by its verse-by-verse, question-and-answer format, rather than any marked difference in the nature of commentary supplied. There are four books on Genesis and two on Exodus.

Philo had access to rich literary resources in Alexandria, but the sources most often employed were "the sacred books"—presumably a reference to the Septuagint (Philo was probably not fluent in Hebrew)—and what he had heard from "the elders of the nation."[94] Philo's philosophical frame, through which he filters the Pentateuch and the rest of the scriptures, is generally Platonist.[95]

The title *Life of Moses* and the placement of this pair of books after βίοι of Joseph and Abraham in the traditional arrangements of the Exposition seem to suggest that the three works should correspond in form and content.[96] There are, however, reasons for pause. On two occasions later in the Exposition, Philo gestures back to the *Moses* (*Virtues* 52; *Rewards* 53) as if to a book that introduced the whole series. And in the preface to the *Joseph*, Philo writes, "Since I have described the lives of these three, the life which results from teaching, the life of the self-taught and the life of practice, I will carry on the series by

---

93   The classic case is Erwin R. Goodenough, "Philo's Exposition of the Law and His De vita Mosis," *HTR* 26 (1933): 109–25.

94   What Philo means by "the elders" is contested. See Christina Termini, "Philo's Thought within the Context of Middle Judaism," in *The Cambridge Companion to Philo*, ed. Adam Kamesar (Cambridge: Cambridge University Press, 2009), 114.

95   Philo is one of the chief representatives of what was called until recently "Middle Platonism," which is distinguished from classical or archaic Platonism by its embrace of some Stoic ideas. See Dillon, *The Middle Platonists*; John Dillon, "Philo and Hellenistic Platonism," in *Philo of Alexandria and Post-Aristotelian Philosophy*, ed. Francesca Alesse, SPhA 5 (Leiden: Brill, 2008), 223–32.

96   In most editions, it is placed after the *Joseph* and before the *Decalogue*. Most scholars, however, see it as a separate work—either preliminary to the Exposition or an independent, apologetic treatise.

describing a fourth life, that of the statesman" (*Joseph* 1.1).[97] This implies that Philo wrote βίοι of Isaac and Jacob in addition to the extant *Abraham*. The *Abraham* begins by describing a schema in which he envisions two triads of men living before Moses and the arrival in history of the written laws: one consisting of Enos, Enoch, and Noah, who represent for Philo hope, repentance, and justice; the other consists of the patriarchs. A cross-reference to the "story of the order in which the world was made," which was "set forth in detail by us as well as was possible in the preceding treatise" (*Abr.* 1.2) seems to point to *Creation* as the book upon which the *Abraham* immediately follows in the series. There is no suggestion that Philo wrote βίοι on Enos, Enoch, or Noah. The preface to the *Joseph* suggests that the decision to write this βίος came after concluding a series of lives on the patriarchs, who together make up the second triad flagged in the beginning of the *Abraham*. Taken together, these observations suggest that the *Life of Moses* stands apart from the *Abraham* and the *Joseph*, as well as the missing βίοι of Isaac and Jacob, as a separate work.[98]

Albert Geljon argues that the *Moses* is Philo's attempt at an "introductory philosophical βίος."[99] The argument appears in a book that is mostly concerned with Gregory of Nyssa's *De vita Moysis*, but the first major section contains the most detailed study of Philo's *Moses* to date.[100] Following Burridge for his definition of βίος and Jaap Mansfeld for the idea of a *schema isagogicum*—an introductory schema used by ancient commentators approaching philosophical corpora—Geljon elaborates Goodenough's view that Philo's

---

97   The *Joseph* seems to function as Philo's commentary on statecraft, the βίος πολιτικός. One scholar has, in part for this reason, taken the *Joseph* together with the *Moses* as Philo's ideal political life in the first case and prophetic life in the second. Valentin Nikiprowetzky, *Le commentaire de l'écriture chez Philon d'Alexandrie: son caractère et sa portée, observations philologiques*, ALGHJ 11 (Leiden: Brill, 1977), 196–97. This is, however, necessary for Nikiprowetzky's argument that the *Moses* is an integral, intended component part of the Exposition. For critique, see Albert C. Geljon, *Philonic Exegesis in Gregory of Nyssa's De vita Moysis*, BJS 333 (Providence: Brown Judaic Studies, 2002), 28–30.

98   This is reflective of the consensus in Philonic scholarship now, that the *Moses* stands either as a companion to the Exposition, an introduction to Moses's writings and/or Philo's commentaries, an introduction specifically to Philo's Exposition, or a totally unconnected, apologetic treatise. Companion: Goodenough, "Philo's Exposition of the Law and His De vita Mosis." Introduction to Moses as mediated by Philo: Geljon, *Philonic Exegesis*. Introduction to the Exposition: Gregory E. Sterling, "'Prolific in Expression and Broad in Thought': International References to Philo's Allegorical Commentary and Exposition of the Law," ERFC 40 (2012): 55–76. An independent, apologetic work (with the *Hypothetica* and *On the Contemplative Life*): Royse, "The Works of Philo," 34.

99   Geljon, *Philonic Exegesis*.

100   This situation will change eventually with Gregory Sterling's translation and commentary for the Philo of Alexandria Commentary Series.

Moses is a "companion piece" to the Exposition, making the more specific claim that it functions as an introductory philosophical βίος with respect to Moses's writings.[101] "Such a *bios* has an introductory function, and treats preliminary issues concerning the author. It should be read before studying the writings of the author himself, and hence it was often placed at the beginning of an edition of his writings."[102] He points to such examples as Thrasyllus's βίοι of Democritus and Plato and Porphyry's *Life of Plotinus*. In addition to providing typical information about the philosopher's ancestry, birth, and death, these works perform functions like providing an annotated bibliography of the philosopher's writings and offering an account of how his particular writings came into being. This explains why Philo's *Moses* includes an account of the origin of the Pentateuch and its translation into Greek (*Moses* 2.25–44). The introductory function is also suggested insofar as Philo gives an outline of the Exposition in the course of his *Moses* (*Moses* 2.45–57) and in undisputed works of the Exposition he refers back to the *Moses*.

In addition to their different positions inside and outside the Exposition, another difference between the *Moses*, on the one hand, and the extant *Abraham* and the *Joseph*, on the other, is that the *Moses* is offered in two books, compared to the single book each for Joseph and Abraham. In addition to having relatively little allegorical interpretation (exceptions are the burning bush episode and the some of the material in *Moses* 2 on the tabernacle and its accouterments) and including material without an immediate bearing on the subject's life (such as the account of the translation of the Septuagint), the *Moses* is considerably longer than those other narratives. At the start of the second volume, Philo summarizes the first volume and suggests that the portrait in *Moses* 1 was of Plato's philosopher-king, "for it has been said, not without good reason, that states can only make progress in well-being if either kings are philosophers or philosophers are kings" (*Moses* 2.2; cf. Plato, *Resp.* 5.473). The second volume treats Moses under three additional headings: the legislative, the high-priestly, and the prophetic.

---

101   Geljon sometimes gives the impression that it is introductory not to Moses's writings, but to Philo's own work on the Mosaic corpus. E.g., "It [the *Moses*] was intended to be an introduction to Philo's exegesis of Moses' writings, i.e., Mosaic philosophy." Later, however, he writes, "Philo's *Mos.* is an introductory *bios*. Moses' life is presented as an example which the reader is encouraged to follow, notably through a further and deeper study of his writings." Geljon, *Philonic Exegesis*, 44, 46.

102   Geljon, 31. Cf. Burridge, *What Are the Gospels?*; Jaap Mansfeld, *Prolegomena: Questions to Be Settled before the Study of an Author or a Text*, PhAnt 61 (Leiden: Brill, 1994); Goodenough, "Philo's Exposition of the Law and His De vita Mosis."

BIOΣ: ETHICS AND MIMESIS   107

Despite these distinctive qualities, both in relation to Philo's other works and in relation to other, contemporary βίοι, no one has seriously objected to the genre classification of the *Moses* as a βίος. This language is found in the title (ΠΕΡΙ ΤΟΥ ΒΙΟΥ ΜΩΥΣΕΩΣ), in the declaration of the subject (Μωυσέως ... τὸν βίον ἀναγράψαι διενοήθην, at *Moses* 1), and in cross-references to the work from elsewhere in the Philonic corpus (cf. *Virtues* 52; *Rewards* 53). The work may well have been intended to introduce the whole Philonic corpus or, as Gregory Sterling has more recently suggested, just the Exposition.[103] While this would at first glance seem to set it apart from many other βίοι in antiquity (no one has suggested that Plutarch's *Solon* was intended to introduce the writings of Solon, or that Nicolaus's *Augustus* the Res Gestae), it poses no obstacle to Philo's ability to approach Moses as ethical exemplar.[104]

One of the references back to the *Moses* from later in the Exposition casts light on what Philo thought he had accomplished in that text:

> All the virtues are virgins, but the fairest among them all, the acknowledged queen of the dance, is piety, which Moses, the teacher of divine lore, in a special degree had for his own, and through it gained among a multitude of other gifts, which have been described in the treatises dealing with his life, four special rewards, the offices of king, legislator, prophet and high priest.
>
> *Rewards* 53

Philo frames this passage with an account of the virtues and vices at variance with each other, a battle playing out in the soul, and never more decisively won by virtue than in the soul of Moses (*Rewards* 52–54). Though his focus in the larger treatise is, as the title suggests, rewards and punishments, Philo's recollection of what he had accomplished in the *Moses* is an account of Moses's virtues. This reading of the *Moses* is supported by a closer investigation of the two-volume βίος itself.

The first volume covers Moses's youth, education, and leadership in the context of the Exodus. The second volume shifts to a more systematic approach to Moses's roles as legislator, high-priest, and prophet. Setting up the first volume, Philo castigates Greek men of letters who knew of Moses and his

---

103   Sterling, "Prolific in Expression and Broad in Thought," 74.

104   There are many other ancient βίοι of philosophers, some extant, many non-extant, introducing the writing of their subject (some of the best known being Porphyry's *Plotinus* and Arrian's *Epictetus*). It would not be surprising to find in those works, parallel to the introductory function, an exploration of how the teacher lived his life and an invitation to imitation.

contributions, but "refused to treat him as worthy of memory, possibly through envy, and also because in many cases the ordinances of the legislators of the different states are opposed to his" (*Moses* 1.2). These same writers lent their talents to "comedies and pieces of voluptuous license, to their widespread disgrace, when they should have used their natural gifts to the full on the lessons taught by good men and their lives" (*Moses* 1.3). Philo thus frames his βίος of Moses with a programmatic remark about genre: comedies, etc., do not teach good morals; good men and their βίοι are important specifically for this function of providing guidance (ὑφήγησις) to the reader.

Philo's paraphrase of Moses's origins and upbringing in *Moses* 1 shows clear signs of improvement on the biblical account. That is, Philo finds virtue and makes it an explicit part of his narrative where the Bible is silent.[105] Moses's virtue is on display already from his early childhood, where Philo makes him "with a modest and serious bearing" apply himself to "hearing and seeing what was sure to profit the soul" (*Moses* 1.20). The site of this virtue is Moses's mind, an object of perpetual fascination and admiration for Philo, and the "trainer" in Moses's exercises in virtue (τοὺς ἀρετῆς ἄθλους) was the reason within him (ἐν ἑαυτῷ λογισμόν; *Moses* 1.48). Moses's mind is "incapable of accepting any falsehood" (*Moses* 1.24) and astonishing to those around him: "his associates and everyone else, struck with amazement at what they felt was a novel spectacle considered earnestly what the mind which dwelt in his body like an image in its shrine could be, whether it was human or divine or a mixture of both" (*Moses* 1.27). The conclusion to the βίος is not Moses's death, but rather the resolution of "his twofold nature of soul and body into a single unity, transforming his whole being into mind, pure as the sunlight" (*Moses* 2.288). In the burning bush episode, Philo's Moses shows none of the fear or reticence of his biblical counterpart (cf. Exod 3.6, 11, 13), and instead questions God only on the basis of what he knows: "he was not ignorant of the fact that his words would be disbelieved by those of his own nation and all others" (*Moses* 1.74). Philo's young Moses amazes everyone with his words and speech: living in a palace, with "numberless incentives to foster their flame [viz., the passions of youthful lust]," he exercised σωφροσύνη and καρτερία (*Moses* 1.25). He was restrained in his eating, in his attitude towards luxury, and in his aversion to

---

105   The fullest treatment of this question of virtue, though with respect to the figure of Moses across Philo's corpus (i.e., not restricted to the *Moses*) and in constant dialogue with other ancient Jewish biblical interpretation, especially Josephus, is Louis H. Feldman, *Philo's Portrayal of Moses in the Context of Ancient Judaism*, CJA 15 (Notre Dame: University of Notre Dame Press, 2007).

BIOΣ: ETHICS AND MIMESIS

boasting (*Moses* 1.28–30). Philo, as these examples demonstrate, uses his *Moses* to pursue an ethical agenda anchored to the mind of the protagonist.

Even moments in the biblical Moses's career that seem to reflect poorly on his character are salvageable in Philo's hands. Where the biblical Moses at the burning bush is frightened and attempts to beg off his assignment (Exod 3.6, 11, 13; 4.1), Philo drops the fright and retains the attempted refusal, but with a twist: "though he believed, he tried to refuse the mission, declaring that he was not eloquent, but feeble of voice and slow of tongue, especially ever since he heard God speaking to him; for he considered that human eloquence compared with God's was dumbness" (*Moses* 1.83). Where the biblical God's response to Moses's repeated attempts to avoid the mission is anger (Exod 4.14), Philo's God approves of Moses's modesty (*Moses* 1.84). Philo offers a comparable justification for the "plundering of the Egyptians" episode, which might appear to be motivated by avarice (φιλοχρηματίαν) or covetousness (ἐπιθυμίαν) in the biblical account (cf. *Moses* 1.141; Exod 12.36). Philo offers two justifiable explanations without choosing between them: "in either case, their action was right, whether one regard it as an act of peace, the acceptance of payment long kept back through reluctance to pay what was due, or as an act of war, the claim under the law of the victors to take their enemies' goods" (*Moses* 1.142).

Moses's virtue is cast in sharper relief when we look at what Philo has done with other characters in the narrative, particularly those whose viciousness Philo exaggerates. The Egyptian killed by Moses, for example, is made to be the cruelest (τὸν βιαιότατον) of the Egyptians (*Moses* 1.44; cf. Exod 2.11–15). Or in another example, Philo magnifies the Egyptian people's collective guilt, concentrated in the person of Pharaoh, for violating the expectations of guest-friendship: "so, then, these strangers, who had left their own country and come to Egypt hoping to live there in safety as in a second fatherland, were made slaves by the ruler of the country and reduced to the condition of captives taken by the custom of war." In this action Pharaoh "showed no shame or fear of the God of liberty and hospitality and of justice to guests and suppliants" (*Moses* 1.36). The crime of the Egyptians has developed from a refusal to free the enslaved Hebrews to, in Philo's account, a shocking violation of guest-hospitality (*Moses* 1.34–39). Later, Philo will develop the contrast between Moses and Pharaoh: Philo's Pharaoh refuses Moses's reasonable request because his "soul from his earliest years was weighed down with the pride of many generations," and "he did not accept a god discernable only by the mind, or any at all beyond those whom his eyes beheld" (*Moses* 1.88). Philo's Moses has noetic vision, access to the realm of the really real; the Pharaoh is trapped in the material world, a fact which is inseparably linked to his vicious (here prideful and insolent) character. The ethical profile in each case is sharpened in Philo's βίος.

The Philonic narrator's access to the inner states of characters in the story plays into this function as well. When Moses performs before Pharaoh's court, Philo adds to the biblical account:

> By this time, the marvelous spectacle had refuted the skepticism in every ill-disposed person's soul, and they now regarded these events not as the works of human cunning or artifices fabricated to deceive, but as brought about by some diviner power to which every feat is easy. But, though they were compelled by the clear evidence of the facts to admit the truth, they did not abate their audacity, but clung to their old inhumanity and impiety as though it were the surest of blessings.
>
> Moses 94–95; cf. Exod 7.8–13

Moses is not the only virtuous character in the story, and Philo enhances the ethical profile of other paragons too, beginning with Moses's parents and their decision to expose their infant son. Their reasoning, Philo notes, is that since "there were persons prying into holes and corners, ever eager to carry some new report to the king, his parents in their fear that their efforts to save one would but cause a larger number, namely themselves, to perish with him, exposed him with tears on the banks of the river, and departed groaning" (*Moses* 1.10). This may strike modern readers as a dubious act of virtue, but it is important to note by way of mitigation that children were not valued in antiquity in the idealized terms that they are in most cultures today. Furthermore, even if we as modern readers are not convinced that this line of reasoning would justify the parents' decision, what is important to notice about the rhetorical structure of the argument is that Philo goes out of his way to introduce an ethical principle where the Bible had none. The same impulse is visible in Philo's handling of the Egyptian princess, the woman who would act as surrogate mother to Moses: she "had been married for a considerable time but had never conceived a child, though she naturally desired one," and she was "always depressed and loud in lamentation, but on this particular day she broke down under the weight of cares; and, though her custom was to remain at home and never even to cross the threshold, she set off with her maids to the river, where the child was exposed" (*Moses* 1.13–14).[106] These extra-biblical comments probe her psyche while constructing it, revealing Philo's concern to

---

106   Trans. LCL, modified.

make her chaste, motivated, and decorous. Philo makes her worry specifically about the prospect of her father's kingdom passing into the hands of strangers, as proof of her filial piety.

Above we saw that at least part of Plutarch's motivation for writing βίοι was to supply readers with models for imitation. Philo makes similar comments in the *Moses*, though sometimes with noteworthy differences. Moses entered

> into the darkness where God was, that is into the unseen, invisible, incorporeal and archetypal essence of existing things. Thus he beheld what is hidden from the sight of mortal nature, and, in himself and his life displayed for all to see, he has set before us, like some well-wrought picture, a piece of work beautiful and godlike, a model (παράδειγμα) for those who are willing to copy it. Happy are they who imprint, or strive to imprint, that image in their souls. For it were best that the mind should carry the form of virtue in perfection (τὸ εἶδος τέλειον ἀρετῆς), but, failing this, let it at least have the unflinching desire to possess that form.
>
> *Moses* 1.158–9; cf. Exod 20.21

Moses enters the Platonic world of ideas, and grasps "the form of virtue in perfection" with his mind. Philo seems to be drawing on not just the Platonic world of ideas (Moses carries the perfect εἶδος of virtue), but also on a Stoic epistemology. Philo also employs the Stoic distinction between the perfect sage and the one advancing towards virtue (in Stoic terms, a προκόπτων). Moses, unlike Plutarch's subjects, is perfect. Philo and his readers, acknowledging that a Moses-like state of perfection in virtue is unattainable, nevertheless can aspire to perfection with Moses as παράδειγμα.[107]

An important part of the Stoic sage's identity that bears on the present discussion was his ability to extirpate the passions. Philo's Moses "tamed and assuaged and reduced to mildness" the passions relating to food, sex, luxury, and boasting that "rage so furiously if left to themselves" (*Moses* 1.26). There may be a certain amount of inconsistency in Philo's portrait, since at times he makes Moses sound as though he has achieved a perfect state of ἀπάθεια, while other passages seem to suggest that Moses was merely excellent at managing his passions, or that Moses only felt appropriate emotions. This is visible in Philo's representation of Moses's response to the injustice he saw inflicted on the

---

107   On Philo's Moses and the Stoic sage, see David Winston, "Sage and Super-Sage in Philo of Alexandria," in *Pomegranates and Golden Bells: Studies in Biblical, Jewish and Near Easter Ritual, Law and Literature in Honor of Jacob Milgrom*, ed. D. P. Wright, D. N. Freedman, and A. Hurvitz (Winona Lake: Eisenbrauns, 1995), 815–24.

Israelites: he sank into depression and anger (ἀθυμῶν καὶ δυσχεραίνων), since he was powerless to punish the wrongdoers or help those suffering (*Moses* 1.40). Still other passages give the impression that Moses's ability to manage the passions was only achievable through divine intervention. He jumps in fright, for example, when his staff turns to a serpent, and is checked only when God inspires him with courage (*Moses* 1.77). However Philo imagined that Moses's handling of his passions, it is evident that Moses is offered to the reader an imitable exemplar of passion management.

In the preface to the *Alexander*, Plutarch drew attention to the notion that "a slight thing" (πρᾶγμα βραχύ) like a word or a gesture can sometimes act as a better guide to ἦθος than great battles and accomplishments. Philo employs a similar principle in his account of Moses at the well in the land of Midian (*Moses* 1.51–57; cf. Exod 2.15–22). "I will describe an action of his at this time," Philo writes, "which, though it may seem a petty matter (εἰ καὶ μικρὸν ὅσα γε τῷ δοκεῖν), argues a spirit of no petty kind (οὐκ ἀπὸ φρονήματος μικροῦ)" (*Moses* 1.51).

Character evaluation is a central element in Plutarch's *Parallel Lives*, and Philo's *Moses* manifests a comparable impulse, making some characters (especially, but not only the protagonist) more uniformly virtuous and other characters more clearly vicious. The firm distinction Philo set between good and bad, for example, is visible in an extra-biblical comment connected to the plagues: "never was judgment so clearly passed on good and bad, a judgment which brought perdition to the latter and salvation to the former" (*Moses* 1.146). Where Exodus's distinction here is simply in terms of Hebrews and Egyptians, with no word of the Hebrews' goodness or the Egyptians' general badness, the latter are precisely the characterizing categories that come into play when Philo casts Moses's story as a βίος. In the same context, Philo interprets the plagues as simultaneously punishments on the wicked Egyptians and *lessons* for the Hebrews: "I think that everyone who witnessed the events of that time could not but have thought of the Hebrews as spectators of the sufferings of others, and not merely spectators in safety, but learners thereby of the finest and most profitable of lessons—piety" (*Moses* 1.146).

If there is a dominant virtue characteristic of Philo's Moses, just as Plutarch appears to have associated characteristic virtues and vices with each of his eminent statesmen, piety (εὐσέβεια) is a compelling candidate. Louis Feldman has made the case that εὐσέβεια acted for Hellenistic Jews as a fifth cardinal virtue, over and above the wisdom, courage, temperance, and justice as discussed in Plato's *Republic*.[108] The discourse on virtues and character was broader than

---

108   Feldman, *Philo's Portrayal of Moses in the Context of Ancient Judaism*, 237.

BIOΣ: ETHICS AND MIMESIS 113

just these five, but they serve as a helpful matrix for approaching the prioritization of virtues in the *Moses*. Philo, later in the Exposition, refers to all the virtues as virgins, but puts εὐσέβεια in a preeminent position as "queen of the dance" (*Rewards* 53), and makes Moses the possessor of this virtue to an unsurpassable degree, pointing back to the *Moses* in support of his point. By virtue of possessing this virtue, Moses was entrusted with the offices king, legislator, high priest, and prophet. Within the βίος, Philo makes εὐσέβεια the "most indispensable virtue in a chief priest" (*Moses* 2.66), and therefore Moses's chief qualification for that office. Philo stresses too that Moses's assessment of others could be made in terms of their εὐσέβεια and ὁσιότης (*Moses* 2.142). The point was made above that Philo's Moses apparently possessed the virtues perfectly, while the good characters around him were at best progressing towards virtue. This is illustrated in connection to piety when Moses rallies the Levites to take action against sin in the camp:

> when they heard the proclamation, they came running with all speed, like troops for whom one signal is enough, showing by their swiftness their zeal and the keenness of the inward feelings which urged them to piety (τὴν προθυμίαν ἐπιδεικνυμένη καὶ τὴν ὀξύτητα τῆς εἰς εὐσέβειαν ψυχικῆς ὁρμῆς).
>
> *Moses* 2.170[109]

The disobedient, fittingly, are described as those "whose piety had little ballast (τῶν πρὸς εὐσέβειαν ἀνερματίστων)" (*Moses* 2.260), and in the context of the golden calf, are described as "men of unstable nature (οἱ μὴ βέβαιοι τὰς φύσεις)," who, "thinking his absence a suitable opportunity, rushed into impiety (ἀσέβειαν) unrestrainedly, as though authority had ceased to be, and, forgetting the reverence they owed to the Self-Existent, became zealous imitators (ζηλωταί) of Egyptian fables" (*Moses* 2.161).[110] The language of zealous imitation is the same as that used in the key text presented above regarding emulation of Moses: "we all know this, that meaner men emulate men of distinction, and set their inclinations in the direction of what they seem to desire," a reality which can have uplifting or disastrous consequences for the followers, depending on the character of their leader (*Moses* 1.160–1). Zealous imitation of Egyptian mores also characterizes the blasphemer in the story Philo adapts from Leviticus 24.10–12. "This half-bred person, having a quarrel with someone of the nation that has vision and knowledge, losing in his anger all control

---

109   Trans. LCL, modified.
110   Trans. LCL, modified.

114   CHAPTER 3

over himself, and being a zealous imitator (ζηλωτὴς ὤν) of Egyptian atheism, extended his impiety (ἀσέβειαν) from earth to heaven" (*Moses* 2.196).[111] Zealous imitation of Phineas's example characterizes the godfearers who attacked their countrymen whose "minds had been misled" and by the arts of Balak's prostitutes had been "perverted to impiety." At Moses's command, these zealous imitators spared the lives only of those who "gave clear proof of their piety" (*Moses* 1.301–3). The language of imitation is not limited to contexts emphasizing piety and its opposites, but it would be safe to conclude that Philo, if asked *what* of Moses's way of life the reader should imitate, would readily point to piety, and all that it entails.

6   Conclusion

The exploration of represented interiority in the βίοι discussed in this chapter has suggested that moral character (ἦθος, τρόπος) is a slice of inner life conventionally central to the genre. Working with Plutarch's *Solon* and Philo's *Moses* as texts that—unlike the Fourth Gospel—are uncontroversially identified as βίοι, it was shown in each case that the writer could work forwards or backwards to construct the ἦθος of the characters (especially, but not only, the protagonists). He might work "backwards," as Plutarch would say, from character-revealing πράξεις and ἔργα like an off-the-cuff remark or a small gesture to fashion ethical constructs, then "forwards" to interpretation of the subject's words and deeds with the help of those constructs. This forward-looking process of interpretation not infrequently involved theorizing the subject's motives for good or ill. Interest in the ἦθος of characters spills deliberately, unstoppably off the page to the ἦθος of readers and rival writers. In Philo's case as much as Plutarch's, the expectation is that the reader will want to imitate the virtues of the book's hero. When we turn in chapter 6 to look at the Fourth Gospel's cognitive material in light of the conventions of βίοι, these patterns will guide the discussion.

---

111   Trans. LCL, modified.

CHAPTER 4

Romance: Thwarted Recognitions and the Πάθη Ποικίλα

Chapter 2 looked at ancient historiography's conventional focus on deeds, with the minds of individuals represented where they contribute to explanations of events. Chapter 3 turned to the ethical exemplarity of subjects in the βίος tradition. Although both of those traditions (along with epic, tragedy, and other amatory genres) inform the genre usually called "the Greek novel" or "romance," the latter represents something new.[1] Some elements characteristic of the novel also show up in history and βίος (see esp. Xenophon's *Cyropaedia*; Ps.Callisthenes's *Life of Alexander*), but what is peripheral there becomes central in romance.[2] Plutarch, in a treatise on ancient Greek comedy, notes that ἦθος and πάθος are both important parts of characterization.[3] It seems fitting, then, to progress from the discussion of ἦθος in the previous chapter to a discussion of πάθος here, attending especially to the cognition-representing literary techniques in the novels that ancient theorists identified as productive of audience emotions. Chief among those techniques are thwarted, suspense-filled, or delayed recognitions (ἀναγνωρίσεις) and the lingering portrayal of abundant, colorful πάθη experienced by characters in their joy, grief, or madness.

This chapter begins with a discussion of existing perspectives on the Gospels and romance, then moves into a general discussion of represented minds in the genre, focusing on πάθη, then ventures into the pathos-rich terrain of two

---

1 On historiographic tendencies in the novels, see John R. Morgan, "Make-Believe and Make Believe: The Fictionality of the Greek Novels," in *Lies and Fiction in the Ancient World*, ed. Christopher Gill and T. P. Wiseman (Austin: University of Texas Press, 1993), 175–229. See Lawrence M. Wills, *The Quest of the Historical Gospel: Mark, John, and the Origins of the Gospel Genre* (London: Routledge, 1997), 11.

2 For pathos in historiography, recall how Josephus lingered on Herod's tortured relationship with Mariamme, the king "dismayed to see that his wife's unreasonable hatred of him was unconcealed" (*Ant.* 15.211–12), and oscillating in agony between anger and love. For pathos in βίος, consider a scene from the *Solon* not directly addressed in chapter 3: Plutarch has Thales contrive to make Solon think that his son had died, sending the sage into paroxysms of grief (*Sol.* 6).

3 Plutarch praises Menander for attending to both ἦθος and πάθος in his characters. See *Comp. Aristoph. et Men.* 853d2.

© KONINKLIJKE BRILL NV, LEIDEN, 2019 | DOI:10.1163/9789004396043_005

116   CHAPTER 4

case studies supplied by Chariton's *Callirhoe* and the anonymous Hellenistic Jewish novel *Aseneth*.[4]

1   John and Romance

Romance has received less attention in connection to the Gospels than history, βίος, or drama. This is partly explained by the lower profile of romance in traditional classical scholarship and partly by the dubious notion that gospels are "serious" while romances are frivolous. Entertainment has not been seen as a viable motive for the Gospels' composition, and readers have been equally reluctant to see novels as deep, formative, or otherwise instructive. The problems with these caricatures have become apparent in the years since the middle twentieth century. The Gospels are now read by many "as literature," with analytical perspectives originally developed for discussing form and narrative functions in the modern novel. Many early Christian texts, including the canonical Acts of the Apostles and even more so the so-called apocryphal gospels and acts, have been read in light of the conventions of the ancient novel.[5] At the same time, classicists have come round to the ancient novels

---

4   *Callirhoe*: The original title is uncertain. It is conventionally given as *Chaereas and Callirhoe*, following the title as printed in the one complete manuscript (Codex Florentinus Laur. Conv. Soppr. 627, saec. 13 [F], dated to the late thirteenth century), but the colophon ("So ends the story I have composed about Callirhoe" [Τοσάδε περὶ Καλλιρόης συνέγραψα]) suggests that the shorter form, using only the heroine's name, may be more original. On the manuscript evidence and the history of the text, see Goold's introduction to the Loeb volume and the introduction to the new critical text in B. P. Reardon, ed., *Chariton Aphrodisiensis: de Callirhoe narrationes amatoriae*, BSGRT (Monachii: Saur, 2004). I refer to the novel in the main text as *Callirhoe*, and in the notes and citations as *Callir.*

Aseneth: The SBL Handbook of Style (2nd ed.) recommends that the title of this work be printed *Joseph and Aseneth* (*Jos. Asen.* for short). This has the potential to introduce confusion between discussion of the text and discussion of those characters. Although it breaks the SBLHS's rule for formatting anonymous texts, I use the form *Aseneth* in the main text and *Asen.* in the notes and citations.

5   On Acts, see Susan Marie Praeder, "Luke-Acts and the Ancient Novel," in *1981 SBL Seminar Papers* (Missoula: Scholars, 1981), 269–92; Richard I. Pervo, *Profit With Delight: The Literary Genre of the Acts of the Apostles* (Minneapolis: Fortress, 1987). On the apocryphal gospels and acts, see, e.g., the essays and bibliography in Maralia P. Futre Pinheiro, Judith Perkins, and Richard Pervo, eds., *The Ancient Novel and Early Christian and Jewish Narrative: Fictional Intersections*, ANS 16 (Groningen: Barkhuis, 2012). Among the canonical gospels, Mark has probably received the most attention in connection to the novels. See, e.g., Mary Ann Tolbert, *Sowing the Gospel: Mark's World in Literary-Historical Perspective* (Minneapolis: Fortress, 1989), 55–79; Scott S. Elliott, *Reconfiguring Mark's Jesus: Narrative Criticism after Poststructuralism*, BMW 41 (Sheffield: Sheffield Phoenix Press, 2011). Richard Pervo writes

with fresh questions and enthusiasm,[6] resulting in discoveries that the novels are informed by ancient rhetorical and philosophical conversations and that they engage their socio-political environments in subtle, "serious," and sometimes subversive ways.[7]

The Gospel of Mark has received more attention in connection to the genre of the ancient novel than its three canonical counterparts. Mary Ann Tolbert's seminal 1989 work compared Mark to romance, and she claims that her findings can be extended to Matthew, Luke, and John.[8] She argues that it would be a mistake to link the Gospels to elite forms of biography, aretology, and memorabilia; proposing instead that we should look to popular Hellenistic literary forms for the "generic repertoire" of Mark's implied reader, particularly the ancient erotic novel.[9] She engages with some scholarship on the novels (esp. Hägg's *The Novel in Antiquity*) and notices formal connections with Chariton's *Callirhoe* and Xenophon's *Ephesiaca* (episodic plot, minimal introduction, a central turning point, a final recognition scene, and a repetitious, conventionalized style), while emphasizing that *"The Gospel of Mark is obviously not an ancient novel of the erotic type."*[10] She thinks the ancient novel gives us the right ballpark, however, and that closer analogues might be in a "biographical type" like Xenophon's *Cyropaedia* or the Alexander Romance.

Lawrence Wills also resists the idea that biographies like those of Plutarch and Suetonius are the best genre analogues for the canonical gospels.[11] Wills departs from Tolbert in arguing for the existence of an *Urgospel* that would have been used independently by both Mark and John,[12] but agrees with her

---

that the canonical gospels "can be understood as fictional biographies roughly analogous to the *Alexander-Romance*, the *Life of Aesop*, or Philostratus's novel about Apollonius of Tyana." Richard I. Pervo, "The Ancient Novel Becomes Christian," in *The Novel in the Ancient World*, ed. Gareth L. Schmeling, MnS 159 (Leiden: Brill, 1996), 689.

6   A spike in interest followed Bryan Reardon's 1983 publication of a collection of ancient novels, now in its second edition: B. P. Reardon, ed., *Collected Ancient Greek Novels*, 2nd ed. (Berkeley: University of California Press, 2008).

7   On philosophy in the ancient novel see, for example, the essays in John R. Morgan and Meriel Jones, eds., *Philosophical Presences in the Ancient Novel*, ANS 10 (Eelde: Barkhuis, 2007). On cultural and political identity, see Tim Whitmarsh, *Narrative and Identity in the Ancient Greek Novel: Returning Romance*, GCRW (Cambridge: Cambridge University Press, 2011).

8   Tolbert, *Sowing the Gospel*, 59.

9   Tolbert, 78.

10   Tolbert, 65 (emphasis original). Cf. Tomas Hägg, *The Novel in Antiquity*, Rev. ed. (University of California Press, 1991).

11   Wills, *The Quest of the Historical Gospel*, 10–18.

12   Cf. Tolbert's handling of similarities between Mark and John: "if such a historical/biographical type of ancient novel existed, it would clearly be the generic home of the

that literarily the Gospels represent a sub-elite culture. The independence of Mark and John makes possible the recovery of traces of the early-first century *Urgospel*, a text he believes was comparable in technique to popular biographical texts like the *Life of Aesop* and *Secundus the Silent Philosopher*.[13]

Michael E. Vines's 2002 book also deals with Mark's genre in conversation with the ancient novel. Although it does not concern the Fourth Gospel directly, much of his theoretical discussion and some of his findings are directed at the genre of "the Gospels" as a set. Vines questions the Gospels-as-Greco-Roman-biographies thesis, and is led to new conclusions by engaging with genre theory, especially the Bakhtinian ideas (1) that genres entail both a compositional form (the techniques that give a text mechanical unity) and an architechtonic form (the ideational perspective that gives a text its axiological unity) and (2) that dialogical relationships exist between text and reader, on the one hand, and between characters, on the other. He follows Bakhtin's historical perspective on the development of the novel in the Hellenistic period, where the "epic chronotope" broke down because of the increased polyglossia in the period, freeing authors from the constraints of traditional literary genres.[14] Mark, also written in this period, responds to the past (specifically, to the "epic values of traditional Judaism") and speaks to its present. Vines connects Mark to the genre of the Jewish novel on the grounds that both employ a "realistic-apocalyptic chronotope," which configures the data in such a way that Mark looks less like a Greco-Roman biography, ancient romance, or Menippean satire (the other three genres discussed in his book) and more like a Jewish novel.[15]

Most recently in connection to Mark, but with a theoretical perspective that could readily be extended to John, Scott S. Elliott argues that previous attempts to use narrative criticism to talk about the Gospels mostly fail to do justice to

---

Gospels and would explain why Mark and John, if they were indeed completely independent of each other, should happen upon the same general format for the story of Jesus." Tolbert, *Sowing the Gospel*, 65–66.

13 Wills, *The Quest of the Historical Gospel*, 12.

14 Michael E. Vines, *The Problem of Markan Genre: The Gospel of Mark and the Jewish Novel*, AcBib 3 (Leiden: Brill, 2002), 120. The chronotope is the "axiologically charged vision of the world," where "time, space, and evaluation merge into an inseperable, organic unity" (62). Cf. M. M. Bakhtin, "Forms of Time and of the Chronotope in the Novel: Notes toward a Historical Poetics," in *The Dialogic Imagination: Four Essays*, ed. Michael Holquist, trans. Caryl Emerson and Michael Holquist, UTPSS 1 (Austin: University of Texas Press, 1981), 84–258.

15 Vines, *The Problem of Markan Genre*, 152–53; 162–63. Wills is largely responsible for establishing "Jewish novel" as an academic category. In addition to *The Quest for the Historical Gospel*, see his *Ancient Jewish Novels: An Anthology* (Oxford: Oxford University Press, 2002); *The Jewish Novel in the Ancient World*, MyPo (Eugene: Wipf and Stock, 2015).

the Gospels as narratives, co-opting the vocabulary of literary critics to perpetuate historical-critical agendas, often softening or forgetting the difference between narrative characters and historical persons. He reads Mark alongside the anonymous *Life of Aesop* and Achilles Tatius's *Leucippe and Clitophon*, not in order to make a claim about genre but to construct "a matrix of interpretability" and trace "a residue of textual effects."[16] The goal is to reconsider the idea of character in a text like Mark without reference to historical persons, and without reading into Mark's characters a lot of assumptions about character predicated on modern ideologies of the self as autonomous agent.[17]

In direct connection to the Fourth Gospel, there have been fewer attempts to make use of the novels in discussions of genre. One exception is Kasper Bro Larsen's work on the "recognition type-scene" employed in the Fourth Gospel.[18] Although this type-scene is most famously visible in Homer's *Odyssey* and classical drama, in the literature contemporary to the Gospels the recognition type-scene is most prominent in the novel. The recognition type-scene in Larsen's project is a "microgenre" and a set of conventions, in the sense described in chapter 1 above. Larsen notes that the relative paucity of recognition type-scenes in ancient βίοι has perhaps contributed to the field's failure to take sufficient notice of the recognition motif.[19] Critical for Larsen's study is the idea that works belonging to one genre (he accepts βίος as the macro- or overriding genre) are able to bring in literary features from other genres. Recognition, which is central to the epistemological plot of the Fourth Gospel, provides one such transferable feature.

Meredith J. C. Warren's 2015 book on John 6 is chiefly interested in the trope of divine antagonism directed at an extraordinary mortal, a trope visible in a wide range of classical texts, but especially the Homeric epics and the romance novels.[20] As in Kasper Bro Larsen's study of the recognition type-scene, the trope of divine-human antagonism is best known from Homeric epic and ancient Athenian tragedy. In literature contemporary to the gospels, however, it is nowhere more prominent than in the novels, which make extensive use of its pathos-generating potential.

---

16   Elliott, *Reconfiguring Mark's Jesus*, 2.

17   Elliott, 2.

18   Kasper Bro Larsen, *Recognizing the Stranger: Recognition Scenes in the Gospel of John*, BibInt 93 (Leiden: Brill, 2008). See also his "The Recognition Scenes and Epistemological Reciprocity in the Fourth Gospel," in *The Gospel of John as Genre Mosaic*, ed. Kasper Bro Larsen, SANt 3 (Göttingen: Vandehoeck & Rupprecht, 2015), 341–56.

19   Larsen, *Recognizing the Stranger*, 9.

20   Meredith J. C. Warren, *My Flesh Is Meat Indeed: A Nonsacramental Reading of John 6:51–58* (Minneapolis: Fortress, 2015).

None of these projects argues that the Gospels *are* romance novels, but all suggest that stylistic features, motifs, type-scenes, and tropes *from* the romances provide comparanda for understanding the Gospels. In that spirit, I turn now to consider the conventions and literary techniques employed by ancient novelists in their manufacture of characters' minds.

2   Conventions for Representing Minds in the Novels[21]

Five complete Greek romances—sometimes called the five ideal romances or erotic novels—survive from a period spanning the first century BCE through the third/fourth century CE,[22] representative of a genre that flourished in the late Hellenistic and early Roman imperial periods.[23] Papyrus finds and sum-

---

21   Unless otherwise noted, translations in this chapter of Chariton, Xenophon of Ephesus, Longus, and Achilles Tatius follow the LCL, and translations of *Aseneth* follow Patricia Ahearne-Kroll, "Joseph and Aseneth," in *Outside the Bible: Ancient Jewish Writings Related to Scripture*, ed. Louis H. Feldman, James L. Kugel, and Lawrence H. Schiffman, vol. 1, 3 vols. (Lincoln: University of Nebraska Press, 2013), 2525–88.

22   Dating the novels is notoriously difficult. The nineteenth century's foremost authority on the novels, Erwin Rohde, wrote that Chariton could not possibly have written before the end of the fifth century CE. The standard date, after papyrus discoveries pushed the terminus ante quem to the second century CE, is the first century CE. See Ewen Bowie, "The Chronology of the Earlier Greek Novels since B. E. Perry: Revisions and Precisions," *AN* 2 (2002): 47–63.

23   The generic unity of the novels is a difficult question to negotiate, in part because (unlike history, βίος, and tragedy) they seem to have been passed over by antiquity's literary critics (a possible exception is in Macrobius's fourth century commentary on Cicero's *Dream of Scipio* [1.2.8]; cf. Tim Whitmarsh, "Introduction," in *The Cambridge Companion to the Greek and Roman Novel*, ed. Tim Whitmarsh [Cambridge: Cambridge University Press, 2008], 3n11). While the pendulum of scholarly opinion has swung from viewing these as "popular" literature of the lower classes towards the other end of the spectrum (cf. Goold's comment that "the broad category to which *Callirhoe* belongs is more appropriately termed light fiction than popular fiction.... Popular it was, but it was a popularity restricted to the top stratum of society. *Callirhoe* cannot have circulated among the lower classes, who were illiterate, uneducated, and unable to afford the purchase of books." [G. P. Goold, "Introduction," in *Chariton: Callirhoe*, LCL 481 (Cambridge: Harvard University Press, 1995), 10]). Ian Repath concurs, though not as stridently, in "Emotional Conflict and Platonic Psychology in the Greek Novel," in *Philosophical Presences in the Ancient Novel*, ed. J. R. Morgan and Meriel Jones, ANS 10 (Eelde: Barkhuis, 2007), 53–84. Repath's argument, however, depends on the authors of these texts being "philosophically literate and writing for a readership which shared that knowledge and appreciated its meaning and impact" (81). The relationship between the five ideal romances and other novelistic works is an important related consideration—there are historical novels

maries in compilers attest to the popularity of the genre and provide partial access to otherwise forgotten romances.[24] Some of these fragmentary texts seem to have followed the plot and thematic contours of the five "canonical" romances: love, travails, adventure, and happy reunion.[25] These five, all set in the pre-Roman period, each spin a yarn about a boy (handsome and noble) falling spectacularly in love with a girl (also beautiful and noble). The protagonist couple is then separated and tried by a series of ordeals jeopardizing their lives and/or chastity before they are finally reunited. The structure of the plot lends itself to narrative displays of πάθος throughout: in the beginning, there is the disruptive passion of first love; in the middle, the consternation of involuntary separation; in the end, the joy of reunion and marital consummation. The Hellenistic Jewish text *Aseneth* participates in many of these same conventions while telling a story informed by the biblical Joseph cycle. *Aseneth*, which will receive closer attention later in this chapter, is stylistically influenced by this tradition of the ancient novel together with the diction and rhythms of the Septuagint and other contemporary Jewish narratives like Judith and Greek Esther.

Ancient novels share with modern novels a focus on individual psychology and human relations.[26] If classical historiography privileges the fortunes

---

(e.g., *Apollonius King of Tyre*; Pseudo-Callisthenes, *Alexander Romance*); bawdy Roman novels (Petronius; Apuleius); Jewish novels (Tobit; Greek Esther; Judith; *Aseneth*), and later Christian apocryphal acts. On the academic politics of genre and the novels, see especially Helen Morales, "Challenging Some Orthodoxies: The Politics of Genre and the Ancient Greek Novel," in *Fiction on the Fringe: Novelistic Writing in the Post-Classical Age*, ed. Grammatiki A. Karla, MnS 310 (Leiden: Brill, 2009), 1–12.

24 Flourishing, but (if one judges from the proportion of surviving papyri that appear to be novels) not necessarily more popular than other literary forms. The survival rate and ratios of papyri, however, are not straightforward guides to "popularity" on any definition of that term. See Ewen Bowie, "Who Read the Ancient Greek Novels?," in *The Ancient Novel: Classical Paradigms and Modern Perspectives*, ed. James Tatum and Gail M. Vernazza (Hanover: Dartmouth College, 1990); Ewen Bowie, "The Readership of the Greek Novels in the Ancient World," in *The Search for the Ancient Novel*, ed. James Tatum (Baltimore: Johns Hopkins University Press, 1994), 435–59; Susan A. Stephens, "'Popularity' of the Ancient Novel," in *The Ancient Novel: Classical Paradigms and Modern Perspectives*, ed. James Tatum and Gail M. Vernazza (Hanover: Dartmouth College, 1990); Susan A. Stephens, "Who Read the Ancient Novels?," in *The Search for the Ancient Novel*, ed. James Tatum (Baltimore: Johns Hopkins University Press, 1994), 405–18.

25 For the fragmentary novels, see Susan A. Stephens and John J. Winkler, eds., *Ancient Greek Novels: The Fragments: Introduction, Text, Translation, and Commentary* (Princeton: Princeton University Press, 1995).

26 The terminological question is important because the labels "romance" and "novel" carry for modern readers connotations of interiority and experience. In modern romantic

novels, the classic story is one of interior transformation and development, the "education of a man" from uncultured and animalistic desire to a nobler love, often accompanied by marriage and fidelity. Such a deeply traced trajectory of inner development is difficult to find in the ancient novel. The application of the labels "novel" and "romance" to ancient texts is a modern convention. In contrast to previous chapters on βίος and ἱστορία, no unambiguous ancient label exists for this genre. They contain πλάσματα and *ficta*, but this by itself is not sufficient. It was sometimes said that upper-crust ancient readers would have been too embarrassed by these texts to acknowledge them, the chief piece of ancient evidence for which is a comment made by the emperor Julian remarking that "for us it will be appropriate to read such narratives as have been composed about deeds that have actually been done; but we must avoid all fictions in the form of narrative (ἀπηγγελμένα πλάσματα) such as were circulated among men in the past, for instance tales whose theme is love, and generally speaking everything of that sort (ἐρωτικὰς ὑποθέσεις καὶ πάντα ἁπλῶς τὰ τοιαῦτα). For just as not every road is suitable for consecrated priests, but the roads they travel ought to be duly assigned, so not every sort of reading is suitable for a priest. For words breed a certain sort of disposition in the soul, and little by little it arouses desires, and then on a sudden kindles a terrible blaze, against which one ought, in my opinion, to arm oneself well in advance" ("Letter to a Priest," 301b–c [trans. LCL]). The view that the novels were intended for or actually read primarily by "juveniles" and the "intellectually underdeveloped" is dismantled by Bowie, "The Readership of the Greek Novels in the Ancient World."

Whether or not there is development in the inner lives of the characters in the Greek novels, the label "novel" or "romance" creates in modern readers an expectation that representation of characters' inner lives will play a prominent role. In this, the reader will not be disappointed, though the phenomenon of free indirect speech—incomplete thoughts, non sequiturs, and the like—is not found here. Instead, the narrator puts characters in position to describe their feelings to themselves or to a companion. Ultimately, the genre's label is less important than observable patterns in its literary form and content. Distinguishing between the modern novel and the ancient novel is important for the same kinds of reasons advanced in the previous chapter for keeping βίοι separate from modern biographies. Some scholars distinguish between the terms, and find that "romance" is an appropriate label but perhaps "novel" is not. Reardon, e.g., explains the apparent deficiencies of Xenophon's *Ephesiaca* by writing that "romance accepts anything. It is not critical, intellectual, as the novel is; there is no guarantee that it will show good taste." B. P. Reardon, *The Form of Greek Romance* (Princeton: Princeton University Press, 1991), 36. But this is too clean and elitist a definition to account for how the genre label "novel" is used in practice to encompass much that is not "critical" nor "intellectual." Cf. David Konstan, *Sexual Symmetry: Love in the Ancient Novel and Related Genres* (Princeton: Princeton University Press, 1994), 5n11.

As an ancillary point, virtually all cognitive narratology has unfolded with the modern novel as its default field of play, and the modern novel is considered by all parties to be a thoroughly modern product. To call these ancient texts "novels" or "romances," then, is to be bold about our terms. A more academic alternative might be "ancient prose fictional narratives," where each term could be safely qualified. Historians of the novel, when they take notice of a figure like Chariton, are typically careful to exclude their writings from the category "novel," wanting to reserve the original of that category for Cervantes or an even later author. There is a good discussion of the history of scholarship and the academic-political stakes in Hägg, *The Novel in Antiquity*, 1–4.

ROMANCE: THWARTED RECOGNITIONS AND THE ΠΑΘΗ ΠΟΙΚΙΛΑ

of groups, there is a shift in the novels to the experiences of individuals.[27] Scholars of the ancient novel point to "the inner process" as one of the features most characteristic of the genre.[28] *Aseneth* will develop this focus on the inner process to an even greater extent, so that the central portion of the text unfolds in the heroine's mind. Sorrow, happiness, hope, fear, irresolution in the face of a difficult choice—these deliberative moments supply manifold opportunities to explore represented cognition.

By volume, most of the represented cognition in the novels belongs to the protagonist couple, but narrative light is cast also on the thoughts of secondary figures, especially jealous gods and human antagonists. Characters' inner lives are visible to the all-seeing eye of the narrator, and in this genre he revels in describing extreme πάθος.[29] Characters often experience rashes of conflicting

27   The experiences of private individuals, as should be apparent already, figure centrally in the plots of the classical novels. This shift towards the experience of the individual has been explained by Reardon as indicative of a crisis of identity in response to the shifting group dynamics of the new imperial world, with the concentration of power at the Roman center disrupting the group identities of newly subject peoples, their fortunes no longer moored to a comprehensible and clearly-delineated group, resulting in their retreat to the world of the autonomous individual and to an idealized past. Note that Romans are absent from the novels, where stories unfold in the pre-Roman Hellenistic world. Hägg summarizes and seems to approve Reardon's view, itself built on Perry's speculations about the social context of the Greek romance: "The bigger the world grows, the smaller the individual feels.... The time has passed when the individual felt he had a meaningful position in society as a 'citizen.'" Hägg, *The Novel in Antiquity*, 89–90. Such propositions seem to me too sweeping to endorse in any but the most cautious of terms.

28   On Chariton in particular, see Hägg, 16. Elsewhere Hägg observes that "the narration of concrete events takes up a comparatively small part of the text; they are generally related in 'summary.' The emphasis is instead on the reactions which they call forth in the minds of the participating characters.... Nearly half the text ... is taken up by direct speech, monologues and dialogues ... 'scene' is the predominant narrative type in the romance." Tomas Hägg, *Narrative Technique in Ancient Greek Romances: Studies of Chariton, Xenophon Ephesius, and Achilles Tatius* (Stockholm: Svenska institutet i Athen and Almqvist & Wiksells Boktryckeri Aktiebolag, 1971), 294. Cf. Edmund Cueva's definition of the ancient novel: "a lengthy prose piece, possessing a rather complex plot involving human beings, their feelings, thoughts, and emotions." Edmund P. Cueva, *The Myths of Fiction: Studies in the Canonical Greek Novels* (Ann Arbor: University of Michigan Press, 2004), 3–4.

29   The suggestion has even been advanced that Chariton wrote with Aristotle's theory of the πάθη in mind. Commenting on the introduction to Chariton's last book (*Callir.* 8.1.4 promises that this eighth and final book "will prove the most enjoyable for my readers, as an antidote to the grim events in the preceding ones" [... καθάρσιον γάρ ἐστι τῶν ἐν τοῖς πρώτοις σκυθρωπῶν]), Reardon writes "it is hard not to think that he is referring to Aristotle," that is, to the theory of κάθαρσις in *Poetics*. B. P. Reardon, "Theme, Structure, and Narrative in Chariton," in *Later Greek Literature*, ed. John J. Winkler and Gordon Willis Williams, YCS 27 (Cambridge: Cambridge University Press, 1982), 21.

πάθη, a trope that does not figure prominently in any other ancient genre.[30] Deliberative thoughts, especially in the context of characters scheming or weighing options, may be distinguished from deictic representations of emotional mental events, on the other. This latter group includes reactions to a protagonist's beauty, sudden onslaughts of anger or grief, and recognition type-scenes. The two varieties of thought interact, particularly in the relatively frequent deliberative scripts that immediately follow an experience of pathos. Or, viewed from the other direction, pathetically-laden moments of recognition presuppose past misunderstandings.[31]

Mental states in the novels are sometimes communicated when characters think or speak amongst themselves in direct or indirect discourse.[32] Far more

---

30 For discussion of the genre's characteristics in general, see Hägg, *The Novel in Antiquity*; Reardon, *The Form of Greek Romance*; Niklas Holzberg, *The Ancient Novel: An Introduction* (London: Routledge, 1995); John R. Morgan and Richard Stoneman, eds., *Greek Fiction: The Greek Novel in Context* (London: Routledge, 1994); Gareth L. Schmeling, ed., *The Novel in the Ancient World*, MnS 159 (Leiden: Brill, 1996). For a continuously updated and nearly comprehensive bibliography, see the Petronian Society Newsletter, online at http://www.ancientnarrative.com/PSN/.

How the thoughts and attitudes of characters are represented in the novels, and whether there are observable patterns in the extant novels, is one area about which little has been said. Some scholars of the novels have, however, adopted narratological perspectives which involve them in related conversations, especially concerning characterization (Koen De Temmerman, *Crafting Characters: Heroes and Heroines in the Ancient Greek Novel* [Oxford: Oxford University Press, 2014]), focalization (e.g., Kathryn S. Chew, "Focalization in Xenophon of Ephesos' *Ephesiaka*," in *Ancient Fiction and Early Christian Narrative*, ed. Ronald F. Hock, J. Bradley Chance, and Judith Perkins, SBLSymS 6 [Atlanta: Scholars, 1998], 47–60), and psychology—especially sexual psychology in Longus (e.g., Holzberg, *The Ancient Novel*, 70–74). It is interesting to see how certain scholars have interpreted the presence or absence of interior perspective when discussing such questions as authorial design and epitomizing, especially with respect to the *Ephesiaca*.

The trope of the emotions in conflict is discussed in Massimo Fusillo, "The Conflict of Emotions: A Topos in the Greek Erotic Novel," in *Oxford Readings in the Greek Novel*, ed. Simon Swain (Oxford: Oxford University Press, 1999), 60–82.

31 For a general introduction to the recognition motif, see Silvia Montiglio, *Love and Providence: Recognition in the Ancient Novel* (Oxford: Oxford University Press, 2013).

32 Monika Fludernik and Alan Palmer in their own ways show that studies of the mind in literature tend to concentrate on reported thought and/or streams of consciousness, both of which are speech acts. As a rule, attention to the "whole mind" means it is preferable to explore representations of *the mind* or *mental events* and *mental states* rather than of represented thought or consciousness, although the latter terms are included. *Inter alia*, this opens the way to analyze represented emotions as part of the minds of the characters in the novels. Monika Fludernik, *Towards a "Natural" Narratology* (London: Routledge, 1996); Alan Palmer, *Fictional Minds*, FN (Lincoln: University of Nebraska Press, 2004), 19.

often, however, mental states are presented obliquely by indicating a given figure's emotional state when she or he says or does something. That emotional state—afraid, excited, anxious, overcome with desire, etc.—is often conveyed with a single participle or adverb modifying a verb of speaking or action. This was a feature we saw in both historiography and βίος. A hallmark of the novels, however, is the asyndetic piling on of πάθη using simple abstract nouns, often with concrete nouns standing in symbolically for emotive states (commonly, e.g., tears, groans), and/or short verbal constructions. These complexes of πάθη are sometimes represented as being in conflict with each other, or as coming in a medley. They are most often attached to individual figures but are sometimes attributed to groups. This sets them apart from narrated thoughts, internal monologues, which are typically attached only to individual figures. Examples of these will be offered below.

In chapter 3, an important precursor to a treatment of character construction in βίοι was a discussion of ancient conceptions of the person and interiority. Here a comparable methodological discussion about the concept of "emotion" is in order. After noting how πάθη differ from modern notions about emotions, we will look at the particular πάθη populating the novels: their frequency, causes, effects, and the figures to which they are ascribed.

Emotions are central to modern understandings of the self and what matters in life.[33] They are, furthermore, psychological phenomena based in neurological and biological realities that applied to the ancients as much as they do to us. There are, however, important differences between ancient and modern understandings of what the emotions are, how many there are, how they are defined, what gives rise to them, how they impact behavior, whether they are "good" or "bad" (and how so), whether one can do anything about them, and (to the extent that they are under individual control) what one should do with/about them. Modern biologists and psychologists might have scientific ways of answering some of these questions, departing sharply from answers provided by ancient thinkers or modern "folk psychologies." Moral philosophers might have peculiar ways of thinking about some of these questions, in which they differ from contemporary non-philosophers. The discourse of emotions is socially constructed, and the distinction to be drawn is more complex than "ancient vs. modern"; rather, it needs to account for both change over time and potential diversity of concurrent conversations within any given society.[34]

---

33 See, e.g., E. Doyle McCarthy, "The Emotions: Senses of the Modern Self," *ÖZS* 27 (2002): 30–49.

34 E. Doyle McCarthy, "The Social Construction of Emotions: New Directions from Culture Theory," *SPEm* 2 (1994): 267–79.

126   CHAPTER 4

In thinking about the broader intellectual climate of the ancient novel, much of our evidence for what ancient Greeks and Romans thought about the emotions comes from philosophers, especially Stoics, who were interested in extirpating the emotions, achieving ἀπάθεια. The ancient Stoics viewed emotions like anger (ὀργή) as the products of flawed reasoning, and held that the experience of anger (or grief, fear, giddy happiness, etc.) could be avoided by reconsidering the reasoning that produced it. One consequence of this view of the πάθη is that children and animals, whose powers of reasoning are as yet undeveloped, are incapable of experiencing an emotion like ὀργή. This sounds very different from most modern views of anger, which might prefer to characterize it as an instinctive, involuntary reaction to pain or offence.[35] Like most of what we know about ancient discourses of emotion, this view reflects an ancient philosophical conversation. It is difficult to know the extent to which it also conveys what nonphilosophers would have meant by ὀργή and other πάθη. In any event, if the view seems counterintuitive, it should act as a brake on too-ready identifications between Greek πάθη and the English terms used to translate them.[36] A Stoic perspective on the emotions is only a part of the range of what people thought about the emotions in antiquity. To arrive at a

---

35   This is the starting point for the illuminating discussions in David Konstan, *The Emotions of the Ancient Greeks: Studies in Aristotle and Classical Literature*, RCLec (Toronto: University of Toronto Press, 2006). For the principle, see pp. ix–xiii, but note that the point is generalized beyond what the evidence can bear when he claims "The Greeks did not conceive of emotions as internal states of excitation. Rather, the emotions are elicited by our interpretation of the words, acts, and intentions of others, each in its characteristic way" (xii). The passage he cites in support of this purportedly characteristic Greek way of conceiving the emotions is a passage from Achilles Tatitus's *Leucippe and Clitophon*, in which the heroine is portrayed very much in a state of internal "excitation," even if the cause of this excitation is speech, a "verbal arrow." The text begins "Leukippe was caught up in an emotional chaos. She was vexed, ashamed, angered ..." (*Leuc. Clit.* 2.29; trans. Winkler; cited in Konstan, p. xii). We shall see that these situations, where a character experiences a medley of concurrent and clashing emotions, are conventional in the novels. Cf. Fusillo, "The Conflict of Emotions: A Topos in the Greek Erotic Novel"; Dirk M. Schenkeveld, "The Lexicon of the Narrator and His Characters: Some Aspects of Syntax and Choice of Words in Chariton's Chaereas and Callirhoe," *GCNov* 4 (1993): 17–30.

36   The idea that emotion and the emotions are culturally determined is not an uncontested claim. Some scholars treat emotion as a universal category and/or emotions as universal subcategories. Although this must be true at some level—the level, say, of chemicals acting in the brain—the moment language enters the equation and labels begin to be applied, there can be little confidence that discursive and experiential practices will maintain stable, cross-cultural correspondences. Two of the epigraphs on Konstan's book are apropos: "Il y a une psychologic implicite dans le langage" and "The fact is that once we name an emotion it takes on a life of its own." See Konstan, *The Emotions of*

fuller picture, we would need to pay attention to what non-Stoic philosophers were saying, what physicians were saying, and how the παθή are represented in other ancient corpora, including popular texts like the ancient novels.

Πάθος often means simply "the thing that happened." This is the sense in which it is used for Chariton's Dionysius, who faints after reading a letter and then, "understanding what had happened" (συνεὶς τὸ πάθος), gives orders predicated on his new understanding (*Callir.* 4.5.9).[37] Aristotle situates the πάθη within a binary metaphysics: active and passive, form and matter, actuality and potentiality.[38] For Aristotle the causes of πάθη lie outside of the bodies experiencing them, which raises questions about whether, how, and to what extent the πάθη may be controlled. Platonists, Peripatetics, Cynics, Stoics, and others would generate answers to these questions, answers in each case bound up with school-specific views of physics, ethics, and the human capacity to manage the self and its circumstances. Aristotle in many ways set the terms and trajectories for the academic discourse of the πάθη by addressing them in the *Nicomachean Ethics* and in the *Rhetoric*. The πάθη discussed in the two texts do not line up, as can be seen in Table 4.1 (πάθη discussed in both works are marked in bold). The fact that each list contains items not found in the other makes it unlikely that Aristotle meant either list to be comprehensive:

TABLE 4.1

πάθη in the *Nicomachean Ethics*	πάθη in the *Rhetoric*
ἐπιθυμία	ὀργή
ὀργή	πραότης
φόβος	φιλία
θάρσος	ἔχθρα
φθόνος	φόβος
χαρά	θάρσος

---

the Ancient Greeks, ix. Cf. Daniel Lagache, *La jalousie amoureuse; psychologie descriptive et psychanalyse. Vol. 2: La jalousie vécue* (Paris: Presses universitaires de France, 1947), 1; William Ian Miller, *The Anatomy of Disgust* (Cambridge: Harvard University Press, 1997), 31.

37   Trans. LCL, modified.

38   It is difficult to avoid beginning anywhere other than Aristotle, whose specter haunts virtually all treatments of the emotions in Greek antiquity. Every section of Konstan's treatment of the emotions among the ancient Greeks, for example, begins with Aristotle.

128   CHAPTER 4

TABLE 4.1 (*cont.*)

πάθη in the *Nicomachean Ethics*	πάθη in the *Rhetoric*
φιλία	αἰσχύνη
μῖσος	ἀναισχυντία
πόθος	χάρις
ζῆλος	ἀχἄριστία
ἔλεος	ἔλεος
	τὸ νεμεσᾶν
	φθόνος
	ζῆλος

In the *Nicomachean Ethics* (1105b21) Aristotle explains that the πάθη are one of three sets of phenomena that happen in the soul (τὰ ἐν τῇ ψυχῇ γινόμενα). The other two are "capacities" (δυνάμεις), which have to do with the extent to which a person is capable of experiencing a given emotion, and "dispositions" (ἕξεις), which have to do with formed states of character—whether a person is disposed to become angry, for example, too violently or not violently enough. Aristotle's ideal is the mean: anger, for example, should be experienced in moderation. As this is a treatise on ethics, the question of how virtue and vice apply is paramount. Aristotle's position is that none of these three states of mind is equivalent with virtue or vice, but "disposition" has the most obvious connection to ethical appraisal, as a person's character can be called virtuous or vicious depending on whether or not it is moderate with respect to the πάθη.

In the *Rhetoric*, Aristotle equates πάθος and ἐπιθυμία. Like desire, one of the functions of a πάθος is to motivate action. This is instructive in the context of the present chapter, where at issue is the question of how narrative representations of πάθη help to drive the plots of the romances. If the *Nicomachean Ethics* was concerned with the place of πάθη in the ethical life, the *Rhetoric* is concerned with their role in belief-creation, that is, as part of the rhetorician's toolkit. Fourteen are discussed, though not with equal attention and not presented in a neat list (as was the case in *Eth. nic.*). The πάθη are discussed in pairs—ὀργή with πραότης, φιλία with ἔχθρα, etc.—a strategy that explains some of the differences in the two lists. In this section of the *Rhetoric*, Aristotle's pattern is to define the πάθος, assess the state of mind of the person who experiences it, determine its object(s), and unpack the reasoning that produces it. Anger, for example, is defined as "desire, accompanied by distress, for conspicuous retaliation because of a conspicuous slight that was directed against oneself

ROMANCE: THWARTED RECOGNITIONS AND THE ΠΑΘΗ ΠΟΙΚΙΛΑ 129

or those near to one" (*Rhet.* 1378a).[39] The state of mind (πῶς τ᾽ ἔχοντες) of people who experience anger is described in terms of distress at being prevented from having something they desire, at being prevented from drinking when thirsty, for example (*Rhet.* 1379a). This way of describing the state of mind makes clear that there is always an object for anger (the person preventing), and that these states are always temporary. To speak of an "angry person," as if anger could form part of the person's permanent ἕξις, is nonsense. There are, however, circumstances that might make a person more easily productive of anger: poverty, illness, embattlement, love, thirst, and in general "longing for something and not getting it" (*Rhet.* 1379a).[40] On this model, what people long for involves, significantly for the study of πάθη in the novels, expectations and their disruption. People "long for" (ἐπιθυμεῖν) their expectations to be met and are delighted (τέρπειν) if what they expect comes to pass but angry if their expectations are disappointed (*Rhet.* 1379a). Aristotle then goes on to explore a number of situations in which people become angry (*Rhet.* 1379a–1380a), and moves on to discuss anger's opposite, πραότης.

The novels do not provide anything like Aristotle's lists of πάθη, yet we do find a variety of incidental lists that paint a picture of some of those most prominent in the romances. A recurring phenomenon in the romances is for a character to experience a medley of πάθη, often stemming from conflicts of desire. Chariton twice uses the colorful expression πάθη ποικίλα, "many-colored emotions" (*Callir.* 3.4.1; 4.5.10), introducing such a medley, but the phenomenon is found in many other narrative situations without this apt label (e.g., μυρίων παθῶν at *Callir.* 8.5.8).[41] From such narrative situations, we can piece together a constellation of the πάθη that feature prominently in the novel. In *Callirhoe* 8.5.8, the context in which a character experiences μυρίων παθῶν, Chariton names ὀργή, μετάνοια, χάρις, and φθόνος specifically. To those four, by looking at other medleys of πάθη, a fuller spectrum can be sketched: from *Callirhoe* 3.4.1, κλαόντων, θαυμαζόντων, πυνθανομένων, ἀπιστούντων;[42] from *Callirhoe* 4.5.10, θυμός, ἀθυμία, φόβος, ἀπιστία,[43] from *Callirhoe* 5.8.2, δάκρυα, χαρά, θάμβος, ἔλεος, ἀπιστία, εὐχαί;[44] and from *Callirhoe* 6.6.1, ὀργιζόμενος, λυπούμενος, φοβούμενος.[45]

---

39   Trans. George A. Kennedy, *Aristotle: On Rhetoric: A Theory of Civic Discourse* (New York: Oxford University Press, 1991).

40   Trans. Kennedy, *Aristotle: On Rhetoric.*

41   My translation.

42   καὶ ἦν ὁμοῦ πάθη ποικίλα κλαόντων, θαυμαζόντων, πυνθανομένων, ἀπιστούντων.

43   κατελάμβανε δὲ αὐτὸν πάθη ποικίλα, θυμός, ἀθυμία, φόβος, ἀπιστία.

44   ἔδοξας ἂν ἐν θεάτρῳ παρεῖναι μυρίων παθῶν πλήρει· πάντα ἦν ὁμοῦ, δάκρυα, χαρά, θάμβος, ἔλεος, ἀπιστία, εὐχαί.

45   ἀπηλλάττετο μυρίων παθῶν μεστός, ὀργιζόμενος μὲν Καλλιρόῃ, λυπούμενος δὲ ἐφ᾽ ἑαυτῷ, φοβούμενος.

The πάθη are expressed more often using participles or verbs than with abstract nouns, and are often represented metynomically with bodily functions (esp. tears to signify grief).[46] When the slave Phocas and the nobleman Dionysius arrange for Callirhoe to learn that Chaereas has been killed, for example, the news results in torn clothing, beaten eyes and cheeks, and flight into the house, a spectacle that prompts Dionysius's decision to "let her emotions take their course (Διονύσιος δὲ ἐξουσίαν ἔδωκε τῷ πάθει)" (*Callir.* 3.10.3).[47] This scene illustrates the difficulty or even futility of trying to reckon how often a given πάθος features in the novel, since without Dionysius's remark, there would be no unambiguous sign that Callirhoe's actions constituted an outburst of something an ancient Greek would label as pathetic.

Using only the πάθη that are identified as such allows us to note their relative frequency and the functions they perform. This list gives the frequency of the terms in *Callirhoe* explicitly labeled as πάθη: ἀθυμία (1); ἀπιστέω (10); ἀπιστία (4); δάκρυα (28); δακρύω (16); ἐλεέω (13); ἔλεος (8); εὐχή (6); εὔχομαι (10); θάμβος (3); θαῦμα (1); θαυμαζόμαι (21); θυμός (4); θυμόω (2); κλαίω (26); λυπέω (34); λύπη (14); μετανοέω (10); μετάνοια (2); ὀργή (8); ὀργίζω (11); πυνθάνομαι (26); φθονέω (13); φθόνος (4); φοβέω (27); φόβος (12); χαίρω (24); χαρά (12); χάρις (42). Again, we could catalogue other πάθη in the novel using more expansive criteria; this list is limited to those terms that are explicitly marked at least once in the novel as πάθη.[48] The figures in parentheses indicate the number of times the term shows up in *Callirhoe* and offer a snapshot of the relative frequency and prominence of certain πάθη in that novel. The word family associated with grief stands out; fear and gratitude also feature prominently. In view of the fact that ordeals occupy most of the narrative, this is unsurprising.

A concept that pervades the novels, despite its surprising absence from both Aristotle's discussions and the explicitly-identified πάθη in Chariton is ἔρως (mentioned 59 times in *Callirhoe*) and its verbal counterpart ἐράω (31). The high frequency is not surprising. First, Chariton personifies Eros as a mischievous deity, who, like Tyche (Fortune) and Aphrodite, acts or is perceived by the characters as acting for and against the characters' interests. Second, ἔρως as a concept is closely related to φιλία, which is an explicit topic in Aristotle's discussions, though not among the explicitly identified πάθη in Chariton.[49]

---

46 Konstan notes the absence of λύπη from Aristotle's lists, but grief—especially if understood as that which is symbolized by wailing and tears—is ubiquitous in the romances. Konstan, *The Emotions of the Ancient Greeks*, xi, cf. 244–58.

47 Trans. Reardon, *Collected Ancient Greek Novels.*

48 The list also includes the noun even if only the verb is marked as a πάθος and vice-versa.

49 Most writers would distinguish ἔρως from φιλία insofar as the former involves sexual desire and the latter is more about a sense of duty than any sort of subjective feeling

ROMANCE: THWARTED RECOGNITIONS AND THE ΠΑΘΗ ΠΟΙΚΙΛΑ

Third, ἔρως in Chariton and other novels, including *Aseneth*, is often "at first sight" (e.g., ἅπαξ ἰδών at *Callir.* 2.4.4), rather than something felt in the context of a welter of mixed emotions experienced between familiars. And though ἔρως is not labeled a πάθος, the πάθος affecting the king when he catches sight of the heroine is described as an ἐρωτικὸν πάθος (*Callir.* 4.6.7), which is a standard effect of a heroine's beauty on the male characters she encounters. The expression is also found in Chariton's introductory label for his story: πάθος ἐρωτικὸν ἐν Συρακούσαις γενόμενον, "a love story which took place in Syracuse" (*Callir.* 1.1.1).[50]

Πάθος is a powerful motivating factor in the novels, visible in a typical case like this: "So the king was moved (ὥρμησεν) to summon Mithridates to trial. But a different sentiment (ἄλλο δὲ πάθος) prompted him to send for the beautiful woman as well" (*Callir.* 4.6.7).[51] Ἄλλος communicates that a πάθος is motivationally equivalent to a ὁρμή to put Mithridates on trial. The use of πάθος to explain a subsequent action in the narrative is reminiscent of Aristotle's link between πάθος and ἐπιθυμία in the *Rhetoric*, when he described the former as having the power to produce an action.

Chariton frequently compares the effect of the emotions on their characters with language reminiscent of Homer's descriptions of his heroes' mortal injuries. One example has already been cited above in connection to a point about status and self-control. Dionysius, love-smitten, "tried to conceal the τραῦμα, as became somebody well-brought up who made especial claim to virtue" (*Callir.* 2.4.1).[52] Already in the first chapter of the book, Callirhoe's beauty has this effect on Chaereas: "So smitten (μετὰ τοῦ τραύματος), Chaereas could barely make his way home. Like a hero mortally wounded (τρωθείς) in battle, he was too proud to fall but too weak to stand" (*Callir.* 1.1.7). Other novelists use this imagery as well. Achilles Tatius, notable for his parenthetical comments about the effects of πάθος on human behavior, describes the effects of love according

---

of affection. See, e.g., Malcolm Heath, *The Poetics of Greek Tragedy* (Stanford: Stanford University Press, 1987), 73–74; Simon Goldhill, *Reading Greek Tragedy* (Cambridge: Cambridge University Press, 1986), 82.

50   David Konstan notes that mutually-reciprocal ἔρως is one of the ways in which the Greek novels stand apart from other species of amatory literature, especially the Roman novels, New Comedy, and love poetry. This may provide an illuminating point of comparison with discussions about reciprocity in the Fourth Gospel. On reciprocity in John, see the long history of scholarship on mutuality between the Johannine Father and Son and between the Son and those who believe in him. See most recently Larsen, "The Recognition Scenes and Epistemological Reciprocity in the Fourth Gospel."

51   Trans. LCL, modified.

52   Trans. LCL, modified.

132   CHAPTER 4

to this program: the soul, wounded by love, becomes susceptible to a variety of
emotions (*Leuc. Clit.* 1.4.4–5).[53]

Representations of emotional trauma are amplified in the novels, eclipsing
representations of physical suffering.[54] Sometimes hints are provided that the
bodies of the protagonists have suffered, but more often "physical pain is written out of the picture, as if it is so far outweighed by mental suffering as to be
negligible."[55] Illustrations might be found in Chariton's descriptions of suffering divinely imposed by Eros, or in Xenophon's Habrocomes crucified with no
mention of physical pain. Habrocomes's only thoughts, as far as his readers
can see, are for Anthia. He consoles himself with the (mistaken) thought that
Anthia is also dead (Xenophon, *Eph.* 4.2).

The passions are frequently described using physical proxies (knees buck-
ling, tears gushing), presenting the emotions as objects externally focalized.
When Callirhoe lays eyes on her bridegroom, and discovers him to be Chaereas,
she "like a dying lamp once it is replenished with oil, flamed into life again and
became taller and stronger" (*Callir.* 1.1.15). The essence of her emotional state,
if not the finer points to which the narrator makes only readers and Callirhoe
herself aware, is on view to the onlookers in the storyworld. "When she came
into the open, all were astounded, as when Artemis appears to hunters in lonely places. Many of the onlookers even knelt in homage. All were entranced by
Callirhoe and congratulated Chaereas" (*Callir.* 1.1.16). She wears her emotions
on her sleeve, so to speak, and her entrancing emotions make her beautiful.[56]

For the novelists, the πάθη are a fertile field to cultivate. We would not be far
wrong were we to describe the genre in terms of manufacturing narrative opportunities to express emotion. The next section will explore mechanisms by
which Chariton achieves those results.

---

53   E.g., Achilles Tatius, *Leuc. Clit.* 1.6; 2.29; 3.11; 5.13; 6.6–7; 6.19; 7.4. Cf. Kathryn S. Chew,
     "Achilles Tatius, Sophistic Master of Novelistic Conventions," in *A Companion to the
     Ancient Novel*, ed. Edmund P. Cueva and Shannon N. Byrne, BCAW (Chichester, West
     Sussex: Wiley Blackwell, 2014), 69.

54   Jason König has done some excellent work on this subject, comparing the novelists on
     this theme to contemporaries like Aelius Aristides and Christian hagiographers. See Jason
     König, "Body and Text," in *The Cambridge Companion to the Greek and Roman Novel*, ed.
     Tim Whitmarsh (Cambridge: Cambridge University Press, 2008), 129–30.

55   König, 130.

56   The reverse of this is also possible, where a character's looks are impaired by negative
     emotions (e.g., Chaereas at *Callir.* 1.1.7–9; Dionysius at *Callir.* 2.7.4).

ROMANCE: THWARTED RECOGNITIONS AND THE ΠΑΘΗ ΠΟΙΚΙΛΑ

3 Chariton's *Callirhoe*

Chariton's *Callirhoe*, which is probably the earliest of the surviving ideal novels,[57] follows the adventures of the titular character, a newlywed Syracusan girl. Jilted suitors lead her young husband Chaereas to doubt her fidelity, with the result that he attacks her, leaving her apparently (from the perspective of the story's characters) dead. She is entombed, revived, abducted by tomb-robbers, and sold as a slave to a wealthy Ionian nobleman named Dionysius. Chaereas pursues her as far as Babylon, where the Persian king is put in the position of having to decide whether she ought to go with Chaereas or Dionysius, a kind and "civilized" man she has subsequently married in an effort to hide the fact that she is pregnant with Chaereas's child. After several additional misadventures, Chaereas and Callirhoe are finally reunited and return to Syracuse.

The novels have inspired an abundance of narratological studies.[58] Narratologists excel at finding broad patterns; in the novels those patterns might be of the "love, travails, happily-ever-after" or "union, separation, reunion" varieties.[59] These are pathos-infused transactions. It comes as no surprise, then, that the novels, consequently, are teeming with πάθη. Chariton even casts his novel in a pathetic register, introducing it as a πάθος ἐρωτικὸν ἐν Συρακούσαις γενόμενον, "a love story which took place in Syracuse" (*Callir.* 1.1.1). Sorrow, happiness, hope, fear, and irresolution figure on almost every page. Consider the reaction of the Persian King on reading a letter: "On reading it,

---

57   The first major monograph on the Greek novels, E. Rohde's *Der griechische Roman* (first ed. 1876), dated Chariton to the very end of the classical period (c. 500 CE), taking the simplicity of Chariton's prose for a sign of literary decadence. See Erwin Rohde, *Der griechische Roman und seine Vorläufer*, 3rd ed. (Leipzig: Breitkopf & Härtel, 1914). That model was challenged by Wilhelm Schmid in his article "Chariton," in PRE, Neue bearbeitung, III 2 (Stuttgart: J. B. Metzler, 1899), 2168–71. Schmid proposed a date in the first century on linguistic grounds. This early dating was subsequently justified by the discovery of papyrus fragments from the mid-second century CE, representing the latest possible date for its composition. The prevailing opinion now is that it stems from the first century BCE or CE. There is a possible reference to a literary work *Callirhoe* in the *Satires* of Persius, which may point to a composition during or before the 50s CE. For the history of scholarship on the dating of Chariton and the other novels, see Reardon, *The Form of Greek Romance*, 9–10; Bowie, "The Chronology of the Earlier Greek Novels since B. E. Perry."

58   E.g., Romain Brethes, "Pour une typologie du rire dans les romans grecs: topos littéraire, jeu narratologique et nouvelle lecture du monde," BAGB 1 (2003): 113–129; John R. Morgan, "Nymphs, Neighbours and Narrators: A Narratological Approach to Longus," *Mn.*, 2003, 171–190; De Temmerman, *Crafting Characters*, 26–45.

59   These are patterns particular to the plot; patterns in characterization also exist (e.g., free, noble boys and girls in the protagonists' roles; pirates, bandits, brigands, governors acting as antagonists; servants and companions acting for both groups in supporting roles).

134   CHAPTER 4

the king was overcome with a variety of emotions (μυρίων παθῶν). He was angry at the capture of what he held most dear and he regretted forcing Chaereas to desert him; then again he was grateful to him for recovering the queen, but he was grieved that he should not be seeing Callirhoe any more; and, above all, he was filled with envy, and muttered, 'Happy Chaereas, he is luckier than I!'" (*Callir.* 8.5.8).

The point of view in this passage can be described either as that of an omniscient narrator or that of the king himself. What used to be discussed under headings like "perspective" and "point of view" is now generally treated using the more precise categories of "focalization" as formulated in Gérard Genette's *Narrative Discourse: An Essay in Method.*[60] Genette identified three modes of focalization: zero, internal, and external. "Zero focalization" or "nonfocalization" refers to the classical narrative, including this scene with the king and the letter, and most of what we encounter in the ancient novels. Internal focalization involves especially situations where the narrator is a character. Internally focalized narratives can be fixed (focalized consistently through a single character), variable (focalized through a succession of characters), or multiple (the same narrative event or object focalized through more than one character). Achilles Tatius's *Leucippe and Clitophon* is focalized through the character Clitophon,[61] and Heliodorus's *Aethiopica* contains variable and multiple internal focalization. Chariton occasionally employs multiple internal focalization when a character recounts for a new audience from his perspective events that have already been narrated earlier and at greater length (e.g., Chaereas to the Syracusans at *Callir.* 8.7.1–8.8.11). External focalization involves a story that is told without special access to the minds of characters in the narrative, and would not apply to any of the ancient texts considered in this book. Confusion between internal and external focalization has led some literary theorists to revise Genette's categories. The most impactful revisions come from Mieke Bal, who adds clarity by distinguishing between focalizors and focalized objects. Focalizors can be external or internal to the narrative, and focalized objects can be either perceptible or non-perceptible. Genette's external focalization would correspond to focalizors with access only to perceptible objects. Again,

---

60   Gérard Genette, *Narrative Discourse: An Essay in Method* (Ithaca: Cornell University Press, 1980).

61   But, importantly, it is an older and wiser version of Clitophon acting as external narrator of his youthful exploits. A narrative internally focalized through a character is not interchangeable with the concept of a "first person narrative," for most of what we think of as "first person narratives" are actually narrated in hindsight. See Mieke Bal, *Narratology: Introduction to the Theory of Narrative*, 3rd ed. (Toronto: University of Toronto Press, 2009), 161.

ROMANCE: THWARTED RECOGNITIONS AND THE ΠΑΘΗ ΠΟΙΚΙΛΑ

these are absent from the ancient texts considered here. Genette's zero focalization corresponds to Bal's external focalizor with access to non-perceptible objects, and Genette's internal focalization corresponds to Bal's internal focalizor with access to non-perceptible objects. The confusion lies in this third category since, as Bal demonstrates, a narrative can have an internal focalizor whose view is restricted to perceptible objects. Non-perceptible objects include any speech that is unspoken, thought reports, feelings, and some of the πάθη. Context determines what is perceptible and non-perceptible. A monologue may be introduced by a verb of speech, but context will determine whether the monologue is a perceptible or non-perceptible object, depending on whether or not other characters are present to hear it. Bal also distinguishes between simple (Mary participates in the rally) and complex (Michele saw that Mary participated in the rally) focalization.[62]

Another way in which the language of focalization is helpful is that it allows for distinctions to be drawn between the narrator's work of *telling* what happened and the characters' work of (*mis*)*perceiving*, (*mis*)*interpreting*, and (*mis*)*understanding* what transpires in the story. The creation of a conceptual divide between "how things are" and "how things appear to be" is essential in the ancient novels, where characters rarely appreciate the full significance of their situations. I will say more below about the processes by which characters in the novels realize narrative "facts" already known to the omniscient narrator and often also to the reader. Simple "character text" is mainly comprised of direct speech, and the focalizor is the character giving the speech. Simple "narrator text" is what we typically think of as third person narration, usually with an omniscient narrator external to the narrative. In the novels, though there are no unreliable narrators, there are many mistaken focalizors.

One of the *loci classici* in the ancient novels to see internal subject focalization at work is the beginning of Heliodorus's novel, which opens *in media res* on a beach scene focalized through the eyes of approaching bandits. In Bal's terms, this scene might be described as having an internal focalizor (the bandits) of a perceptible object (the beach scene). The narrator, who is distinct from the bandits, knows the scene's significance, as do other characters (the hero and heroine, unbeknownst to the bandits, lie alive among the dead bodies). Here and elsewhere, Heliodorus contains the most extreme examples of restricted observer focalization, though the phenomenon of focalizing through characters (rather than just through the omniscient narrator) is present in all extant ancient novels. The beauty of the heroes, for example, is appreciated largely through the perspective of other characters finding them attractive.

---

62 Bal, 160–61.

Callirhoe's beauty is described in external narrator speech (e.g., at *Callir.* 1.1.1; 6.2.2), but more often with internal focalization (e.g., Dionysius at *Callir.* 1.4.2; the bandit Theron at *Callir.* 1.11.6–7; the countrywomen on Dionysius's estate at *Callir.* 2.2.3–4; the king at *Callir.* 6.3.5; the eunuch Artaxerxes at *Callir.* 6.5.2; the king's wife Statira at *Callir.* 8.4.13–14). The use of internal focalization in these situations allows the narrator to "show" rather than simply "tell" his readers about the characters as aesthetic objects.[63]

Appreciating the play of focalization in the novels entails developing a sense of the desires that motivate internal focalizing subjects. The extant novels appear to operate with divine and human levels of motivation—both gods and humans act on their desires. Chariton's novel is framed by the desires of the suitors, of Eros, and of the political rivals Hermocrates and Ariston. After introducing himself ("Chariton of Aphrodisias, clerk of the lawyer Athenagoras") and his subject ("I am going to relate a love story which took place in Syracuse"), Chariton's narrative proper begins with the fictional daughter of the historical Hermocrates, a leader famous in the ancient world for a naval triumph against Athens in 413 BCE.[64] "Hermocrates, ruler of Syracuse, victor over the Athenians, had a daughter named Callirhoe, a marvel of a girl and the idol of all Sicily" (*Callir.* 1.1.1). What makes Callirhoe marvelous is her beauty: "her beauty was not so much human as divine, not that of a Nereid or a mountain nymph either, but of Aphrodite herself." And this divine beauty functions like a beacon to eligible bachelors everywhere: "Reports of this incredible vision spread far and wide. Suitors came pouring into Syracuse, potentates and

---

63   Kathryn Chew has argued that Xenophon starts out with zero degree focalization and then drops it for a variable internal focalization. Chew, "Focalization in Xenophon of Ephesos' *Ephesiaka*." Massimo Fusillo observes that Chariton's narrator, in a comparison with the Homeric narrator, "presents a more varied profile," preserving "a basic narratorial omniscience," but often coming "close to the viewpoint of his characters in short passages where he introduces subjective elements." Fusillo, "The Conflict of Emotions: A Topos in the Greek Erotic Novel," 68. For "this distinctive psychological aspect of Chariton's narrative," Fusillo points the reader to Hägg, *Narrative Technique in Ancient Greek Romances*, 114–19; Isolde Stark, "Zur Erzählperspektive im griechischen Liebesroman," *Ph.* 128 (1984): 260; C. Ruiz-Montero, *La estructura de la novela griega* (Salamanca: Ediciones Universidad de Salamanca, 1988), 318–19; Massimo Fusillo, *Il romanzo greco: polifonia ed eros* (Venice: Marsilio Editori, 1989), 120–22.

64   This sets the novel on a more concretely "historical" footing than any of the other five ideal romances. Although some commentators have used it to describe Chariton as "historical fiction" or the like, in my view its more fundamental function is to conjure up for readers familiar with Greek history a well-rounded narrative world: the presence of a named minor character (Hermocrates) who is also a historical figure is no more significant than the presence of a place name which corresponds to a place in the real world (e.g., Syracuse, Athens, Ionia, Egypt).

princes, not only from Sicily, but from Italy, the continent, and the peoples of the continent" (*Callir.* 1.1.2). Her beauty engenders desire, setting the plot in motion. Alongside these desiring human actors are gods, notably Eros, who "wanted to make a match of his own devising (ὁ δὲ ῎Ερως ζεῦγος ἴδιον ἠθέλησε συμπλέξαι)" (*Callir.* 1.1.3). The heroine's beauty is often the narrative fact that catapults the protagonists into a dangerous dilemma. Another consequence of the beauty of the hero and heroine in all the novels is that it brings them perilously close to the divine plane.

As in most ancient Greek literature, the novels reflect no simple binary between human and divine. Some humans—inevitably the hero or heroine in the novels—are so godlike in appearance that they are mistaken for deities. Callirhoe is mistaken for a goddess by dozens of characters (e.g., by Leonas at *Callir.* 1.14.1; Dionysius at *Callir.* 2.3.6; boatsmen and a crowd in *Callir.* 3.2.15; the Persian king at *Callir.* 6.3.5). She is usually taken for Aphrodite, though she is also compared obliquely to Artemis (*Callir.* 1.1.16; 4.7.5; 6.4.7) and Thetis (*Callir.* 3.3.6; 6.3.5). Some gods act directly in the narrative, with their thoughts, dispositions, motives, and πάθη as much on display as those of their human counterparts. We saw above how the plans of Eros ran against those of Callirhoe's suitors; his disposition ("being a god who likes to win" at *Callir.* 6.4.5; cf. 1.1.4; "naturally optimistic" at *Callir.* 2.6.4; "naturally curious" at *Callir.* 3.9.4; "delights in deceit and trickery" at *Callir.* 4.4.5) and his thought processes (e.g., at *Callir.* 2.4.5) are also on display.

Human and divine desires are often in conflict in this genre. Chariton illustrates this with Eros and Chaereas at the beginning of his novel, and again later when Aphrodite acts against Dionysius.[65] This motif is prominent in other genres as well, particularly in epic and tragedy.[66]

The ability to exercise self-control over one's πάθη was culturally prized in the Hellenistic world, where the novels are set, and the Roman imperial world, where most of these novels were written. This ability was linked to gender and social status.[67] One could expect that women and people of low social classes

---

65 Dionysius thinks mistakenly that his accomplishments on behalf of the Persian king Artaxerxes, who is deciding whether Callirhoe will go to himself or to Chaereas, will cause the Great King to decide in his favor. But Aphrodite upsets his expectations. Also, it is revealed at the end of the narrative that it was Aphrodite who, angered at Chaereas's jealous attack on his new bride, decided to take pity on him after "having harassed by land and sea the handsome couple she had originally brought together" (*Callir.* 8.1.3). This theme is not unique to the novels; it can, like so much else in the novels, be traced back to Homer.

66 Cf. the discussion of Euripides's *Hippolytus* in chapter 5, below.

67 The gendered dimension of the emotional discourse in Chariton, especially concerning ὀργή, is the focus of J. H. D. Scourfield, "Anger and Gender in Chariton's *Chaereas and Callirhoe*," in *Ancient Anger: Perspectives from Homer to Galen*, ed. Susanna Braund

138   CHAPTER 4

would be unable to control πάθη, a stereotype observable in Heliodorus's towns-women, who are so overwhelmed by Theagenes's handsomeness that they pelt him with apples and flowers (*Aeth.* 3.3.8).[68] Conversely, it is assumed that men of high class should be able to exercise restraint. The heroines of the novels are on several occasions able to turn this to their advantage. Nowhere is it better illustrated than by Chariton's Dionysius, who refuses to touch Callirhoe with-out her consent and reproaches himself for wanting to yield to base desires. When Callirhoe finally agrees to marry Dionysius, his "passion raged fiercely and would not suffer the wedding to be delayed; self-control is painful when desire can be satisfied. He was a civilized man; but he had been overwhelmed by a storm—his heart was submerged, but still he forced himself to hold his head above the towering waves of his passion" (*Callir.* 3.2.6).[69] This scene is im-portant for the metaphorical language in which it describes Dionysius's pathos and for the invocation of the sententia that "self-control is painful when desire can be satisfied," but what is important to notice at present is the expectation of self-control over desires (ἐξουσίαν ἐπιθυμίας) for the "civilized man" (ἀνὴρ πεπαιδευμένος).[70] This dimension of Dionysius's nobility is highlighted by the contrast with the servant Leonas, who counsels him that he can take her if he pleases (*Callir.* 2.6.2).[71]

Callirhoe partakes in the noble restraint of πάθη as well, despite her gen-der. Dionysius at one point recognizes in her a "kinship of character" (τρόπου συγγένεια). Some of her πάθη, including her initial attraction to Chaereas, she tries to conceal (*Callir.* 1.1.14; 1.3.6; 1.11.2; 2.5.7; 6.6.8; cf. Heliodorus, *Aeth.* 4.6.1; 6.9.4). This nobility, however, does not result in absolute demurral. In fact, Callirhoe's nobility leads her to flare up (ἠγανάκτησεν) on several occasions, "full of spirit" (φρονήματος πλήρης) whenever she senses an affront to her character (e.g., *Callir.* 1.3.6; 2.5.8–9). Both her tendency to flare up and her Dionysius-like

---

and Glenn W. Most, YCS 32 (Cambridge: Cambridge University Press, 2004). For a more general treatment of ancient anger management, see William V. Harris, *Restraining Rage: The Ideology of Anger Control in Classical Antiquity* (Cambridge: Harvard University Press, 2009).

68   "And all those women of the lower orders who were incapable of controlling and con-cealing their emotions (τὸ τῆς ψυχῆς πάθος ἐγκρατείᾳ κρύπτειν ἀδύνατοι) pelted him with apples and flowers in the hope of attracting his goodwill."

69   Trans. Reardon, *Collected Ancient Greek Novels.*

70   Cf. Chariton's earlier remark about the same character: "Dionysius had been wounded [by love], but tried to conceal the wound, as became an educated man (πεπαιδευμένος ἀνήρ) who made especial claim to virtue" (*Callir.* 2.4.1).

71   Another good example is found in the reaction of the (high status) Persian king Artaxerxes to advice from the (low status) eunuch Artaxates that the only way to remedy his desire would be to take the object of desire: "Do not accuse me of lacking self-control (μηδεμίαν μου καταγνῷς ἀκρασίαν). I am not overcome to that extent!" (*Callir.* 6.3.8).

restraint are marvelously illustrated in a scene where she is propositioned by the king's eunuch on behalf of his master. His words "pierced Callirhoe's heart like a sword-thrust, but she pretended not to understand (προσεποιεῖτο δὲ μὴ συνιέναι)," leading the eunuch to think he had failed to express his meaning clearly enough (δόξας δὲ ὁ εὐνοῦχος ὅτι ἀσαφῶς εἴρηκεν ὃ ἤθελε). When he tries again, "Callirhoe's first impulse (τὸ μὲν πρῶτον ὥρμησεν) was, if she could, to pluck out the eyes of this corrupter; but as a polite and intelligent woman (πεπαιδευμένη καὶ φρενήρης), she quickly remembered where she was, who she was, and who was talking to her (ταχέως λογισαμένη καὶ τὸν τόπον καὶ τίς ἐστιν αὐτὴ καὶ τίς ὁ λέγων). So she restrained her anger (τὴν ὀργὴν μετέβαλε) and gave the oriental an evasive reply" (*Callir.* 6.5.7–8). The scene is remarkable not only for characterizing Callirhoe as πεπαιδευμένη (like Dionysius), but also for walking the reader through the process by which she mastered her anger.

Some scholars have seen in Chariton's Chaereas an instance of "development" along this trajectory from lack of control to mature, "civilized" control over his anger.[72] Processes of education, maturation, and change of disposition are evidently themes in the novels, as will also be illustrated strikingly in Aseneth's case.

Earlier we noted that the novels frequently put divine and human desires in conflict. Slighted by Chaereas and Callirhoe's σωφροσύνη, the god Eros, who "likes winning and enjoys unexpected triumphs" (*Callir.* 1.1.4), launches an assault on their souls.[73]

Describing Eros as loving to win or Dionysius as one who keeps his feelings in check are examples of characterization by disposition. Again, individual gods and humans have individual dispositions, though these are often stereotyped and thus predictable. Hermocrates the statesman is patriotic and authoritative (*Callir.* 1.1.12), Callirhoe as a general's daughter is φρονήματος πλήρης (*Callir.* 1.3.6; 2.8.1), Theron the chief bandit is οἷα δεινὸς ἀνὴρ (*Callir.* 1.9.6); the serving-woman Plangon is "a quick-witted creature" (ἐντρεχής) and able to read between the lines of her master's orders (*Callir.* 2.6.5). Disposition is to a great extent—not to say totally—predetermined in the novels' storyworlds by

---

72 Scourfield, "Anger and Gender in Chariton's *Chaereas and Callirhoe*," 173–75. Hägg takes a different view: "In Chariton too we observed a strong interest in psychology, but with him it is always a matter of one particular type or character being put in different situations, of his or her different reactions being aptly described. But there is never a development in the sense that a character is changed by enduring changing fortunes. Chaereas may seem to be two different people in the first and second half of the novel, the emotional lover and the brave warrior, but what changes is his situation, not his character." Hägg, *The Novel in Antiquity*, 53.

73 Trans. LCL, modified.

social status, gender, and group affiliation. Chariton writes aphoristically of women that they are easy prey when they think they are loved (*Callir.* 1.4.2); of slaves that with money and no supervision they will launch themselves unrestrainedly into debauchery (*Callir.* 4.5.4–5); of barbarians that they are naturally "woman-crazy" (γυναιμανές; *Callir.* 5.2.6); of those brought up under despotism that they think nothing is impossible for the king (*Callir.* 6.6.10); and implicitly of Egyptians (who make up the bulk of Chaereas's fighting force in book 7) that they need to be managed by a wise Greek in order to have success in battle. The eunuch, planning a sexual rendezvous for Callirhoe and the king, Chariton tells us, was thinking ὡς εὐνοῦχος, ὡς δοῦλος, ὡς βάρβαρος (*Callir.* 6.4.10). Chaereas, by contrast, when he is courageous, loyal, and showing good sense, is being true to his noble nature and upbringing (φύσεως ἀγαθῆς καὶ παιδείας; *Callir.* 7.2.5). The stereotyping of disposition corresponds to Theon's dictum, discussed in chapter 1 above, about the kinds of speech appropriate to characters according to their social stations: "Different ways of speaking would also be fitting by nature for a woman and for a man, and by status for a slave and a free man, and by activities for a soldier and a farmer, and by state of mind for a lover and a temperate man, and by their origin the words of a Laconian, sparse and clear, differ from those of a man of Attica, which are voluble" (Theon 116).[74]

Just as the narrator takes for granted that the dispositions of lower-class women or noble men or barbarians are specific and predictable, sententiae in the novels frequently purport to explain why a character acts or feels a certain way. Explaining why Dionysius's passion raged fiercely, we saw above, Chariton explains that "self-control is painful when desire can be satisfied" (*Callir.* 3.2.6).[75] Later, explaining how it is that Theron revealed himself to Chaereas and the boarding party, despite knowing that it would mean his eventual death, the narrator observes that "man is by nature a life-loving creature and even in the worst misfortunes does not despair of a change for the better, since the god who created men has implanted this illusion in all so that they should not run away from the misery of life" (*Callir.* 3.3.16). Then, when Theron is being questioned before the Syracusans, the narrator offers this principle as a way of explanation for his action: "He held out for a long time and almost succeeded in overcoming the tortures. But conscience is a powerful force in everyone, and truth prevails in the end" (*Callir.* 3.4.13). Or consider this scene, involving the novel's heroine: after hearing about the appearance of two foreigners at the shrine of Aphrodite in Ionia, "Callirhoe suspected the truth, for people are apt

---

74   Trans. George A. Kennedy, *Progymnasmata: Greek Textbooks of Prose Composition and Rhetoric*, WGRW 10 (Atlanta: SBL, 2003).

75   Trans. Reardon, *Collected Ancient Greek Novels*.

ROMANCE: THWARTED RECOGNITIONS AND THE ΠΑΘΗ ΠΟΙΚΙΛΑ

to believe what they want to" (*Callir.* 3.9.3). Such statements usually originate with the narrator, but sometimes they are internally focalized using a character, as when Callirhoe tells Dionysius about her conversation with the priestess of Aphrodite's shrine: "Rejoining Dionysius, she told him only what she had heard from the priestess, fully aware that love is naturally curious and that Dionysius himself would try to ferret out what had taken place" (*Callir.* 3.9.4). There is no reason to think in this case that the narrator would want to distance himself from this *sententia* about the nature of love, although in other cases it may be that a narrator rejects what a character takes for a truism.[76]

A common tactic for producing emotion is to engineer situations where characters are faced with apparently impossible choices. Take Chaereas, for example, torn between his desire to pursue Callirhoe (alive in Ionia, according to the captured pirate Theron) and staying home with his infirm and dying father and his Hecuba-channeling mother (*Callir.* 3.5.5).[77] Chaereas responds by attempting suicide, a response which has been discussed in terms of what it says about gender and genre and the potentially comedic function it serves— suicide as a sort of banana peel pratfall.[78] Whether or not it is a knowing send-up of "typical" women and emotional Homeric heroes, whether or not it is a literary wink at the stage of New Comedy, this episode illustrates the narrative pattern of manufacturing artificial dilemmas to excite characters' emotions.

The most frequent situation in which these tensive moments are created is the assault on the will of a protagonist, often in chastity ordeals.[79] The two competing desires are to live and to maintain one's sexual integrity.[80] Chariton

---

76   The narrator distances himself from some "barbarian" assumptions, such as that underestimation Artaxates makes of Greek pride and nobility (*Callir.* 6.4.10).

77   The request of Chaereas's father, "Just wait a few days so that I can die in your arms; then bury me and go" is reminiscent of the man Jesus calls to be a disciple, who asks that he be allowed first "to go and bury my father" (Matt 8.21; cf. Luke 9.59). The request of Chaereas's mother, "I beg you, my child, do not leave me here all alone, but put me on the boat. I shall be a light load, but if I prove a burden and a nuisance, throw me into the sea you sail on.' So saying, she tore open her dress and said, holding out her breasts, 'Son, have respect for these and take pity upon me if ever I gave you the teat to soften your sorrows'" is reminiscent of Hecuba's request to Hector before his final encounter with Achilles (*Callir.* 3.5.5–6; cf. *Iliad* 22.82–83).

78   See especially Konstan, *Sexual Symmetry*, 16–17. On suicide in Chariton and other novels, see Suzanne MacAlister, *Dreams and Suicides: The Greek Novel from Antiquity to the Byzantine Empire* (New York: Routledge, 1996).

79   Hägg, *The Novel in Antiquity*, 160.

80   Xenophon's Anthia finds herself in just such a predicament more often than any other character in the novels. For a brief discussion, see Helen Morales, "The History of Sexuality," in *The Cambridge Companion to the Greek and Roman Novel*, ed. Tim Whitmarsh (Cambridge: Cambridge University Press, 2008), 53.

elaborates this convention when he puts Callirhoe in Ionia, adding a pregnancy as a third competing interest. If she were not pregnant, the narrative makes clear, Callirhoe would never have yielded to Dionysius's desire. There are no parallels in the extant novels of a heroine capitulating to a male character other than her first lover, but no other heroine finds herself in quite the same predicament as Callirhoe in Ionia. Pregnant by Chaereas, she faces the difficult choice of attempting an abortion, of carrying the baby to term and risking Dionysius's potentially deadly jealousy or anger, or of marrying Dionysius and leading him to think himself the father of the baby born seven months into the marriage. Only after staging a lengthy internal debate, in which she theorizes the desires of both Chaereas and the unborn baby, does she decide on the third option.[81] Such extended internal deliberations are relatively rare in the novels (cf. *Callir.* 1.7.1–3), but when they do occur they can mirror debates that play out among multiple speakers in larger groups of characters (e.g., the pirates upon finding Callirhoe [*Callir.* 1.10.1–8]; the trial before Artaxerxes in book 6). An expectation of the genre seems to be that the central couple must survive until the end of the story, from which it follows that a way must be found out of each dilemma faced by the protagonists. The protagonists' values make this a challenge, however, since as a rule their love for each other always makes their reasoning more efficient: they are nearly always willing to die before compromising their fidelity.[82] The situation with Callirhoe and Dionysius is complicated insofar as Callirhoe did not face the immediate threat of rape or murder. Her predicament is her pregnancy, and the consequences to her and her child's social status if she is found pregnant without the Ionians' knowledge of her true marital status. The solution for which she opts, coaxed by Dionysius's slave Plangon, is less about keeping herself alive for Chaereas and more about keeping the child alive. The story could have been written without the pregnancy, but then Callirhoe would have had no compelling motivation to alter her situation as the slave/guest of Dionysius.

---

81   This internal debate is analyzed for what it says about consciousness and female agency in the ancient novel by Margaret A. Doody, "The Representation of Consciousness in the Ancient Novel," in *Remapping the Rise of the European Novel*, ed. J. Mander (Oxford: Voltaire Foundation, 2007), 35–45.

82   Even Achilles Tatius's Clitophon, who thinks that he has lost his beloved Leucippe, will not readily yield to the beautiful and wealthy widow Melite, but "he ignores her, nourishing fantasies that Leucippe will come back to life (*Leuc. Clit.* 5.11). He sails with Melite for Ephesus, steadfastly resisting her attempts to seduce him. The twist, typical of Achilles' whole work, is to have Clitophon recognize Leucippe alive (*Leuc. Clit.* 5.17–18) before putting him in bed with Melite (*Leuc. Clit.* 5.27).

The emotion-ridden dilemmas faced by Chariton's characters are often elaborated in what we might anachronistically call interior monologues. These can be compared with monologues in drama, a case of the theater's conventions informing the conventions of the novelist. These texts have been noticed before, not from the perspective of represented thought so much as within the framework of direct speech, indirect speech, and free indirect speech. The thoughts-as-speeches tend to be marked as direct speech with a third-person, singular form of φημί.[83] These situations where the thoughts of a character are introduced by a verb of speaking are difficult to distinguish clearly from those in which a character's thoughts are introduced by a verb of thinking.

Extended thought reports are more frequently encountered in the novels than in any of the other genres explored in this book. When they do occur, they are often signaled merely by the fact that a character is alone and begins to speak. Sometimes the verb of speaking is accompanied by a reflexive pronoun, as in the prelude to the example above: "arguing with herself (λέγουσα πρὸς ἑαυτήν), 'Am I to allow a descendant of Hermocrates to be born a slave?'" (*Callir.* 2.9.2). Sometimes the character simply begins to speak while alone, as in the example given above of Callirhoe working through her three options: "Going upstairs to her room and shutting the door, Callirhoe held the image of Chaereas against her womb and said (φησί), 'Behold, we are three—husband, wife, and child! Let us plan together what is best for us all'" (*Callir.* 2.11.1). Both episodes offer private thoughts, rather than declamations, since the verbs of speaking can be interchanged with verbs of thinking, even within a given thought report (φησί at *Callir.* 2.11.1, but ταύτην μὲν οὖν τὴν ἡμέραν καὶ τὴν νύκτα ἐν τούτοις ἦν τοῖς λογισμοῖς at 2.11.4, referring to the same thought process).[84]

---

83 Identifying indirect character speech in the novels is a trickier business. Longus has less direct speech than the other novelists. See Graham Anderson, "The Management of Dialogue in Ancient Fiction," in *A Companion to the Ancient Novel*, ed. Edmund P. Cueva, BCAW (Chichester: Wiley Blackwell, 2014), 217–30.

84 Cf. Christopher Gill's discussion of interior deliberation in Homer. Interior, he says, because there is no one around with whom to share the deliberative process. Christopher Gill, *Personality in Greek Epic, Tragedy, and Philosophy: The Self in Dialogue* (Oxford: Clarendon, 1996), 46–47, 58–60. But not all interior monologues are deliberative. Others are, as I indicate above, better described as "emotionally expressive" or similar. Perhaps there is a parallel here to Aristotle's division of speeches into three species: deliberative, judicial, and epideictic. It is worth recalling too, in connection to the internal "deliberative" monologues, that in Plato the personality is a complex of interactive parts, capable of independent and sometimes conflicted motivation (252–9; cf. Christopher Gill, *The Structured Self in Hellenistic and Roman Thought* [New York: Oxford University Press, 2006], 390–91).

As a rule, thought reports give characters artificial opportunities to wax poetic about their predicaments, to lay out their desires and aversions. This is the dynamic at work in Callirhoe's speech at the end of book 2, but further examples can be easily found. Consider Callirhoe's realization of her fresh plight after being "rescued" by Theron and his robber band. Her private lament functions to lay out a case for how her present ordeal, far from being an improvement on dying, is actually worse (*Callir.* 1.11.2–3). These thoughts, and many more like them, are for the reader's benefit. They function in a way comparable to the rhetorical arguments of the courtroom, the schoolhouse, or the market square, blending reasoning for/against a given course of action with rhetorical and dramatic flair (cf., e.g., the pair of speeches by the suitors from Rhegium and Acragas at *Callir.* 1.2.1–6, or the tomb robbers at *Callir.* 1.10.1–8).[85]

From a structural perspective, characters' reported knowledge and thoughts help keep alive in readers' minds what Bryan Reardon calls "the accumulating burden of incidents."[86] Though the device is found in each of the ideal novels, Heliodorus's *Aethiopica* is the most sophisticated in employing "discrepant awareness" as a technique, using one character's ignorance to furnish another character with a springboard for a speech. Sometimes these speeches traverse ground already familiar to readers (and in these cases, will do that same work of keeping alive the accumulating burden of incidents); in other cases, they will introduce new information that helps the reader contextualize other narrative data. This story, unlike the other novels, is not linear.[87] In the *Aethiopica*, stories told among characters become a primary vehicle for unfolding the action. Questions predicated on a character's ignorance and desire to understand become the literary conceit by which the narrative develops. Heliodorus surpasses his generic counterparts in the extent to which he strategically withholds information *from readers* as well as from characters within the storyworld. The opening beach scene is one example of the narrator withholding information from the reader, but the technique is pervasive in the novel: Cnemon withholds information from Calasiris; Calasiris withholds information from Chariclea; Theagenes and Chariclea withholds information from Cnemon; Theagenes, Chariclea, and Cnemon withhold information from Thermouthis; and Theagenes attempts to withhold information from Calasiris.

---

85 On rhetoric in the novels, see Ronald F. Hock, "The Rhetoric of Romance," in *Handbook of Classical Rhetoric in the Hellenistic Period: 330 BC–AD 400*, ed. Stanley E. Porter (Boston: Brill, 2001), 445–66.

86 Reardon, *The Form of Greek Romance*, 27.

87 To borrow terms from the Russian Formalists, the fabula (the raw data of the story, evenly following a linear chronology) is not in line with the syuzhet (order of narration, the way a story is organized).

ROMANCE: THWARTED RECOGNITIONS AND THE ΠΑΘΗ ΠΟΙΚΙΛΑ   145

Chariton in *Callirhoe* strategically withholds information as well, though only among characters, never from readers. Callirhoe withholds the fact of her pregnancy from all but Plangon in book 2, for example, and Chaereas keeps silent about his background when he is put on Mithridates's chain gang and later when he is sentenced to crucifixion in book 4.

Represented thought, in dialogue as well as in interior monologues, provides a means of spinning out and sustaining distinctions between illusion and reality, between "how things appear" and "how things are," so that these distinctions may be resolved later with great panache. Readers usually have access to both types of knowledge. Again, Heliodorus spends more time creating illusions for readers than do the other novelists. Recognitions (ἀναγνωρίσεις)—both of characters' identities and of narrative facts more generally—are a primary tool for resolving these two levels.

Recognitions sometimes occur instantly (when, for example, tokens are in evidence) and are sometimes drawn out. In Chariton, the reader is always at least one step ahead of the recognizing character. Waking up in the tomb, for example, Callirhoe only gradually recognizes how she arrived there (*Callir.* 1.8.1–4). The reader, however, knew from the moment she lost consciousness that her death was only apparent (*Callir.* 1.4.12–1.5.1).[88] Similarly, Callirhoe's recognition that she has been sold as a slave appears to develop gradually (*Callir.* 1.14.6–10). Here again readers are a step ahead in their understanding of the situation. In the course of her monologue, she reveals her realization that she is sold, but unlike the readers she knows not to whom. These thought reports might be called monologues of realization to distinguish them from monologues of deliberation. Both types are productive of emotions.

In cases of gradual recognition, the cascade of discursive moves culminating in full recognition often begins with a statement from one character to another that turns out to be more significant to the hearer than to the speaker. Chariton furnishes an example of this when a priestess of Aphrodite finds Callirhoe crying and strikes up a conversation. In it she mentions that two foreigners had visited the shrine "and one of them nearly expired at the sight of your statue, so like a goddess on earth has Aphrodite made you" (*Callir.* 3.9.1). The priestess seeks to cheer Callirhoe with this anecdote for what it says about *her* (Aphrodite has made you internationally renowned for beauty), when in fact Callirhoe—to the priestess's surprise—is excited by the anecdote for what it accidentally tells her about the persons behind the compliment. "Callirhoe's heart was pierced by these words, and with staring eyes, like one possessed, she cried, 'Who were the strangers? Where had they sailed from? What did they

---

88   Cf. the several incidents of *Scheintod* of Leucippe in Achilles Tatius, discussed below.

say?'" (*Callir.* 3.9.2). This flurry of questions, following on Callirhoe's partial recognition, is related to the genre's πάθη ποικίλα convention discussed above.

At climactic moments Chariton slows narrative time to linger before, during, and after a character learns an important piece of information, especially where a consequential narrative fact is understood or misunderstood. This phenomenon *includes* but is not limited to recognition scenes. Take for example the scene in which Callirhoe learns by stages that she is to marry Chaereas. In keeping with her maidenly modesty, she tells no one her feelings. Only Aphrodite has heard her desire to have "this man" as her husband (*Callir.* 1.1.7). It is not clear that she knows anything about him beyond the fact that he is handsome (εὔμορφον, πάντων ὑπερέχον, *Callir.* 1.1.3). Though the two fall swiftly in love (ταχέως οὖν πάθος ἐρωτικὸν ἀντέδωκαν ἀλλήλοις, *Callir.* 1.1.6), they do not exchange words or share their feelings with each other. Chaereas can tell his parents that he wishes to have Callirhoe as a wife (how does he learn her name?), but Callirhoe suffers a lonelier fate, "for she had to keep silent for shame of being exposed" (*Callir.* 1.1.8). Imagine how she must have felt, then, when news arrived that she was to be married! The reader knows of Hermocrates's decision and its implications for Callirhoe, but she remains "knowing nothing," and "silently weeping" on her bed (*Callir.* 1.1.14). The nurse announces the wedding but not the identity of the groom. Chariton employs Homeric imagery to describe her response: "'at this her knees collapsed and the heart within her,' for she had no idea to whom she was being married" (*Callir.* 1.1.14), underscoring the distance between what the reader knows and what Callirhoe knows.[89] Perhaps contextual knowledge of her situation leads readers to theorize her mind in such a way that she assumes Hermocrates has selected one of the young suitors in residence in Syracuse, a group to which Chaereas does not belong. Chariton's elaborations on the response are cast in physical terms: she becomes mute, "darkness covered her eyes," and she nearly stops breathing. Chariton's omniscient narrator casts an eye into the minds of the onlookers, using what was described above as variable internal focalization: those who saw these physical reactions think she is just being modest. The reader remains in the privileged position of knowing both that Callirhoe's reaction is based on a false assumption and that her attendants are misinterpreting their mistress's behavior.

---

89   On Homer in the novels generally and in Chariton in particular, see the comments made above and Graverini, "From the Epic to The Novelistic Hero." Molinié, in his Budé edition of Chariton, notes 28 Homeric texts cited by Chariton on 31 occasions. Georges Molinié, *Chariton: Le roman de Chairéas et Callirhoé*, Budé (Paris: Belles lettres, 1979), 12. Cf. Bowie, "The Readership of the Greek Novels in the Ancient World," 454n14.

ROMANCE: THWARTED RECOGNITIONS AND THE ΠΑΘΗ ΠΟΙΚΙΛΑ

Once the maids have prepared Callirhoe to meet the groom, her gradual recognition reaches its climax. A crowd outside her door parts to reveal Chaereas, led by his parents. "Chaereas ran forward and kissed her; recognizing the man she loved, Callirhoe, like a dying lamp once it is replenished with oil, flamed into life and became taller and stronger" (*Callir.* 1.1.15). Neither her thoughts nor feelings are narrated directly; only the fact of recognition and a bevy of emotionally-induced physical changes focalized through the onlookers. She appears taller and stronger, the lamp metaphor suggests that she exudes brightness and light, and the sight of her occasions a response "as when Artemis appears to hunters in lonely places." The god-likeness prompts many to kneel in homage (προσεκύνησαν). "All were entranced by Callirhoe and congratulated Chaereas" (*Callir.* 1.1.15–16). The προσκύνησις suggests that the onlookers are treating her as a goddess. Twenty-two lines pass by in which everyone but Callirhoe knows that she will be married to Chaereas. At last, she recognizes her beloved and responds positively.

The narrative slows in a comparable way when Chaereas falls into the trap set by the jilted suitors: he moves from trusting his wife to becoming convinced of her infidelity, to attacking her, to believing that she is dead, to learning the truth about how he had been fooled by torturing the maidservants. While Chaereas rides his epistemological roller coaster, the reader remains in an epistemologically advantageous position—knowing that Callirhoe never wavered in her fidelity, understanding the motivations and machinations of the suitors in creating the misunderstanding, and knowing that her death was only apparent (*Callir.* 1.5.1).

A third gradual recognition transpires as the narrative shifts again to Callirhoe, who goes on to infer what transpired and how she came to be trapped in the tomb, culminating in grief over her fortune (*Callir.* 1.8.3–4). Here again the narrator has not disguised the fact that Callirhoe's death was only apparent, but none of the characters in the story yet know this.[90] She "lay without speech or breath, presenting to all the appearance of death" (*Callir.* 1.5.1).

---

90   Reardon's summary of Chariton in *The Form of the Romance* seems to miss this point: "To their [the robbers'] astonishment the first thing they see is Callirhoe—alive! She had, we learn, merely been in a deep coma from which she has just awakened as the robbers enter" (18). This is oversimplified on two levels—first, the robbers hear Callirhoe before they see her (she is in the shadows at the back of the cave), and they presumably see the treasures between the voice and the door. More importantly, their discovery is not *our* discovery; we have known all along that Callirhoe's death was only apparent, and consequently take pleasure in our epistemic advantage over the robbers.

Recognitions in the novels are ubiquitous and multiform. It is not only protagonists who experience recognition, nor is the phenomenon restricted to individuals. The capture and trial of Theron leads to a gradual and collective recognition, as the Syracusans come to realize by stages his identity and role in Callirhoe's abduction. Theron's alibi begins to break down when an anonymous fisherman in the crowd recognizes him and says to his neighbors, "I have seen this fellow before, hanging around our harbor." The remark begins to circulate. Someone shouts out that Theron is lying, and torturers are summoned when Theron denies the accusation. Finally, he gives the Syracusans what they need to complete their gradual recognition, omitting only the name of the man to whom he sold Callirhoe (*Callir.* 3.4.7–14). And here, as is usual for Chariton, the reader already knows. Some of Chariton's most impressive examples of recognition are found at the end of the novel, in the mutual recognition of Chaereas and Callirhoe aboard the ship Chaereas commands—again, the reader knows already what Chaereas does not (that Callirhoe is among the captives) and what Callirhoe does not (that her captor is Chaereas) (*Callir.* 8.1.7–10).

The Syracusans in the previous paragraph experienced what we might label a simple delay of recognition. But more often in the novels, delayed recognitions can be complicated by employing the devices of misperception and misunderstanding. Chariton's most famous recognition scene furnishes an example: Led by his friend Polycharmus into the room where Callirhoe is captive, "he [Chaereas] saw her, lying down and wrapped up though she was, his heart was stirred by the way she breathed and looked, and he was seized with excitement. *He would certainly have recognized her, had he not been utterly convinced that Dionysius had recovered Callirhoe.* Quietly going to her, he said, 'Courage my dear, whoever you are! We are not going to use force on you. You shall have the husband you want.' While he was still speaking, Callirhoe recognized his voice and uncovered her face" (*Callir.* 8.1.8).[91] The point to notice here is the initial misrecognition. The delay between misrecognition and its resolution here is short and explained in cognitive terms: Callirhoe's breathing and form should have been the tokens Chaereas needed, but his false beliefs about Callirhoe and Dionysius delayed recognition.

Recognitions are not limited to the personal identities of characters in the story; they extend also to circumstances. One recurring example is the apparent death (*Scheintod*) motif, which is the starting point for a process of delayed

---

91   Trans. LCL, modified, emphasis added.

ROMANCE: THWARTED RECOGNITIONS AND THE ΠΑΘΗ ΠΟΙΚΙΛΑ 149

recognition.[92] Chariton gives an example of this in the first pages of his novel, when townspeople take the comatose Callirhoe for dead (*Callir.* 1.5.1) and will not recognize their mistake for some time. Shortly afterward they bury her, the grave robbers mistake the entombed Callirhoe for a δαίμων (*Callir.* 1.9.4) and only later realize that she is a human girl. Another example of recognition of a narrative circumstance is found in the scene discussed above in connection to control of the emotions: propositioned by the eunuch, Callirhoe recognizes the danger she is in and disguises her recognition, leading the eunuch to misperceive her state of mind (*Callir.* 6.5.10). The phenomenon prevails in other novels too. For example, Xenophon has the prefect of Egypt misapprehend the guilt of Habrocomes, Habrocomes wrongly supposes Antheia to be dead (*Eph.* 4.2.1–2), and Antheia wrongly supposes Habrocomes to be dead (*Eph.* 4.5.1–3).

Thought reports often extend the narrative time in which misunderstandings and misperceptions are in effect. Typically readers know "the truth" already and so these moments reinforce their epistemological advantage; sometimes readers do not understand and are either confused or share the misperception with a character.[93] In order not to make a liar out of the narrator,[94] the reader usually knows the "truth." Consider, for example, the first apparent death of Callirhoe. Unless Chariton focalizes through spectator characters (and here he does not), he cannot make a reader think that she died. He can only say that she appeared to have died. An exception might be possible, though, if the narrative is focalized on one character through another character as with Heliodorus's bandits in the opening scene of the *Aethiopica* or Achilles Tatius's Clitophon, watching his beloved Leucippe die (e.g., *Leuc. Clit.* 3.15; 5.7).[95] *Scheintod* figures

---

92 Though there are other circumstances where mistaken perception delays recognition. For example, the robber guard Anchialus is mistaken in thinking Antheia will readily sleep with him (Xenophon, *Ephesiaca* 4.5.2).

93 As in Achilles Tatius, *Leuc. Clit.* 3.15.5–6; 5.7.4–18.2; 7.4.3–6.

94 The concept of the "unreliable narrator," associated with stories like Henry James's *The Turn of the Screw* and Nabokov's *Lolita*, was not theorized before modernity. Some first-person narrators from ancient works have been read as unreliable narrators, (e.g., the soldier in Plautus's *Miles gloriosus*), but accepting this may result in a situation where every first-person narrator can be labeled unreliable. A better solution is to allow for a range of different ways in which a narrator can be unreliable, as William Riggan attempted to do in *Pícaros, Madmen, Naïfs, and Clowns: The Unreliable First-Person Narrator* (Norman: University of Oklahoma Press, 1981). The term "unreliable narrator" was first used in the 1961 first edition of Wayne C. Booth, *The Rhetoric of Fiction*, 2nd ed. (Chicago: University of Chicago Press, 1983), 156–57.

95 Hägg says that with Achilles Tatius, "whenever suspense demands it, we are back in the restricted narrative perspective," i.e., the narrative is focalized through a character like Clitophon. Hägg, *The Novel in Antiquity*, 43.

in each of the novels, usually providing occasions for affected parties to be overwhelmed by grief. In worlds where lovers despair of life without the love and presence of the other, these episodes frequently lead to suicide attempts (e.g., *Callir.* 1.5.2; 3.3.1; *Aeth.* 3.6–8).[96] A primary function of secondary characters like Cnemon for Theagones (*Aeth.* 2.1) or Polycharmus for Chaereas (*Callir.* 5.10.10; 7.1.7–8) is to keep the protagonist alive at such times.

Sometimes the misperceptions that delay recognition are created and sometimes they arise without obvious agency. They simply occur, for example, when Dionysius mistakes Callirhoe for Aphrodite (*Callir.* 2.3.6). Those occasions where they are created (e.g., Plangon tricks Callirhoe at *Callir.* 2.10.7; Leucippe tricks the bandits with Clitophon at Achilles Tatius, *Leuc. Clit.* 3.5) give explicit attention to the inter-cognitive relationships among characters. An elaborate created instance is when Phocas creates the impression that Chaereas has died (*Callir.* 3.9.5–3.10.3). At the same time, and again on almost every page of the novels, the reader becomes aware of what a character wants or knows (or does not know) inferentially, that is, without the narrator or any other focalizor explaining what a character knows. A common pattern begins with a character making claims the reader knows to be untrue. For example, at one point, Theron claims to be a Cretan traveler who survived because of his piety (*Callir.* 3.3.17–18).[97] Chaereas, to whom he is speaking and who recognizes the goods in the ship's cargo as those left in Callirhoe's tomb, apparently believes him. No mention is made of suspicion or of what Chaereas did and did not know about Theron. He simply responds by acting on information the reader knows to be false. Later, in Chaereas's speech to the Syracusan assembly, we learn that his response to Theron can be summed up as, "This fellow, whoever he is, was found among them half dead. I spared no pains to revive him and have brought him to show you."[98] The "whoever he is" perhaps reflects some distrust, but it is a distrust that is never made explicit. The point is that Chaereas, by his actions, is shown to hold erroneous beliefs, while the reader knows the truth, producing discrepant awareness and an opportunity for delayed recognition.

---

96   See Konstan, *Sexual Symmetry*, 16–17; MacAlister, *Dreams and Suicides*.

97   There are at least two jokes in this claim: one is the intertextual riff on Epimenides's Paradox, "Epimenides the Cretan says that all Cretans are liars" (cf. Titus 1:12–13); the other is the irony that Theron has in fact survived because of his *lack* of piety. When his crew began to die of thirst, "they repented of their deeds, and reproached each other with the futility of it all. Now all the rest were dying of thirst, but even in this plight Theron proved a rogue. He secretly stole from the water, and thus robbed his fellow robbers" (*Callir.* 3.3.11).

98   Trans. LCL, modified.

In the lead-up to Chariton's protagonists' wedding, as described in the previous section, a series of mistaken conclusions are drawn. (1) When Chaereas tells his father Ariston that he must have Callirhoe as a wife, "his father groaned and said, 'I fear you are done for, my son. Hermocrates will surely never give you his daughter when he has so many rich and royal suitors for her. You must not even make the attempt, in case we suffer a public humiliation'" (*Callir.* 1.1.9). Ariston's conclusion neglects the persuasive power of the Syracusan assembly, which prevails on the patriotic Hermocrates to consent to the marriage Chaereas desired (*Callir.* 1.1.11–12). (2) Then there is the physical despondency of Callirhoe, described above, predicated on her mistaken assumption that she is to marry someone other than Chaereas. Later in the narrative, her reaction to the news of her wedding is described analeptically as a near-death experience from which she luckily escaped, foreshadowing her much more dramatic return from near death in the sealed tomb (*Callir.* 1.8.1). (3) The attendants draw the false conclusion that Callirhoe's physical reaction is a sign of her modesty. (4) Finally, the onlookers' obeisance strongly intimates that they have mistaken Callirhoe for a goddess (*Callir.* 1.1.16). These four instances of mistaken conclusion play out one after the other in a very compact section of the novel. All are relatively straightforward misunderstandings. Only one is explicitly rectified, in Callirhoe's discovery that her assumption concerning the identity of her fiancé is wrong. The novel abounds with mistaken beliefs like these.

In addition to delaying resolution and recognition, mistakes raise narrative stakes. The four mistaken conclusions sketched in the previous paragraph each make the eventual union all the more amazing. Ariston's mistake helps the reader appreciate that the odds are longer than usual in the matter of securing Chaereas's hoped-for marriage. Callirhoe's mistake helps the reader appreciate the depth of her desire for Chaereas. The attendants' mistake helps the reader appreciate that Callirhoe was characteristically modest, reinforcing the narrator's earlier comment about her modesty (cf. *Callir.* 1.1.8).

The mistaken conclusions discussed above are innocent and uncontrived. Often in the novels, however, mistakes are engineered and even malicious. After the wedding of Callirhoe and Chaereas, the next major episode is the conspiracy devised by the girl's neglected suitors—the ones indicated in Ariston's initial response to Chaereas's expressed desire to marry Callirhoe. The plan they hatch involves an initial theorizing of both Chaereas and Callirhoe's minds: "Callirhoe may be even-tempered and incapable of base suspicion," one of the suitors says, "but Chaereas, brought up in the gymnasium and not unacquainted with youthful follies, can easily be made suspicious and lured into youthful jealousy" (*Callir.* 1.2.6). Their plot involves giving Chaereas the idea

152   CHAPTER 4

that his new wife has been unfaithful. When Chaereas next left town, the suitors come by night and create a tableau at the bride's house to give the impression that reveling had transpired in his absence: "they garlanded the vestibule, sprinkled it with perfumes, soaked the ground with wine, and let drop half-burned torches" (*Callir.* 1.3.2). Their plan has its desired effect of misdirection; Chaereas draws the false conclusion. But after hearing Callirhoe's indignant reaction to the unjust accusation, the lovers reconcile, and so the suitors find themselves back where they started. Their response is to craft a more compelling subterfuge, which culminates in that terrible and memorable scene in which Chaereas angrily kicks his unsuspecting wife, sending her into a coma and apparent death (*Callir.* 1.4.11–12).

The subcategory of created misperceptions necessarily involves characters theorizing the minds of other characters. When the suitor from Acragas lays out his scheme, he speculates that Callirhoe "doesn't know what malice and suspicion are," but figures that Chaereas, a regular at the gymnasium, will be more easily provoked to suspicion (*Callir.* 1.2.6). The suspicions receive some implicit confirmation when the narrator, explaining how Plangon manipulated Callirhoe's decision, says that "Callirhoe was quite unsuspicious of Plangon's advice (οὐδὲν ὑπώπτευε Καλλιρόη), since she was a well-bred young girl and ignorant of servile cunning (μεῖραξ εὐγενὴς καὶ πανουργίας ἄπειρος δουλικῆς)" (*Callir.* 2.10.7). These examples illustrate that theories of mind are often predicated on stereotypes about the dispositions of social groups, ages, and genders, and (in Chariton at least) narrator and characters seem to agree on the content and practicality of these stereotypes: well-bred young girls think one way, servile old women another; Greek modes of thought are not those of barbarians; lovestruck men think in different terms from men not in love. In reasoning about where he will attempt to offload his booty, Theron theorizes the Athenians ("a nation of gossips, and they love lawsuits ... nosey parkers") and the Ionians (they "love luxury and don't look for trouble"). Chariton also furnishes (both in narrator speech and in character speech) theorizations of the dispositions of barbarians, Greeks, Egyptians, eunuchs, and women (see, e.g., *Callir.* 6.4.10; 6.7.12; and the discussion above).

Related to "created misperception" is the calculated withholding of information. Polycharmus, for example, reacting to the news of the attendant at Aphrodite's shrine that Dionysius had recently married a slave whose image Chaereas recognizes as Callirhoe's, keeps silent for he "did not wish it known who they were until they had talked over the situation thoroughly and were agreed on a course of action" (*Callir.* 3.6.5). Later, Callirhoe asked Dionysius to free Plangon, hoping "that Plangon's improved fortunes in addition to her natural affection would secure her loyalty" (*Callir.* 3.8.1). Other examples of the

ROMANCE: THWARTED RECOGNITIONS AND THE ΠΑΘΗ ΠΟΙΚΙΛΑ 153

phenomenon lie in Theron's withholding the name of the Ionian man to whom he sold Callirhoe; Callirhoe withholding from Dionysius the facts of her former marriage and her pregnancy; Leonas withholding the sighting of the Athenian ships offshore; and Callirhoe again at the end of the novel withholding from Dionysius the true paternity of her son, whom she entrusts to his care. These examples suggest that the novels' protagonists and antagonists both participate in creating misperceptions.

The conventions of representing what characters know, when they know it, and what attendant emotions accompany coming to know it are paralleled and played with in the text to which we now turn, the anonymous novel *Aseneth*.

4   *Aseneth*

Aseneth, like Philo's *Life of Moses* in the previous chapter and the *Exagoge* of Ezekiel the Tragedian in the next, is generally read as a product of Alexandrian Judaism, composed sometime between 100 BCE and the decimation of Egyptian Jews under Trajan (115–7 CE). It is possible, then, that it was written by a contemporary of Chariton and the Fourth Evangelist. That provenance has been challenged by Ross Shepherd Kraemer, who shows how the novel might be the product of a Christian or Jewish God-fearing writer from Syria or Asia Minor active at some point between the fourth and sixth centuries CE, a view based largely on the absence of references to the book in texts produced before the fifth century.[99] On either reading, the text is useful for talking about the generic conventions of the classical novel, both in terms of what it reflects from writers like Chariton and in what from that tradition it subverts. Texts like *Aseneth* and the fragmentary novels show that the romance genre was more diverse than we might think if we restricted ourselves to the five complete, "ideal" novels. Within that diversity, these other novels retain the genre's characteristic emphases on emotional excess and thwarted recognitions of various types, as we will see illustrated here in the case of *Aseneth*.

The first part of *Aseneth* is centrally concerned with the conversion of an Egyptian priest's daughter and her subsequent marriage to Joseph, followed

---

99   Ross Shepard Kraemer, *When Aseneth Met Joseph: A Late Antique Tale of the Biblical Patriarch and His Egyptian Wife, Reconsidered* (New York: Oxford University Press, 1998), 286–92. Kraemer leaves open the possibility of non-Christian Jewish authorship, by a writer perhaps from the land of Israel. Most scholars who have published on the issue since Kraemer's book remain convinced of the earlier situation of *Aseneth* in Hellenistic Judaism. See, e.g., John J. Collins, "Joseph and Aseneth: Jewish or Christian?," *JSP* 14 (2005): 97–112.

154 CHAPTER 4

by a second part focused on intrigues initiated by the son of Pharaoh.[100] The central concerns of the first part are the meeting, conversion, and marriage of Aseneth; the second part has chiefly to do with the infatuation conceived for Aseneth by the anonymous son of Pharaoh, a bandit character,[101] and his enlistment of Joseph's half-brothers Dan, Gad, Naphtali, and Asher (i.e., the sons of Bilhah and Zilpah) in an ill-fated plot to take Aseneth for himself and intrigue against Joseph and Pharaoh. The biblical hook for the story is just a few short remarks in Genesis 41 and 46.

> Pharaoh gave Joseph the name Zaphenath-paneah; and he gave him Aseneth daughter of Potiphera, priest of On, as his wife. Thus Joseph gained authority over the land of Egypt.
>
> Gen 41.46

> Before the years of famine came, Joseph had two sons, whom Asenath daughter of Potiphera, priest of On, bore to him. Joseph named the first-born Manasseh, "For," he said, "God has made me forget all my hardship and all my father's house." The second he named Ephraim, "For God has made me fruitful in the land of my misfortunes."
>
> Gen 41.50–52

> To Joseph in the land of Egypt were born Manasseh and Ephraim, whom Asenath daughter of Potiphera, priest of On, bore to him.
>
> Gen 46.20

The Bible says nothing more about Asenath daughter of Potiphera. In the Septuagint, she becomes Aseneth, daughter of Pentephres, priest of Heliopolis, and these are (with minor variations) the names adopted for the characters in the text that concerns us here.[102] The material of Genesis 37–50 figures in

---

100 But Wills argues that the novel "should not be divided into a first half and a second half, as it is by many scholars, but into an early and late layer. The love-and-adventure story associated with the second half actually begins in chapter 1 but is then overwhelmed in most of the intervening chapters by the introduction of a symbolic conversion story." Wills, *The Jewish Novel in the Ancient World*, 184.

101 As noted by Patricia D. Ahearne-Kroll, "'Joseph and Aseneth' and Jewish Identity in Greco-Roman Egypt" (PhD diss, The University of Chicago, 2005), 107. The bandit as a character type is described by Alain Billault, "Characterization in the Ancient Novel," in *The Novel in the Ancient World*, ed. Gareth L. Schmeling, MnS 159 (Leiden: Brill, 1996), 120.

102 Although in at least one manuscript (445), a scribe has crossed out several instances of the name Pentephres and substituted "Potifar." See Ahearne-Kroll, "Joseph and Asenath," 258n20; Christoph Burchard, *Joseph und Aseneth*, PVTG 5 (Leiden: Brill, 2003), 71.

other ways in *Aseneth*, however, particularly in making up part of the assumed backstory.[103] In what follows, I discuss some of the resonances with a bearing on cognitive characterization of the novel's subjects. In any event, it would be too simple to call this an instance of "rewritten Bible" or an "elaboration" of these few verses.[104]

There once was a time when *Aseneth* was treated straightforwardly as a part of the genre of Greek novel in the same tradition as those works by Chariton, Xenophon, Achilles Tatius, Longus, and Heliodorus.[105] The "religious" content of the work, however, and the possibility of its composition some centuries before the apparent heyday of the classical novel in the second century CE both presented obstacles to its easy inclusion in this genre. One way of resolving the apparent problem was to make *Aseneth* an accidental predecessor of the novel and perhaps even "a source of inspiration for the Alexandrinian authors of novels."[106] Another way of responding to the *Aseneth*-as-romance thesis has been to probe at what might be obscured by a straightforward identification of the text with that genre.[107] Patricia Aheare-Kroll is a recent defender of the thesis that *Aseneth* belongs to the romance genre.[108] Others, less ready to assign *Aseneth* to a general genre "romance," have tried to make it representative of something like a "sapiential novel" or a "national hero novel" with an

---

103 The narrative begins by setting the novel in "the first year of the seven years of abundance" (*Asen.* 1.1), a reference that would only make full sense to a reader familiar with the biblical account. Nearly every chapter of the novel contains elements that are comprehensible only to a reader familiar with the biblical account. Some of these resonances are discussed by Susan Docherty, who sees them as criteria for belonging to "the genre of rewritten bible." See also Chesnutt, who writes that the biblical references are "not incidental but are central to the narrative and crucial for a full appreciation of it," and Kraemer, who writes that biblical references "constitute the principle building blocks of the stories" in *Aseneth*. Susan Docherty, "*Joseph and Aseneth*: Rewritten Bible or Narrative Expansion?," *JSJ* 35 (2004): 27–48; Randall D. Chesnutt, *From Death to Life: Conversion in Joseph and Aseneth*, JSPSup 16 (Sheffield: Sheffield Academic Press, 1995), 258; Kraemer, *When Aseneth Met Joseph*, 20.

104 See the discussion in chapter 2 above and Eva Mroczek, *The Literary Imagination in Jewish Antiquity* (Oxford: Oxford University Press, 2016).

105 Marc Philonenko, *Joseph et Aséneth: Introduction, texte critique, traduction et notes*, StPb 13 (Leiden: Brill, 1968), 43–47; S. West, "Joseph and Asenath: A Neglected Greek Romance," *ClQ* 24 (1974): 71–77.

106 Nina Braginskaya, "*Joseph and Aseneth* in Greek Literary History: The Case of the 'First Novel,'" in *The Ancient Novel and Early Christian and Jewish Narrative: Fictional Intersections*, ed. Maralia P. Futre Pinheiro, Judith Perkins, and Richard Pervo, ANS (Groningen: Barkhuis, 2012), 85.

107 Kraemer, *When Aseneth Met Joseph*, 9–12.

108 Ahearne-Kroll, "'Joseph and Aseneth' and Jewish Identity in Greco-Roman Egypt." See also her remarks on genre in Ahearne-Kroll, "Joseph and Aseneth," 2525–26.

156   CHAPTER 4

"allegorical layer" superimposed by a later writer.[109] The symbolic content and
the centrality of conversion in *Aseneth* have pushed some away from locating
it in the genre, while others have seen the "religious" content as unproblem-
atic on the basis of "religious" content in other novels—the Psyche and Cupid
story embedded in Apuleius's *Metamorphoses*, for example, or the conversion narrative in book 11 of that same work, or the propagandistic function of
Heliodorus's *Aethiopica*.[110] Some would prefer to put it in an artificial category
called the Jewish novel together with works like Tobit, Judith, Greek Esther,
and Greek Daniel.[111]

There are important similarities between *Aseneth* and the classical novels
in structure and theme. Fidelity and chastity are primary virtues in both. The
heroine is beautiful and falls instantly in love with a handsome bachelor. The
story is less about Joseph and more about Aseneth, a proportionality that reflects the prominence given to Callirhoe over Chaereas in Chariton's novel. The
protagonists of both *Aseneth* and the classical novels are regularly likened to or
mistaken for goddesses.[112] Like *Callirhoe*, the story of *Aseneth* has a "historical"
hook in the Genesis narrative comparable to the hook provided by the historical Hermocrates in *Callirhoe*.[113]

But there are also important differences when we set *Aseneth* against the
backdrop of the ideal novels, including the heroine's self-initiated conversion
from an idolatrous, Egyptian past to a future as a bride worthy of her Israelite
fiancé. There is no close analogue for this in the five ideal novels, although
some have discussed a sort of conversion in Chaereas's character, from his initial, petulant disposition to something more mature by the end of that story.[114]

---

109   Sapiential novel: Richard I. Pervo, "Joseph and Aseneth and the Greek Novel," in *1976 SBL
      Seminar Papers*, ed. G. W. MacRae (Missoula: Scholars, 1976), 171. National hero novel with
      overlay: Wills, *The Jewish Novel in the Ancient World*, 184. Wills takes the category "national
      hero romance" from Martin Braun, *History and Romance in Graeco-Oriental Literature*
      (Oxford: Blackwell, 1938).

110   Christoph Burchard, "Joseph and Aseneth," in *OTP*, ed. James H. Charlesworth, vol. 2
      (Garden City: Doubleday, 1983), 183–84.

111   Wills, *The Jewish Novel in the Ancient World*; Wills, *Ancient Jewish Novels*. In connection to
      Mark, see also Vines, *The Problem of Markan Genre*.

112   Aseneth on account of her post-conversion beauty, but note also that she occupies the
      position of a goddess when she is first introduced: living in the sanctuary-like upper room
      of a tower, the room and her person decorated with the paraphernalia of idolatry and at-
      tended by seven virgin companions.

113   For a more extensive catalogue of similarities between *Aseneth* and the classical romance,
      see Ahearne-Kroll, "'Joseph and Aseneth' and Jewish Identity in Greco-Roman Egypt,"
      88–142.

114   Habrocomes undergoes a comparable "education" at Eros's initiative, and Daphnis and
      Chloe are also "educated in the ways of love" in Longus's novel. See the essays in Alan
      H. Sommerstein and Catherine Atherton, eds., *Education in Greek Fiction*, NCLS 4 (Bari:

Even if characters in the novels develop over the course of the narrative, however, they are apparently acceptable to each other from the beginning. And so another difference is that Joseph in *Aseneth* does not fall in love with his future wife at first sight; his initial response is to ask that she be sent away (*Asen.* 7.2). It is not unusual in the classical novels for protagonists to resist the advances of admirers, but it is unusual for one of the central couple to resist the advances of the other. Xenophon features a male protagonist who, like Joseph, sees himself as superior to conventional marriage. But when he meets Anthia, the result is the same irresistible love we saw between Chaereas and Callirhoe in our discussion of Chariton above. Furthermore, if love motivates the ideal novels' protagonist couples to endure ordeals for the sake of mutual fidelity, in *Aseneth* the heroine's love for Joseph motivates her to endure a solitary week-long psychological ordeal, involving an angelic visitation, psychedelic bees, and an enigmatic, bleeding honeycomb. Joseph is not portrayed as experiencing the same depth and range of emotions as Aseneth or his male counterparts in the classical novels. This is no doubt partly to be explained by his characteristic self-control, in which respect he more closely resembles Dionysius than Chaereas.

Because of the prominence of Aseneth's conversion in the first part of the text, a default way of contextualizing *Aseneth* has been as a Jewish tract extolling proselytism.[115] Other hypotheses advanced are that it was written to justify the existence of the schismatic Jewish temple at Heliopolis,[116] to counsel Jews worried about the status of converts and the midrashic problem of exogamy,[117] to instruct Jews more generally in how to co-exist in a polyethnic and polytheistic environment,[118] to attract converts to Judaism by representing conversion as like initiation to a mystery,[119] to promote the ideal of Christian virginity,[120]

Levante, 1997), particularly John Morgan's essay, "Erotika Mathemata: Greek Romance as Sentimental Education."

115 E.g., George W. E. Nickelsburg, *Jewish Literature between the Bible and the Mishnah: A Historical and Literary Introduction*, 2nd ed. (Minneapolis: Fortress, 2005), 337.

116 Gideon Bohak, *Joseph and Aseneth and the Jewish Temple in Heliopolis*, EJL 10 (Atlanta: Scholars, 1996).

117 Chesnutt, *From Death to Life*. For the prohibitions against exogamy, see Gen 24.3–4, 37–38; 27.46–28.1; cf. Jub. 20.4; 22.20; 30.7–16; Tob 4.12–13.

118 Ahearne-Kroll, "'Joseph and Aseneth' and Jewish Identity in Greco-Roman Egypt," 6; Ahearne-Kroll, "Joseph and Aseneth," 2527.

119 This last item is obviously a more focused form of the standard view that *Aseneth* has a missionary function. G. D. Kilpatrick, "Living Issues in Biblical Scholarship: The Last Supper," *ExpTim* 64 (1952): 6. See also the discussion in Chesnutt, *From Death to Life*, 217–53.

120 E. W. Brooks, ed., *Joseph and Asenath, the Confession and Prayer of Asenath, Daughter of Pentephres the Priest*, vol. 7, 8 vols., TED 2 (London: Macmillan, 1918).

158   CHAPTER 4

or by and for use by the Therapeutae, an ascetic community described by Philo.[121] All of these theses have managed to find articulation with more or less emphasis on the text's participation in the romance genre.

An important feature of the internal landscape for characters in novels is the stated or demonstrated disposition of leading figures. Knowledge of a character's disposition helps readers predict a character's responses to the emotional ordeals in store, just as knowing the disposition of the subjects in the βίος tradition was used to help decide what they did in situations where the historical record was ambiguous. After introducing her in relation to her father and his station and describing her beauty and the effect it had on the local bachelors (*Asen.* 1.3–6), Aseneth's disposition is described as disdainful and despising (ἐξουθενοῦσα καὶ καταπτύουσα) towards every man, boastful and arrogant (ἀλαζὼν καὶ ὑπερήφανος) before everyone (*Asen.* 2.1; cf. her confession at 12.5). This is reminiscent of the initial disposition of Xenophon's Habrocomes, whose disposition is narrated after his introduction in relation to his parents, his good looks, and the desire of the other Ephesians and Asians to associate with him: "He held a high opinion of himself, glorying both in his spiritual accomplishments and even more so in his physical beauty. Everything generally reckoned fine he despised as inferior, and nothing seen or heard seemed to him worthy of Habrocomes" (*Eph.* 1.1.4). This irks Eros, who arranges for him to suffer by making him fall in love with Anthia. Other characters are introduced in terms of their dispositions as well, including Pentephres (*Asen.* 1.3), Levi (*Asen.* 22.13), and Simeon (*Asen.* 23.7), but the most important dispositions for the reader to keep track of are Aseneth's, described at the outset and fundamentally altered in the course of her weeklong conversion experience (note especially how she repents of that disposition at *Asen.* 12.5), and Joseph's, which remains constant for the duration of the narrative (see, e.g., *Asen.* 4.7). Other characters' dispositions are communicated only obliquely, including Pharaoh's and his son's (cf. *Asen.* 1.7–9).

The analysis above revealed the expectation that much of this genre's adventure transpires internally, as when Callirhoe's private monologues take the narrative spotlight.[122] A comparable pattern prevails in *Aseneth*. When she first

---

121   Matthias Delcor, "Un roman d'amour d'origine thérapeute: Le Livre de Joseph et Asénath," *BLE* 63 (1962): 3–27. This last view is defended briefly by Wills, *The Jewish Novel in the Ancient World*, 176–77. Note the critique in Randall D. Chesnutt, "The Dead Sea Scrolls and the Meal Formula in *Joseph and Aseneth*: From Qumran Fever to Qumran Light," in *The Bible and the Dead Sea Scrolls: The Dead Seas Scrolls and the Qumran Community*, ed. James H. Charlesworth (Waco: Baylor University Press, 2006), 397–426.

122   Cf. the remarks above and Hägg, *The Novel in Antiquity*, 16; Fusillo, "The Conflict of Emotions: A Topos in the Greek Erotic Novel," 64.

ROMANCE: THWARTED RECOGNITIONS AND THE ΠΑΘΗ ΠΟΙΚΙΛΑ   159

sees Joseph, Aseneth, "groaned aloud and said in her heart (ἐν τῇ καρδίᾳ αὐτῆς), 'What will I do now, miserable as I am?'" (*Asen.* 6.1–2), launching an internal monologue comparable to Callirhoe's in the tomb (*Callir.* 1.8.3–4). Wearing her mourning tunic, Aseneth is locked in her room in the seven days while Joseph is away. Much is made of the fact that "her mouth was closed and she did not open it during the seven days and the seven nights of her humble state" (*Asen.* 11.2). While in this posture, "she said in her heart while not opening her mouth, 'What am I to do, lowly as I am, or where am I to go?'" (*Asen.* 11.3). Later, after her prayer, we learn that Aseneth was "afraid to open her mouth and utter the name of God" so that she continues to speak "in her heart without opening her mouth" (*Asen.* 11.15). Thus in *Aseneth* there is a plot-driven reason for making her speech an internal affair, comparable to Callirhoe's private prayers to Aphrodite (e.g., *Callir.* 1.1.7). In *Aseneth*, it leads to a decision to open her mouth to the Most High and speak his holy, awe-inspiring name (*Asen.* 11.17–19), then repeat much of what she had formerly said to herself privately (*Asen.* 12.1–13.15), interspersed with praise for her divine addressee. Aseneth also speaks to herself when she finds the honeycomb requested by her heavenly visitor: "Aseneth was astonished and said in her heart (ἐν τῇ καρδίᾳ αὐτῆς), 'Did this comb, then, come out of this man's mouth, because its aroma is like the breath of this man's mouth?" (*Asen.* 16.11).[123] When she suggests this to the man in the next scene, "the man smiled at Aseneth's understanding" (*Asen.* 16.12) and a moment later says, "Happy are you, Aseneth, because the secret mysteries of the Most High have been revealed to you" (*Asen.* 16.14).[124] Aseneth is the subject of most of the inner glimpses in the novel (see also *Asen.* 10.13; 16.9; 17.10; 18.1), but access to the minds of Joseph (*Asen.* 7.8) and Simeon (*Asen.* 23.7–8) figure as well.

The internal speeches in *Aseneth*, as in *Callirhoe*, in addition to foregrounding the states of mind of characters in the narrative, serve as a convenient device for helping the reader track the "accumulating burden of incidents" in the story.[125] For example, in a prayer to God, Aseneth retraces the events leading to her current state: the sackcloth, ashes, and mourning tunic, the removal of

---

123 ἐν τῇ καρδίᾳ αὐτῆς is missing in some witnesses. See Uta Barbara Fink, *Joseph und Aseneth: Revision des griechischen Textes und Edition der zweiten lateinischen Übersetzung*, PVTG 5 (Berlin: De Gruyter, 2008), 121.

124 On the revelatory motif in Aseneth, see Randall D. Chesnutt, "Revelatory Experiences Attributed to Biblical Women in Early Jewish Literature," in *"Women like This": New Perspectives on Jewish Women in the Greco-Roman World*, ed. Amy-Jill Levine (Atlanta: Scholars, 1991), 107–25; Edith McEwan Humphrey, *Joseph and Aseneth*, GApPs (Sheffield: Sheffield Academic Press, 2000).

125 See remarks above and Reardon, *The Form of Greek Romance*, 27.

the clothes and ornaments readers had "watched" her put on,[126] the sullying of her sanctuary-like room with tears and ashes smuggled from downstairs, her disposal of her gods, her naïve remarks about Joseph to her father, and so on. All of these events had been communicated to the reader previously by the narrator. The repetition in private character speech helps the reader with the accumulating burden of events in the same way that characters relating past events to each other helps the reader. When characters relate past events to each other, however, (as when Aseneth summarizes to Joseph the visit of the heavenly man, *Asen.* 19.5–7), the reader must also reckon with whether and to what extent the speaker is filtering her speech. Filtering speech is not an issue when characters rehearse narrative events to themselves.

Recognitions (ἀναγνωρίσεις) of people and narrative facts, whether drawn out or instantaneous, are important in the novels for advancing the plot. While *Aseneth* has no obvious counterpart to the famous scene where Chaereas recognizes Callirhoe among his prisoners of war, where a person's concealed identity is revealed, the Jewish novel does contain many instances of recognition construed more broadly. Sylvia Montiglio speaks of *Aseneth* lacking "the canonical recognition of the protagonists that in the Greek specimens ends their separation," but having instead a "vertical recognition" that takes place when Aseneth first sees Joseph on his chariot, a sight that sets her transformation in motion.[127] On Montiglio's reading, the shift from a horizontal to a vertical recognition is a way in which the genre's recognition convention is bent.

Another way in which recognition, construed broadly, is at work in the novel concerns nobility. This important piece of the protagonists' disposition and identity is immediately visible to those with the eyes to see it. In the novels, even when protagonists are in dire straits, they are "recognized" as noble by various onlookers. Dionysius, for example, recognizes that Callirhoe cannot be a mere slave (*Callir.* 2.3.6; cf. 5.3.2–9). In a comparable way, Aseneth recognizes Joseph as a "son of God." "For who among men on earth will beget such beauty, and which woman's womb will bear such light?" (*Asen.* 6.3–4).

Recognition also figures in Aseneth's encounter with the man from heaven (*Asen.* 14.3–17.10), but it is difficult to say exactly of what sort. The man praises Aseneth early in their encounter for her understanding (*Asen.* 16.12, 14), but when he flies off in a chariot "like a flame of fire," with four horses "like lightning," Aseneth has a deeper recognition, saying "I am foolish and audacious because I have spoken boldly and said that a man came into my room from heaven, and I did not know that a god came to me. And see now he is traveling

---

126   On the male gaze in *Aseneth*, see Kraemer, *When Aseneth Met Joseph*, 202.

127   Montiglio, *Love and Providence*, 205–7.

ROMANCE: THWARTED RECOGNITIONS AND THE ΠΑΘΗ ΠΟΙΚΙΛΑ

back to heaven to his place" (*Asen.* 17.9). The verse is problematic, since it is presented as a further recognition but one that seems to work as a step backwards on her path towards monolatry.[128] In any case, an important possibility introduced by this text is that recognition is not always total; *partial recognitions* seem to play a role in the genre as well, as when characters recognize a piece of Callirhoe's identity (e.g., that she is Greek, that she is freeborn and noble, that she is pregnant), but not the whole story.

Joseph's recognition of Aseneth on his return to Pentephres's house, after being away for the week during which Aseneth experienced her conversion, excellently illustrates the phenomenon. Failing to recognize her immediately, he performs what Kasper Bro Larsen labels the move of cognitive resistance: "Aseneth came out from the entrance to meet Joseph, and Joseph saw her and was amazed at her beauty and said to her, 'Who are you? Quickly, tell me!'"[129] She answers instead by telling him what happened in his absence, including the heavenly man's promise "to go also to Joseph and speak into his ears my words about you," which, as Aseneth points out, means that "And now, you know, my lord, whether that man has come to you and has spoken to you about me" (*Asen.* 19.1–11). Joseph then blesses her and reveals that the angel followed through on his promise. The two embrace and share a series of kisses in which Joseph imparts to her the spirit of life, the spirit of wisdom, and the spirit of truth. No medley of emotions is narrated, but the two, when they come together, "came to life in their spirit" (*Asen.* 19.10), which is structurally and functionally comparable.

The prophetic stature of Joseph's brother Levi also figures into the discourse of recognition. At *Aseneth* 23.8, "Levi saw the consideration of his (Simeon's) heart because Levi was a prophet and he would observe (things) clearly with his mind and his eyes and he would read what is written in the heart of people." Later, he perceives in his prophetic spirit the plot of Dan, Gad, and Pharaoh's son, and warns the would-be victims (*Asen.* 25.6). Near the end of novel, Levi recognizes that Aseneth wants to save the brothers who had recently been working for Pharoah's son. He also apprehends that those brothers are hiding nearby: "Levi realized (it), and he did not report it to his brothers. For he was afraid lest they cut them down in their anger" (*Asen.* 28.15). Levi's recognition gives rise to fear, illustrating the genre's conventional pairing of recognition and emotion.

---

128 *Aseneth* 17.9 is missing from some manuscripts, and in those where it does appear, her recognition is that the visitor was an angel of the LORD, or a man from heaven, or a divine being. See Ahearne-Kroll, "Joseph and Aseneth," 2587n147; Burchard, *Joseph und Aseneth,* 228.

129 Larsen, *Recognizing the Stranger,* 64–66.

As in the other novels, a common tactic for delaying recognition and its attendant emotions lies in the introduction of misunderstandings. A straightforward example may be found in the scene where Aseneth lies on her bed in her locked room, groaning and weeping. The readers know that this is due to a combination of causes, including being rebuffed by Joseph and her grief and anger felt in connection to her idolatrous past. Aseneth's reply to her companions' inquiry after her wellbeing, however, is that she has a pain in her head and weakness in her limbs preventing her from getting out of bed (*Asen.* 10.6–7; cf. 18.4). This is shown to be untrue, however, when a moment later she gets up and opens the door quietly to dress in her mourning tunic (*Asen.* 10.8). The interaction between Chariton's Callirhoe and her serving women as they prepare her for her marriage is comparable (*Callir.* 1.1.13–15). At *Aseneth* 11.4, Aseneth mis-imagines her parents' minds (cf. *Asen.* 20.7 for the correction). As Aseneth is recounting her past wrongs, she numbers among them that, "unknowingly was I led, and I have spoken blasphemous words against my lord, Joseph, because I, miserable as I am, did not know that he is your son, since people told me that 'Joseph is a son of the shepherd from the land of Canaan'" (*Asen.* 13.13). This is a misunderstanding that Aseneth later corrects herself, when she sees Joseph with her own eyes (*Asen.* 6.1). In the second part of the novel, Pharaoh's son creates a misperception to recruit the sons of Bilhah and Zilpah for his plot against Joseph. "Pharaoh's son lied to them and said, 'See, blessing and death are before your face.... For I heard Joseph your brother speaking to Pharaoh my father about you saying, 'Dan, Gad, Naphtali, and Asher are children of my father's servants, and they are not my brothers. I will wait for the death of my father, and I will wipe them out from the earth and all their offspring" (*Asen.* 24.7–8). The younger brothers, Naphtali and Asher, seem to experience a change of heart before Dan and Gad, since they attempt to dissuade them from attacking Joseph already in chapter 25. Dan and Gad's more vivid recognition follows God's intervention, brought about in response to Aseneth's prayer: "The LORD God heard Aseneth's voice, and immediately their [Dan and Gad's] swords fell from their hands onto the ground and burned to ashes. And the sons of Bilhah and Zilpah saw this great event, and they were very afraid and said, 'The LORD wages war against us on behalf of Aseneth!'" (*Asen.* 27.11–28.1). The narrative as it stands does not allow us to say whether the misperception created by Pharaoh's son is ever cleared up. What we can see is that it triggers a chain of events delaying the brothers' recognition of a key narrative circumstance, namely, God's special care for Joseph and Aseneth.

At the end of her week-long psychodrama, Aseneth is distressed about her appearance and imagines Joseph's reaction: "Woe to me, the lowly one, <because> my face is fallen. Joseph will see me and scorn me" (*Asen.* 18.7). Readers

ROMANCE: THWARTED RECOGNITIONS AND THE ΠΑΘΗ ΠΟΙΚΙΛΑ   163

familiar with Joseph's character and disposition may doubt the prediction; as the narrative stands, however, readers do not get to find out if this was a true misperception or not, since Aseneth goes on to become divinely beautiful after this scene and before Joseph sees her (*Asen.* 18.9–10).

Some of the created misperceptions take place before the narrative begins. When Aseneth initially refuses to see Joseph, it is because she thinks he is an "alien and a fugitive and sold (as a slave)," a "shepherd's son" who has "slept with his mistress, and his master threw him into the prison of darkness" and was brought out of prison because he could do what old ladies could have done, namely, interpret dreams (*Asen.* 4.10). To the reader who knows the biblical story of Joseph, this is a fascinating series of details. The author has theorized the mind of an Egyptian skeptical reader of the biblical account, or perhaps the mind of an Egyptian misled by Potiphar's wife's account.

Recognitions, as we have seen, are one of several means by which emotions are triggered in the novels. As was typical in the novels, many characters in *Aseneth* experience suffering on account of the protagonist's beauty. Joseph's beauty causes horrible suffering (ὡς ἑώρων τὸν Ἰωσήφ, κακῶς ἔπασχον ἐπὶ τῷ κάλλει αὐτοῦ) among "all the wives and daughters of Egyptian men" (*Asen.* 7.3), and Aseneth's beauty (despite the paradoxical fact that she was kept out of sight) attracts suitors from all over Egypt, including even the king's son (*Asen.* 1.6–7). After her conversion, Aseneth's beauty elicits amazement in all who see her, including Joseph (*Asen.* 19.4; cf. 18.10, 11; 20.7; 21.4). Aseneth also suffers at the initial prospect of being married to Joseph: "much red sweat poured over her upon her face, she became very angry, and she looked sidelong at her father with her eyes" (*Asen.* 4.9). A similar extreme reaction plays out when Joseph rebuffs her: "She was deeply stricken and very distressed and groaned aloud, and she looked intently at Joseph with her eyes opened and her eyes were full of tears. And Joseph looked at her and he had compassion for her, and he too was stricken because Joseph was gentle and merciful, and he feared God" (*Asen.* 8.8).

Virtually every arrival or revelation of a piece of information is met with an emotion. Pentephres was "extremely glad" (ἐχάρη χαρὰν μεγάλην σφόδρα) to hear of Joseph's approach (*Asen.* 3.3).[130] Aseneth "rejoiced" (ἐχάρη) to hear that her father and mother had returned from the field of their inheritance

---

130   The prominence of the emotions is comparable to what one finds in the novels, but the
       syntax with which they are expressed is much closer to the Septuagint. When characters
       rejoice, they "rejoice with a great rejoicing" (e.g., at *Asen.* 3.3; 4.1; 7.8; 15.11). A similar pat-
       tern prevails for representing fear, trembling, groaning, and grieving. For references see
       the following note and Ahearne-Kroll, "Joseph and Aseneth," 2583n35.

(*Asen.* 3.5), Pentephres and his wife were "very glad" (ἐχάρησαν ... χαρὰν μεγάλην) to see their daughter (*Asen.* 4.1), Aseneth "rejoiced" (ἐχάρη) to see what her parents had brought with them from the field (*Asen.* 4.2), and so on. Amazement (τὸ θαμβεῖν) in Aseneth is used only in responses to her post-conversion beauty (*Asen.* 18.10; 19.4; 20.7; 21.4) and in her response to Jacob's beauty when she sees him for the first time (*Asen.* 22.7–8). The emotions are frequently emphasized with a Hebraizing syntactical structure familiar from the Septuagint: to be "very afraid" is to "fear a great fear" (ἐφοβήθη φόβον μέγαν).[131] More extreme displays of πάθος are Aseneth's first reaction to Pentephres's suggestion that she be married to Joseph and her reaction to seeing Joseph pull up in his chariot. In the first instance, "much red sweat poured over her upon her face, she became very angry, and she looked sidelong at her father with her eyes" (*Asen.* 4.9). In the second case, "she was deeply stricken and her soul was broken; her knees weakened, her whole body trembled, and she was very afraid" (*Asen.* 6.1). The emotions that feature most frequently in *Aseneth* are χαρά (*Asen.* 3.3; 4.1; 7.8; 15.11; 21.3; 24.5), θάμβος (*Asen.* 18.10; 19.4; 21.2; 22.7, 8), and φόβος (*Asen.* 6.1; 10.1; 14.10; 18.11; 24.1), but one also encounters characters experiencing ἔλεος (*Asen.* 8.8); ὀργή and θύμος (at *Asen.* 4.9; 23.9–10; 28.7; cf. the potential for anger in 28.17); λύπη (*Asen.* 8.8; 9.1; 16.2; 18.3; 24.1, 11; cf. plans to cause grief in 24.19); and general distress (τὸ κατανύσσειν at *Asen.* 8.8; τὸ ταράσσειν at 24.11; 26.8; cf. 11.10).

Chariton offered the figure of Dionysius as a study in how a civilized person ought to control his emotions, and part of what made his character so compelling (in a way that neither Chaereas or the pirates can match) was the real struggle he experiences between what he ought to do (exercise self-control) and what he wants to do (take Callirhoe for himself). Both Joseph and Levi model self-control in *Aseneth*, and Pharaoh's son illustrates what can happen when one fails to control the emotions. Joseph's self-control is highlighted in Pentephres's description of his disposition: "Joseph is a god-fearing man, self-controlled, and chaste (θεοσεβὴς καὶ σώφρων καὶ παρθένος), ... adept in wisdom and knowledge, and the spirit of God is upon him and the favor of the LORD is with him" (*Asen.* 4.8). He does not show any erotic affection for Aseneth prior to her conversion. He is "mightily stricken" (κατενύγη ἰσχυρῶς) because of her, is "greatly grieved" (ἐλυπήθη σφόδρα), and has "great compassion for her" (ἠλέησεν αὐτὴν σφόδρα), but the unambiguous reason given for his concern is that he is πραῢς καὶ ἐλεήμων καὶ φοβούμενος τὸν θεόν (*Asen.* 8.8). Levi's self-control is even more pronounced. While Joseph controls his own emotions, Levi controls both his own emotions and the emotions of his brother Simeon.

---

131 Further instances of the construction with στεναγμός, χαρά, φοβός, τρόμος, and λύπη at 3.3; 4.1; 6.1; 7.8; 10.1, 3; 11.1; 14.10; 15.11; 18.11; 21.3; 24.1, 5.

When Levi sees Simeon growing angry, he "stepped on Simeon's right foot with his foot and pressed it, and he signaled to him to cease from his anger. And Levi said to Simeon quietly, 'Why are you furious with anger against this man? We are god-fearing men, and it is not fitting for us to repay evil for evil" (*Asen.* 23.9). He then speaks boldly to Pharaoh's son "with a disciplined calmness of heart" (*Asen.* 23.10). Levi is also able to interact with his sister-in-law without becoming enflamed by desire for her.

Aseneth shows that the genre expectations of the Greek novel concerning delayed recognitions and management of emotions, among other cognitive themes, can be put to work effectively in a narrative about trading idolatry for exclusive worship of the God of Israel.

5   Conclusion

The whole action of the Greek novel can compellingly be characterized in terms of drawing out states of misperception and misunderstanding, delaying recognition by various means, until a climactic moment. The predictable but flexible erotic plots are calculated to maximize pathetic expression in the characters, excelling both at creating the circumstances necessary for flourishing discrepant awareness and at maintaining those discrepancies. The protagonists' encounters with each other, both at the initial meeting and at subsequent reunion(s), stir their emotions. Serial ordeals also provoke emotional responses, providing occasions for the protagonists to describe their plight and how it makes them feel, often in finely tuned rhetorical form and often with interior monologues. Encounters with the protagonists produce emotional responses in the novels' cast of supporting characters. Much of this material is non-perceptible or only partially perceptible to the figures who interact with suffering characters in the novels, and is shared with the reader by means of a narrator. In the next chapter, we will turn to consider patterns of represented cognition in classical tragic drama, a medium antecedent to the novels and without a narrator. Without a narrator, direct dialogue needs be skillfully managed to conjure up phenomena comparable to those studied in this chapter, including discrepant awareness, misperceptions, misunderstandings, and recognitions.

CHAPTER 5

Drama: Discrepant Awareness and Dramatic Irony

This chapter, after looking at a range of ways scholars have connected the Fourth Gospel to classical Greek tragedy, explores dramatic patterns of representing minds, both in general and in close readings of Euripides's *Hippolytus* and Ezekiel the Tragedian's *Exagoge*. The best known ancient tragedians in antiquity and still today are fifth-century Athenians: Aeschylus, Sophocles, and Euripides. Their corpora, of which a substantial portion remains, influenced virtually all subsequent classical drama. Partly for that reason, and also because more of their plays have survived than plays by their Hellenistic counterparts, more time is spent in this chapter on Euripides than Ezekiel, both in the general exploration and in the first of the two probes.[1] Ezekiel is more difficult to study, both for having gone virtually unnoticed as a dramatist in later antiquity and for the fact that only fragments of a single play survive (he may have written others).[2] Euripides is easier to study, both because of the volume of surviving work (nineteen plays are extant) and because of a more robust reception history. Although only a fraction of his lifetime output (Euripides wrote over ninety plays), the surviving plays are enough to give readers a good sense of the genre's conventions for representing character cognition. Ezekiel is worth studying, however, both for illustrating how certain conventions of the genre may have been changing in the Hellenistic period and for illustrating the difference between working freely from mythoi, on the one hand, and a written, "historical" narrative, on the other. If the Fourth Gospel's conventions for writing minds is dramatically inflected, a question to be considered at length in the next chapter, Ezekiel will help us appreciate in a preliminary way the scope latent in the genre for structural and stylistic innovation.

---

1 Satyrus of Callatis comments in his Hellenistic-period *Life of Euripides* that Euripides's contemporaries did not sufficiently appreciate him as a master of his craft. This may imply that by Satyrus's day Euripides was widely considered a master of the medium. See Satyros and Stefan Schorn, *Satyros aus Kallatis: Sammlung der Fragmente mit Kommentar* (Basel: Schwabe, 2004).

2 The idea that Ezekiel wrote other plays is based on Alexander Polyhistor's description of him as ὁ τῶν τραγῳδιῶν ποιητής (apud Eusebius, *Praep. ev.* 9.436d).

© KONINKLIJKE BRILL NV, LEIDEN, 2019 | DOI:10.1163/9789004396043_006

DRAMA: DISCREPANT AWARENESS AND DRAMATIC IRONY 167

1   John and Drama

Many early Christian leaders warned their flocks to stay away from Greek drama. Tertullian, for example, instructs catechumens that the theater is incompatible with the Christian life of meekness, peace, and purity. Drama, he warned, was a portal to immorality.[3] Augustine, whose Neoplatonist philosophy of art predisposed him against the theater, argued that the language of the stage was an inadequate system of signs for representing Christian realities.[4] Though such early readers would not have talked about the Fourth Gospel (or any Scriptural text, presumably) as cast in dramatic form, there is a significant modern tendency to do just that.[5]

Modern Johannine scholars can mean at least two things by "dramatic" as a descriptive term applied to the Fourth Gospel. Some argue that the Fourth Gospel in whole or in part conforms to the program laid out for tragedy by Aristotle in the *Poetics* (cf. the discussion in ch. 1 above) or formally resembles the classical, fifth-century models of Greek tragic drama by Aeschylus, Sophocles, and Euripides. These scholars find in John, *inter alia*, five-act structures; devices like stichomythia, enjambment, and rhetorical questions; stage directions; and the subordination of action to speech. On the other hand are those who employ "dramatic" as a synonym for "vivid" or "exciting," without reference to any particular ancient genre.[6] This chapter is concerned mainly

---

3   In *de Spectaculis*. A work by Novatian with the same title also survives from the same period. Cf. also John Chrysostom's comment that "The church is not a theater, where we listen merely for pleasure" (*Homilia de Statuis ad Populum Antiochenum*). Quoted in T. D. Barnes, "Christians and the Theater: E. Togo Salmon Papers I," in *Roman Theater and Society*, ed. William J. Slater (Ann Arbor: University of Michigan Press, 1996), 161–80.

4   Augustine talks about the theater in *Confessions, City of God, Concerning the Teacher*, and *On Christian Teaching*, as well as in occasional speeches and letters. For Augustine's antipathy to the theater, see Donnalee Dox, *The Idea of the Theater in Latin Christian Thought: Augustine to the Fourteenth Century* (Ann Arbor: University of Michigan Press, 2004). The object of critique in writers like Tertullian and Augustine is the perceived content (incest, murder, idolatry, and the like) rather than the form "drama" as such. This distinction has allowed some later theologians to conceive of the form in more positive terms, while maintaining Tertullian and Augustine's aversion to the immoral classical content. This is the kind of argument one finds in the self-exculpatory appendix to Kevin J. Vanhoozer's *Faith Speaking Understanding: Performing the Drama of Doctrine* (Westminster John Knox Press, 2014). See also James K. A. Smith, "Staging the Incarnation: Revisioning Augustine's Critique of Theatre," *LitTh* 15 (2001): 123–39.

5   Other early Christian authors, especially in the East, were less averse to casting Scripture dramatically. See, e.g., Ephrem the Syrian's dramatic dialogue poems, Jacob of Serugh's dramatic verse homilies, or Romanos the Melodist's *kontakia*.

6   Also to be noted under this second banner is J. Louis Martyn's description of the Fourth Gospel as "a two level drama," and the conversation it started when it was published in

168   CHAPTER 5

with the group that makes the case for a full or partial genre-based connection, not dealing directly with the second group, where "dramatic" means something like "exciting."[7]

In 1907, F. R. Montgomery Hitchcock argued that the Fourth Gospel should be read as a drama in the mode of Greek tragedy. To make his case, he focused on the Johannine language of "the hour" as a structuring device. His ideas took shape more concretely in his 1923 article, "Is the Fourth Gospel a Drama?," where he argues that it conforms to Aristotle's criteria in *Poetics* 12 and 18 and Horace's in *Ars poetica* 189–90.

> We ... see how closely he follows the canons of Aristotle, ... that adherence to the then recognised canons of the drama would establish the dramatic character and unity of this Gospel, whose writer, while attending to his characters, did not neglect the structure of his plot, which according to Aristotle (*Poetics*, vi. 9,15) is "the soul of a tragedy"—i.e., that in which the dramatic conflict is unfolded.[8]

References to the "hour" of Jesus "mark the dramatic development of the work," he wrote, which can be understood in five parts: "there is the beginning, the development towards the central point, the central point, the development towards the end, the end."[9] It would be easy to read Hitchcock's article today as though its primary interest were the genre of John. Read in light of the concerns that drove academic conversations in his milieu, however, and looking to the frequently underscored consequences of its reading of John, it becomes apparent that Hitchcock was less invested in settling a question about *genre* and more concerned to establish the literary *unity* of John over and against

---

1968. See J. Louis Martyn, *History and Theology in the Fourth Gospel*, 3rd ed., NTL (Louisville: Westminster John Knox, 2003). When scholars have engaged Martyn's thesis subsequently and found reasons that John is or is not "a two-level drama," they are less interested in genre than whether or not the Fourth Gospel describes the experiences of the Johannine community at the end of the first century CE symbolically in its discourse about the life of Jesus. Cf. Tobias Hägerland, "John's Gospel: A Two-Level Drama?," *JSNT* 25 (2003): 309–22.

7   If there are few attempts to establish such a link in John's case, there are even fewer for the Synoptics. One exception is Gilbert G. Bilezikian, *The Liberated Gospel: A Comparison of the Gospel of Mark and Greek Tragedy* (Grand Rapids: Baker Book House, 1977).

8   F. R. M. Hitchcock, "Is the Fourth Gospel a Drama?," *Theol.* 7 (1923): 15.

9   Hitchcock, 16.

those source- and form-critics who were discovering layers of tradition and compilation in the Gospels.[10]

In 1930, Clayton R. Bowen argued that the Fourth Gospel "is not a narrative at all," not a story composed from scratch, but rather a miscellany of *material connected dramatically*. That is to say, the material is itself the kind of thing one finds in classical drama (e.g., dialogue and monologue, entrances and exits, sketches of settings and characters), and the apparently abrupt disjunctions in the text are like abrupt shifts in drama, where the authorial unity of the texts was not the matter of dispute that it was in John's case.[11] The thesis was part of an attempt to explain John's style, particularly the long discourses, the dialogic material, and the aporias, none of which feature so extensively in the Synoptics. Whereas the "dramatic" connections in Hitchcock's assessment conferred "unity" on the Fourth Gospel, in Bowen's work a dramatic paradigm explains John's apparent disunity. These are two sides of the same coin.

C. Milo Connick's 1948 article points to a handful of predecessors other than Hitchcock and Bowen who link John to drama, most of them in the less technical sense described above.[12] Connick attempts to advance the conversation by looking at the "purpose" of the Evangelist, the Evangelist's use of synoptic material (assuming that John knows Mark, Luke, and probably Matthew), and his use of dramatic techniques. The purpose of the Gospel, which he finds articulated at John 20.31, is "to produce a twofold conviction: (1) that Jesus is the Christ (the fulfiller of the hopes and promises of Israel), and (2) that he is the Son of God (the fulfiller of the destiny of mankind)." He deems this "wholly consonant with that of a dramatist who selects his material with an eye to persuading his public."[13] This assumes, however, what is to be demonstrated: Is it the function of dramatists to select material with an eye to persuasion? And if so, persuasion of what sort? To what ends? Ancient rhetoric and drama intersect

---

10   F. R. M. Hitchcock, "The Dramatic Development of the Fourth Gospel," *Exp.* 4 (1907): 266–79; Hitchcock, "Is the Fourth Gospel a Drama?" On the unity question and the trajectory of scholarship traced here on the next several pages, see Colleen M. Conway's excellent article "The Production of the Johannine Community: A New Historicist Perspective," *JBL* 121 (2002): 479–95.

11   Clayton R. Bowen, "The Fourth Gospel as Dramatic Material," *JBL* 49 (1930): 292–305.

12   C. Milo Connick, "The Dramatic Character of the Fourth Gospel," *JBL* 67 (1948): 159–69. Connick points to Adolf Jülicher, *An Introduction to the New Testament* (New York: G. P. Putnam's Sons, 1904), 389; D. A. Hayes, *John and His Writings* (New York: The Methodist Book Concern, 1917), 94; G. R. B. Charnwood, *According to Saint John* (Boston: Little, Brown, & Co., 1925), 61; R. H. Strachan, *The Fourth Evangelist: Dramatist or Historian?* (New York: George H. Doran Co., 1925), 14–15, 31; G. H. C. Macgregor, *The Gospel of John* (London: Hodder and Stoughton, 1928), xxii.

13   Connick, "The Dramatic Character of the Fourth Gospel," 160.

170   CHAPTER 5

in mutually constitutive ways, but no extant Greek drama has a purpose statement leveled at the audience's beliefs about the present, extra-dramatic identity of a person from the play.[14] Connick's second area of inquiry, John's use of
Synoptic material, reinforces his first point: John has been selective in omitting, adding, and altering Synoptic sources, and shows that his aim is not "a
well-rounded account" of the life and teachings of Jesus, but rather to retain
only what seems to him suitable for embodying his thoughts, omitting whatever does not fit.[15] Connick's third area of inquiry at first glance seems promising
in connection to this chapter, since "dramatic techniques" are precisely what
we are exploring as they relate to the representation of characters' cognition.
But thought representation is not a part of the eight techniques Connick discusses under "dramatic techniques." The eight techniques are: (1) catastrophe
announced at the beginning, and the whole of the narrative tending irresist-
ibly towards the tragic ending, which is constantly kept before the reader;
(2) concentrated action as the narrative moves forward; (3) contrasts of the
light/dark variety; (4) symmetry in the recurrence of certain characters and dramatic scenes (Nathanael, Jesus's mother, meals with the disciples); (5) variety
in settings and modes of discourse (story, sermon, conversations at night and
at noontime); (6) dramatic irony (especially in the comments of Caiaphas, the
chief priests and Pharisees, and Pilate); (7) indications of time and place; (8)
dialogue pattern following the structure observable in the interactions with
Nicodemus, the Samaritan Woman, the Jews, Jews who believed Jesus, Martha,
and sometimes the disciples. Connick does not illustrate these techniques
with examples from classical dramas, nor does he build a case for why they
are necessary or typical of the genre. One could, however, easily find instances
of these techniques when turning to the dramas, and this is precisely what
some more recent scholars have done. In this book, we are most interested in
those techniques that bear on the cognitive domain of narrative. Connick's
first, third, sixth, and eighth items can all readily be connected to that domain.

A generic link with tragedy does not necessitate that the Fourth Gospel was
written for performance, a point the early-twentieth century scholars noted.

---

14   On the intersection of rhetoric and drama, see George L. Parsenios, *Rhetoric and Drama
      in the Johannine Lawsuit Motif*, WUNT 258 (Tübingen: Mohr Siebeck, 2010); David Sansone,
      Greek Drama and the Invention of Rhetoric (Chichester: Wiley Blackwell, 2012).

15   Here Connick follows W. Heitmüller, "*Das Johannes-Evangelium*," where he reads "Wenn
      unser Evangelist ... so manchen synoptischen Stoff übergeht, so erklärt sich das aus
      seinem Zweck. Er verwertet nur das, was ihm geeignet erscheint seine Gedanken zu
      verkörpern, und last fort, was sich diesem Zweck nicht fügt" (Heitmüller, "*Das Johannes-
      Evangelium*," cited in Otto Baumgarten, *Die Schriften des Neuen Testaments* [Göttingen:
      Vandenhoeck and Ruprecht, 1920], 26).

DRAMA: DISCREPANT AWARENESS AND DRAMATIC IRONY

Classical drama, unlike most other ancient genres, including those discussed in the previous three chapters, was bound by certain institutionally-given restrictions if they were to be eligible for performance. Turning from the fifth-century exemplars to the Fourth Gospel, the most obvious differences from a formal perspective have to do with meter and narrational strategies. John does not follow a metrical scheme. Differences in narrational strategies—John's lack of a chorus and use of a third-person narrator—are of greater interest. These formal differences are so striking that one wonders why connect John to drama at all. Among these early scholars, the motivation seems clear enough, visible in Connick's conclusions to his first two sections: in addition to solving "unity" concerns, the link to drama helped some biblical scholars troubled by apparent discrepancies between the Synoptics and John. Higher criticism, mostly in Germany where *Literarkritik*[16] had pulled the Gospels apart, devastating such cherished notions as "authorial unity." The differences between John and the Synoptics, to a certain kind of critic, amounted to proof that parts of the Gospels were made up, the stuff of myth, in need of demythologizing. By suggesting that John was composed in a different, dramatic mold, the scholars surveyed above "saved" John from the bonfire of myth.

The second half of the twentieth century saw new kinds of arguments being made about John and drama. Perhaps to the chagrin of "unity" scholars like Hitchcock and Bowen, Bultmann's view that the Gospels were composite and edited documents became the scholarly consensus, and redaction criticism had its heyday—chiefly in work on the Synoptics, but in Johannine studies too. The idea that John was "drama" in some technical sense, however, lived on in some circles. The "literary unity" concern receded, but the "John's differences from the Synoptics" concern—latent in some work from the earlier period—took on a new sense of urgency. In 1983, W. R. Domeris used the John-as-dramatist argument to account for peculiarities of the Fourth Gospel: "if ... John wrote as a dramatist in order to highlight certain aspects of the person of Jesus, including his deity and pre-existence, then John's variation from the Synoptic tradition might have another provenance."[17] Here also for the first time we begin to find direct engagement with classical dramatists: Domeris opens by quoting from Euripides's *Andromache* (though he misidentifies the play as Euripides's *Alcestis*) and closes by quoting from Sophocles's *Antigone*,

---

16 Not to be confused with the "literary criticism" introduced to biblical studies by Stibbe, Culpepper, et al. in the 1980s. Members of this latter group quite deliberately set aside questions of redactional history and approach the Gospels as literary unities.

17 William R. Domeris, "The Johannine Drama," *JTSA* 42 (1983): 29.

signaling that by "drama" he means in the first place the canonical plays by Aeschylus, Sophocles, and Euripides.

Domeris's argument is based chiefly on three observations: (1) proportionally speaking the Gospel is mostly direct speech; (2) the speakers are named; and (3) the Gospel can easily "be reproduced in dramatic form." These three factors form the basis for his contention that "John has deliberately fashioned his Gospel after the model of the Greek dramas and particularly the Tragedies."[18] Domeris does not use the language of genre, preferring instead to speak of John's "form" ("John does not abandon the form of a Gospel") and tragedies as a "model" after which a Gospel might be fashioned.[19] Domeris was not the first to suggest that dramatic conventions might explain some of the classic problems in Johannine exegesis stemming from perceived departures with the Synoptic tradition. He does, however, break new ground in connecting John's prologue with prologues found in some classical dramas. John's "dramatic model accounts largely for the style of the prologue and releases us from the attempt to detect an aramaic [sic] poetical original."[20] Domeris does not remark on characterization or the representation of thoughts in either classical dramas or in John.

Fifteen years earlier, an unassuming little book had been published which would set the agenda for a dominant stream of Johannine scholarship for much of the rest of the twentieth century. In *History and Theology in the Fourth Gospel*, J. Louis Martyn uses the image of a "two-level drama" to talk about the social history of the Johannine community, where the story of Jesus is playing out on the surface of the text and the story of the Johannine community is encoded as a second-level story reflected in that first-level story. Although much of his treatment of the Fourth Gospel, particularly chapter 9, uses the imagery of theatrical production, neither Martyn nor the major adopters of his thesis (esp. Raymond Brown) use "drama" in a technical, genre-identifying sense.[21]

---

18   Domeris, 29–30. Later, he specifically puts "biography" off the table: "all this is consistent with a writer whose prime concern is to present not a biography, but an understanding of the ethical, soteriological and cosmic issues surrounding the hero of his play." Domeris, 30.

19   Domeris, 30.

20   Domeris, 30. For a lengthier discussion of John's prologue with comparison to dramatic prologues, see Elizabeth Harris, *Prologue and Gospel: The Theology of the Fourth Evangelist*, JSNTSup 107 (Sheffield: Sheffield Academic Press, 1994). Though Harris insists that John deliberately and self-consciously employed something like a Euripidean prologue to his work, she does less to substantiate this claim than to explore how John 1.1–18 prepares readers for the rest of the Gospel.

21   Martyn does not discuss the genre of John as a whole text. He does use the language of genre to describe a pattern he detects, but this is a genre that is *sui generis* to John, without

DRAMA: DISCREPANT AWARENESS AND DRAMATIC IRONY   173

The Martyn thesis, however, was enormously influential in the 1980s and 1990s, when interest in literary criticism and the gospels peaked. One of those influenced was Mark Stibbe, who put John in conversation with Euripides's *Bacchae*, arguing that John adopted and subverted the plot or *mythos* of that tragedy.[22] A central emphasis of Stibbe's early work on the Fourth Gospel is that its narrative form and social function are inseparable.[23] The attention to narrative form takes its lead from Culpepper and the still-young field of Johannine literary studies, though rejecting the New Critical tendency he sees in them of focusing on the text apart from social circumstances. The sociological context within which Stibbe locates the social function of John's narrative is a version of the Johannine community paradigm. Stibbe is aware that critiques have been leveled at Martyn's thesis,[24] and yet advances a bold vision of the Johannine community's social history, whose members he thinks are estranged from contemporary Judaism and in some cases their natural families. In these straits, the power of the Gospel's narrative is to reinforce the authority of the beloved disciple (identified as Lazarus), "to recreate the sense of family and home in a people faced with the crisis of metaphorical and actual homelessness," and create a sense of "homecoming" with John 19.25.[25] Where Hitchcock had discerned a five-act structure in the Gospel as a whole, Stibbe focuses his attention on chapters 18–19, where he finds a five-act structure in smaller compass. He connects these chapters with what he calls "Dionysiac poetics," connecting John's Jesus to Euripides's Dionysus insofar as both have divine and human parents, both come into the world without being recognized, both seek to alleviate suffering, and both involve a death (in the *Bacchae*, the

---

precedent in the synoptics or other ancient literature, and without an ancient category label. "By creating a sequence of scenes based on the miracle story, someone created a *literary genre* quite without counterpart in the body of the Gospels. We may indeed call it a drama" (32; emphasis original). The language of genre disappears after the introduction to the book, though he will later compare the form of the Gospel to the thought-world of Jewish apocalypticism (130–6). The language of "drama" pervades the book, but without reference to Athens, literary criticism, or any of the classical dramatists.

22   Stibbe makes no claim that a relationship of literary dependence exists between John and the *Bacchae* (139), but does see in John the same "deep structure that generated tragic stories in ancient Athens—the purpose, passion, perception paradigm centring on the killing of a king and derived from the myth of Dionysus." Mark W. G. Stibbe, *John as Storyteller: Narrative Criticism and the Fourth Gospel* (Cambridge: Cambridge University Press, 1992), 139.

23   In this he anticipates one of the major trajectories of modern genre scholarship, rhetorical genre studies, the foundational text for which is Carolyn R. Miller, "Genre as Social Action," *QJSp* 70 (1984): 151–67.

24   Stibbe, *John as Storyteller*, 56–61.

25   Stibbe, 148–67; quotations from 166 and 167.

σπαραγμός of Pentheus) and an ascent into heaven. Of particular interest for this book is the failure of recognition, about which I shall have more to say, both in this chapter in connection to other dramatic productions and in the next chapter in connection to John.

More recently, Dennis R. MacDonald has developed a more sophisticated and elaborate thesis connecting the Fourth Gospel to the *Bacchae*. Returning to the source-critical and *literarkritischen* approaches that dominated Johannine scholarship in the mid-20th century, MacDonald argues that the Fourth Gospel's earliest recoverable version—a text he labels the *Dionysian Gospel*—was in conversation with Dionysian discourse represented especially, but not exclusively, by the language of Euripides's *Bacchae*.[26] MacDonald offers a tentative reconstruction of the *Dionysian Gospel* and produces an intertextual commentary on the mimetic relationship he sees existing between it and the *Bacchae*. Parallels abound, and MacDonald points them out with an expert eye. The cognitive dimension of the two texts, however, is not given sustained attention. MacDonald's interest is more squarely placed on things *done* by characters in the two traditions, and a case is developed that the *Dionysian Gospel's* Jesus outperforms the *Bacchae's* Dionysus at every turn.

Interest in John in connection to drama waxed and waned in the twentieth century, but it has become a staple of Johannnine studies in this century largely thanks to an important book by Jo-Ann Brant, who deliberately and conscientiously engages questions of genre.[27] Brant argues that comparing John with classical dramatists in a structuralist mode reveals confluences in the dramatic structure of each. Though Brant has done more to associate John with drama as a genre than anyone else, she stops short of claiming that it is a drama in a technical sense: "I take the argument for reliance upon dramatic conventions as far as I can without violating the form in which we now find the gospel," she writes, going on to cite Stibbe's dictum that "A drama is a story without a storyteller," and John has a storyteller (i.e., the narrator).[28] For Brant, the upshot is that the Fourth Gospel can be read as a performance piece—among her goals is to demonstrate the usefulness of theater criticism for Johannine analysis.[29] The book looks in particular at how speech is conveyed (ch. 2), how characterization works (ch. 3), and how Jesus's death is portrayed (ch. 4).

---

26 Dennis R. MacDonald, *The Dionysian Gospel: The Fourth Gospel and Euripides* (Minneapolis: Fortress, 2017).

27 Jo-Ann A. Brant, *Dialogue and Drama: Elements of Greek Tragedy in the Fourth Gospel* (Peabody: Hendrickson, 2004).

28 Brant, 7. Cf. Stibbe, *John as Storyteller*, 130.

29 Brant, *Dialogue and Drama*, 8.

DRAMA: DISCREPANT AWARENESS AND DRAMATIC IRONY 175

According to Brant, drama offers a helpful context for explaining the antagonistic language of the Fourth Gospel. She draws on theater theorists who do not limit themselves to ancient drama, especially the distinction drawn by Roman Ingarden and Eli Rozik between fictional, theatrical, and performance axes of dramatic texts.[30] She explores "the conventions of drama by which speech constructs the world of the play and its action" and how "the long speeches and dialogues of the gospel, like those in Greek tragedy, use antitheses and verbal duels to represent the conflict and to organize the characters' thoughts so that they can be comprehended by an audience and recited by a reader or actor."[31] Though her focus is not "thought" as an element of characterization and a domain of narrative per se, but rather what Aristotle in the *Poetics* calls διανοία (cf. ch. 1 of this book), her approach sheds light on this important dimension of the Gospel's plot and characterization.

Brant offers a fine discussion of the debates and conflicts in John. By setting these in conversation with ancient Greek tragedy, new light is cast on the orienting desires and dispositions of Johannine figures in conflict. She also explores the consequences of the narrator's reduced role, which creates space for the characters to articulate the plot in their speech.[32] For example, in her discussion of ἀναγνώρισις in John, Brant observes that "recognition is a cognitive act and therefore something private. In a narrative, an omniscient narrator can reveal what occurs in a character's head. In a performance piece, recognition must be played out on the dramatic and theatrical axes so that the audience can see or hear the event happen."[33] Actions that follow the recognition and the way that characters speak at the moment of recognition are two of the primary means by which recognition is represented in drama.

George Parsenios is another scholar who has managed to shed a great deal of light on the Fourth Gospel by attending to classical drama.[34] Like the other

---

30   Brant, 8–10. Cf. Roman Ingarden, "The Functions of Language in the Theater," in *The Literary Work of Art: An Investigation on the Borderlines of Ontology, Logic, and Theory of Literature*, trans. George G. Grabowicz (Evanston: Northwestern University Press, 1973), 377–96; Eli Rozik, "The Functions of Language in Theatre," *ThResInt* 18 (1993): 104–14.

31   Brant, *Dialogue and Drama*, 11.

32   Brant, 3.

33   Brant, 51.

34   George L. Parsenios, *Departure and Consolation: The Johannine Farewell Discourses in Light of Greco-Roman Literature*, NovTSup 117 (Leiden: Brill, 2005); George L. Parsenios, "'No Longer in the World' (John 17:11): The Transformation of the Tragic in the Fourth Gospel," *HTR* 98 (2005): 1–21; Parsenios, *Rhetoric and Drama in the Johannine Lawsuit Motif*; George L. Parsenios, "The Silent Spaces between Narrative and Drama," in *The Gospel of John as Genre Mosaic*, ed. Kasper Bro Larsen, SANt 3 (Göttingen: Vandenhoeck & Rupprecht, 2015), 85–97.

authors here, he does not claim that John *is* a drama in a technical sense but rather believes that attending to conventions in drama and related genres will illuminate certain themes and motifs in the Fourth Gospel. He explores "dramatic departures" in connection to Jesus's remark, "Rise, let us go forth" (John 14.31), to show how John "bends" the testament genre in the direction of the tragic.[35] He also looks to tragedy as a model for making sense of the apparently confused references to time in the Farewell Discourses, the temporal "fusion of horizons" between Jesus's past and present: "The entire gospel is written from the postresurrection perspective, so that the events of the hour of Jesus influence the story long before they are actually narrated." In Jesus's long goodbye, then, the audience of the Fourth Gospel, like the audience of a Greek tragedy, witnesses the last words delivered by a speaker who is both alive and dead already. The "twist" in John is that, while both Jesus and the protagonists of Euripides's *Alcestis* or *Hippolytus* or Sophocles's *Trachiniae* are "no longer" (οὐχέτι) in the world, the classical figures speak from a perspective of departing the light and going to Hades; John's Jesus on the other hand is "the light of the world" and speaks from the perspective of his hour of glorification.[36] Parsenios's 2005 book, *Rhetoric and Drama in the Johannine Lawsuit Motif*, intervenes in a discussion about the juridical motif in John, explored most fully in Andrew Lincoln's *Truth on Trial*, to show that legal rhetoric and tragic drama (both independently recognized as important for John) were deeply intertwined in antiquity, an intertwinement typically neglected by Johannine scholars who situate John in either a dramatic or a legal context.[37] The "signs" in John are, furthermore, evidence of a sort that Aristotle identifies as the "tokens" which are so often decisive in determining the denouement in the tragedies; the questioning that Jesus pursues at different points in the Gospel (e.g., at John 8.50) can be illuminated by contrast to the legal character of seeking and questioning pursued by speakers in the dramas (e.g., Oedipus in Sophocles, *Oedipus rex*).[38] Parsenios's most recent contribution explores three "silent moments" in the Gospel (John 1.19–21; 14.30–31; and 3.31–36) where one would expect to find the voice of the narrator and does not.[39] This absence of the narrator will continue to be a point of interest going forward with the present study.

---

35 Parsenios, *Departure and Consolation*. Cf. Harold W. Attridge, "Genre Bending in the Fourth Gospel," *JBL* 121 (2002): 3–21.

36 Parsenios, "'No Longer in the World' (John 17:11)," quotation from p. 7.

37 Parsenios, *Rhetoric and Drama in the Johannine Lawsuit Motif*; Andrew T. Lincoln, *Truth on Trial: The Lawsuit Motif in the Fourth Gospel* (Peabody: Hendrickson, 2000).

38 Parsenios, *Rhetoric and Drama in the Johannine Lawsuit Motif*.

39 Parsenios, "The Silent Spaces."

DRAMA: DISCREPANT AWARENESS AND DRAMATIC IRONY 177

Kasper Bro Larsen's work on ἀναγνώρισις, introduced above in chapter 4, needs also be mentioned here, since the recognition type-scene he sees employed and transformed in the Fourth Gospel is grounded in the dramatic tradition. It is a crucial element of some of the most famous Greek tragedies, especially those in the Electra-Orestes cycle and in Sophocles's *Oedipus rex*.[40] Larsen's attention to ἀναγνώρισις in John and in drama is not new—he is quite consciously following in the footsteps of Hitchcock, who mentions ἀναγνώρισις, and Culpepper, who touches on ἀναγνώρισις briefly in his *Anatomy* and in more detail with some later works—but Larsen's is the most detailed and careful treatment of the phenomenon in connection to John to date.[41] Larsen does not focus on the macro-genre of the Fourth Gospel, finding it more fruitful here to explore the many microgenres that are present and "bent," to use Harold W. Attridge's term.

Harold W. Attridge's important 2002 article on "genre bending" does not address John in connection to tragedy explicitly. He does, however, gesture to Stibbe in remarking that John's plot is "often dramatic."[42] In a 2015 article, Attridge takes stock of the impact "genre-bending" has had on the way New Testament scholars have thought about John's genre in the interim, and advances the new idea that John takes up the "macro genre" that is visible in the earliest gospels and "bends" it in the direction of drama with a prologue that offers a formal hypothesis; dramatic irony like that found in the *Bacchae*; the "delayed exit" device as described by George Parsenios; and "dramatic encounters" involving recognition scenes, as explored by Kasper Bro Larsen.[43] The effect of these bends, Attridge suggests, is a transformative encounter with the risen Christ.

Scholars' caveats warning us not to read John simplistically as a formal tragedy are justified. The gospel is not in meter, there are no singing parts, there is

---

40   Kasper Bro Larsen, *Recognizing the Stranger: Recognition Scenes in the Gospel of John*, BibInt 93 (Leiden: Brill, 2008), 2. Cf. Bernhard Zimmerman, "Anagnorisis," in *DNP* 1:642–43. As they both point out, Homer's *Odyssey* furnishes the recognition scenes which would become prototypical in subsequent Greek literature, especially drama and the novel.

41   Cf. Hitchcock, "The Dramatic Development of the Fourth Gospel"; Hitchcock, "Is the Fourth Gospel a Drama?" Culpepper relates John to biography and drama, focusing on the recognition motif, in "The Plot of John's Gospel" and "The Gospel as Literature," chapters in R. Alan Culpepper, *The Gospel and Letters of John* (Nashville: Abingdon, 1998).

42   Attridge, "Genre Bending in the Fourth Gospel," 5.

43   Harold W. Attridge, "The Gospel of John: Genre Matters?," in *The Gospel of John as Genre Mosaic*, ed. Kasper Bro Larsen, SANt 3 (Göttingen: Vandehoeck & Rupprecht, 2015), 27–45. Cf. Parsenios, "'No Longer in the World' (John 17:11)"; Larsen, *Recognizing the Stranger*.

178   CHAPTER 5

no chorus,[44] it does not unfold its total narrative in a single location over the course of a single day,[45] it features a third person narrator, and so on. To these differences, we might add that the classical exemplars of Greek tragedy are products of Athens in the fifth century BCE; the Fourth Gospel, most scholars agree, comes from Asia Minor sometime near the end of the first century CE. The six-hundred-year gap, however, is not as serious an obstacle as one might initially think. Homeric poetry predates the classical tragedians and yet exerted an ever-stronger purchase on the literary imaginations of writers in the Hellenistic period and beyond.[46] The myths represented in Greek tragedy, which were largely spun out of the Homeric epics, are a piece of that same fabric. From a social perspective, there are several reasons why dramatic conventions set out half a millennium earlier could exert influence on the form of a first century text: theaters were ubiquitous; dramas were read privately as well as performed publicly; the three great tragedians we know achieved their celebrated status at an early date and were frequently revisited and restaged (alongside newer works, which continued to be produced).[47] Other early

---

44   Stibbe, however, understands the Jews in the Lazarus narrative functioning "as a kind of dramatic chorus, commenting on the action involving Jesus and the two sisters." See Mark W. G. Stibbe, *John's Gospel*, NTRea (London: Routledge, 1994), 96.

45   It was typical of fifth-century Athenian plays to unfold their action in the course of a single day, from sunrise to sunset, and in a single location. In the literature, this is called the Unity of Time and Place principle (cf. Aristotle's remarks on appropriate structure and scope of a tragedy, *Poet.* 1450b–1451a). But this was not a necessary feature, as Ezekiel's *Exagoge* shows.

46   For the influence of Homer on early Christian literature, see the work of Dennis Ronald MacDonald: *Christianizing Homer: The Odyssey, Plato, and the Acts of Andrew* (New York: Oxford University Press, 1994); *The Homeric Epics and the Gospel of Mark* (New Haven: Yale University Press, 2000); *Mimesis and Intertextuality in Antiquity and Christianity*, SAC (Harrisburg: Trinity Press International, 2001); *Does the New Testament Imitate Homer?: Four Cases from the Acts of the Apostles* (New Haven: Yale University Press, 2003); *Mythologizing Jesus: From Jewish Teacher to Epic Hero* (Lanham: Rowman & Littlefield, 2015). More recently, Macdonald has turned his attention from Homer to Virgil. See Dennis Ronald MacDonald, *Luke and Vergil: Imitations of Classical Greek Literature*, NTGL 2 (Lanham: Rowman & Littlefield, 2015).

47   On the ubiquity of theaters, T. D. Barnes quotes Pausanias (*Descr.* 10.4.1) to make the point that "every self-respecting Greek city of the Roman East, however small and insignificant, had its theater, while larger cities also had an odeum, and still larger ones several theaters. A passage of Pausanias [makes clear] how central a theater was to a city's self-esteem: 'From Chaeronea two and a half miles bring you to the city of Panopeus in Phokis: if you can call it a city when it has no government offices, no gymnasium, no theater, no market-square, when it has no running water at a water-head and the inhabitants live on the edge of a torrent in hovels like mountain huts.'" Barnes, "Christians and the Theater: E. Togo Salmon Papers I," 161.

DRAMA: DISCREPANT AWARENESS AND DRAMATIC IRONY 179

Christian writers besides the Fourth Evangelist were familiar with tragedians to the point of being able to quote from, for example, Sophocles (cf. *1 Clem.* 37.4), Euripides (cf. Acts 26.14) Menander (cf. 1 Cor 15.33), Epimenides (cf. Titus 1.12), and Aratus (cf. Acts 17.28).[48] Even the Christian anti-drama sentiments of Tertullian and Augustine, mentioned above, are predicated on familiarity with the theater. Classical drama was ubiquitous in the Hellenistic landscape of the first centuries CE.

Athenian tragedy touches all the other genres discussed in this project. One can readily find studies exploring tragic influences in Thucydides, Polybius, Josephus, Plutarch, Lucian, the novels, and many other authors and genres.[49] Intergeneric fraternization is a regular aspect of belonging to a genre, which is why it was suggested above that genre "sets" or "ecologies" are more helpful than genres as independent "pigeon holes." Although analysis sometimes requires that we discuss genres as distinct entities that "influence" each other in particular cases, the reality is more complex.

2   Conventions for Representing Minds in Drama[50]

> *Clytemnestra:* I am afraid: I look to my interest, not his.
>   They say he is angry at his father's murder.
> EURIPIDES, *EL.* 1114–15

---

48   Both Parsenios and Brant deal in a similar way with the question of access. See Parsenios, "'No Longer in the World' (John 17:11)," 3–4; Brant, *Dialogue and Drama*, 12–15. Scholarship on the reception of the Greek tragedies is an industry in its own right, but for a general account focusing on the move from a fifth-century Athenian context to the international art-form recognizable and observable throughout the Greco-Roman world in later antiquity, see P. E. Easterling, "From Repertoire to Canon," in *The Cambridge Companion to Greek Tragedy*, ed. P. E. Easterling (Cambridge: Cambridge University Press, 1997), 211–27.

49   E.g., John H. Finley Jr., "Euripides and Thucydides," *HSCP* 49 (1938): 23–68; Phillip de Lacy, "Biography and Tragedy in Plutarch," *AJP* 73 (1952): 159–71; F. W. Walbank, "History and Tragedy," *Hist.* 9 (1960): 216–34; J. M. Mossman, "Tragedy and Epic in Plutarch's Alexander," in *Essays on Plutarch's Lives*, ed. Barbara Scardigli (Oxford: Clarendon, 1995), 209–28; Francesca Calabi, "Theatrical Language in Philo's in Flaccum," in *Italian Studies on Philo of Alexandria*, ed. Francesca Calabi, SPhAMA 1 (Leiden: Brill, 2003), 91–116; Louis H. Feldman, "The Influence of the Greek Tragedians on Josephus," in *Judaism and Hellenism Reconsidered*, JSJS 107 (Leiden: Brill, 2006), 413–43. Note also the thesis of Moses Hadas that 4 Maccabees is influenced by Greek tragedy in the way it sets a scene and carries action forward through dialogue. Moses Hadas, ed., *The Third and Fourth Books of Maccabees*, JAL (New York: Harper, 1953).

50   Unless otherwise noted, translations in this chapter of Aeschylus, Sophocles, and Euripides follow the LCL, and translations of Ezekiel the Tragedian follow Howard Jacobson, *The Exagoge of Ezekiel* (Cambridge: Cambridge University Press, 1983), 49–67.

180   CHAPTER 5

Locked in heated discussion with the titular character of Euripides's *Electra*, Clytemnestra announces her own state of mind and in the next line what she takes to be that of Orestes. The most distinctive formal feature of drama is that the whole of the narrative is conveyed in direct speech. There is no narrator to peer into characters' heads. Audiences must rely on the dramatis personae to report their own thoughts or to theorize each other's minds in speech.[51]

Much of the work a narrator would normally do in describing the scene and context is accomplished by use of *deictic speech*.[52] When Hippolytus approaches the altar of Artemis with a garland, he uses deictic speech to describe his actions for the audience: "For you, lady, I bring this plaited garland (τόνδε πλεκτὸν στέφανον) I have made, gathered from a virgin meadow" (Euripides, *Hipp.* 73–74). When Electra sets the scene in the *Orestes*, she explains the body the audience sees lying beside her: "Poor Orestes lies here ('Ορέστης ὅδε) sick, ravaged by a fierce disease, prostrate on his bed, his mother's blood goading him with fits of insanity" (Euripides, *Orest.* 34–37).[53] She has just rehearsed the fateful genealogy of her family, culminating in the death of Clytemnestra at Orestes's hand. Such speech serves the stage director as well as the audience. Deictic speech may point to anything on view in the situation unfolding in any given scene, both as it refers to the speaker and to others on- or off-stage. In Electra's speech, the physical arrangements of the stage are indicated (here, the prostrate body of Orestes) and the state of mind is pointed out as well (here, Orestes is τροχηλατεῖ μανίαισιν, "driven with madness"). Elsewhere, deictic speech might indicate buildings, the approach of a new character,[54] or natural phenomena like an earthquake.[55]

---

51   When the dramas were performed, of course, actors and producers had additional means by which they could communicate states of mind, including voice modulation, the use of different masks, and physical movement on stage. For the extra-textual performance dynamics of theater production in ancient Greece, see the well-curated bibliography in Alan H. Sommerstein, *Greek Drama and Dramatists* (New York: Routledge, 2002), 174–75.

52   For a discussion of deictic speech as it relates to the movements and gestures of Greek tragic actors, its incorporation into the text, and the possibility of its contribution to the advancement of the "dramatic action" (i.e., the provocation of a plot-related response in the dialogue partner), see Joe Park Poe, "Word and Deed: On 'Stage-Directions' in Greek Tragedy," *Mn.* 56 (2003): 420–48.

53   Trans. Robin Waterfield, *Euripides: Orestes and Other Plays*, owc (Oxford: Oxford University Press, 2001).

54   See Richard Hamilton, "Announced Entrances in Greek Tragedy," *HSCP* 82 (1978): 63–82.

55   It is unclear to what extent the producer might have arranged for what moderns would call "special effects" in a play's production. When the earthquake takes place in Euripides's *Bacchae* (the so-called Palace Miracle, the first of Dionysius's epiphanies in the play), for

DRAMA: DISCREPANT AWARENESS AND DRAMATIC IRONY 181

Deictic language often indicates states of the body that reflect states of mind, both in self-observation and in observing others. Orestes's posture in Electra's deictic speech is one such state of the body, reflecting his grief. A few lines later she adds more details: "He weeps when his body gains some respite from its disease and he is in his right mind; but sometimes he leaps up from his bed and runs around like a colt freed from the yoke" (Euripides, *Orest.* 43–45).[56] As in the novels, tears are a common outward indicator of an interior state, and characters frequently draw attention to them.[57] Clytemnestra, speaking to Electra about Iphigenia, provides an example of a speaker using deictic language to self-report a cognitive state (Euripides, *Elect.* 1011–50). Her report is synchronic with the cognitive state it describes. Thought reports are not limited to what is synchronic, however—they can be forward-looking, backward-looking, or iterative. These diachronic perspectives can also be combined, as they are in this report of Electra: "The greater part of my life has been spent on weeping and wailing and tears in the night, as without husband or children I draw my pitiable life out into an interminable future" (Euripides, *Orest.* 202–7).[58]

Deictic language pointing to the mental state of another may be found in many of the prologues of classical drama, as when Poseidon sketches a scene that includes Hecuba while setting up the *Daughters of Troy*:

> *Poseidon:* Nearby, beside the gates, for any to look upon
> who has the heart, she lies face upward, Hecuba
> weeping for multitudes her multitude of tears.
>
> EURIPIDES, *Tro.* 36–38[59]

Poseidon speaks with privileged access to Hecuba's mind. He knows and describes the causes of her tears. Hecuba's daughter has been taken away and,

---

example, we are left to wonder if and how this might have been indicated outside of the reaction of the chorus (*Bacch.* 671–701). For discussion, see the commentary by E. R. Dodds, *Euripides: Bacchae*, 2nd ed. (Oxford: Clarendon, 1986), 147–51.

56 Trans. Waterfield, *Euripides: Orestes and Other Plays*.

57 For further examples, see Euripides, *Orest.* 60 (Electra on Helen's tears); *Med.* 24–33 (the nurse on Medea's tears); *Med.* 1012 (the Paidagogos on Medea's tears).

58 Trans. Waterfield, *Euripides: Orestes and Other Plays*. See also Creusa's distinction between past and present states of mind at Euripides, *Ion* 1609–13. As it bears on questions of humans' shifting attitudes towards the gods in the plays of Euripides, see Donald J. Mastronarde, *The Art of Euripides: Dramatic Technique and Social Context* (Cambridge: Cambridge University Press, 2010), 166–67.

59 Trans. David Grene and Richmond Alexander Lattimore, eds., *Euripides*, 3 vols., CGT (Chicago: University of Chicago Press, 1959).

although she does not yet know it, slaughtered at Achilles's tomb (*Tro.* 39–40). Her husband Priam and sons are dead. Only Cassandra, "reeling crazed at King Apollo's stroke," remains with her (*Tro.* 42).[60] Tears are readily accessible to players in the plays, divine or not. Divine characters like Poseidon in prologue to the *Trojan Women* have divine access to the states of mind of the human characters and are unerring in divining the reasons for those states of mind. Human characters, on the other hand, while equally capable of using deictic speech to draw attention to their own or others' tears, often mistake the cause for those tears in others. We see this play out, for example, when Ion mistakes the cause of Creusa's tears (Euripides, *Ion* 246). Regardless of whether the person indicating the tears is human or divine, however, the fact remains that someone needs to say something about the tears if the audience is to appreciate their effect. The use of masks and the distance between spectator and stage would have made it difficult to see tears on the cheek of an actor.[61]

"True causes of tears" belongs to the non-perceptible domain, which tends to be accessible to the divine gaze, but is a frequent source of confusion and misunderstanding on the part of the human figures who predominantly occupy the stage in most dramas. A god may see through to the reality, but most interactions are between human characters. This is why it matters that, as a rule, *thoughts vocalized in speech are filtered thoughts*. This principle is evident in narrative genres where omniscient narrators are able to communicate to the reader what characters are withholding. In the novels, the narrator can interject after a speech, for example, to indicate that Callirhoe had filtered any mention of Chaereas out of what she said to Dionysius, or to indicate that Theron had filtered from his confession to the people of Syracuse the identity of the person to whom he had sold Callirhoe (*Callir.* 2.5.11; 3.4.14). The disconnect between verbal appearances and inner realities parallels the disconnect lamented by the titular character in Euripides's *Medea*: "O Zeus, why, when you gave people sure signs of gold that is counterfeit, is there no stamp ($\chi\alpha\rho\alpha\kappa\tau\dot{\eta}\rho$) on the human body by which one could identify base men?" (*Med.* 516–9).[62] The Greek dramatists were well aware of the potential for discrepancy between what people say and what they know. One challenge for the dramatist lay in

---

60   Trans. Grene and Lattimore, *Euripides.*

61   "When one character refers to another as having tears running down his or her face or looking triumphant, it is clear that the audience members were the ones to supply, as it were, the visualized emotion, since the mask of an actor was unable to display it (the actor could, however, express the required emotion through voice, stance, and gesture)." John Davidson, "Theatrical Production," in *A Companion to Greek Tragedy*, ed. Justina Gregory (Oxford: Blackwell, 2005), 208–9.

62   Trans. LCL, modified.

DRAMA: DISCREPANT AWARENESS AND DRAMATIC IRONY

how to share with the audience information about a character's thoughts or feelings that he or she would normally keep private. A variety of devices might be deployed, three of which we discuss here as divine priming, question and answer, and the monologue.

Divine priming occurs in Poseidon's prologue to *The Daughters of Troy*, where Poseidon casts his divine eye into Hecuba's mind to reveal the cause of her posture and tears. Hermes furnishes another example with his revelation to the audience of Euripides's *Ion* that "Here Phoebus raped Creusa, daughter of Erechtheus, at the place where under Pallas' acropolis stand Athens' northern cliffs, the Long Cliffs, as the lords of Attica call them. Without her father's knowledge (ἀγνὼς δὲ πατρί), for so the god wished it (τῷ θεῷ γὰρ ἦν φίλον), she carried to term the burden of her belly" (Euripides, *Ion* 11–13).[63] In addition to the material facts of the plot leading up to this moment, Hermes supplies the audience with divine access to the minds of both Phoebus and Erechtheus. Later in the prologue, Hermes helps the audience navigate the mistaken conclusions drawn by the priestess at Delphi where the infant was deposited:

> She noticed the infant and wondered at the effrontery of the local girl, whoever it was, who had abandoned her secret offspring at the god's temple. She felt she ought to remove him from the bounds of the precinct, but pity melted her harshness; and the god was on the child's side too, working to prevent his removal from the temple, so she took him in and brought him up. She does not know that the father is Phoebus, and doesn't know who the mother is either; nor does the boy know who his parents are (οὐκ οἶδε Φοῖβον οὐδὲ μητέρ᾽ ἧς ἔφυ, ὁ παῖς τε τοὺς τεκόντας οὐκ ἐπίσταται).
>
> EURIPIDES, *Ion* 42–50[64]

Without this information, the theater-goer would see only the priestess picking up the baby and bringing him up in the temple. Observers would lose more than the information that neither the priestess nor the boy knew his true parentage, information necessary for the plot and the eventual recognition scenes. They would also lose access to the priestess's character-defining thought process on encountering the infant.[65]

---

63 Trans. LCL, modified.

64 Trans. Waterfield, *Euripides: Orestes and Other Plays*.

65 This type of prologue will become even more important in New Comedy, where mistaken identities and misunderstandings often drive the plot. See the comments on the informing function of "prologue gods" in Mastronarde, *The Art of Euripides*, 107–14.

184   CHAPTER 5

Human characters can prime the audience as well, but their perspectives are inevitably limited. Iphigenia, at the prologue to *Iphigenia in Tauris*, explains the play's primary conceit: "People believe (ὡς δοκεῖ) that I was sacrificed by my own father to Artemis, in the great pursuit of Helen.... But Artemis deceived their eyes with a deer to bleed for me and stole me through the azure sky" (Euripides, *Iph. taur.* 5–6, 28–30).[66] But she herself labors under the delusion that her brother Orestes is dead. She has experienced a dream (described at *Iph. taur.* 42–62) from which she falsely concluded that Orestes had died (*Iph. taur.* 54–55).

A common device for revealing states of mind is an exchange between two characters, especially a protagonist and his or her friend. The confidantes and aides in the drama—one thinks especially of Pylades to Orestes in Euripides's *Iphigenia at Tauris* or of Orestes to Electra in Euripides's *Electra*—serve a number of important narrative functions, including saving heroes from premature honor-suicides and of speaking for the hero when the latter is too overwhelmed to speak for himself.[67] This figure is usually a single person, although in some plays the chorus can play the role (e.g., the chorus to Hecuba in Euripides's *Tro.* 1239 and *passim*, or the chorus of slave women to Helen in Euripides's *Hel.* 179ff and *passim*). The confidante's role in eliciting the protagonist's thoughts is double-edged. On the one hand, close friends often know the minds of their friends better than anyone else. The two can even be said to "share a mind," eliminating the need to dialogue. On the other hand, there is typically a relationship of perfect trust,[68] so that when they do dialogue, readers need not worry that honesty is being filtered out of the thoughts, feelings, desires, or intentions they share.

A variation on relational structure that achieves the removal of the thinking or feeling subject's filter without coalescing the minds of the protagonist and partner is to make the protagonist "crazed." When Cassandra tells Hecuba to

---

66   Trans. Grene and Lattimore, *Euripides*.

67   Cf. Admetus and Heracles in the *Alcestis*; Orestes and Pylades in the *Orestes*; Theseus and Heracles in *Heracles*; Demophon and the relatives of Heracles in *Children of Heracles*.

       The novels offered an obvious use of this same device, as, e.g., with Polycharmus to Chaereas. Even there, where a narrator could communicate everything the reader needs to know, it can be "dramatically" effective to pitch these as conversations. The plot can sometimes demand this device too, in the event that a partner needs to "know" what the protagonist is feeling. Novelists have the option of using narrator-faciliatated indirect speech to accomplish the same function. Indirect speech is present in drama; it is, however, related by other characters.

68   This closeness is often based on shared identity markers (e.g., Helen and her chorus of slaves are united by Greekness in barbarian Egypt) or familial metaphors (e.g., Orestes and Pylades are united by fictive kinship in *Iph. taur.* 498).

DRAMA: DISCREPANT AWARENESS AND DRAMATIC IRONY 185

cheer up because she plans to kill Agamemnon and "avenge my brothers' blood and my father's in the desolation of his house" (Euripides, *Tro.* 359–60), no one can accuse her of self-censoring.[69] Madness strips the filters from one's speech. It is no accident that so many of drama's most memorably honest characters are out of their senses.

The monologue is a third device for facilitating access to the thoughts of characters in drama.[70] Although it is relatively rare for a character to address him- or herself directly (examples at Euripides, *Med.* 409–19; Euripides, *Tro.* 98–152), there are many cases where characters speak alone on the stage, including many of Euripides's prologues.[71] There are also instances in drama where either a speaker or a chorus appears alone on the stage to address the audience, though the traditional view among classicists is that the tragedians never broke what we would call the "fourth wall." The lines spoken by Electra at Euripides's *Orestes* 128–32 are sometimes put forward as an example, but even this passage can be explained as an idiomatic use of the second person address.[72] The audience of a tragic production, however, is never truly absent. Even if nobody on stage breaks character to address the audience directly, the spectators are always in some sense "present while absent." Viewed the other way around, allowing for the possibility that figures on stage break character in some qualified sense to address the audience at moments like the lines of Electra just mentioned, there is nevertheless no real interaction with the

---

69   Trans. Grene and Lattimore, *Euripides*. This complex example underscores the larger point I am trying to make. Cassandra in the context of this passage is suspected of being "crazed" and "passionate" (*Tro.* 348) and driven out of her wits by Apollo (*Tro.* 408). This characterization explains how she can make such risky remarks in the hearing of Agamemnon's representative, Talthybius.

70   Modern literary critics distinguish between the monologue and the soliloquy, so that the former is a speech made in the presence of others and the latter is a speech made by a character alone. Ancient critics, however, made no sharp theoretical distinctions between them, and "monologue" is used in this project in accordance with what would have been the term used by an ancient Greek critic. For an influential study of these techniques in tragedy, see Wolfgang Schadewaldt, *Monolog und Selbstgespräch; Untersuchungen zur Formgeschichte der griechischen Tragödie*, NPU 2 (Berlin: Weidmann, 1926).
       Note also that short monologues are sometimes called "asides," and monologues addressed to an idea (such as love) or an object (such as a cultic statue) are sometimes called "apostrophes." Examples of all of these devices may be found in the tragic corpus.

71   Not only in Euripides. Cf. the prologue delivered by the watchman in Aeschylus's *Agamemnon*.

72   Addresses to the audience figure more prominently in Old Comedy than in ancient tragic productions, especially in the device of the *parabasis*, where the poet addresses the audience through the chorus. For a defense of the traditional view that one finds audience address in Comedy but not Tragedy, see David Bain, "Audience Address in Greek Tragedy," *ClQ* 25 (1975): 13–25.

spectators. Information moves unidirectionally; the audience is "absent while present." And this raises the possibility that characters *on* stage can be "absent while present." Medea's sons are a case in point: physically present, their smiles and soft skin present by δεῖξις in Medea's speech, they are at the same time absent, oblivious to the terrible significance of their mother's words (*Med.* 1021–80). Perhaps the most famous monologue in Euripides is that of Medea to herself on the brink of filicide (*Med.* 1021–80):

> *Medea:* And now, spare nothing that is in your knowledge,
> Medea: make your plan, prepare your ruse.
> Do this dreadful thing. There is so much
> at stake. Display your courage. Do you see
> how you are suffering? Do not allow
> these Sisyphean snakes to laugh at you
> on Jason's wedding day. Your father is noble;
> your grandfather is Helios. You have
> the knowledge, not to mention woman's nature:
> for any kind of noble deed, we're helpless;
> for malice, though, our wisdom is unmatched.
>
> *Med.* 409–19[73]

Devices for representing thoughts in drama have thus far been treated in general terms, drawing on a wide variety of classical exemplars, mainly from the Euripidean corpus.[74] I now turn to two specific cases, Euripides's *Hippolytus* and Ezekiel's *Exagoge*, moving in each case from contextualizing the particular play to discussion of the roles played in it by represented thought.

---

73   Trans. Diane Arnson Svarlien, *Euripides: Alcestis, Medea, Hippolytus* (Indianapolis: Hackett Publishing, 2007).

74   A great proportion of classical scholarship on the dramas is concerned with identifying what is distinctive and characteristic of one dramatist over and against the other two. This mode of scholarship bears a structural resemblance to gospels scholarship that works almost exclusively with the four canonical Gospels to identify the theological or ideological or formal *Tendenz* of each. In both cases, ancient precedents may be found for the comparative enterprise. E.g., Clement's comment about John being the spiritual gospel, in the one case, or Aristotle's comparison between Sophocles, who "presents people as they ought to be," and Euripides, who "presents people as they are" (*Poet.* 1460b34–36).

DRAMA: DISCREPANT AWARENESS AND DRAMATIC IRONY 187

3   Euripides's *Hippolytus*

Most of what we know about the life of Euripides (ca. 480–406 BCE) is derived from references made by several contemporaries, especially Aristophanes.[75] Most of what we know about his interests comes from his plays. The *Hippolytus* was among his best-appreciated plays, both in his own lifetime (it won the first prize when it debuted at the City Dionysia in 428 BCE) and afterwards (inspiring, among others, Seneca (ca. 4 BCE–65 CE) and Jean Racine (1639–1699) to produce their own versions of the drama).[76]

Hippolytus is a play about who knows what and when they know it; about love, fear, hatred, belief, and disbelief as forces that create states of mind; and the consequences of discrepant awareness. Thoughts in this play bring life-destroying consequences; the chorus is not flippant when it exclaims to Phaedra, who has fallen in love with her stepson Hippolytus, "Death take me, my friend, before I come to share your thoughts! (ὀλοίμαν ἔγωγε πρὶν σᾶν, φίλα, κατανύσαι φρενῶν)" (*Hipp.* 364–5). What one knows, or *thinks* one knows, determines one's actions, typically with tragic consequences.

The play begins with Aphrodite, who feels slighted by the chastity-loving Hippolytus in favor of the virginal Artemis, and so has devised a plot against Hippolytus's life. She has caused Hippolytus's stepmother Phaedra to conceive a passionate desire for Hippolytus while Theseus the king (her husband and Hippolytus's father) is away (in voluntary exile for an unrelated murder). Hippolytus rejects a servant's warning about the danger of neglecting Aphrodite. Phaedra, sick with love, is questioned by a nurse and finally reveals the reason for her sorry condition. The nurse, contrary to Phaedra's wishes, propositions Hippolytus on Phaedra's behalf, after making Hippolytus swear an oath not to reveal any of what she has come to say. Hippolytus is shocked and appalled, and is furious at being prevented by his oath from telling Theseus. Phaedra, on learning what the nurse had attempted, writes a letter falsely accusing Hippolytus of rape then hangs herself. Theseus returns

---

75   A later biographical tradition exists, building largely on extrapolations from the man's works and especially from those same characterizations developed in Old Comedy. For a collection and moderate weighing of the evidence see R. E. Wycherley, "Aristophanes and Euripides," *GR* 15 (1946): 98–107. For a more recent but idiosyncratic treatment, see Ranja Knobl, "Biographical Representations of Euripides. Some Examples of Their Development from Classical Antiquity to Byzantium" (PhD diss, Durham University, 2008).

76   For the reception of the *Hippolytus*, especially with reference to Racine's *Phèdre*, see Peter Burian, "Tragedy Adapted for Stages and Screens: The Renaissance to the Present," in *The Cambridge Companion to Greek Tragedy* (Cambridge: Cambridge University Press, 1997), 228–83.

188 CHAPTER 5

and discovers his dead wife and the letter. Believing what he reads, he invokes Poseidon to curse Hippolytus. Hippolytus enters and argues with Theseus, but the oath prevents him from telling the whole exculpatory truth. Theseus exiles Hippolytus. A messenger arrives to inform Theseus that Hippolytus has been in a freak chariot accident and lays dying on the beach. Theseus is happy at the news until Artemis arrives and exposes the whole plot, effecting Theseus's recognition—now too late—that his son is innocent, that Phaedra had lied, and that the whole tragedy had been set in motion by the jealousy of Aphrodite. Hippolytus is brought in on a stretcher and forgives Theseus in his final moments before dying.

Two goddesses figure prominently in the play. Both possess direct access to the minds of the human figures (e.g., Aphrodite of Phaedra at *Hipp.* 26–27; 38–39), and even delight in shaping the dispositions of those minds (e.g., Aphrodite of Phaedra at *Hipp.* 28). The prologue, delivered by Aphrodite, is important for setting out the motivating desires of the principal actors (herself at *Hipp.* 8–11 and 43; Hippolytus at 14–15; Phaedra at 26–42); for describing the means by which she plans to avenge herself on Hippolytus, in manipulating Theseus's perceptions so that he turns against his son; and third, for giving her an initial opportunity to justify her destructive plan. The prologue primes the audience with privileged knowledge of Hippolytus's and Phaedra's states of mind (the one, single-minded in his disposition to Artemis, goddess of virginity and the hunt; the other, "pricked cruelly by the goads of a shameful love"), which will be necessary for understanding the discrepant awareness that governs much of the dialogue in the play. The justificatory strategy of Aphrodite will be countermanded by Artemis at the epilogue, when she reveals the truth to her noble devotees, though they by then have been irremediably crushed under Aphrodite's machinations.

The divine perspectives at the beginning and end of the play serve the audience in the first case and Theseus in the second case with an "objective" perspective on the dispositions and motivations of the drama's principal parties, both those on-stage (Phaedra, Hippolytus, Theseus) and in the wings (Aphrodite, Artemis, Poseidon). Aphrodite can report her own feelings: she hates Hippolytus because he neglects to honor her (*Hipp.* 43). And she can report the feelings of others: "Phaedra groans in bitterness of heart, and the goads of love prick her cruelly and she is like to die. But she breathes not a word of her secret and none of the servants know of the sickness that afflicts her" (*Hipp.* 38–40).[77] If the goddess's access to minds is privileged and

---

77   Trans. Grene and Lattimore, *Euripides.* Feelings and thoughts need not be sharply distinguished; both stand on the side of a psychological model in which one's cognitive states

DRAMA: DISCREPANT AWARENESS AND DRAMATIC IRONY 189

straightforward, however, what she does with that knowledge is not. The focalization of "objective" access to minds is markedly different when we compare Aphrodite's attitude to Hippolytus with that of Artemis.[78]

The dramatis personae in the play have access to their own thoughts and feelings, and express them both privately and in conversation. Hippolytus, after failing to convince Theseus of his innocence and reflecting on the banishment imposed by his father, declares, "So, I'm condemned and there is no release. I know the truth and dare not tell the truth" (*Hipp.* 1090–1).[79] His subsequent speeches—first a prayer to Artemis, then a farewell to his companions (*Hipp.* 1098–101)—suggest the presence of others on stage, but his "dare not tell the truth" refers back to his oath to the nurse, which he several times curses for its muzzling effect.[80] Artemis, whether she is standing in view of the audience or represented by a statue (the play could be staged either way), already knows the whole truth and so his thoughts are not concealed from her. The lines, "I'm condemned and there is no release. I know the truth and dare not tell the truth," then, represent an interior view, Hippolytus voicing his own thoughts aloud while processing his interaction with his father.

More often, speakers report their feelings to others on stage: Phaedra speaks of her fear (*Hipp.* 517–8) and her misery (*Hipp.* 570); Hippolytus speaks of his

---

are dynamic and liable to change. On the other side of that model are character or disposition, which are (theoretically) unchanging. A complication to this two-category model, a model for which one can easily find support in ancient philosophical discourse, however, is that sometimes πάθη become characteristic for a character indefinitely. Usually, tragedy has struck before the play begins, and the protagonists will be characterized by a named πάθος for the duration. Examples are Phaedra here, afflicted by love, or Hecuba in *Trojan Women*, afflicted by grief after the "death" of Troy. With attention to diachronic markers within the plays themselves, however, the two-category approach to characterization works. The speakers, looking back in storytime to before the plays began, can speak of the onset of emotional states like Phaedra's love or Hecuba's grief. These temporary states of mind, in the psychological model assumed by the dramatist, are all the more tragic when combined with the virtuous, noble ἦθος of the afflicted protagonists.

78   The use of Genette's "focalization" language is helpful in dispelling the specter of objectivity. Focalized speech is *de facto* subjective speech.

79   Trans. Grene and Latimore, *Euripides.*

80   Most famously in conversation with the nurse. When she senses that he is inclining towards laying the facts out before Theseus, she reminds him of his promise. His response, "My tongue an oath did take, but not my heart" (*Hipp.* 612 [Coleridge]) was much quoted in antiquity (e.g., Plato, *Theaet.* 154b; Aristotle, *Rhet.* 1416a; Aristophanes, *Frogs* 1471). Despite the apparent implication, however, Hippolytus does not break his oath. Even though he feels it has been got from him unjustly, he will not perjure himself. See Torrance's discussion in Alan H. Sommerstein and Isabelle C. Torrance, "The Tongue and the Mind: Responses to Euripides, Hippolytus 612," in *Oaths and Swearing in Ancient Greece*, BzAlt 307 (Berlin: de Gruyter, 2014), 289–94.

190   CHAPTER 5

hatred of women (*Hipp.* 633–4; 640) and grief for his father's suffering (*Hipp.* 1405); the chorus speaks of its fear (*Hipp.* 855) and anger (*Hipp.* 1146). The gods in this storyworld also have feelings, a principle Aphrodite articulates in the prologue (*Hipp.* 8) and makes the motivating force behind her stratagem. Because their speaking parts are largely limited to the prologue and epilogue, however, the gods' emotions are most important for helping the audience appreciate why the human characters find themselves in the predicaments they do. The gods' emotions also function in human characters' theorizations of the gods' minds, and those theorizations impact what human figures say and do to each other.

Zeus's love for Semele is invoked by the nurse when she advises Phaedra to seek out a chance to act on her desire with Hippolytus (*Hipp.* 450–55).[81] Poseidon's love and disappointment for Theseus (*Hipp.* 1317–23), Artemis's fear of Zeus (*Hipp.* 1331) and love of Hippolytus (*Hipp.* 1398), and Aphrodite's anger at Hippolytus (*Hipp.* 1417) all play parts in the play. Some are self-reported, as in the case of Artemis's love for Hippolytus or Aphrodite's missing joy (*Hipp.* 5–10) and hate towards Hippolytus (*Hipp.* 43); more often they are reported by others, as with Zeus's love, Poseidon's love and disappointment, and Artemis's fear mentioned above.[82] Characters theorize the minds of each other at greater length on several occasions in the play, as when Theseus's messenger argues for Hippolytus's innocence (*Hipp.* 1251–4), or when Hippolytus imagines what Theseus must be thinking (*Hipp.* 1003–11, 1192–3, 1413).

Theorizing the minds of others in a dramatic play can accomplish several kinds of work. Of the samples noted in the previous paragraph, Hippolytus's response to Theseus's angry monologue deserves a closer look. This is a classic case of discrepant awareness serving to heighten the dramatic tension. The audience, with Hippolytus, knows what happened while Theseus was away. Like Hippolytus, but for different reasons, they are unable to tell the king what

---

81   How this figures into the nurse's rhetorical strategy becomes clear later in the speech, where she exhorts Phaedra: "Come dear, give up your discontented mood. Give up your railing. It's only insolent pride to wish to be superior to the Gods. The Gods have willed it so" (*Hipp.* 473–76 [Grene]). This highlights how the gods' minds can be invoked as part of the traditional mythic structure accepted by Phaedra and playgoer alike (everyone knows that Zeus loved Semele), and also how the gods' minds can be theorized in the narrative present ("The Gods have willed it [viz., Phaedra's attraction to Hippolytus] so"). Most important, however, is to notice how these theorizations function rhetorically in the nurse's own agenda: her misguided, ignoble desire to see her mistress well again (a pragmatic wish), even if this comes at a cost to honor.

82   See also Aphrodite of Phaedra at *Hipp.* 25–30; the nurse of Hippolytus at *Hipp.* 305–10; Phaedra of Aphrodite and Hippolytus at *Hipp.* 725–30; Theseus of Hippolytus at *Hipp.* 935–80.

DRAMA: DISCREPANT AWARENESS AND DRAMATIC IRONY   191

he needs to know.[83] If the audience is muzzled by virtue of being seated in the theater, behind the fourth wall, Hippolytus is silenced by his oath.[84] Theseus's monologue is filled with theorizations of the wicked thoughts and feelings motivating Hippolytus's imagined bad behavior (e.g., "'She is dead,' you thought, 'and that will save me'" [*Hipp.* 955–60]).[85] Hippolytus, in his response, seizes on this line in Theseus's accusation, gives it a twist, and runs with it: "You ought then to show how I was corrupted (δεῖ δή σε δεῖξαι τῷ τρόπῳ διεφθάρην). Did her body surpass all other women's in beauty? (πότερα τὸ τῆσδε σῶμ᾽ ἐκαλλιστεύετο πασῶν γυναικῶν;)" (*Hipp.* 1008–10). Hippolytus enters into the narrative world constructed by Theseus, in which he has consorted with Phaedra, and invites Theseus to consider several dimensions of that world he neglected in his initial accusation. First, what motivation would Hippolytus have had for yielding to Phaedra in particular? Was it her beauty? The rhetorical question invites a negative response. Hippolytus continues: "Or did I hope that by taking an heiress as mistress I would succeed to your house? (ἢ σὸν οἰκήσειν δόμον ἔγκληρον εὐνὴν προσλαβὼν ἐπήλπισα;)" (*Hipp.* 1010–2). This language takes the theorization of mental states to a second level of abstraction. Theseus listens as Hippolytus imagines what Theseus suspects a guilty Hippolytus would desire (here with the language of τὸ ἐπελπίζειν). Euripides has had Hippolytus and Theseus fabricate a fictional world within their "real" world on the stage: a fiction within a fiction.

The encounter between Theseus and Hippolytus helps clarify what, for Theseus, was a more plausible motive for Hippolytus's supposed actions. An audience might recall from the prologue (at *Hipp.* 10–13) or from their more general knowledge of the Hippolytus mythos that Hippolytus is the illegitimate

---

83   Theseus's absence and νόστος is thematically related to the Odyssean precedent. In both cases, chaos develops in the home during the king's absence. The twist is that Phaedra is not like Penelope, and Hippolytus is not like the suitors. And the authorial perspective of the *Hippolytus* is much more sympathetic to Phaedra as the desiring party; the *Odyssey* is less sympathetic to the suitors as the desiring party. Desire in both cases is clearly marked as inappropriate, but the responsibility for this inappropriate desire devolves on Aphrodite in the *Hippolytus* in a discursive move that mirrors Homer's assignment of responsibility to the gods for the Trojan War and Odysseus's difficult journey home.

84   A not-so-subtle moral lesson in this play is that it is dangerous to confide in servants. The nurse's relentless questioning of her mistress is what, from one perspective, sets her destruction in motion. From another perspective, Aphrodite is to blame; from another perspective, Phaedra is to blame, either for falling in love in the first place or for capitulating to the nurse's badgering. In any case, Phaedra learns this lesson when, despite her explicit request *not to tell this to Hippolytus* (*Hipp.* 520), the nurse goes off and does just that (cf. *Hipp.* 589–95); Hippolytus learns the same lesson when he comes to regret giving his oath to the nurse at *Hipp.* 605–15. "I know the truth and cannot tell it!" (*Hipp.* 1090).

85   Trans. Grene and Lattimore, *Euripides.*

192   CHAPTER 5

child of Theseus and an Amazonian. Theseus's heir would have been a legitimate child from Phaedra. Hippolytus is quick to add: "I would have been a fool, a senseless fool, if I had dreamed it" (*Hipp.* 1013–4).[86] He goes on to explain that the burdens of a ruler from his perspective outweigh the freedoms enjoyed by other men (*Hipp.* 1014–24). He swears to Zeus that he is innocent (*Hipp.* 1024–31), but stops short of intimating why Phaedra has killed herself: "Whether your wife took her own life because she was afraid, I do not know. I may not speak further than this. Virtuous she was in deed, although not virtuous; I that have virtue used it to my ruin" (*Hipp.* 1032–5).[87] This is as close as his fateful oath permits him to come in giving Theseus the full truth, and it draws attention to the gap between what characters know and what they say. Speech in the presence of other characters, as demonstrated above, is always potentially filtered speech.[88] Theseus has heard nothing of Phaedra's passion for Hippolytus. The cryptic remark, "Virtuous she was in deed, although not virtuous," will be understood by Theseus in a different light from how Hippolytus intends it. From Hippolytus's perspective, at issue is Phaedra's adulterous desire, and the contrast is between her virtuous "deed" (that is, she was virtuous in not acting on the passion) and her unvirtuous desire. From Theseus's perspective, the contrast drawn by Hippolytus might rather be understood in terms of her virtuous history as a wife, on the one hand, and on the other her unvirtuous decisions to deprive Theseus of a wife and lie in her letter. Theseus does not believe Hippolytus, but that would not prevent him from understanding Hippolytus to intend the remark in these terms.

The previous chapter noted the problem of whether ancient "character" and, by extension, literary characters, are changeable. Did Chariton's Chaereas undergo a process of maturation or was it just that his permanent character gradually crystalized over the course of the narrative? The *Hippolytus* exhibits a comparable ambiguity between fixity and change in the inner processes of its dramatis personae. On the one hand, Hippolytus and Phaedra are characterized as virtuous and resolute. These characterizations are indicated initially by Aphrodite, who hates the one and treats the other as collateral damage.[89]

---

86   Trans. Grene and Lattimore, *Euripides.*
87   Trans. Grene and Lattimore, *Euripides.*
88   Cf. Orestes holding back from revealing his identity to Iphigenia (Euripides, *Iph. taur.* 482–787); Electra holding back from articulating what "a maiden ought not" about the women in Aegisthus's life (i.e., her mother, Clytemnestra) (Euripides, *El.* 945–46).
89   Cf. her remark in the prologue: "Renowned shall Phaedra be in her death, but none the less die she must. Her suffering does not weigh in the scale so much that I should let my enemies go untouched escaping payment of that retribution that honor demands that I have" (*Hipp.* 46–50).

DRAMA: DISCREPANT AWARENESS AND DRAMATIC IRONY

Their dispositions are reinforced in their respective conversations with attendants in their first appearances in the play. Hippolytus's single-minded devotion to Artemis and virginity are foregrounded in his debut on the stage (*Hipp.* 58–113) and in his subsequent conversation with his servant (*Hipp.* 88–120). The servant draws special attention to the danger of neglecting Aphrodite, so that from Aphrodite's perspective Hippolytus is without excuse. The same is true of Phaedra, who is questioned about the reason for her dejection, first by the chorus and then more aggressively by the nurse. None of the women around Phaedra know what the audience knows until, by chance and persistence, the nurse discovers the truth in the climactic conclusion to a long stichomythia (*Hipp.* 309–52). Still, Phaedra's basic disposition appears not to have changed. She is still sick with love for Hippolytus and still knows the impropriety of her desire. She maintains this position resolutely unto death, despite the nurse's best efforts to change her perspective, a fine example of how dispositional states can be ethically inflected.

From another perspective, however, both Hippolytus and Phaedra do change. Phaedra, once her desire has been revealed to the nurse and the chorus, describes a process of trying to deal with it. "I shall also tell you the way my thoughts went (λέξω δὲ καί σοι τῆς ἐμῆς γνώμης ὁδόν)" (*Hipp.* 391). She first planned to keep silent and, when that failed, she determined to overcome the inappropriate desire by applying reason and good sense. When that too failed, she determined to starve to death (*Hipp.* 390–402). This fact gets overlooked in some treatments of the play. Phaedra is already resigned to die when the play begins. Despite the nurse's attempt to change her mind, she never deviates from her suicidal trajectory. All that changes is her decision to bring down the arrogant Hippolytus with her (*Hipp.* 727–30).

Change is at work in Hippolytus's mind too. In his own words at the beginning of the play, he acknowledges Aphrodite, but "from afar (πρόσωθεν)" (*Hipp.* 103), because of his commitment to chastity. By the end of the play, following Artemis's explanation of Aphrodite's responsibility for his destruction, he wishes "that the race of men could curse the gods" (*Hipp.* 1415), with Aphrodite clearly in view.[90] Theseus appears to change, and the audience can even watch his mind move through successive states of belief to disbelief to false belief to belief, and from happiness to confusion to anger to feeling "neither sorrow

---

90   Not only has Artemis just told Hippolytus of Aphrodite's plot, but the goddess interrupts him here to mollify him with the promise that "you shall not be unavenged, Cypris [Aphrodite] shall find the angry shafts she hurled against you for your piety and innocence shall cost her dear. I'll wait until she loves a mortal next time, and with this hand—with these unerring arrows I'll punish him" (*Hipp.* 1416–21).

nor grief" (*Hipp.* 1260) and finally to unalloyed grief. But there is constancy here too; the changes are explained in the end by reference to the meddling of Aphrodite:

> *Artemis*   He was deceived, a god contrived it so.
> *Hippolytus* How great, unhappy father, your misfortune!
> *Theseus*   I am gone, my son, I have no joy in life.
> *Hippolytus* For your mistake I pity you more than me.
> *Theseus*   Would I could die, my son, instead of you!
> *Hippolytus* Poseidon your father's gifts, what woe they brought!
> *Theseus*   Would that the curse had never come to my lips!
> *Hippolytus* You would have killed me still, such was your anger.
> *Theseus*   Yes, for the gods had robbed me of my wits.
>
> Hipp. 1406–14

While the tragic figure's character and disposition appear to remain constant, his thoughts and emotions are liable to change. Gods, moreover, are able interfere with thoughts and emotions (so Aphrodite will say of Phaedra's love, "This was my devising" [*Hipp.* 28], and Artemis referring to Aphrodite will excuse Theseus's behavior because it stemmed from a deception contrived by a δαίμων [*Hipp.* 1406]). Humans, likewise, can interfere with thoughts and emotions, but not character or disposition, though their success in doing so seems to be less assured than that of divine meddlers. In other words, both human and divine actors do more than *theorize* the minds of others; they attempt with varying degrees to *affect* or *control* the minds of others in respect of their thoughts and emotions.

Characters try to change each other's minds and reframe issues in each other's minds, as is visible in the interactions of Theseus and Hippolytus discussed above. Other examples are when the nurse tries to convince Phaedra that seeking an opportunity to slake her lust is preferable to death (*Hipp.* 433–81), when the servant tries to convince Hippolytus of the danger in offending a goddess (*Hipp.* 88–105), when the nurse tries to reframe Phaedra's anger after failing to win Hippolytus's consent (*Hipp.* 695–701). By means of her note, Phaedra tries to frame the reason for her suicide in Theseus's mind. Hippolytus, in his defense, tries to reframe the reason for the death in Theseus's mind, although his oath makes this difficult. These issues are ultimately reframed in Theseus's mind by Artemis, the epilogue's *dea ex machina*, helping him to understand his son's guiltlessness and his own rashness in jumping to conclusions, invoking Poseidon's curse, and banishing Hippolytus.

For tracking the representations of interiority, the most impressive feature of this play is its use of discrepant awareness.[91] There is agony and ecstasy for the reader in watching characters reason from faulty premises. The logic may be right, but it pushes the reasoning character to a tragic outcome. This is true especially for Theseus (*Hipp.* 875–98), but it applies also in subtler ways with other characters. Hippolytus's reasoning neglects the importance of the premise the servant tries to impress on him: that Aphrodite will not suffer his neglect lightly (*Hipp.* 88–120). Discrepant awareness also makes it possible for a reader to watch a character move closer to the truth by degrees, as when Theseus discovers the corpse of his wife, and later the reasons for her death. That process begins at the center of the play and is not resolved until Artemis speaks in the epilogue (*Hipp.* 1286–1341). Theseus's comment to the messenger who brings him news of Hippolytus's accident shows that in his intermediate state he still fails to understand Hippolytus or the truth: "Could it be that someone whose wife he ravished as he did his father's became his enemy?" (*Hipp.* 1164). Theseus does not yet understand that he is himself responsible for the tragedy, insofar as he invoked Poseidon against Hippolytus. At this point in the drama, the audience is also in the dark regarding the manner of Hippolytus's death. But it is only a partial, artful suspension of the epistemic advantage enjoyed by the audience over characters in the drama, for Aphrodite had primed the audience in the prologue to pay attention to Theseus's curse (*Hipp.* 887–90; 43–45). Aphrodite's plan, articulated in the prologue, supplies the audience with a macro-context to interpret this and every detail with a bearing on the plot, so that they are at an advantage over poor Theseus and his family.

4 Ezekiel the Tragedian's *Exagoge*

Little is known about the Hellenistic tragedian Ezekiel apart from the fragments of a play, the *Exagoge*, amounting to 269 lines in iambic trimeter, which survived because they were copied from one of his tragedies by Alexander Polyhistor. Eusebius of Caesarea knew about Ezekiel via Alexander, and he is known to modern scholarship via excerpts in Eusebius's *Praeparatio*

---

91 The origins of the term lie in structuralist approaches to English literature. See, e.g., K. P. S. Jochum, *Discrepant Awareness: Studies in English Renaissance Drama*, NSAA 13 (Frankfurt am Main: Lang, 1979); Madeleine Doran, "'Discrepant Awareness' in Shakespeare's Comedies," *MPh* 60 (1962): 51–55.

evangelica.[92] Both Eusebius and Clement of Alexandria speak of Ezekiel as a writer of tragedies.[93] If he wrote other tragedies, however, they have been lost.[94] Educated guesses place him in Alexandria at some point in the second century BCE.[95] Eusebius's interest was to show that Greek writers were engaged with Jewish history and writers. Polyhistor's reason for excerpting Ezekiel was probably his interest in Moses traditions. Neither excerptor was motivated to preserve an instance of Hellenistic Jewish drama for its own sake. Nevertheless, the surviving fragments supply a body of text sufficiently ample for us to make some preliminary remarks about Ezekiel's work in the cognitive domain of his dramatis personae. Just as we were in Josephus's case able to highlight genre-driven and ideology-driven interventions by comparing his *Jewish Antiquities* with its hypotext, so too with Ezekiel we can take a close look at his representation of thoughts and compare these with LXX Exodus, which at times he follows quite closely.[96]

A scene-setting speech by Moses, which apparently functioned as a prologue to the play, comes first in assemblages of the surviving fragments. This

---

92 Eusebius, *Praep. ev.* 9.28; 29.4–16. Eusebius is citing from Alexander Polyhistor's *Peri Ioudaiōn.* Clement's *Stromata* contains more fragments, all of which overlap with the two longer texts from Polyhistor cited by Eusebius. The attribution to Ezekiel of frg. 18 (concerning Moses and the serpent) from Epiphanius's *Panarion* is disputed. For the manuscript evidence, see Carl R. Holladay, ed., *Fragments from Hellenistic Jewish Authors. Volume II: Poets*, SBLTT 30 (Atlanta: Scholars, 1989), 2–3. For a more detailed discussion of transmission, see Pierluigi Lanfranchi, *L'Exagoge d'Ezechiel le Tragique: Introduction, texte, traduction et commentaire*, SVTP 21 (Leiden: Brill, 2006), 73–99. The text of Polyhistor can be found in the New Jacoby or in Karl Müller, ed. *Fragmenta Historicorum Graecorum*, vol. 3 (Paris: A. F. Didot, 1849), 210–44.

93 Eusebius *Praep. ev.* 9.436; Clement, *Strom.* 1.25.155.

94 The suggestion has been recently made that the fragments of Ezekiel are taken from an original tetralogy of four related works. This idea would be another way of accounting for the plural and, perhaps more importantly, it would account for the apparent violation of the "unity of time and place" rule that one observes in typical reconstructions of the work as a single play. See Thomas D. Kohn, "The Tragedies of Ezekiel," *GRBS* 43 (2002): 5–12. The suggestion is rejected by Howard Jacobson, "Ezekiel's *Exagoge*, One Play or Four?," *GRBS* 43 (2003): 391–96.

95 More precision is not necessary. The *terminus ante quem* is provided by Alexander Polyhistor, active in the first half of the first century BCE. It is likely that Ezekiel's work drew on a Greek translation of Exodus, putting the *terminus post quem* in the third century with the translation of the Septuagint. See Jacobson, *The Exagoge of Ezekiel*, 5–17; John J. Collins, *Between Athens and Jerusalem: Jewish Identity in the Hellenistic Diaspora* (Grand Rapids: Eerdmans, 2000), 224; Lanfranchi, *L'Exagoge d'Ezechiel le Tragique*, 10. No direct evidence puts him in Alexandria; for critical remarks of "alexandrocentrisme" among earlier generations of scholars of Hellenistic Judsaism, see Lanfranchi, 11–13.

96 There is no consensus on whether Ezekiel could read Hebrew. Jacobson, *The Exagoge of Ezekiel*, 40–47.

DRAMA: DISCREPANT AWARENESS AND DRAMATIC IRONY

prologue describes in general terms the history of the Jews in Egypt from the time of Jacob's arrival to the circumstances of Moses's childhood, coming of age, killing of an Egyptian, and subsequent flight. This, the speaker says, explains why "now in my wandering I have come to this foreign land" (Ezek. Trag. 58), where the drama begins.[97] Moses meets Sepphora, who explains to him that he is in Libya, a land peopled by black Ethiopians and ruled by her father, a priest. After a gap in the text, the drama resumes with a conversation in which Sepphora is explaining to a character named Chum that her father has given her as a bride to "this stranger," whom the audience understands to be Moses (Ezek. Trag. 66–67). After another gap, the drama resumes with Moses recounting a vision of a throne atop Sinai, occupied by a crown-wearing, scepter-wielding noble man who installed Moses on the throne with the crown and scepter. Moses reports being able to see all the earth and heavens from the throne and receiving obeisance from the ranks of stars. Raguel offers a positive interpretation of the dream. After another break, the encounter at the burning bush is dramatized, in which God commissions Moses and Aaron to go to Egypt. Moses's conversation with Pharaoh does not survive, but is assumed in subsequent fragments. The surviving fragments resume with a messenger speech, detailing the Egyptians' pursuit of the Hebrews and their subsequent destruction in the sea. This speech is presumably delivered to an authority back in Egypt. The final surviving fragments contain a scout's report, delivered to "Great Moses" concerning discoveries of an airy valley, a shady meadow, springs of water and a phoenix with the help of "some sort of sign, a pillar of fire" (Ezek. Trag. 243–69). The end of the text is lost.

Ezekiel's participation in the genre of the great Athenian tragedians is uncontested. Howard Jacobson assembles evidence for Ezekiel's first-hand acquaintance with Aeschylus's *Persians*, and convincing arguments have been made that Ezekiel also knew Sophocles and Euripides and that their work informed his style.[98] The prologue is "Euripidean" insofar as it is cast as a monologue delivered by a character alone on stage for the benefit of the audience, though (again, as in classical precedents) the speaking character (here Moses) does not break the fourth wall to address the audience directly.[99] Formal and ideological confluences between Ezekiel and his classical predecessors have

---

97   Translation and text in Jacobson, 50–67.

98   Jacobson, 3, 23–28, 185n7. *The Persians* is the only other "historical" tragedy to survive from antiquity, though it is probably a mistake to draw too firm a distinction between "historical" and "mythical" productions. The messenger scene in Ezekiel is, in the eyes of most commentators, clearly based on a similar scene in *The Persians*. See Jacobson, 24, 136–41.

99   But note also the prologues in Aeschylus's *Agamemnon* and *Eumenides.*

been explored, usually in scholarship on variety in Hellenistic Judaism.[100] These studies tend to focus on what Ezekiel has added, omitted, or changed from the biblical account: for example, the omission of the circumcision requirement when the Passover is introduced; the change in manner of exposing the baby Moses (from the basket in the river to clothed at the riverside); or the addition of a messenger to report after the fact the destruction of the Egyptian army.[101]

A tragedian like Euripides would have drawn on a variety of "sources," including Homer, written and oral mythic traditions, and earlier dramas. A Hippolytus mythos existed prior to his penning of either the surviving *Hippolytus* or the now-lost *Hippolytus Veiled*.[102] Euripides's productions, however, are very much

---

100 E.g., Emil Schürer, *The History of the Jewish People in the Age of Jesus Christ (175 BC–AD 135)*, ed. Géza Vermès et al., vol. 3.1 (Edinburgh: T. & T. Clark, 1986), 565; Jacobson, *The Exagoge of Ezekiel*; Holladay, *Fragments from Hellenistic Jewish Authors. Volume II: Poets*; Collins, *Between Athens and Jerusalem*. The omission of Ezekiel from modern handbooks and introductions to Greek drama is revealing. This is not surprising for books that restrict themselves to historical studies of the genre in its fifth century context; it is less acceptable in the books that attend to the evolution and reception of Greek drama. One looks in vain for Ezekiel in, e.g., Simon Goldhill, *Reading Greek Tragedy* (Cambridge: Cambridge University Press, 1986); Sommerstein, *Greek Drama and Dramatists*; Justina Gregory, ed., *A Companion to Greek Tragedy*, BCAW (Oxford: Blackwell, 2005); Nancy Sorkin Rabinowitz, *Greek Tragedy*, BICW (Malden: Blackwell, 2008); Ian Christopher Storey and Arlene Allan, *A Guide to Ancient Greek Drama*, 2nd ed., BGCL (Chichester: Wiley Blackwell, 2014).

101 Circumcision omitted (Ezek. Trag. 156–60; cf. Exod 12.43–9): Jacobson, *The Exagoge of Ezekiel*, 135; Collins, *Between Athens and Jerusalem*, 225. Midwives omitted: Jacobson, *The Exagoge of Ezekiel*, 75. Manner of exposure changed, basket omitted, clothes added (Ezek. Trag. 16; cf. Exod 2.3–5): Jacobson, 75; Jo-Ann A. Brant, "Mimesis and Dramatic Art in Ezekiel," in *Ancient Fiction: The Matrix of Early Christian and Jewish Narrative*, ed. Jo-Ann A. Brant, Charles W. Hedrick, and Chris Shea, SBLSymS 32 (Leiden: Brill, 2005), 135. Messenger speech added (Ezek. Trag. 193–242; cf. Exod 14.5–15.21): Jacobson, *The Exagoge of Ezekiel*, 136–52. The fragmentary nature of the text, however, makes it difficult to say definitively whether any given detail was omitted.

Jacobson rejects the possibility first noted by Wieneke of a connection between Ezekiel and the dramatic motif of a baby decorated with tokens to facilitate later recognition. Cf. Joseph Wieneke, "Ezechielis Iudaei poetae Alexandrini fabulae quae inscribitur Exagoge : fragmenta" (Diss, Münster: Monasterii Westfalorum, Aschendorff, 1931).

102 Conventional wisdom has it that the *Hippolytus Veiled* (Ἱππόλυτος καλυπτόμενος) came first and was a popular failure. The view is based on an evaluation of the surviving Hippolytus play (sometimes called Ἱππόλυτος στεφανοφόρος, "Hippolytus Garlanded") in light of comment by Aristophanes of Byzantium in his hypothesis to the *Hippolytus* that "it seems to have been written second since what was unseemly and worthy of blame in the other is corrected (διώρθωται) in this play." See Hanna M. Roisman, "The Veiled Hippolytus and Phaedra," *Hermes* 127 (1999): 397n2. For a full account of the scholia to the play, see Jacopo Cavarzeran, *Scholia in Euripidis "Hippolytum": Edizione critica, introduzione, indici* (Berlin: de Gruyter, 2016).

his own creations. There was no mythos "fixed" in every detail and universally known, which the Athenian tragedians could consult and "rewrite." But there is a further complication. Sometimes, even within a play, Euripides will change a widely accepted tradition in some important way. One thinks of the *Helen*, where the real Helen is in Egypt and a double in Troy, or of *Iphigenia at Tauris*, where Artemis has whisked Iphigenia away to Tauris at the last minute, fooling the onlookers at the sacrifice with the blood of a deer sacrificed in Iphigenia's place. In both cases, Euripides departs from the conventional narrative as reflected by Homer and other early poets and even provides an explanation for the perceived discrepancy *in* the play.[103] The situation is in some ways less complicated with Ezekiel, whose primary source was LXX Exodus. There are few major departures from the biblical account in terms of the plot, or of who lives and dies, and none of the departures is explained in the text, as Helen explains how she came to be in Egypt, or as Iphigenia recounts her safe relocation to Tauris. Although we should not assume that Ezekiel's Greek text of Exodus matched ours word for word, or that he was uninfluenced by other traditions about the Exodus, we are on firm ground in speaking of the differences between the *Exagoge* and our LXX Exodus as clues to where Ezekiel saw potential for developing dramatic aspects of the story.

Within the context of scholarship on Ezekiel in a Hellenistic Jewish context, there is a tendency to focus on how his changes to Exodus 1–15 might be apologetically motivated. However fruitful this method may appear to be, it has the potential to obscure what drives some of the changes. So Jacobson, when discussing the changes to the account of the exposure of baby Moses and his subsequent rescue by the princess, takes pains to show how all the changes are designed to defend Jochabed (and perhaps by extension the Jews as a group) from the charge of cruelty: "he absolves the mother of the charge of endangering her child's life."[104] This, he says, is why Moses is put in a safe place *beside* the river rather than in a basket *in* the river, and why Ezekiel's Moses is sheltered by vegetation: "the Biblical ἕλος becomes λάσιον εἰς ἕλος δασύ, the exaggerated emphasis on the vegetative overgrowth is designed to suggest a relatively warm and protected area." Moses is "kept neat, warm, dry, and comfortable" in

---

103   Euripides, *Hel.* 31–67; *Iph. taur.* 6–56.

104   Jacobson, *The Exagoge of Ezekiel*, 75–76. And again with Miriam: the difference between Ezekiel and Exodus (i.e., whether she watched from afar (μακρόθεν; Exod 2.4) or was near by (πέλας; Ezek. Trag. 18) leads Jacobson to claim, "Once again we detect the honor of the family being defended. Miriam did not watch fearfully from afar, but stood close by and alert" (Jacobson, 76). If this is Ezekiel's purpose, though, it is not applied uniformly. Note that Ezekiel's Moses is at least as fearful than his biblical counterpart.

200   CHAPTER 5

what is "clearly an attempt to indicate [Jochabed's] concern for his welfare."[105]
These interpretive comments seem strained, not least because one could easily assemble a set of passages where the moral failings of Israelite characters are
amplified, as when Moses murders the Egyptian: "First, I saw two men fighting,
one a Hebrew, the other an Egyptian. I saw that we were alone, no one else
was present. So I rescued my kinsman and slew the other" (Ezek. Trag. 42–45;
cf. Exod 2.11–15). Exodus's moral justification for Moses's action—amplified in
readers like Philo (*Moses* 1.43–44; cf. ch. 3 of this book) and Artapanus (apud
Eusebius, *Praep. ev.* 9.27.18)—have here been removed.[106] In short, changes
to the Exodus narrative need not be explained apologetically in every case.
Indeed, some of the innovations are more satisfyingly explained by recourse to
the conventions of the genre into which Ezekiel brings Moses's story.

Scholarship on Ezekiel also tends to make his primary interpretive context
one where "rewriting" biblical texts and stories was a flourishing activity. This
is more promising than simply comparing and contrasting Ezekiel with LXX
Exodus. Kristine Ruffatto, for example, situates Ezekiel in conversation with
Enochic traditions, focusing on Moses's vision (Ezek. Trag. 68–82).[107] Jacobson
does this habitually, especially when looking to see how other recipients of
the tradition handled a discrepancy between Ezekiel and Exodus. For example,
where Ezekiel omits the detail from Exodus 1 about the midwives, he notes that
this part of the narrative is dropped or modified in *Jubilees*, the medieval docu-
ment *Jerahmeel*, Philo's *Life of Moses*, and Josephus's *Antiquities*.[108]

These arguments about the apologetic functions of the text often focus on
apparently excised biblical details. Focusing on what is present in the text,
including "additions" the biblically literate reader would notice, what seems
most striking about Ezekiel are his renderings of dramatic conventions in

---

105   Jacobson, *The Exagoge of Ezekiel*, 76.
106   Compare the decision of Josephus in the *Antiquities* to omit the incident, and note Philo's
       allegorical interpretation of Exod 2.11–12 (*Leg.* 3.12.37), which differs from the account in
       his *Moses*.
107   Kristine J. Ruffatto, "Polemics with Enochic Traditions in the Exagoge of Ezekiel the
       Tragedian," *JSP* 15 (2006): 195–210.
108   *Jub.* 46; *Jerahmeel* 42; Philo, *Moses* 1.5–8; Josephus, *Ant.* 2.205–7. See Jacobson, *The
       Exagoge of Ezekiel*, 75. Lanfranchi suggests that Jacobson is perhaps too confident in his
       own ability to situate the *Exagoge* in his contemporary exegetical landscape, particularly
       in connection to midrashic literature: "Si une critique peut être avancée à Jacobson, elle
       concerne sa confiance excessive en la possibilité d'expliquer l'interprétation qu'Ezéchiel
       donne de l'Exode, à partir de l'exégèse juive traditionnelle, notamment des midrashim."
       Lanfranchi, *L'Exagoge d'Ezechiel le Tragique*, 337.

DRAMA: DISCREPANT AWARENESS AND DRAMATIC IRONY 201

presenting the story.[109] The introduction of the messenger speech is a case in point. The destruction of the Egyptian army is crucial to the narrative of the *Exagoge*; from a dramatic view of the action, it represents a climax. It would, however, be virtually impossible to act out on the stage, for much the same reasons as (for example) Poseidon's assault on Hippolytus's chariot. Just as Euripides used a messenger speech to describe what transpired on the beach (*Hipp.* 1157–1254), so here Ezekiel introduces an Egyptian messenger to relay an account of what happened at the Red Sea (Ezek. Trag. 193–242).[110] Technically, this means Ezekiel contradicts the biblical account, where the Egyptian army was annihilated to a man (cf. Exod 14.28), but that is not the point. The chief reason is to incorporate a pathetic account of the annihilation, and the pathos is heightened by putting the report in the mouth of a representative of the vanquished.[111]

The messenger speech also highlights what is the most important kind of structural change, however, for this analysis: the elimination of Exodus's omniscient narrator and the focalization of the whole action through speakers on a stage. The messenger speaks of "my army" overtaking the Hebrews, and says "I inquired" as to the size of the army (Ezek. Trag. 202–4). This contrasts with the biblical account, where the Egyptian army functions as a faceless extension of Pharaoh's hard-heartedness. Here, the whole spectacle, including a dramatic *peripeteia*, is put on view. The messenger speaks of what he saw on arriving at the shore of the Red Sea:

> They [the Hebrews] were lying in groups (ἦσαν ἠθροισμένοι) by the shore of the Red Sea. The men, worn out, were giving food to their children

---

109   Whether the intended audience of the play was Jewish or Gentile, the expected extent of their education in Greek and biblical traditions, their social status, and the particular occasion (if any) for the production of the play are questions about which no definite answer can be given. The working assumption of most scholars, though, is that the intended audience was made up of Hellenized, Diasporic Jews familiar with the Septuagint; curious non-Jewish neighbors would have been a likely secondary audience.

110   None of this matters if the *Exagoge* was not written for performance, as some have suggested. The messenger speech inclines me to think the play was designed to be staged. Arguing that it was designed for theatrical representation specifically at Passover, see Lanfranchi, *L'Exagoge d'Ezechiel le Tragique*, 57–72, esp. 64–68. For ancient Jews and the theater in general, see Mireille Hadas-Lebel, "Les Juifs et le théâtre dans l'antiquité," *CJu* 14 (2003): 14–17. For the messenger speech as a device in Greek tragedy (though without reference to Ezekiel), see James Barrett, *Staged Narrative: Poetics and the Messenger in Greek Tragedy*, JPICL (Berkeley: University of California Press, 2002).

111   Cf. Brant, "Mimesis and Dramatic Art in Ezekiel," 142–45.

202   CHAPTER 5

and wives. Flocks and household utensils were all around. They themselves were all unarmed and on seeing us cried out (αὐτοὶ ... ἰδόντες ἡμας
ἠλάλαξαν) tearfully toward the heaven and their ancestral God. There was
great turmoil among the men.

> Ezek. Trag. 205–13

The recasting of this information in first-person language adds poignancy to
the account, and sets up a strong contrast between "them" (the Hebrews) and
"us" (the Egyptians). "We in contrast were delighted.... We pitched our camp....
We waited, desiring a morning battle. We were confident in our numbers and
our fearsome weapons" (Ezek. Trag. 214–19). Then comes the reversal: "Divine
wonders and portents began to occur" (Ezek. Trag. 220). A large pillar "suddenly appeared" (Ezek. Trag. 222). Then Moses, the messenger reports, took his
rod and split the Red Sea in two. "All of *them* rushed energetically and swiftly
through the sea's pathway. *We* entered the path quickly, on their track. *We* hastened forward, but encountered night" (Ezek. Trag. 224–31, emphasis added).
The strong contrast between the Hebrews and the Egyptians remains, but now
it is becoming apparent that fortunes are shifting. "Suddenly, the wheels of the
chariots would not turn, as if they were bound fast. From the heavens came a
great flash, as if of a fire. It seemed that God was helping them" (Ezek. Trag.
232–36). Once the Hebrews were safely through the sea, "one man" (τις) cried
out, as he watched a large wave envelop the army, "Let us run back home and
flee the power of the Supreme One. For He is helping them, but is wreaking
our destruction" (Ezek. Trag. 238–41). But it was too late. "The path was washed
away and the army perished" (Ezek. Trag. 241–42). The fragments do not preserve the frame of this report, but a safe guess is that the recipient is whomever Pharaoh had left in charge in Egypt. The audience witnesses not only the
material *peripeteia*, in the loss of an army, but a pair of cognitive *peripeteiai* as
first the anonymous Egyptian and then the recipient of the messenger's speech
have their expectations dashed.

The next piece of narrative preserved is of a Hebrew scout making a report
to Moses, in which again the omniscient perspective of a narrator is traded in
for the limited perspective of a human actor: "Great Moses, take note of the
place we have discovered, by that airy valley. It is over there, as, I think, you can
see (ὥς που καὶ σὺ τυγχάνεις ὁρῶν). From there a light flashed out at night, some
sort of sign, a pillar of fire (τόθεν δὲ φέγγος ἐξέλαμψέ νιν κατ᾽ εὐφρόνης σημεῖον
ὡς στῦλος πυρός). There we discovered a shady meadow and springs of water"
(Ezek. Trag. 243–48). The scout waxes poetic about how wonderful the place is,
and an ecphrastic report is appended describing a phoenix. The report is filled
with apparent guesswork and surmise of the sort one would expect from an

DRAMA: DISCREPANT AWARENESS AND DRAMATIC IRONY 203

observer not in tune with the omniscient narrator of Exodus. The technique is comparable, on the one hand, to the thinking out loud of various characters in the Euripidean plays discussed above (e.g. Electra's husband at Euripides, *El.* 341–4), and on the other hand to the straightforward, third-person narration in Exodus, where the divine plan (including especially the source and function of the pillar of fire) is made explicit.

The process of thinking out loud, which we spoke of in chapter 4 above in terms of slowing narrative time, is apparent also in the scene with Moses at the burning bush: "Ha, what is this portent from the bush, miraculous and hard for a man to believe? The bush has suddenly burst into furious flame, yet all its foliage stays green and fresh. What is going on? I shall approach and examine this great miracle. For it is hard to believe" (Ezek. Trag. 90–95). What the narrator in Exodus communicates is what Moses communicates by his own speech in Ezekiel. The passage combines three functions: it uses deictic language to paint a picture for the audience, it gives stage directions to the producer, and it gives access to Moses's mind in real time. Again, we might compare a passage like this to the "real time" processing of characters like Electra's husband (see above) or the famous last speech of Medea (see above). The opening expletive (ἔα) added by Ezekiel heightens the dramatic effect in the scene.[112]

Like Euripides, Ezekiel provides his audience with a prologue that gives them a privileged cognitive vantage point from which to watch the unfolding drama. In the first lines of the prologue, Moses theorizes Pharaoh's mind: "King Pharaoh, when he saw our people increasing in number, devised many plans against us" (Ezek. Trag. 7–8). A few lines later, Moses theorizes a recognition by the princess: "When she saw me, she took me up and recognized that I was a Hebrew" (Ezek. Trag. 21–22). To set the scene for the Hebrews' exit from Egypt, Moses looks back in time to an earlier generation.[113] What may we infer from the fact that these revelations about the minds of Pharaoh and the princess are in a prologue? Perhaps, we may be tempted to ask, it depends on whether or not Moses is divine. For there is a convention, discussed above, in which gods and goddesses open a drama with a prologue that informs the audience about the state of the drama's characters' minds and hearts. When human speakers do this kind of work in prologues, they tend to do a good job of relaying the emotions and desires of other actors in the play (e.g., Electra

---

112 Notice the same particle at Euripides, *Orest.* 1573; *Bacch.* 644; *Med.* 1004.

113 Comparing Ezekiel to Euripides, Jacobson writes that "it is particularly Euripidean to have a character open the play with a sweeping historical account directed to the audience." Jacobson, *The Exagoge of Ezekiel*, 69. It is an open question whether the original play opened with the text of Fragment 1. There are no compelling reasons to think that it did not. See further Jacobson, 70–72.

in the *Orestes*), but they tend to make mistakes in theorizing minds *when it is important for the plot* (as we saw with Iphigenia failing to understand her dream). Some readers of the *Exagoge* have seen in it the divinization of Moses, which might make his access to the minds of others a moot point. But this imports a concern about "Hellenistic Jewish theology" into the interpretation, a state of affairs almost certainly attributable to the fact that Ezekiel's modern readers tend to be scholars of Hellenistic Judaism first and this particular text second. In any case, Moses's limited, human perspective becomes apparent later in the play when, like Iphigenia, he responds to a dream vision with fear and failure to understand (Ezek. Trag. 68–89; cf. Euripides, *Iph. taur.* 143–77).[114] His father-in-law Raguel steps in at that point to interpret. A second mitigating observation is that there is nothing necessarily superhuman about Moses's account of Pharaoh or the princess's minds. In the first case, Moses could infer that Pharaoh "devised many plans against us" from his contemporaries' and predecessors' lived experience of suffering because of those plans; in the second case, Moses's description of the princess seeing and recognizing the baby Moses as a Hebrew can all be understood as Moses's acceptance of what he had heard about the event when he was older. Support for this approach is found in a telling inclusion at line 15, describing how his mother hid him as a baby for three months: "So she has told me (ὡς ἔφασκεν)." The same explanation applies to everything Moses says about his infancy, including the cognitive states of the actors involved in those years. And finally, despite the suggestiveness of the vision, we should note that God, speaking to Moses from the burning bush, explains that he will not be allowed to see God's face because he is mortal (θνητόν; Ezek. Trag. 102).[115]

Secrecy plays an important role in the account of Moses's infancy. Jacobson draws a comparison to the prologue of the *Ion*, where there is also a "secret pregnancy" (but secrecy of a different sort and very different circumstances in terms of paternity and threat to safety) along with the exposure and rescue/

---

114 As is typical in the dramas, all parties involved assume that the dream matters, that it has some bearing on their reality, and yet there is some confusion about how to interpret it properly. For other dreams and visions, and the uncertainty they engender, see Sophocles, *El.* 417–23, Aeschylus, *Cho.* 523–50, Aeschylus, *Pers.* 181–210.

115 God, in that conversation, also exhibits the superhuman knowledge one associates with divine figures like Aphrodite in the prologue to the *Hippolytus*. A voice addresses the astonished Moses by name, revealing a divine knowledge of his identity and purpose. "The voice of God rings out to you from the bush" (Ezek. Trag. 99), the voice goes on to say in scene-setting language, identifying the speaker and the source. One can imagine how this information would be critical to comprehending the scene if one were not familiar with the biblical account.

DRAMA: DISCREPANT AWARENESS AND DRAMATIC IRONY 205

discovery of the child.[116] The priestess's failure to recognize Ion offers an interesting comparandum for the princess's recognition of Moses as a Hebrew (although she fails to realize the connection between Moses and his nurse/mother, fetched by Miriam).

Later in the prologue, Moses says more along the same lines: "When my infancy had passed, my mother brought me to the princess' palace, after telling me all about my lineage and God's gifts" (Ezek. Trag. 32–35). Here again we see Ezekiel attentive to Moses's mind: an explanation is added to the biblical account to explain how Moses acquired the knowledge of the circumstances of his birth. We saw above that dramatists were free—encouraged even—to innovate in the cognitive domain of their plots while leaving the material facts of the plot intact. This, along with the account of Moses's princely education, narrated in the next lines (Ezek. Trag. 36–39), represents Ezekiel making just such a move in connection to Exodus 2.9–10.

Moses buries the Egyptian "so no one else should notice and disclose the killing" (Ezek. Trag. 47). Here his character shows a concern for what others know, but in vain (we are not told how the word got out; perhaps the Hebrew man saved by Moses has talked). Compare Phaedra's concern for what others know in the *Hippolytus*: when she learns that word has gotten out about her desire for her stepson, she takes decisive, fatal action. When Moses attempts to intervene in another conflict, he addresses one of the combatants: "Why are you striking a weaker man?" (Ezek. Trag. 50). The response reveals that news of Moses's deed has circulated: "Who made you our judge and overseer? Or are you going to kill me, as you killed the man yesterday?" (Ezek. Trag. 51–53). Moses reacts "in fear" and reports to the audience the question that went through his mind: "How has this become known?" (Ezek. Trag. 54). The man's fear-provoking question in this genre is worth commenting on for its dramatic irony, since (as anyone familiar with the Moses saga knows) no less a figure than God has appointed Moses judge and overseer for the Hebrews. It is not fear that drives Moses out of Egypt in this drama, however; it is rather the fact that the report "quickly reached the king and he sought to take my life" (Ezek. Trag. 55–56). This concludes the prologue, having explained how Moses arrived in his present circumstances and what characteristic desires and dispositions are operative in Egypt. Comparing it to the prologues in classical drama, however, reveals that Ezekiel could have done more to indicate the goals and motivations of Pharaoh and Moses, and to foreshadow the looming conflict that will result from their incompatible orientations.

---

116   Jacobson, *The Exagoge of Ezekiel*, 70.

After meeting a group of seven maidens and learning from Sepphora that he stands in Libya, where her father Raguel is king, the text breaks off. When it resumes, a character named Chum is exhorting Sepphora to reveal something, to which Sepphora replies, "My father has given me as a spouse to this stranger" (Ezek. Trag. 66–67). It is difficult to guess at what it was Chum was asking Sepphora to reveal, especially since his is a character otherwise unknown in Moses traditions. Some have suggested, from Sepphora's response, that he is a rejected suitor.[117] Whatever the case, his line hints that Ezekiel participates in the dramatic tradition of filtering speech to suit the context and to maintain discrepant awareness between characters. This conversation is comparable to the exchange between Phaedra and her nurse, discussed above, in which Phaedra begs the nurse not to reveal a shameful piece of knowledge about her desires. It is a productive speculation to wonder if here (as there), a conflict is playing out between what one wants (Phaedra wants Hippolytus) and what one's duty demands (that Phaedra bear her emotions silently, do whatever she can to suppress or destroy them, and maintain her lawful marriage). Perhaps Sepphora in this play is between duty (her father has given her to Moses as a wife) and her desire (for Chum?). If so, the parallel with Phaedra is illuminating.

God predicts Pharaoh's fear and its motivating function: "King Pharaoh will suffer nonè of the plagues I have described, until he sees his firstborn son a corpse. Then in fear he will quickly send forth the people" (Ezek. Trag. 149–51). The obvious emphasis here is on fear as a response to God's intervention, but also worth noting are (1) God's access to what his enemies' hearts are now (hubristic, hardened, arrogant) and what they will be, once his plan has been realized (fearful, brought low), which has a structural parallel to Aphrodite's plan for her enemy Hippolytus (cf. other instances of divine antagonism); and (2) the tragic prolonging of Pharaoh's *agnoia*.

5   Conclusion

The defining literary characteristic of the dramatic traditions discussed in this chapter, compared to previous chapters, is the absence of a narrator to facilitate access to the cognitive domain of narrative. We looked at several of the literary techniques used by dramatists to curate cognitive access, including (1) divine priming, especially in the prologues; (2) the drawing out of information in dialogues between characters; and (3) the monologue. In each

---

117   Howard Jacobson, "The Identity and Role of Chum in Ezekiel's 'Exagoge,'" *HUSLA* 9 (1981): 139–46.

case, these helped furnish a vocabulary for approaching the phenomena of discrepant awareness and dramatic irony. Discrepant awareness tends to make dramatic irony possible. The ungrasped knowledge is conventionally of life-and-death significance, and when that knowledge is inevitably recognized in a moment of ἀναγνώρισις, it is typically too late for the recognizing character to avert the tragedy. Although this chapter focused on figures like Theseus, Hippolytus, and Pharaoh, the point could be strengthened by looking more broadly in the tragic tradition to figures like Oedipus in Sophocles's Theban plays or Pentheus in Euripides's *Bacchae*.

CHAPTER 6

Genre, Innovation, and Johannine Characterization

If genres have characteristic ways of manufacturing characters' minds, as this book has argued, interpreters of texts where the "genre question" is at issue would do well to pay attention to those patterns. Apart from certain scholarly activities, like writing a book about genre or composing the obligatory discussion of genre in a commentary, scholars typically do not give much explicit thought to genre.[1] Consequently, genre-conditioned conventions at play in ancient texts can go unacknowledged in common forms of scholarly production.[2] The preceding four chapters outlined patterns for representing and using the minds of characters to organize narratives in four ancient genres and identified strategies used by biblical scholars to link or identify the Fourth Gospel with those genres. Although genre-determined conventions for representing characters' minds have not figured in Johannine scholarship as such, occasional intersections have been noted between existing conversations and the present work. The goal for this concluding chapter is to push those conversations further, setting John's techniques for representing minds in conversation with the genre-conditioned patterns articulated in previous chapters. This comparative exercise produces in combination and, I hope, in each case individually, a more nuanced sense of Johannine conceptual and literary innovation in the cognitive domain.

1   Historiography

Reading John with the conventions of historiography in mind, one would expect to find in its representation of character cognition a focus on causes for

---

1   Sune Auken argues that all communication is mediated by genre, and that most of our interpretation through genre is tacit and rarely understood as such. See Sune Auken, "Genre and Interpretation," in *Genre And...*, ed. Sune Auken, P. S. Lauridsen, and A. J. Rasmussen, CStG 2 (Copenhagen: Ekbátana, 2015), 154–83; Sune Auken, "Contemporary Genre Studies," in *The Gospel of John as Genre Mosaic*, ed. Kasper Bro Larsen, SANt 3 (Göttingen: Vandehoeck & Rupprecht, 2015), 47–66.
2   This causes problems in some studies of a given theme or an idea in antiquity. For an example of a study of rage in the classical world that does give attention to genre-driven conventions, see William V. Harris, *Restraining Rage: The Ideology of Anger Control in Classical Antiquity* (Cambridge: Harvard University Press, 2009).

© KONINKLIJKE BRILL NV, LEIDEN, 2019 | DOI:10.1163/9789004396043_007

GENRE, INNOVATION, AND JOHANNINE CHARACTERIZATION

actions and events represented in the Gospel. This immediately runs into the obstacle of identifying what "events" count for explanation in causal terms. Chances of making a comprehensive and universally-satisfying list are slim. At any rate, the Fourth Gospel contains little of the phenomena typically explained in the historiographical tradition investigated above—battles, king-making, the drawing up of constitutions, and so on. Or does it? Kingship is explored at least in thematic and ironic terms (e.g., at John 1.49; 6.15; 12.13–15; 18.33–19.22), and it is perfectly possible to read see the dualistic worldview set up by the Evangelist in terms of cosmic battle.[3] But even if these count as "events," the historian will struggle to understand *when* these events take or took place. They seem to fall into the category of "the already and not yet,"[4] which is difficult to square with the chronological perspectives employed by writers like Josephus and Polybius.

At any rate, a non-exhaustive list of key events in the Fourth Gospel might include the Son's descent from and ascent to heaven;[5] the sending of John the Baptist (John 1.6) and the Paraclete (John 14.26; cf. 14.16; 15.26; 16.7); records of Jesus's movements (e.g., John 4.1–3; 12.9–19); actions performed by Jesus and other characters (e.g., the temple incident at John 2.14–22; the congregation of the Sanhedrin at John 11.47); the σημεῖα concentrated in the first half of the

---

3 On kingship, see Beth M. Stovell, *Mapping Metaphorical Discourse in the Fourth Gospel: John's Eternal King*, LingBS 5 (Leiden: Brill, 2012). On Johannine dualism, see John Ashton, *Understanding the Fourth Gospel*, 2nd ed. (Oxford: Oxford University Press, 2007), 387–414.

4 Martyn sketches a picture of the Fourth Evangelist's apocalyptic worldview that accounts for this tension, suggesting that "events on the heavenly stage not only correspond to events on the earthly stage, but also slightly precede them in time, leading them into existence, so to speak. What transpires on the heavenly stage is often called 'things to come'. For that reason events seen on the earthly stage are entirely enigmatic to one who sees only the earthly stage." J. Louis Martyn, *History and Theology in the Fourth Gospel*, 3rd ed., NTL (Louisville: Westminster John Knox, 2003), 130. Other illuminating studies of Johannine temporality: George L. Parsenios, "'No Longer in the World' (John 17:11): The Transformation of the Tragic in the Fourth Gospel," HTR 98 (2005): 1–21; Douglas Estes, *The Temporal Mechanics of the Fourth Gospel: A Theory of Hermeneutical Relativity in the Gospel of John*, BibInt 92 (Leiden: Brill, 2008).

5 Cf. Wayne A. Meeks, "The Man from Heaven in Johannine Sectarianism," *JBL* 91 (1972): 44–72. "The uniqueness of the Fourth Gospel in early Christian literature consists above all in the special patterns of language which it uses to describe Jesus Christ. Fundamental among these patterns is the description of Jesus as the one who has descended from heaven and, at the end of his mission which constitutes a *krisis* for the whole world, reascends to the Father" (44). See also Ernst Käsemann, *The Testament of Jesus: A Study of the Gospel of John in the Light of Chapter 17*, trans. Gerhard Krodel (Philadelphia: Fortress, 1968); Marinus de Jonge, *Jesus, Stranger from Heaven and Son of God: Jesus Christ and the Christians in Johannine Perspective*, trans. John E. Steely, SBSt 11 (Missoula: Scholars, 1977); Godfrey C. Nicholson, *Death as Departure: The Johannine Descent-Ascent Schema*, SBLDS 63 (Chico: Scholars, 1983).

210   CHAPTER 6

Gospel; and the rejection/condemnation of Jesus (e.g., John 9.45–54).[6] Not all
of these are explained in the Fourth Gospel with reference to a cognitive act.
Here we will consider the cognitive acts that *do* function in John in a calculus
of providing causal explanations for events.

The most important category of cognition that offers explanatory power for
events in John, as in historiography, is *desire*. Desires could be indicated by explicit references to the will (τὸ θέλημα) and implicitly by reference to the ends
pursued by various characters. In John, what characters desire functions on
several levels in unison and interacts with the motif of appearances and reality.

The "will of man" and "will of God" are set in contrast in the prologue, priming readers to attend to differences between divine and human desires in the
subsequent narrative. A distinction is drawn between those who "received" the
true light to which John bore witness, on the one hand, and those who did
not. The context makes clear that this "true light" is a person, the same person as the λόγος who is the grammatical subject of John's first sentence, the
person eventually identified as "Jesus" and "God the only son" (John 1.17–18).
Shuffling the temporal lenses, we read that those who received the light are
the children of God, born "not of blood or of the will of the flesh or of the will
of man, but of God (οὐδὲ ἐκ θελήματος σαρκὸς οὐδὲ ἐκ θελήματος ἀνδρὸς ἀλλ᾽ ἐκ
θεοῦ)" (John 1.9–13). The contrast between being born from θελήματος σαρκός
or θελήματος ἀνδρός, on the one hand, and being born ἐκ θεοῦ, on the other,
alerts the reader to the mapping of the will onto a quintessential Johannine
binary.[7] The historiographical focus on causes helps us to appreciate who is responsible for the change that matters in Johannine perspective: God, not "the
flesh," and certainly not "the will of a man (or husband)," is responsible for
bringing about the birth ἄνωθεν that will prove so confusing to Nicodemus in
John 3.[8]

---

6   Traditionally seven signs (John 2.1–11; 4.46–54; 5.1–15; 6.1–15; 6.16–21; 9.1–41; 11.1–57), though
    there are good reasons to be skeptical of overschematization. For discussion, see Raymond
    E. Brown, *The Gospel According to John I–XII: A New Translation with Introduction and
    Commentary*, AB 29 (Garden City: Doubleday, 1966), 1:cxxxix–cxliii.

7   On Johannine dualism generally, see Ashton, *Understanding the Fourth Gospel*, 387–411.

8   This raises an important set of questions—important, at least, from the perspective of later
    Christian theology—about free will and determinism. For a discussion of determinism and
    the human responsibility to choose appropriately, arguing that John affirms both perspec-
    tives, see Harold W. Attridge, "Divine Sovereignty and Human Responsibility in the Fourth
    Gospel," in *Revealed Wisdom: Studies in Apocalyptic in Honour of Christopher Rowland*, ed.
    John F. Ashton, AGJU/AJEC 88 (Boston: Brill, 2014), 183–99.

The Father's desires play an important role in Jesus's articulation of his mission. In conversation with "the Jews,"[9] Jesus describes his relationship with the Father in several ways. He is doing the Father's work (John 5.17; cf. 4.34; 9.4; 17.4); he is imitating the work of the Father (John 5.19); he is loved by the Father and is being shown what the Father is doing (John 5.20); and giving life to the dead is a prominent instance (perhaps the defining instance) of the Father's actions Jesus imitates (John 5.21, 25–26; cf. 10.17–18; 11.43–44). The Father has given the power of judgment over to the Son (John 5.22, 27) as a mechanism for securing honor for the Son (John 5.23). The scarlet thread running through these relational constructs is the conformity of Jesus's will to the Father's, a correspondence made explicit when Jesus says, "I can do nothing on my own. As I hear, I judge; and my judgment is just, because I seek to do not my own will but the will of him who sent me (ὅτι οὐ ζητῶ τὸ θέλημα τὸ ἐμὸν ἀλλὰ τὸ θέλημα τοῦ πέμψαντός με)" (John 5.30).[10]

That Jesus's will is distinct from that of the sender deserves pause. A longstanding debate in Johannine studies concerns whether or not and in what sense Jesus is "divine." Some readers have formed the impression that the Johannine Jesus is "God going about on the earth," in Ernst Käsemann's

---

9   The character group οἱ Ἰουδαῖοι is named over four times more often in John (71 times) than in Matthew, Mark, and Luke combined (16 times, most of which are in the title "king of the Jews"). In John, they are often, but not always, cast in a negative light. Some scholars, following Urban C. von Wahlde, have argued that the term should be rendered "the Judeans," which solves some problems (e.g., that Jesus and his disciples are not numbered in John among οἱ Ἰουδαῖοι) while creating new problems (e.g., some instances appear to include Galileans among οἱ Ἰουδαῖοι; cf. John 6.41, 52). Other scholars, following Malcolm Lowe, have argued that οἱ Ἰουδαῖοι refers primarily to the Jewish leaders, though this also fails to account for every instance. Given that οἱ Ἰουδαῖοι could already in the first century be used generically for the people we call "Jews," regardless of whether they came from Judea (see Shaye Cohen), I employ the traditional form "the Jews" without quotation marks to refer to John's Ἰουδαῖοι. See Adele Reinhartz and Raimo Hakola for a more discussion. Urban C. Von Wahlde, "The Johannine 'Jews': A Critical Survey," *NTS* 28 (1982): 33–60; Urban C. Von Wahlde, "The Jews in the Gospel of John: Fifteen Years of Research (1983–1998)," *ETL* 76 (2000): 30–55; Malcolm Lowe, "Who Were the IOUDAIOI?," *NovT* 18 (1976): 101–30; Shaye J. D. Cohen, *The Beginnings of Jewishness: Boundaries, Varieties, Uncertainties*, HCS 31 (Berkeley: University of California Press, 1999), 70; Raimo Hakola, *Identity Matters: John, the Jews, and Jewishness*, NovTSup 118 (Leiden: Brill, 2005); Adele Reinhartz, *Cast Out of the Covenant: Jews and Anti-Judaism in the Gospel of John* (Lanham: Lexington Books Fortress Academic, 2018).

10   On the Johannine theme of judgment, see Harold W. Attridge, "The Gospel of John: Genre Matters?," in *The Gospel of John as Genre Mosaic*, ed. Kasper Bro Larsen, SANt 3 (Göttingen: Vandehoeck & Rupprecht, 2015), 43.

212   CHAPTER 6

enduring phrase,[11] while others have emphasized his humanity.[12] Evidence exists to commend both views, and the handling of Jesus's will is instructive for demonstrating the tension. The passage just cited (John 5.30) lays emphasis on a distinction between Jesus's θέλημα and God's. The situation becomes more complicated in John 6, when some of the same themes resurface and are developed:

> Everything that the Father gives me will come to me, and anyone who comes to me I will never drive away; for I have come down from heaven, not to do my own will, but the will of him who sent me (ὅτι καταβέβηκα ἀπὸ τοῦ οὐρανοῦ οὐχ ἵνα ποιῶ τὸ θέλημα τὸ ἐμὸν ἀλλὰ τὸ θέλημα τοῦ πέμψαντός με). And this is the will of him who sent me, that I should lose nothing of all that he has given me, but raise it up on the last day (τοῦτο δέ ἐστιν τὸ θέλημα τοῦ πέμψαντός με, ἵνα πᾶν ὃ δέδωκέν μοι μὴ ἀπολέσω ἐξ αὐτοῦ ἀλλὰ ἀναστήσω αὐτὸ [ἐν] τῇ ἐσχάτῃ ἡμέρᾳ). This is indeed the will of my Father, that all who see the Son and believe in him may have eternal life; and I will raise them up on the last day (τοῦτο γάρ ἐστιν τὸ θέλημα τοῦ πατρός μου, ἵνα πᾶς ὁ θεωρῶν τὸν υἱὸν καὶ πιστεύων εἰς αὐτὸν ἔχῃ ζωὴν αἰώνιον, καὶ ἀναστήσω αὐτὸν ἐγὼ [ἐν] τῇ ἐσχάτῃ ἡμέρᾳ)."
>
> John 6.37–40

Added to the discussion now is that third party introduced proleptically in the prologue: those who must receive or reject Jesus. Compared to the prologue, however, the perspective here has shifted: still present is the action of the receiver (believing), but it is now joined to Jesus's responsibility "to lose nothing of all that he has given me." Jesus's will remains distinct from, yet in step with, the Father's.[13] Jesus could, conceivably, decide to "drive away" those who come to him, but because his will has been conformed to that of the sending Father, he does not. Viewed through the historiographical lens, the passage also connects Jesus's will with what we suggested above could be construed as one of the central Johannine events: Jesus's descent from heaven. "I have descended from heaven (καταβέβηκα ἀπὸ τοῦ οὐρανοῦ)," Jesus says, "not in order that I

---

11   Käsemann, *The Testament of Jesus*, 9. The German "der über die Erde schreitende Gott" is more often rendered by scholars with something like "God striding over the face of the earth."

12   See especially Marianne Meye Thompson, *The Humanity of Jesus in the Fourth Gospel* (Philadelphia: Fortress, 1988).

13   Cf. also Jesus's troubled soul at John 12.27. Perhaps the "trouble" is the result of conflict between Jesus's will and the Father's.

GENRE, INNOVATION, AND JOHANNINE CHARACTERIZATION

might do my own will, but rather the will of the one who sent me (οὐχ ἵνα ποιῶ τὸ θέλημα τὸ ἐμὸν ἀλλὰ τὸ θέλημα τοῦ πέμψαντός με)" (John 6.38).

Jesus's will may be distinct from the Father's, but the fact that it is conformed to the Father's implies that it never has a causal effect unaligned with the causal force of God's will. This dynamic radiates outward in John's narrative to believers. In his Farewell Discourses, Jesus explains to his inner circle how this works. After talking about the pain they will experience on his departure, Jesus says to the disciples, "On that day you will ask nothing of me. Very truly, I tell you, if you ask anything of the Father in my name, he will give it to you" (John 16.23–24). The connection to what the Evangelist has established about the relationship between Father and Son is clear, but the idea in "if you ask of the Father anything in my name, he will give it to you" calls for more elaboration. The disciples have seen Jesus making requests of the Father throughout the narrative (implicit in the raising of Lazarus, e.g., at John 11.39–44; cf. 11.22), and will see it again before the curtain falls (e.g., in chapter 17; see esp. 17.5). Now the disciples are invited into that dynamic as well. Jesus's requests have had demonstrably causal effects. They have been effective because what Jesus wants aligns with what God wants. Since God always gets what he wants, the prayer asking for God to get what he wants is necessarily effective.[14] Jesus's will has been brought into step with the Father's, and now the disciples are invited to align theirs as well. This is even more clearly the case in Jesus's earlier promise to the disciples, "If you abide in me, and my words abide in you, ask for whatever you wish, and it will be done for you" (John 15.7). To have one's will conformed to the Father's is, therefore, an important aspect of the Johannine idea of "abiding" (τὸ μενεῖν).

Does John offer any picture of what it might look like for followers of Jesus to have their wills conformed to the Father's? Jesus's prophetic remark to Peter suggests an affirmative answer: "You used to go wherever you wished (περιεπάτεις ὅπου ἤθελες); when you are older, someone will take you where you do not wish to go (ὅταν δὲ γηράσῃς, ἐκτενεῖς τὰς χεῖράς σου, καὶ ἄλλος σε ζώσει καὶ οἴσει ὅπου οὐ θέλεις)" (John 21.18).[15] This verse is typically read as a remark

---

14   On Johannine "determinism," see Attridge, "Divine Sovereignty and Human Responsibility in the Fourth Gospel."

15   Many readers of John conclude that chapter 21 is a later addition to a text that originally ended with John 20.31. For discussion of the issues (Was it added later? How much later? By the same or a new author? What is the "historical" status of the narrative in ch. 21?), see, e.g., Craig S. Keener, *The Gospel of John: A Commentary* (Peabody: Hendrickson, 2003), 1219–24. The conclusion that it is a late addition has much to commend itself, but the approach here is to take the Gospel in its final form. Whatever the circumstances of the composition and affixation of John 21 to the rest of the text, that chapter is both ancient

about Peter's martyrdom, a reading supported by the parenthetical comment in the following verse: "he said this to indicate the kind of death by which he would glorify God" (John 21.19). As with much of what John's Jesus says, however, another level of meaning may be present. Jesus's words may be taken as a part of the discourse of transforming desires, so that the promise is that Peter's faculty for "willing" will be no longer be the causal force in determining what happens with his life. That prerogative will go to "another." On one level of interpretation, that "other" is the person who ushers Peter to the cross.[16] At a more profound level, that "other" is God himself, who will lead Peter like Jesus to the cross, to glorify God. The parallels to the passion are clear: at one level, the Jews and Pilate act as the apparent causes of Jesus's death, while at the more profound level, God himself is the agent whose desires advance the story into death and beyond, to glorification and resurrection. The transformation of Peter's will predicted by Jesus in chapter 21 picks up on an earlier conversation between the two: "Simon Peter said to him, 'Lord, where are you going?' Jesus answered, 'Where I am going, you cannot follow me now; but you will follow afterward' ("Οπου ὑπάγω οὐ δύνασαί μοι νῦν ἀκολουθῆσαι, ἀκολουθήσεις δὲ ὕστερον)" (John 13.36). This again can be read on multiple levels—in the first instance, Jesus will be going to his trial and execution; in the register of τὸ θέλειν, however, Jesus is "now" doing the will of the sender as Peter will "later" do the will of the sender. The language of "following" here, as often in ancient literature, is a piece of the discourse of desire. People "seek" (ζητεῖν) and "follow after" (ἀκολουθεῖν) what they desire.[17]

The focus on desire as a causal force clarifies the objects of the Johannine Father's desire. Jesus's first promise to "do whatever you ask in my name (ὅ τι ἂν αἰτήσητε ἐν τῷ ὀνόματί μου τοῦτο ποιήσω)" is offered together with an explanation: "So that the Father may be glorified in the Son (ἵνα δοξασθῇ ὁ πατὴρ ἐν τῷ υἱῷ)" (John 14.13). When the disciples have aligned their desires with what Jesus and God want, their desires result in the glorification of God. It takes only a small step further to see that if the result of granted requests is God's glory,

---

      and interweaves well with the style and motifs developed in the first twenty chapters, an integration illustrated in the issue of Peter's will discussed here.

16   Eusebius collects the early Christian traditions about the crucifixion of Peter and Paul at *Hist. eccl.* 2.25.5–8. Cf. also Acts of Peter 35–40 for the account of Peter's crucifixion upside down.

17   For a long list of contemporary Jewish texts in which "seeking" and "following" God are promoted in lieu of seeking or following one's own desires, see Keener, *The Gospel of John*, 1:469. See also the remarks about zealous imitation (ζηλωτὴς ὤν) in Philo's *Moses*, discussed in chapter 3 above.

GENRE, INNOVATION, AND JOHANNINE CHARACTERIZATION

then what God and those with conformed wills desire *is* the glory of God. Read alongside the passage discussed above, what comes into view is that God is glorified and his will satisfied when Jesus loses nothing of what he has been given, but raises it up on the last day, and when all who see the Son and believe in him have eternal life (cf. John 6.37–40). Some of these events are narrated in the Gospel; others (especially the "raising" to happen on the "last day") lie beyond the horizon.

Jesus models this structure of desire in his prayer for the disciples following the Farewell Discourses: "Now glorify me, Father, in your own presence, with the glory that I had in your presence before the world came into being (νῦν δόξασόν με σύ, πάτερ, παρὰ σεαυτῷ τῇ δόξῃ ᾗ εἶχον πρὸ τοῦ τὸν κόσμον εἶναι παρὰ σοί)" (John 17.5). The "ask and receive" structure as articulated earlier in John has built into it a promise that the disciples' joy will be fulfilled: "On that day [when Jesus returns after having been taken away] you will ask nothing of me. Very truly, I tell you, if you ask anything of the Father in my name, he will give it to you. Until now you have not asked for anything in my name. Ask and you will receive, so that your joy may be complete" (John 16.23–24). In the prayer of chapter 17, Jesus expresses a desire that those whom the Father has given him might dwell with him and see his glory (John 17.24). Since we have already seen that Jesus gets what he asks for, that his desires have causal effect, this bodes well for those followers.

If Jesus and his followers in John are portrayed as bringing their desires into line with God the Father, the structure of Johannine dualism suggests the possibility of an opposite process of desire-conformation. Such a configuration of desire is precisely what we find fashioned on the lips of the Johannine Jesus in polemical dialogue with the Jews: "You are from your father the devil, and you choose to do your father's desires (τὰς ἐπιθυμίας τοῦ πατρὸς ὑμῶν θέλετε ποιεῖν). He was a murderer from the beginning and does not stand in the truth, because there is no truth in him. When he lies, he speaks according to his own nature, for he is a liar and the father of lies" (John 8.44). The relationship of the Jews to the devil parodies the relationship of Jesus and his followers to God the Father. In both cases the desires of those in the child's position are conformed to those of the paternal figure. Where the object of God's desires is life for those who come to Jesus, the devil's desires are for murder. This casts an ominous shadow forward in John, where the desires of the devil and the Jews will come to apparent fruition in the orchestration of Jesus's execution.

The achievement of the devil's desires is only apparent, however (a ψεῦδος, to use the language of John 8.44), inasmuch as the death is followed by resurrection and eternal life, all inclining towards God's glory. The apparent triumph of evil (or, to stay in the register of desire, the apparent achievement of the will

216   CHAPTER 6

of personified evil) is a feature more reminiscent of Jewish apocalyptic writing than of Hellenistic historiography.[18] And it may be not insignificant that some of these apocalypses, especially those written in the aftermath of national disaster (Daniel after the desecration of Solomon's Temple; 4 Ezra after the destruction of Herod's Temple; Revelation in the context of religiously-motivated persecution) can be described as participating in a historiographical discourse about the totality of human history.[19] I cannot pursue the full implications of this connection now, except to note that it recommends itself as an avenue for further comparative work on the Fourth Gospel and those apocalyptic texts.[20]

The frustration of the devil and the Jews' desires is prefigured in John 7, where Jesus has raised the ire of the chief priests and Pharisees so that they sent servants to arrest him (John 7.32). When these men cross paths with Jesus, he is provoking dissension in the crowd on the topic of "where the Messiah will come from." "There was a division in the crowd because of him. Some of them wanted to arrest him, but no one laid hands on him" (John 7.43–44). The Pharisees' servants return empty-handed. The larger issue is, as in the possibly-related Lukan passage (Luke 4.29) and the later Johannine episodes (John 8.59; 10.39), one of God's timing. The "hour" of glorification has not yet arrived. But our attention to which desires are "effective" in John draws attention to an additional level of significance. The historiographical lens makes these episodes important for their contributions to the cognitive characterization of God, the devil, and their agents, whose wills are conformed for better or worse.

The Jews' θέλημα, however, will not remain always as powerless as it is in chapter 7. It appears to achieve its desired outcome with the arrest, trial, and execution of Jesus. The Jews are successful in compelling Pilate to give them what they desire and take action against Jesus, despite the governor's initial resistance (e.g., at John 18.35). The tipping point seems to be when the Jews are able to leverage Pilate's desire to remain a "friend of Caesar" (John 19.12). A chain of desire, then, connects Pilate to the Jews to the devil.[21]

When Jesus's announcements that the Jews want to kill him (John 7.19; cf. 8.37, 40) were discussed above, nothing was said about the incredulity those

---

18   For the apparent triumph of evil in Jewish apocalyptic writing, cf., e.g., 1 Enoch 100.5; 108.2; Dan 11.27; 4 Ezra 6.27–28; 1QM XIII, 14–18; Gal 1.4; 2 Thess 2.8–12.

19   See, e.g., Christopher Rowland, *The Open Heaven: A Study of Apocalyptic in Judaism and Early Christianity* (New York: Crossroad, 1982), 136–46.

20   John's connection to apocalyptic literature: Ashton, *Understanding the Fourth Gospel*, 307–29. Cf. Martyn, *History and Theology in the Fourth Gospel*, 130–36.

21   Cf. Wayne A. Meeks, "'Am I a Jew?'—Johannine Christianity and Judaism," in *Christianity, Judaism and Other Greco-Roman Cults: Studies for Morton Smith at 60*, ed. Jacob Neusner, vol. 1, SJLA 12 (Leiden: Brill, 1975), 161; Keener, *The Gospel of John*, 1111.

GENRE, INNOVATION, AND JOHANNINE CHARACTERIZATION

remarks provoke in his interlocutors: "the crowd answered, 'You have a demon! Who is trying to kill you?'" (John 7.20; cf. 8.48). This is where things get interesting. The Johannine Jesus apparently knows what people desire in a way that transcends what they themselves are aware of at the moment of speaking. In Bal's language, this makes their desires non-perceptible focalized objects in the narrative.[22] In another context, where the disciples are puzzling among themselves as to the meaning of one of Jesus's teachings, the narrator brings Jesus into the scene: "Jesus knew that they wanted to ask him, so he said to them, 'Are you discussing among yourselves what I meant when I said, "A little while, and you will no longer see me, and again a little while, and you will see me"?'" (John 16.19). This is one of several instances in John where the reader sees in action a principle articulated at the end of chapter 2: "When he was in Jerusalem during the Passover festival, many believed in his name because they saw the signs that he was doing. But Jesus on his part would not entrust himself to them, because he knew all people and needed no one to testify about anyone; for *he himself knew what was in everyone*" (John 2.23–25, emphasis added; cf. 6.64). The interpretive repercussions of this observation for understanding Jesus's conversations in chapters 7 and 8 are that Jesus is making explicit the real desires of those with whom he is speaking, even if they have not yet become aware of their own desires.[23]

Chapter 9 thematizes the issue of causation explicitly when the disciples ask Jesus about a blind man, "Who sinned, this man or his parents, that he was born blind?" (John 9.2). The question assumes a causal link between sin and blindness, asking only about the agent responsible for the sin.[24] Jesus's reply rejects the premise and turns the question into a teachable moment with a characteristic Johannine twist: "Neither this man nor his parents sinned. He was born blind so that God's works might be revealed in him" (John 9.3). God's works have been linked already in John to the discourse of desire. Thus Jesus's reply replaces an expected structure of causation with a new one, grounded in God's will. With this in mind, it is remarkable that once the man has had his sight restored and is subsequently interrogated by the Jews, who believe

---

22   See the discussion on focalizors and focalized objects in chapter 4 above.

23   The "clairvoyance" of the Johannine Jesus is a subject to which I hope to return in a future project. For two recent discussions in connection to Luke, see Collin Blake Bullard, *Jesus and the Thoughts of Many Hearts: Implicit Christology and Jesus' Knowledge in the Gospel of Luke*, LNTS 530 (New York: T. & T. Clark, 2015); Michal Beth Dinkler, "'The Thoughts of Many Hearts Shall Be Revealed': Listening in on Lukan Interior Monologues," *JBL* 134 (2015): 373–99.

24   For a discussion and collection of ancient texts in which such a connection is established or questioned, see Keener, *The Gospel of John*, 777–79.

Jesus to be "a sinner" (John 9.16, 24), the man defends Jesus by recourse to this principle: "We know that God does not listen to sinners, but he does listen to one who worships him and obeys his will" (John 9.31). The man does not know what he is saying (cf. John 9.25, "One thing I do know, that though I was blind, now I see"), and yet his claim for Jesus is nevertheless true on a deeper level than he yet understands.[25] Jesus, obedient to God's will, has God's ear because obedience means his will has been brought into step with God's effective will.

The Fourth Gospel contains much more that could be read in terms of a contrast between God's causally effective will and the causally ineffective or only-apparently effective will of his enemies, but I move now to complicate the picture by considering the conventions for manufacturing minds in the βίος tradition.

2   Βίος

The ancient biographical tradition, we saw in chapter 3 above, is deeply ethical in orientation; its business is to investigate the moral character of famous men as a technique for the reader's own moral formation. As it happens, attention to the ethical dimension of the Fourth Gospel is now on the rise, making this an excellent moment to bring ethics and genre into conversation.[26] Despite

---

25   The remark is thus "ironic" in the same sense as remarks by Nicodemus (John 3.2), the paralytic (John 5.7), and the High Priest (John 11.50). The whole exchange between the man and the Jews in chapter 9 is deeply ironic. Note especially his question, which puts their θέλημα at issue, and their answer: μὴ καὶ ὑμεῖς θέλετε αὐτοῦ μαθηταὶ γενέσθαι; καὶ ἐλοιδόρησαν αὐτὸν καὶ εἶπον, Σὺ μαθητὴς εἶ ἐκείνου, ἡμεῖς δὲ τοῦ Μωϋσέως ἐσμὲν μαθηταί (John 9.27b–28). On Johannine irony generally: G. W. MacRae, "Theology and Irony in the Fourth Gospel," in *The Gospel of John as Literature: An Anthology of Twentieth-Century Perspectives*, ed. Mark W. G. Stibbe, NTTS 17 (Leiden: Brill, 1993), 103–13; Paul D. Duke, *Irony in the Fourth Gospel* (Atlanta: John Knox Press, 1985).

26   Craig Koester confidently predicts a new surge of interest in the question of Johannine ethics in his review article of the important 2012 volume edited by van der Watt and Zimmerman (for which, see below). Craig R. Koester, "Rethinking the Ethics of John: A Review Article," *JSNT* 36 (September 1, 2013): 85–98. For other recent contributions to the Johannine ethics conversation, see especially Wayne A. Meeks, "The Ethics of the Fourth Evangelist," in *Exploring the Gospel of John: In Honor of D. Moody Smith*, ed. R. Alan Culpepper and Carl Clifton Black (Louisville: Westminster John Knox, 1996), 317–26; Johannes Nissen, "Community and Ethics in the Gospel of John," in *New Readings in John: Literary and Theological Perspectives: Essays from the Scandinavian Conference on the Fourth Gospel in Århus 1997*, ed. Johannes Nissen and Sigfred Pedersen (Sheffield: Sheffield Academic Press, 1999), 194–212; D. Moody Smith, "Ethics and the Interpretation of the Fourth Gospel," in *Word, Theology, and Community in John*, ed. John Painter, R. Alan

GENRE, INNOVATION, AND JOHANNINE CHARACTERIZATION

the fact that most scholars working on the question would identify John as a βίος, little of their work takes as its starting point the idea that a primary function of βίοι was to explore the imitable ἦθος of the figures represented. An important exception is Richard Burridge's *Imitating Jesus: An Inclusive Approach to New Testament Ethics*, one lengthy chapter of which is devoted to the Fourth Gospel.[27] Building on his *What are the Gospels?*, Burridge recognizes that βίοι were written at least in part to provide ethical models for imitation, and he attempts to show that

> John's careful portrait of how Jesus treated individuals and the mixed, inclusive nature of his community form the perfect backdrop for his ultimately mimetic purpose in writing this biographical narrative that we should follow Jesus' example of self-sacrificial love within a mixed inclusive community of others who are also responding to his call and reaching out to his world.[28]

Burridge sees the message of the Fourth Gospel as fitting well with his "basic argument that both the historical Jesus and the rest of the New Testament are more about seeking a response of faith than in giving moral instructions."[29] While John has distinctive vocabulary and stylistic features, Burridge warns that "one must be careful not to overstress" the differences between John,

---

Culpepper, and Fernando F. Segovia (St. Louis: Chalice Press, 2002), 109–22; Hans Boersma, "A New Age Love Story: Worldview and Ethics in the Gospel of John," *CTJ* 38 (2003): 103–119; J. G. van der Watt, "The Gospel of John's Perception of Ethical Behaviour," *In Die Skriflig* 45 (2011): 431–447; J. G. van der Watt and Ruben Zimmermann, eds., *Rethinking the Ethics of John: "Implicit Ethics" in the Johannine Writings*, WUNT 291 (Tübingen: Mohr Siebeck, 2012); Christopher W. Skinner and Sherri Brown, eds., *Johannine Ethics: The Moral World of the Gospel and Epistles of John* (Minneapolis: Fortress, 2017); Sookgoo Shin, *Ethics in the Gospel of John: Discipleship as Moral Progress*, BibInt 168 (Leiden: Brill, 2018). See Skinner and Brown for a history of scholarship; see Shin for a well-curated bibliography. The subject is also broached in general treatments of "New Testament Ethics," including Jack T. Sanders, *Ethics in the New Testament: Change and Development* (Philadelphia: Fortress, 1975); J. L. Houlden, *Ethics and the New Testament* (New York: Oxford University Press, 1977); Wolfgang Schrage, *The Ethics of the New Testament*, trans. David Edward Green (Philadelphia: Fortress, 1988); Richard B. Hays, *The Moral Vision of the New Testament: Community, Cross, New Creation: A Contemporary Introduction to New Testament Ethics* (San Francisco: HarperSanFrancisco, 1996); Frank J. Matera, *New Testament Ethics: The Legacies of Jesus and Paul* (Louisville: Westminster John Knox Press, 1996); Richard A. Burridge, *Imitating Jesus: An Inclusive Approach to New Testament Ethics* (Grand Rapids: Eerdmans, 2007).

27 Burridge, *Imitating Jesus*, 285–346.
28 Burridge, 346.
29 Burridge, 345.

220 CHAPTER 6

on the one hand, and the Synoptics and the historical Jesus, on the other.[30] "Yes, the fourth gospel is very different," he writes in the conclusion, "and yet at the same time we have discovered just another reinterpretation of our basic thesis."[31] In trying not to "overstress" difference, however, it is all too easy to fall for the opposite temptation and attempt to force John into a Procrustean bed.

Burridge's thesis to the effect that John wrote a βίος for readers to follow "Jesus' example of self-sacrificial love within a mixed inclusive community of others who are also responding to his call and reaching out to his world" has appeal from the perspective of the modern Christian committed to progressive ethical issues like inclusivity, community, relationship-building, non-violence, and speaking truth to power. It is not always clear, however, how Burridge uses the precedent of the ethical function of βίοι to arrive at these conclusions. There is also a slippage (perhaps difficult to avoid in the "New Testament ethics" genre) from the historical reading of John as a βίος with ethical implications for its first-century readers to the transhistorical reading where the model in John is for "us" and "all Christians."[32] The categories of analysis also present difficulties. What, for example, does "love" mean in John? Burridge frequently uses the terms "love" and "Jesus" interchangeably.[33] This is a practice familiar to Christians now in no small part *because* of Johannine literature, but we should recall how odd such a usage would have been in the context of ancient βίοι.[34] On that note, one wonders why Burridge does not make direct use of other ancient βίοι in this chapter to make his point about the ethical message of John.[35]

---

30   Burridge, 288. On confluence between John's ethical message, the ethical message of the historical Jesus, and the ethical message of Paul, see Burridge, 328.

31   Burridge, *Imitating Jesus*, 346.

32   Burridge, 345. For a strong critique of attempts to use the Fourth Gospel in fashioning a modern Christian ethic, see Meeks, "The Ethics of the Fourth Evangelist."

33   E.g., "In the fourth gospel, Jesus is depicted as the love of God, coming to dwell among human beings to bring them his divine truth." Burridge, *Imitating Jesus*, 346; cf. 320, 322, 325, and passim.

34   Jesus is never called "Love" in so many words in the New Testament, but one could draw this connection by working backwards from 1 John 4.8 ("God is love") to the Fourth Gospel's establishing a state of unity between Jesus and God the Father.

35   When he does draw in noncanonical material, his evaluation turns disturbingly caustic. "It is notable that John does not give any licence to the natural reaction to hate one's enemies, in the vituperative manner of the Qumran material (see, e.g., *Hymns*, XIV; *Manual of Discipline*, IX, 15–22)." Burridge, *Imitating Jesus*, 329. This looks like more of an attempt to bring John into line with the good Christian ethic of loving one's enemies (commanded explicitly in Matt 5.43–44; Luke 6.32–36), than a balanced assessment of what one finds at Qumran. It also conveniently glosses over some of the uncomfortable promises one can find in the New Testament about what will happen to God's enemies.

GENRE, INNOVATION, AND JOHANNINE CHARACTERIZATION 221

Perhaps a better way to study the ethical example set by John's Jesus is to take a cue from the paradigmatic role protagonists tend to play in βίοι, but then focus our attention on what we find in John, without worrying about John's compatibility with the rest of the New Testament or with laudable, progressive Christian values traditionally anchored elsewhere in the history of theology. For example, it is not clear that the community promoted by the Fourth Gospel is mixed and inclusive; in fact, there is much to suggest that the Johannine community (on a stronger or weaker version of the community hypothesis) is hostile towards Jews, synagogue, Romans, and anyone else who falls on the blind, dark, ignorant, disobedient, non-recognizing side of John's apocalyptic binary.[36] We might also consider whether John knows synoptic traditions and, if so, what is the significance of his "silence" on ethical points enjoined in the Synoptics.[37]

One of the things that sets βίοι and encomia apart from historiography, as we have seen in this study, is the focus on the ἦθος and τροπός of individual actors around whom the texts are arranged. Moral character is so central that, despite obvious family resemblances between βίος and history-writing, ἦθος and τροπός can take precedence in this narrower genre over the question of whether a story "really happened" or is fictitious. In looking at Solon, we noted Plutarch's parenthetical, methodological comment that he includes the audience with Croesus because it reflects the character of Solon, even though he has doubts about the episode's historicity.[38] One consequence of looking at John through the lens provided by βίοι is that some of the stories may be there because the Evangelist took them as characteristic of Jesus, even where he had no reason to think that they really happened.

---

36   On John's dualism, see, e.g., Ashton, *Understanding the Fourth Gospel*, 387–418. On the antagonistic community ethics of John, see Meeks, "The Ethics of the Fourth Evangelist." For a reading of John sensitive to what is not inclusive, see Adele Reinhartz's "engaged reader" in Adele Reinhartz, *Befriending the Beloved Disciple: A Jewish Reading of the Gospel of John* (New York: Continuum, 2001), 131–59.

37   Burridge finds persuasive views like that expressed by Victor Furnish: The love command "need not be regarded in itself as *excluding* love for 'neighbours' and 'enemies.'" Cited in Burridge, *Imitating Jesus*, 329. Cf. Victor Paul Furnish, *The Love Command in the New Testament*, NTL (London: SCM Press, 1973), 154. Emphasis Furnish's.

38   Tim Duff speaks of Plutarch privileging this account of the subject's character over "clear chronological evidence to the contrary." Tim Duff, *Plutarch's Lives: Exploring Virtue and Vice* (Oxford: Clarendon, 1999), 312. Christopher Pelling, however, calls this an overstatement and wonders if Solon made the trip in his "notoriously spritely old age." Christopher Pelling, "Truth and Fiction in Plutarch's Lives," in *Plutarch and History: Eighteen Studies* (Swansea: Classical Press of Wales, 2002), 162n2. In either event, Plutarch's privileging of the "characteristic" criterion over the "historical" here is clear.

If βίοι characteristically exposit their subjects' moral characters and offer those expositions to readers for moral formation through imitation, and if we want to read the Fourth Gospel with that set of expectations as a lens, we ought then consider (1) whether and how John portrays Jesus's moral character and (2) in what ways it is designed to be paradigmatic for readers.

The discussion of John and historiography above looked at the act of supplying motivations and desires for narrated actions. With the lens supplied by the conventions of βίος, we find that those same motivations are ethically inflected in the Fourth Gospel. Having a causally "effective" will in the Fourth Gospel, we saw, depends on the degree to which one's will has been conformed to the Father's. That act of conformity is simultaneously an imitation of Jesus. Imitating a structure of willing *ipso facto* catapults the imitator into ethical territory.

The remark of the man born blind, discussed in the section above, is illuminating again in this connection. After Jesus has healed the man and while he is in conversation with the Pharisees and high priests, the man says, "We know that God does not listen to sinners, but he does listen to one who is devout (θεοσεβής) and does his will (τὸ θέλημα αὐτοῦ ποιῇ)" (John 9.31). Viewed through the historiographical lens, the deeper meaning noted in the comment was that Jesus's will is causally effective because it has been conformed to God's will. The logic of the remark in a biographical register, however, complements the historiographical reading: Jesus's effective healing means that God listened to Jesus, and if God listened to Jesus, Jesus must be θεοσεβής and doing the will of God. This is comparable to Plutarch's reasoning "backwards" from an action or remark to an understanding of a person's ἦθος.[39] The biographical lens, then, focuses attention on the ethical content in the remark: Jesus is devout, and in a more profound sense than the formerly blind man yet realizes. Taking these readings in tandem allows the tentative conclusion that piety is a piece of John's ethical vision and entails conforming one's will to God's.

Both Plutarch's *Solon* and Philo's *Moses* present their respective subjects in paradigmatic terms for the reader's benefit. Both, in their discourse of exemplarity, explore the virtues embodied by the subject. Chapter 3 above showed that Plutarch used the *Solon* to think through what one's attitudes towards wealth should be, and that Philo used the tractate *Moses* to explore the virtues appropriate to the roles of Moses as philosopher-king, prophet, high-priest, and lawgiver. The blind man's remark has put θεοσέβεια on the table as a virtue explored in John. If Jesus's θεοσέβεια plays a role in John, however, it is understated. Piety is not invoked explicitly anywhere else in John, though there are (1) several episodes in which Jesus is critical of traditional practices of Jewish

---

39   Cf. the discussion above in connection to *Alex.* 1.1–2.

GENRE, INNOVATION, AND JOHANNINE CHARACTERIZATION

piety and (2) a range of actions attributed to (and so offered as paradigmatic by) Jesus that various ancient authors link to the practice of piety.

On the first point, Jesus's critique of "vain" Pharisaic piety is a characterizing motif better associated with the Synoptics, but it may also be found in the Fourth Gospel, latent in Jesus's "signs" involving the stone water jars used by the Jews for purification (John 2.6) or on the Sabbath ordinance (John 5.9–16; 7.23; 9.14–16; cf. 19.31). In John, this critique is couched in terms of the antagonists' ignorance of true piety. What one knows is linked to how one acts and, correspondingly, how one is judged. It also forms a piece of a discourse of replacement, so that for John Jesus replaces Jewish purification traditions, Jerusalem and the Temple as the proper space of worship, the Sabbath ordinance, the feasts of the Jews, and so on.[40] The replacement, however, is an apples-for-oranges transaction. Jesus does not trade in one traditional concrete praxis for another, equally specific system of pious expression.

On the second point, some of what Jesus does in John can be linked to ancient discussions of piety. Honoring one's parents, including the care for parents in their old age, for example, is a requirement of piety in texts from across the ancient world.[41] Jesus's act of arranging for his mother's care from the cross might then be read as an act of piety (John 19.26–27), and, as Craig Keener notes, "By taking over Jesus' own role of caring for his mother, normally passed on to a younger brother, the 'beloved disciple' models how true disciples adopt the concerns of Jesus as their own and follow in his steps."[42] Keener's comment introduces the beloved disciple as an object of imitation, a character and a role I will return to below. All that is needed at present is to register that the scene sets up a structure of characterization in which Jesus charges the beloved disciple to care for his mother and so imitate his filial piety—if that is what this is.[43] Two mitigating factors are that Jesus's own care for his mother has not been emphasized in John, and no ethical comment is attached to this scene.

40　So Brown, *The Gospel According to John I–XII: A New Translation with Introduction and Commentary*, lxx and passim.

41　See the references collected from sources as wide ranging as Hierocles and *Genesis Rabbah* by Keener, *The Gospel of John*, 1144n679. For caring for one's parents in light of ancient Jewish conceptions of piety, see Pieter A. H. de Boer, *Fatherhood and Motherhood in Israelite and Judean Piety* (Leiden: Brill, 1974).

42　Keener, *The Gospel of John*, 1144.

43　This posture of filial piety is one area in which John's Jesus may offer a "corrective" to certain synoptic traditions in which Jesus causes his parents agony (Luke 2.48), "rejects" his mother and brothers (Mark 3.31–35 and parr.), and seems to encourage his disciples to do the same (Mark 10.29 and parr.; Luke 14.26). Another set of traditions can be found in the Synoptics where filial piety is apparently encouraged (Mark 7.11–12; 10.19; parr.), which seem to be closer to the reading of John 19 suggested here.

The Evangelist does not use it to comment on the beloved disciple's ethics, nor does he offer it explicitly to the reader as an example to model. For what it is worth, Josephus in another context explains that εὐσέβεια (which I take as virtually synonymous with θεοσέβεια) touches every aspect of Jewish life (*Ag. Ap.* 2.181). If θεοσέβεια is the content with which the Evangelist fills out Jesus's ethical profile, it may be as ambiguous or all-encompassing a signifier as the "love" command in chapter 13, to which we now turn.

What is certain in looking at the question of John and ethics is that—and here other early representations of Jesus, such as those in the Synoptics, Q, and the Gospel of Thomas offer a helpful counterpoint—John's Jesus does not offer much by way of explicit paraenesis. In Bultmann's famous (if exaggerated) formulation, "Jesus as the Revealer of God *reveals nothing but that he is the Revealer*" and "in his Gospel [John] presents only the fact (*das Dass*) of the Revelation without describing its content (*ihr Was*)."[44] This oversimplifies the Fourth Gospel, for reasons that will become clear in the coming pages. Its general thrust, however, is well placed and suggests a difference between John's Jesus and the figures in the βίοι discussed above. Both Plutarch's Solon and Philo's Moses are presented as teachers who instruct their listeners about the themes they model in their own lives. A look to figures like Plutarch's generals and kings in other βίοι would find that enacted ethics remains a central component also in βίοι even where the protagonist is not remembered primarily as a teacher or lawgiver.

Conversations about Johannine ethics typically begin either from this relative lack of explicit ethical injunction in the Fourth Gospel compared with other gospels, or from the implications of the "love command" articulated twice in John. After washing the disciples' feet, Jesus alludes to Moses's legislative function, saying, "I give you a new commandment, that you love one another. Just as I have loved you (καθὼς ἠγάπησα ὑμᾶς), you also should love one another" (John 13.34). The "just as I have ___" construction is as close as John comes to endorsing the paradigmatic structure that we expect in βίοι. Just prior to the command, Jesus had washed the disciples' feet as an example (ὑπόδειγμα), and framed it in terms of his being "lord" and "teacher" (John 13.13–15). Later, in the context of the Farewell Discourses, Jesus gives his listeners an idea of what love entails: "No one has greater love than this, to lay down one's life for one's friends" (John 15.13).

All of Jesus's public teaching in John has to do with himself, and even his private teaching to the disciples lacks the specificity of Jesus's teaching as

---

44   See Rudolf Bultmann, *Theology of the New Testament* (London: SCM Press, 1955), 2:66. Emphasis original.

GENRE, INNOVATION, AND JOHANNINE CHARACTERIZATION   225

represented in other early Christian texts.[45] On closer analysis, even the love command, for all its apparent outward force, is a continuation of Jesus's self-revelation, gesturing forward to his passion and the possibility that readers who count themselves among the disciples should expect opportunities to follow Jesus's example (cf. John 21.18–19). Whatever else love means in John, the ethical act explicitly invites imitation, which is the structure we would expect to see in a βίος. More elusive, however, is the nature of the content filling out the structure: an ambiguous love that involves performing menial services for one's inferiors and the highest possible form of which is to die on behalf of one's friends. Attempting to provide specificity in particular activities, it would seem, is to resist John's move away from particulars to orienting principles. The Fourth Gospel does not demand that believers take up footwashing and seek out martyrdom. It demands instead the kind of dispositional surrender to God that results in a willingness to act in these ways.

The Johannine character to have attracted most attention in terms of imitability is, perhaps surprisingly, not Jesus but the enigmatic and nameless figure conventionally called the beloved disciple.[46] He is mentioned as such half a dozen times in the second half of the text (John 13.23; 19.26; 20.20; 21.7, 20, 24), and readers have with varying degrees of persuasiveness linked him to other named or unnamed Johannine characters. His function has been read variously as a guarantor, and/or author, and/or founder the Johannine community, and/or leader in that community.[47] Whatever else he may be, an enduring hypothesis is that he serves readers as the exemplary disciple, that he models the ideal response to the revelation of Jesus in John.[48] Keener's positioning of the beloved disciple was noted above, when he takes charge of Jesus's mother (John

---

45   D. Moody Smith, *Johannine Christianity: Essays on Its Setting, Sources, and Theology* (Edinburgh: T. & T. Clark, 2006), 178–81. Cited and discussed further by Meeks, "The Ethics of the Fourth Evangelist," 318.

46   The identity of this figure is one of the enduring puzzles of Johannine scholarship. See Harold W. Attridge, "The Restless Quest for the Beloved Disciple," in *Essays on John and Hebrews*, WUNT 264 (Tübingen: Mohr Siebeck, 2010).

47   The author function is assigned chiefly on the basis of a coda to the Gospel: "This is the disciple who is bearing witness to these things; and we know that his testimony is true" (John 21.24).

48   Ismo Dunderberg offers a fine discussion of the beloved disciple as "ideal figure," and draws on the typology developed by John Collins and George Nickelsburg to show that not all "ideal" figures are paradigmatic. He concludes that John's beloved disciple is first of all a character in John's narrative, yet an "ideal" character in connection to authorship. Ismo Dunderberg, *The Beloved Disciple in Conflict?: Revisiting the Gospels of John and Thomas* (Oxford: Oxford University Press, 2006), 116–48. Cf. John J. Collins and George W. E. Nickelsburg, "Introduction," in *Ideal Figures in Ancient Judaism: Profiles and Paradigms*, SCS 12 (Chico: Scholars, 1980).

19.26–27), as a "model" for "how true disciples adopt the concerns of Jesus as their own and follow in his steps."[49] Raymond F. Collins in 1976 extended this view to a broader approach to characters in John.[50] Rejecting the notion that the characters functioned as "symbols" of various spiritual institutions and categories, he develops the view that each of John's characters offers a model of response to Jesus to be emulated or rejected. The ideal reader will want to imitate the ideal disciple, represented by the beloved disciple. Collins's article has been widely influential and continues to shape what people write about Johannine characters and characterization.[51] Although his thesis in its strong form is indefensible, as has been shown elsewhere, it raises a set of questions worth consideration.[52]

Jesus as exemplar in John provides readers with ambiguous characteristic qualities for imitation: perhaps "piety," and certainly "love." If the beloved disciple also offers a model for imitation, in what ways does he function? As noted briefly in chapter 3 above, secondary characters routinely offered protreptic and apotreptic ethical models in the βίος tradition. Even so, John's presentation of the beloved disciple (and other secondary characters) offers little to work with. A number of his actions are presented positively, often in situations where he seems to "better" than Peter.[53] Neither Jesus nor the Evangelist, however, explicitly endorses his actions as exemplary.

Precious little detail has emerged concerning the specifics of the actions or ethical orientations readers would be expected to cultivate by imitation. The behaviors enjoined on characters and readers of John mostly have to do with recognizing and believing Jesus. Although few details are provided about

---

49   Keener, *The Gospel of John*, 1144.

50   First published as Raymond F. Collins, "The Representative Figures of the Fourth Gospel. Part I," *DRev* 94 (1976): 26–46; Raymond F. Collins, "The Representative Figures of the Fourth Gospel. Part II," *DRev* 94 (1976): 118–132. Eventually reprinted together as Raymond F. Collins, "Representative Figures," in *These Things Have Been Written: Studies on the Fourth Gospel* (Grand Rapids: Eerdmans, 1990), 1–45.

51   See the discussions, e.g., in Christopher W. Skinner, ed., *Characters and Characterization in the Gospel of John*, LNTS 461 (London: Bloomsbury, 2013), xix–xxii. The Beloved Disciple's "ideal" quality has been extended to other questions too. Richard Bauckham, e.g., as part of his inquiry into the historiographical qualities of the Fourth Gospel, makes this figure the "ideal" eyewitness to Jesus whose testimony supports its historiographical character. Richard Bauckham, "The Fourth Gospel as the Testimony of the Beloved Disciple," in *The Gospel of John and Christian Theology*, ed. Richard Bauckham and Carl Mosser (Grand Rapids: Eerdmans, 2008), 120–39.

52   For discussion and critique, see Christopher W. Skinner, "Introduction," in *Characters and Characterization in the Gospel of John*, LNTS 461 (London: Bloomsbury, 2013), xxi–xxii.

53   Emphasized in Kevin Quast, *Peter and the Beloved Disciple: Figures for a Community in Crisis*, JSNTSup 32 (Sheffield: JSOT Press, 1989).

GENRE, INNOVATION, AND JOHANNINE CHARACTERIZATION

what action looks like that is motivated by that knowledge, every indication is that one's cognitive orientation to Jesus has profound consequences for how one lives in the world. The Fourth Gospel's silence on the particulars of the expected ethical outcomes may be read as a failure of prescriptivism or as a Socratic opportunity to reorder one's lived experience in light of newly-clarified knowledge and belief produced in dialogical collision with the divine Logos. These critical issues will be taken up in the final part of this chapter, where the dramatic lens will help us make sense of the minds of those Jesus encounters in the Fourth Gospel's dialogue material. But first I turn to discuss John in conversation with the conventions of romance, which help illuminate the responses generated at moments of encounter with Jesus as an image and emissary of the divine.

3   Romance

Relatively fewer Johannine scholars have worked with the ancient novel as an interpretive matrix for the Fourth Gospel, for plain enough reasons. Standard features of content and structure associated with romance—a boy and girl, both beautiful and noble, fall in love, travel and experience ordeals, especially attempts on their chastity, and are reunited at last for a happy ending—are missing. John's Jesus does not have a co-starring female protagonist. Although he travels about Galilee, Samaria, and Judea, Jesus's perambulations are relatively bereft of adventure. Compared with the Synoptics, it would be a stretch to call anything Jesus experiences in the Fourth Gospel an "ordeal." There are angry Jews and confused disciples, but no pirates, shipwrecks, or barbarians. Neither nobility nor beauty is ever explicitly thematized. The list could go on.

But this is where attending to a smaller slice of the data might prove illuminating. It is telling that the Johannine scholars who have found the novels useful for comparison have hit upon cognitive phenomena like ἀναγνωρίσις and divine-human antagonism.[54] Chapter 4's exploration of cognitive themes in the Greek novel tradition took further steps down those paths, particularly in the attention given to the larger scope covered by recognition and the narrative functions of desire and emotions. Recognition was shown to entail more

---

54   Recognitions: Kasper Bro Larsen, *Recognizing the Stranger: Recognition Scenes in the Gospel of John*, BibInt 93 (Leiden: Brill, 2008); Kasper Bro Larsen, "The Recognition Scenes and Epistemological Reciprocity in the Fourth Gospel," in *The Gospel of John as Genre Mosaic*, ed. Kasper Bro Larsen, SANt 3 (Göttingen: Vandehoeck & Rupprecht, 2015), 341–56. Divine-human antagonism: Meredith J. C. Warren, *My Flesh Is Meat Indeed: A Nonsacramental Reading of John 6:51–58* (Minneapolis: Fortress, 2015).

than the instant recognition of persons. It could be gradual or instant, partial or total, and person-directed or circumstance-directed. This complexity opens up new possibilities for seeing "recognition" at work in the Fourth Gospel. Emotions frequently figured in and around recognition scenes in the novels, often as part of a medley of many-colored emotions. They surface in responses to the protagonists' beauty, in expressions of reciprocal ἔρως, and in relation to the discourse of self-control.

In chapter 4 above, I argued that the whole action of the Greek novel might compellingly be characterized in terms of drawing out states of misperception and misunderstanding, delaying recognition by various means, until, seemingly against all odds, the lovers are finally united with an abundance of passion. Although it sounds trite to speak of John as a love story, focusing on these two elements in the Fourth Gospel—encountering and recognizing a lover—may prove instructive.

Almost every time an ancient novel's heroine (and sometimes the hero) meets someone new, that person is overwhelmed at what they see. Callirhoe, for example, has this effect not only on Chaereas (*Callir.* 1.1.7), but also on nearly every other man or woman she meets in the course of the novel (e.g., Statira at *Callir.* 5.9.1). The onlooker frequently mistakes her for a goddess and may also be stirred by desire to plot-advancing action (e.g., Dionysius at *Callir.* 2.3.6). The effect is only superficial, however, because the extant Greek novels progress unfailingly towards the τέλος of lovers happily reunited, whatever challenges are presented by this secondary cast of desiring creatures en route.

The Fourth Gospel, comparably, presents the story of Jesus as a series of encounters—with the first disciples (John 1.35–42), with Philip and Nathanael (John 1.43–51), with Jesus's mother (John 2.1–5), with the wedding servants (John 2.6–8), and so on. An important difference is that in his story, Jesus is a god mistaken for a man. In the course of subsequent dialogue these other characters either persist in their misrecognition or come to recognize what the reader already knows from the prologue: Jesus is "God the only Son," sent by the Father to "explain God in full" (θεὸν οὐδεὶς ἑώρακεν πώποτε· μονογενὴς θεὸς ὁ ὢν εἰς τὸν κόλπον τοῦ πατρὸς ἐκεῖνος ἐξηγήσατο) to those below (John 1.18).

Encounters with protagonists in the Greek novels are accompanied in many cases by extravagant displays of emotion, as when Mithridates faints upon seeing Callirhoe (*Callir.* 4.1.9), or when Aseneth trembles and goes weak in the knees when she first sees Joseph (*Asen.* 6.1). In Chariton, with his affinity for Homeric language and imagery, these emotional moments are often colored by the language of Homeric physical trauma relocated to the soul of the sufferer. Although John's characters can be emotional in their responses to Jesus, the Evangelist says little of what they feel, leaving the reader to infer their states of

GENRE, INNOVATION, AND JOHANNINE CHARACTERIZATION

mind from the dialogue. This dynamic will be discussed in the next section of this chapter, when we read John in conversation with drama.

Emotions, though represented with economy, are not absent from the Fourth Gospel. A common function of represented emotions in the novels was to highlight conflict in the sufferer. Chariton twice uses the expression πάθη ποικίλα to describe such situations, especially where a simple πάθος is complicated by a conflicting interest, forcing a difficult choice, as when Callirhoe's pity (ἔλεός) for her child is amplified while she is at a loss over whether to marry Dionysius or abort her pregnancy: "My choice lies between two vital matters, my honor or the life of my child" (*Callir.* 2.10.7).[55] Although the Fourth Gospel has no exact parallel to such a dilemma of ἔλεός, the novelistic lens may help bring into focus some of the "complications" wrought on the emotions of Johannine characters.

Pilate's dilemma offers a useful case study of a πάθος complicated by the Evangelist. On the one hand he desires to release Jesus (note the desire-indicating language of "seeking" in John 19.12), but is pulled in another direction by the Jews who demand Jesus's death. Like Callirhoe, he wriggles to get off the hook. First, he asks the Jews to "take him yourselves and judge him according to your law" (John 18.31). Later, Pilate pronounces his inability to find a case against Jesus and proposes that Jesus be the beneficiary of a custom in which the governor releases a prisoner to the Jews at Passover (John 18.38–39). When the Jews reject the proposal, Pilate tries flogging and mocking Jesus and reasserting his inability to find a case against Jesus (John 19.1–6). So far, the Evangelist has said nothing explicitly about Pilate's emotional state. When the governor hears the Jews reject his latest attempt to placate—"We have a law, and according to that law he ought to die because he has claimed to be the Son of God" (John 19.7)—the audience is confirmed in what they may have suspected already: Pilate is afraid. As Callirhoe's ἔλεός grew complicated while her window of opportunity to raise her child with Dionysius as father crept shut, so here Pilate's fear is complicated and intensified: μᾶλλον ἐφοβήθη (John 19.8). The Jews have been steadily tightening the screws, blocking his attempted dodges, and now introduce a charge that Jesus claims divine sonship. The charge is laden with irony. Were the Jews initially reluctant to put the charge on the table, wanting Pilate to act on the basis of their ambiguous word that, "if this man were not a criminal, we would not have handed him over to you" (John 18.30)? In the language of "Son of God" introduced now that the dialogue is well underway, does Pilate sense a threat to the emperor and his cult? Are

---

55   Trans. LCL.

230   CHAPTER 6

the Jews conscious of the significance these particular words hold for a Roman official's ears?[56] To be sure, the charge is of a piece with Johannine irony, where "he ought to die" (not for the reasons they put forward, but for God's glory), and "he has claimed to be the Son of God" (which from John's perspective he is, though the Jews do not accept it). Do they operate on a third and intermediary level in Pilate's mind, not necessarily intended by the Jews (recall their initial reticence to specify the charge) and equally ironically misguided from the Evangelist's perspective, but nevertheless significant to Pilate in connection to the emperor cult? It is impossible to say.

Despite his magnified fear, Pilate continues to equivocate and, after a second interview with Jesus, carries on seeking to release him.[57] His hand is forced, however, when the Jews spell out for him the logic of Jesus's claims to kingship and divine sonship: If you release this man, you are not a friend of Caesar, for everyone who makes himself a king stands against Caesar (ἐὰν τοῦτον ἀπολύσῃς, οὐκ εἶ φίλος τοῦ Καίσαρος· πᾶς ὁ βασιλέα ἑαυτὸν ποιῶν ἀντιλέγει τῷ Καίσαρι)" (John 19.12). Whether or not the Jews knew earlier the significance "son of God" might have for a Roman governor, and whether or not they understand now what it means to Pilate to be a "friend of the emperor," they evidently understand enough to allude darkly to the consequences of ignoring or releasing a subject who "makes himself king." This plays into the anxieties that motivate Pilate's action, compelling him to choose friendship with Caesar over friendship with Jesus.[58]

To be a friend (φίλος), whether with Jesus or Caesar, is to be in a relationship characterized by φιλία. This is not the ἔρως of the novels, but it belongs to the same semantic field. Φιλία plays a critical role in the Johannine conceptual landscape, inflecting Johannine characterizations. John the Baptist describes himself as the φίλος of the bridegroom in a transparent illustration where the bridegroom is Jesus (John 3.29); Jesus speaks of Lazarus as ὁ φίλος ἡμῶν (John 11.11); and again of the disciples as Jesus's φίλοι if they do what he commands (John 15.14). The sisters of Lazarus know that their brother is "he whom

---

56   Cf. Adela Yarbro Collins, "Mark and His Readers: The Son of God among Greeks and Romans," HTR 93 (2000): 85–100; Warren Carter, *John and Empire: Initial Explorations* (New York: T. & T. Clark, 2008), 5–6, 194–95; Michael Peppard, *The Son of God in the Roman World: Divine Sonship in Its Social and Political Context* (New York: Oxford University Press, 2011).

57   The progressive, habitual aspect of the imperfect in ἐκ τούτου ὁ Πιλᾶτος ἐζήτει ἀπολῦσαι αὐτόν should be given its full force here.

58   On friendship in John, see also the discussion above in connection to Johannine ethics and Martin M. Culy, *Echoes of Friendship in the Gospel of John*, NTMon 30 (Sheffield: Sheffield Phoenix Press, 2010).

GENRE, INNOVATION, AND JOHANNINE CHARACTERIZATION 231

you [Jesus] love (ὃν φιλεῖς)" (John 11.3); and the Jews take Jesus's weeping as evidence of Jesus's love for Lazarus ("Ἴδε πῶς ἐφίλει αὐτόν) (John 11.36). Φιλία characterizes the relationship between the Father and the Son (John 5.20), and exists on both sides of the Johannine line in the sand: "If you belonged to the world," Jesus tells the disciples, "the world would love you as its own (εἰ ἐκ τοῦ κόσμου ἦτε, ὁ κόσμος ἂν τὸ ἴδιον ἐφίλει)" (John 15.19). The implication is that the world does not love Jesus's followers. This verse has played an important role in conversations about the Johannine community, reinforcing the suggestion that followers of the Johannine Christ are not feeling very well loved by "the world." Even without crossing that bridge from text to *Sitz im Leben*, this verse effectively puts "love" on both sides of the Johannine binary. The world loves its own and Jesus's followers love their own. At John 12.25, Jesus announces that "he who loves his life will lose it." Pilate, by choosing to be a φίλος of Caesar instead of a φίλος of Jesus, chooses to love his own "life" instead of "life" in Jesus's person and so excludes himself from the Father's love. That love is reserved in the Fourth Gospel for those who have first loved Jesus and believed in his divine origin: "For the Father himself loves you, because you have loved me and believed that I have come from God (αὐτὸς γὰρ ὁ πατὴρ φιλεῖ ὑμᾶς, ὅτι ὑμεῖς ἐμὲ πεφιλήκατε καὶ πεπιστεύκατε ὅτι ἐγὼ παρὰ [τοῦ] θεοῦ ἐξῆλθον)" (John 16.27).

Some scholars have attempted to draw a sharp distinction between φιλία and ἀγάπη, which is more frequent word for "love" in the Fourth Gospel.[59] But we have already seen that φιλία could be used either of God for those who believe in Jesus or of "the world" for its own. The disciple ὃν ἠγάπα ὁ Ἰησοῦς (John 13.23; cf. 19.26; 21.7) is also described as the disciple ὃν ἐφίλει ὁ Ἰησοῦς (John 20.2). The Father "loves" (φιλεῖ) the Son (John 5.20) and the Father "loves" (ἀγαπᾷ) the Son (John 3.35; 10.17). On the other side of the coin, people have "loved" (ἠγάπησαν) the darkness more than the light (John 3.19), showing that τὸ ἀγαπᾶν is not a special quality felt exclusively by Jesus and his followers. In Jesus's conversation with Peter (John 21.15–17), which will be examined at greater length below, the words appear to be used interchangeably. Ἀγάπη is applied to other named individuals (Jesus loves Mary, Martha, and Lazarus at John 11.5), as well as generalized groups (e.g., the secret disciples loved human glory more than the glory of God at John 12.43).

In addition to being imitable, love in the Fourth Gospel is ideally mutual. Jesus loves his own (John 13.1), and expects them to reciprocate: "If you love

---

59   See the discussion, e.g., in Raymond E. Brown, *The Gospel According to John XIII–XXI: A New Translation with Introduction and Commentary*, AB 29A (Garden City: Doubleday, 1970), 1102–3.

232 CHAPTER 6

me," he says, "you will keep my commandments" (John 14.15–31). His "new commandment," as discussed above in connection to Johannine ethics, is that the disciples will "love one another" (John 13.34; 15.12; cf. 15.17). Loving Jesus leads to being loved by the Father (John 14.21; cf. 17.23, 26) and "to remain" in Jesus's love is to participate in the pre-existent mutual love that exists between the Father and the Son (John 15.9–10; cf. 17.24). Love is scalable, and in the Johannine world of ideas, the greatest ἀγάπη is to lay down one's life for one's φίλοι (John 15.13). This is more like the feeling in the novels between heroes and their companions than that between hero and heroine; Chaereas and Polycharmus (cf. *Callir.* 3.6.7; 7.1.7; 8.8.12–13) rather than Chaereas and Callirhoe; Aseneth and her maid (cf. *Asen.* 10.4) rather than Aseneth and Joseph. Chapter 4 above showed that it was a primary function of these friends to keep the hero alive when he despaired of life in the absence of the beloved (e.g., *Callir.* 6.2.8–9). The friends of the Johannine Jesus seek to keep him alive too, when they suspect that he is throwing his life away, but in the Fourth Gospel Jesus never despairs and the disciples' action only highlights their failure to fully appreciate his divine mission. On this reading, the "lovers" separated and eventually reunited are Jesus and the Father; Jesus's friends are invited to "share his joy," as the friend of the bridegroom shares in the joy of the wedding (cf. John 3.29). This reading has as an important consequence the decentering of Jesus's followers in the hierarchy of the Evangelist's interests: the primary relationship celebrated in John is that which exists between Father and Son. Jesus's followers take up the mantle of a Polycharmus, except that where Polycharmus was able to keep his wits about him and see his lovestruck comrade through to safety and back into the arms of the beloved (e.g., *Callir.* 4.2.1–3), Jesus's followers struggle to wrap their heads around the determined logic that steers Jesus's descent into the world and return to the Father.

Love, fear, and grief are the emotions felt most frequently in the novels. Fear and love have already been discussed, but the Johannine discourse of grief is also worth sounding for resonances with the novelistic pattern described above. Helpful in this connection is the conversation between the resurrected Jesus and Peter on the subject of Peter's love.

Ὅτε οὖν ἠρίστησαν λέγει τῷ Σίμωνι Πέτρῳ ὁ Ἰησοῦς, Σίμων Ἰωάννου, ἀγαπᾷς με πλέον τούτων; λέγει αὐτῷ, Ναί, κύριε, σὺ οἶδας ὅτι φιλῶ σε. λέγει αὐτῷ, Βόσκε τὰ ἀρνία μου. λέγει αὐτῷ πάλιν δεύτερον, Σίμων Ἰωάννου, ἀγαπᾷς με; λέγει αὐτῷ, Ναί, κύριε, σὺ οἶδας ὅτι φιλῶ σε. λέγει αὐτῷ, Ποίμαινε τὰ πρόβατά μου. λέγει αὐτῷ τὸ τρίτον, Σίμων Ἰωάννου, φιλεῖς με; ἐλυπήθη ὁ Πέτρος ὅτι εἶπεν αὐτῷ τὸ τρίτον, Φιλεῖς με; καὶ λέγει αὐτῷ, Κύριε, πάντα σὺ οἶδας, σὺ γινώσκεις ὅτι φιλῶ σε. λέγει αὐτῷ, Βόσκε τὰ πρόβατά μου.

GENRE, INNOVATION, AND JOHANNINE CHARACTERIZATION

> When they had finished breakfast, Jesus said to Simon Peter, "Simon son of John, do you love me more than these?" He said to him, "Yes, Lord; you know that I love you." Jesus said to him, "Feed my lambs." A second time he said to him, "Simon son of John, do you love me?" He said to him, "Yes, Lord; you know that I love you." Jesus said to him, "Tend my sheep." He said to him the third time, "Simon son of John, do you love me?" Peter felt hurt because he said to him the third time, "Do you love me?" And he said to him, "Lord, you know everything; you know that I love you." Jesus said to him, "Feed my sheep."
>
> John 21.15–17

This encounter, which culminates in Jesus's prediction about Peter's martyrdom, was discussed above in connection to the bending of Peter's will to God's, in imitation of Jesus and for God's glorification. Reviewing the emotional content woven into the conversation that precedes the prediction, we see Peter's apparently simple love interrogated, frustrated, and complicated. The nature of the primary πάθος in question, ἀγάπη or φιλία, was discussed above; what is important to note now is that the encounter with Jesus complicates the emotion. In the course of the interrogation, the love Peter professes is complicated by grief, so that Peter feels ἀγάπη, φιλία, and λύπη simultaneously. Callirhoe's ongoing reflection on her situation and her pity for her child eventually lead her to choose the arrangement with Dionysius. In a comparable way, the Johannine Jesus's continued probing of Peter's love and its connection to a consequent ethical action (for the benefit of Jesus's "lambs" and "sheep"; cf. John 10.1–16) leads by degrees and with grief to a more profound acknowledgment of what Jesus knows, from "you know that I love you" to "you know everything." Confessing belief in Jesus, which is tantamount to believing in the truth of the message Jesus claims to bring from the Father to those who would receive it, and subsequent action stemming from one's love of Jesus are, as we saw above, key to the ethical paradigm operative in the Fourth Gospel.

Encounters with Jesus, like encounters with protagonists in the novels, are often productive of a desire that will steer the direction of subsequent conversation or action. Peter's encounter with Jesus leads to his "feeding the sheep" and "tending the lambs" of Jesus in the Gospel's unnarrated future, after their conversation and before the predicted martyrdom. In the novels, engendered desire pushes the plot forward in predictable ways, often motivating an attempt to possess a protagonist, often sexually.[60] Sometimes these would-be

---

60   The "chastity ordeal." See, e.g., Tomas Hägg, *The Novel in Antiquity*, Rev. ed. (University of California Press, 1991), 79, 160. An important innovation on this convention is its

234   CHAPTER 6

possessors attempt to use force, but more often they employ verbal persuasion. Their desires are almost always frustrated. In the few cases where they are
successful (Dionysius enjoys a short marriage with Callirhoe; the young and
rustic Daphnis is given an education in lovemaking by a mature, urbane city
lady; Melite eventually succeeds with Clitophon), extenuating circumstances
excuse the protagonist who capitulates. The pattern may be profitably compared to the flummoxed desires of the Johannine Jews in the Fourth Gospel.
Their encounters with Jesus produce a desire to have him killed, in which they
are (temporarily) apparently successful.

What the novels' characters do with their awakened desire is ethically inflected, a test of character. Johannine characters, in varying states of understanding and misunderstanding, form desires as a result of conversation with
Jesus—not, it should be noted, as a result of seeing him. In fact, the Gospel
seems to warn about the dangers involved in trusting too easily in one's outward senses. The Thomas story is important here (John 20.24–29) but perhaps
the most important locus for the development of this theme is in chapter 9,
especially in the judgment with which that chapter concludes:

> Καὶ εἶπεν ὁ Ἰησοῦς, Εἰς κρίμα ἐγὼ εἰς τὸν κόσμον τοῦτον ἦλθον, ἵνα οἱ μὴ
> βλέποντες βλέπωσιν καὶ οἱ βλέποντες τυφλοὶ γένωνται. Ἤκουσαν ἐκ τῶν
> Φαρισαίων ταῦτα οἱ μετ᾽ αὐτοῦ ὄντες, καὶ εἶπον αὐτῷ, Μὴ καὶ ἡμεῖς τυφλοί
> ἐσμεν; εἶπεν αὐτοῖς ὁ Ἰησοῦς, Εἰ τυφλοὶ ἦτε, οὐκ ἂν εἴχετε ἁμαρτίαν· νῦν δὲ
> λέγετε ὅτι Βλέπομεν· ἡ ἁμαρτία ὑμῶν μένει.

> Jesus said, "I came into this world for judgment so that those who do
> not see may see, and those who do see may become blind." Some of the
> Pharisees near him heard this and said to him, "Surely we are not blind,
> are we?" Jesus said to them, "If you were blind, you would not have sin.
> But now that you say, 'We see,' your sin remains."
>
> John 9.39–41

Such passages are often invoked in scholarly discussions about the extent to
which John is proto-gnostic or docetic, or in connection to the motif of divine "sight" in the Fourth Gospel.[61] The "seeing" that matters in John, as many
have noticed, has to do with whether or not one apprehends (understands,

---

   repurposing as an ascetic chastity ideal in early Christian apocryphal acts like those of
   Paul and Thecla.

61   See, e.g., Keener, *The Gospel of John*, 247–51.

GENRE, INNOVATION, AND JOHANNINE CHARACTERIZATION   235

recognizes, believes in) Jesus. Merely seeing Jesus with one's outer senses, as the Jews do here, is not enough. The ideal position is that of the authorial "we" at the beginning and the end of the Gospel. In the prologue, this "we" beheld the glory of the Word become flesh (Καὶ ὁ λόγος σὰρξ ἐγένετο καὶ ἐσκήνωσεν ἐν ἡμῖν, καὶ ἐθεασάμεθα τὴν δόξαν αὐτοῦ, δόξαν ὡς μονογενοῦς παρὰ πατρός, πλήρης χάριτος καὶ ἀληθείας, John 1.14), and nestled in the final lines of the Gospel is the bold declaration, "We know that his testimony is true (οἴδαμεν ὅτι ἀληθὴς αὐτοῦ ἡ μαρτυρία ἐστίν)" (John 21.24). "Knowing," the action attributed to the authorial "we" here, is conflated with the language of "seeing" and "beholding" throughout the Gospel. This is the context in which the dialogue in chapter 9 ought to be read, bursting at its literary seams with double entendre and dramatic irony. The novels routinely situate the birth of desire in the moment of visually perceiving the hero or heroine. The Fourth Gospel relocates vision to better account for the desires that matter (glory, life) in the Johannine conceptual universe. Only in dialogue with the Word are one's true desires stirred and aligned either with the clear-sighted authorial perspective or with the damned liars who "say they can see but cannot" and so remain in their sins (John 8.21; 9.41; cf. 8.34; 15.22; 16.8–9) and darkness (John 12.35, 36; cf. 1.5; 3.19; 8.12).

Whatever their differences in using encounters with a protagonist to cultivate desire, both John and the Greek novels make abundant use of misunderstanding in those encounters. Characters in the novels frequently mistake the heroine for a goddess, and something like the inverse of this seems to be at play in the Fourth Gospel. Jesus's divine identity is clear enough to the reader, for whom Jesus is described early as God (John 1.18). That identity is developed in a variety of ways throughout the Gospel. Sometimes the misunderstanding involves the idea that Jesus is a (mere?) man, as expressed by the Samaritan Woman to her townspeople (John 4.29), obliquely by Nicodemus in presenting a legal point of order to the Pharisees (John 7.51), by the man born blind in describing his healer to the Jews (John 9.11), by the Pharisees when they are debating amongst themselves whether "this man is from God" or not (John 9.16), and again by the Pharisees when they claim to know that "this man" is a sinner (John 9.24),[62] by the Pharisees and chief priests who call a meeting to decide about "this man" who is performing many signs (John 11.47–50), or by a girl in Caiaphas's courtyard who asks whether Peter was among the disciples of "this

---

62   Contextually, "this man" points to Jesus. On a profounder level, however, "this man" could well apply to themselves, the world, or even their addressee, whom the Jews eventually attack with the remark, "You were born entirely in sins, and are you trying to teach us?" (John 9.34), after which they drove him out. The remark, then, would be like that of the High Priest at John 11.50: wrong about Jesus at face value, but profoundly true on a level unappreciated by the speaker.

man" (John 18.17). These uses are not especially surprising, however, since a central point about Jesus's identity in John is that in his person the pre-existent Logos (John 1.1; 17.5) has "become flesh" and dwelt among us (John 1.14). Jesus even adopts this terminology when he describes himself to the Jews as "a man who has told you the truth that I heard from God" (John 8.40).

Even more important than Jesus's humanity or divinity, however, is that he is *both* simultaneously. This is too much for the Johannine Jews to process, resulting in situations like this: "The Jews answered him, 'It is not for a good work that we are going to stone you, but for blasphemy, because you, though only a human being, are making yourself God' (ἀπεκρίθησαν αὐτῷ οἱ Ἰουδαῖοι, Περὶ καλοῦ ἔργου οὐ λιθάζομέν σε ἀλλὰ περὶ βλασφημίας, καὶ ὅτι σὺ ἄνθρωπος ὢν ποιεῖς σεαυτὸν θεόν'" (John 10.33). The Jews here show that on some level they understand Jesus's revelation of himself as God but cannot accept it. They are right to see that Jesus is ἄνθρωπος; they are wrong, from the Gospel's theological perspective, in thinking that he can be no more than that. Therein lies the misunderstanding, which in John is an ethical failing with fatal consequences.

The human sphere, in which Jesus is present only for a brief season (cf. John 10.35–36), does not figure in the Johannine Jesus's divine calculus of value: "I do not accept glory from people (δόξαν παρὰ ἀνθρώπων οὐ λαμβάνω)," Jesus says (John 5.41). This stands in contrast to those of the authorities who, although they believed in Jesus, "were not confessing him because of the Pharisees, so that they would not be put out of the synagogue (διὰ τοὺς Φαρισαίους οὐχ ὡμολόγουν ἵνα μὴ ἀποσυνάγωγοι γένωνται)" (John 12.42). The expression ἀποσυνάγωγος occurs several times in the Fourth Gospel (cf. John 9.22; 16.2), but is explained here only in these terms: "For they loved the glory of people more than the glory of God (ἠγάπησαν γὰρ τὴν δόξαν τῶν ἀνθρώπων μᾶλλον ἤπερ τὴν δόξαν τοῦ θεοῦ)."[63] The contrast with Jesus's attitude towards δόξα τῶν ἀνθρώπων is clear. Thus, even these figures who "believe" in Jesus in some sense misunderstand what it means to be his followers. To cast this point in terms introduced earlier in this chapter, they fail to imitate Jesus and fail to align their wills (represented here by what they "loved") with the divine perspective.

In the Fourth Gospel, as in the novels, some of the misunderstandings generated in the course of the narrative are eventually resolved, while others remain unsettled. Chariton, for example, leaves unresolved Dionysius's state of mind

---

63 At one point this term was one of the strongest arguments in favor of Martyn's "two-level drama" hypothesis, on the basis that the historical Jesus's followers could not have been "put out of the synagogue" during his lifetime. But for an argument that expulsions during Jesus's lifetime are historically plausible, see now Jonathan Bernier, *Aposynagōgos and the Historical Jesus in John: Rethinking the Historicity of the Johannine Expulsion Passages*, BibInt 122 (Leiden: Brill, 2013).

GENRE, INNOVATION, AND JOHANNINE CHARACTERIZATION 237

with respect to "his" son at the end of book 8. *Aseneth* leaves unresolved the fate of Joseph's repentant brothers, hiding in the bushes (*Asen.* 28.16–17). These examples are relatively innocuous, and their existence makes the happy ending possible. Bringing this insight to the Fourth Gospel may offer a fresh way of handling some of the ambiguous characters we encounter there. Within scholarship on characterization in the Fourth Gospel, there has been some confusion about how it stands with various characters at the end of the Gospel. The sharply dualistic worldview encourages readers to ask of each character and perhaps also of themselves (cf. John 20.31) whether that person came to "believe that Jesus is the Christ the Son of God" and, so believing, "have Life in his name" (John 20.31; cf. 3.16 and *passim*). With some of the characters, however, their final status is ambiguous. Did Nicodemus manage to surmount the confusion generated by his night-time conversation with Jesus in chapter 3? He reappears twice, briefly, later in the Gospel advocating on Jesus's behalf (John 7.50–51) and tending to his body after death (John 19.38–40). But is he, as the Evangelist might say, "walking in the light"? His continued association with the Jews, in chapter 7, and his association in chapter 19 with Joseph of Arimathea, a "disciple of Jesus, but a secret one because of his fear of the Jews" (John 19.38), incline us to answer negatively. The secret disciples, as we saw above, have the wrong priorities. They care about the glory that comes from people not that which comes from God. And Nicodemus, in his final vignette, is tending to the body rather than what really counts in the end for John. His care for the body here is powerfully suggestive of his continuing misunderstanding. But the fact remains that we simply do not know. And the novelistic lens lets us be content with that. The important outcome is that Jesus has been reunited with the Father. Their love was never in danger any more than that of the protagonists in any of the Greek novels, their confidence in being reunited was assured, and the friends made during Jesus's sojourn are—like so many Polycharmuses or Dionysiuses—given the opportunity to benefit by proximity to that reciprocal love. An important difference, of course, is that while none of the novels' secondary characters are offered a permanent place in the erotic union of the novels' protagonists, the friends of Jesus are invited to remain forever in the agapic embrace of the Johannine Father and Son.

4 Drama

Chapter 5, exploring the range of conventions for manufacturing characters' minds in drama, dwelt especially on the literary techniques dramatists used to foreground characters' inner lives without recourse to an omniscient narrator.[64] Among these techniques we noted (1) divine priming, mainly in the prologues; (2) the drawing out of information in dialogues between characters; and (3) the monologue. Although the Fourth Gospel has a narrator,[65] all three of these techniques are in effect there as well. The three can overlap, as, for example, when dialogue lapses into monologue, or when a monologue is delivered by an agent capable of divine priming, as is usually the case with the so-called "prologue gods." These compensatory techniques have consequences for the play of discrepant awareness, recognition, filtered speech, and deictic speech.

Probably no prologue in the history of writing has attracted as much comment as that of the Fourth Gospel, with its powerful, poignant evocation of Genesis, the gospel tradition, and Plato. Many have attempted to describe its programmatic function in relation to the rest of the Gospel, but it has not been read as an instance of the dramatic prologue like those, for example, composed by Euripides and delivered by gods and goddesses to frame his dramatic productions.[66] The Fourth Gospel's prologue is delivered in narrator speech. The Johannine narrator, however, like most third-person narrators in ancient narratives, possesses something approaching a divine perspective. Like the prologue gods in Euripides, he has access to what is non-perceptible about characters in his storyworld. He employs this throughout the text to good effect, as we have seen already in this chapter. The task at hand is to inquire in what sense the voice in the prologue primes the audience with knowledge of thoughts, characters, dispositions, motivations, or feelings of characters who are mentioned in it, and to what extent doing so builds discrepant awareness between the audience, on the one hand, and characters like Nicodemus or Nathaniel, on the other.

---

64 Ancient theorists described the distinction in terms of μίμησις and διηγήσις, where tragedy belongs to the former as an "imitation" of life (real life is missing a narrator), and is set off against all other writing that is "narrative."

65 The seminal discussion is R. Alan Culpepper, *Anatomy of the Fourth Gospel: A Study in Literary Design* (Philadelphia: Fortress, 1983). For a recent discussion of fleeting moments where the narrator is apparently *absent* in John, see George L. Parsenios, "The Silent Spaces between Narrative and Drama," in *The Gospel of John as Genre Mosaic*, ed. Kasper Bro Larsen, SANt 3 (Göttingen: Vandehoeck & Rupprecht, 2015), 85–97.

66 Brant comes close: "In design and function, the prologue of the Fourth Gospel bears significant resemblance to those of Euripides. The prologue initiates the audience into the privileged realm of knowing that makes irony possible, orients the audience to the broader narrative in which the action is situated and prepares it to enter the action in medias res, and calls the audience into being and gives it a role." Jo-Ann A. Brant, *Dialogue and Drama: Elements of Greek Tragedy in the Fourth Gospel* (Peabody: Hendrickson, 2004), 17.

GENRE, INNOVATION, AND JOHANNINE CHARACTERIZATION

There is more than one viable way of counting the characters in the prologue. A list erring on the side of inclusivity gives us the Word (John 1.1, 2); God (John 1.1, 2, 6, 12, 13, 18); humanity (John 1.4); the darkness (John 1.5); John (John 1.6, 15); the world (John 1.9, 10); his [the light's] own (John 1.11); those who received [the light] (John 1.12); the children of God (John 1.12); those who believe (John 1.12); "us" (John 1.14); Moses (John 1.17); and Jesus Christ (John 1.17). Some of these "characters" are co-extensive and/or collapsed into each other, yielding identifications between "the Word," "God," "the light," and "Jesus Christ"; an identification of "those who received [the light]" and "the children of God," "those who believe," and "us." The identification of the Word with God is stated (John 1.1), but then the two are spoken of, here and throughout the Gospel, as distinct.

Of programmatic importance is the surprising failure of "his own" (οἱ ἴδιοι) to be identified with the receiving, believing, children of God. This gestures forward to the rejection of Jesus by the Jews in the Gospel.[67] Divine prologues in drama could gesture forward in time, as when Aphrodite predicts that "the young man who wars against me shall be killed by his father with curses the sea lord Poseidon granted him as a gift" (Euripides, *Hipp.* 43–45), but the focus in such forward-looking remarks tends (as in that example) to be on the future life-and-death outcomes that stem from a present state of mind. John's prologue says nothing about characters' initial states of mind, and speaks as if all the necessary cognitive moves (testifying, accepting, recognizing, believing, seeing) have already happened.[68]

The prologue offers a programmatic play on words in verse 5, where we read that the darkness did not "overcome" (κατέλαβεν) the light, since "the light" turns out to be the Word-God-Jesus-Christ and καταλαμβάνειν can have the sense of "apprehend (intellectually)," "accept," or "conquer." Most interpreters see this as an instance of Johannine wordplay, what some ancient rhetoricians called *traductio*.[69] Whether or not "darkness" is anthropomorphized in parallel to the "light," the Evangelist puts to good use the metaphor of physical darkness as a failure of cognition. And so the prologue describes already one dimension

---

67 Westermann argues that John 1.11–12 outlines John's story (coming to his own in chs. 1–6; rejected by them in chs. 7–12; empowering those who receive him in 13–17). Claus Westermann, *Gospel of John in the Light of the Old Testament*, trans. Siegfried S. Schatzmann (Peabody: Hendrickson, 1998), 7. See also Keener, *The Gospel of John*, 395.

68 Parsenios argues that this is because the words are spoken from a "postresurrection perspective." Parsenios, "'No Longer in the World' (John 17:11)," 7.

69 For a list of scholarly works that take this position, see Keener, *The Gospel of John*, 387n243. For *traductio*, see Isocrates, *Peace* 8.101; Cicero *Verr.* 2.64.155; cited in Keener, *The Gospel of John*, 387n244.

of the cognitive plot the subsequent narrative will relate as having happened: those who do not receive Jesus thereby show themselves to belong to the realm of intellectual darkness. It is not insignificant that Nicodemus comes to Jesus "by night" (John 3.2; cf. 19.39); that, in the dark (σκοτία ἤδη ἐγεγόνει), the disciples experience rough seas and terror in Jesus's absence (John 6.17); that when Judas is exposed as the betrayer he leaves "and it was night" (John 13.30); that Mary Magdalene cannot find Jesus in the dark (σκοτίας ἔτι οὔσης) (John 20.1); and that the disciples, fishing without Jesus and catching nothing, are fishing by night (John 21.3). The reference to darkness "overcoming" the light surfaces again when Jesus offers this advice: "The light is with you for a little longer. Walk while you have the light, so that the darkness may not overtake you (ἵνα μὴ σκοτία ὑμᾶς καταλάβῃ). If you walk in the darkness, you do not know where you are going" (John 12.35). And, if there were any question about what "the light" is here (the disciples have not had the priming benefit offered the reader by John 1.8–9), he explains a few verses later: "I have come as light into the world, so that everyone who believes in me should not remain in the darkness" (John 12.46). Ignorance in John is not just a qualitative judgment; it is an identity marker for the Other.

The failure of darkness to overcome or grasp the light is described again in the prologue, this time in unambiguously cognitive terms, in verse 10: "He was in the world, and the world came into being through him; yet the world did not know/recognize him (ἐν τῷ κόσμῳ ἦν, καὶ ὁ κόσμος δι' αὐτοῦ ἐγένετο, καὶ ὁ κόσμος αὐτὸν οὐκ ἔγνω)." Larsen translates ἔγνω here as "recognize," and makes a compelling case that this is a piece of the recognition motif that pervades the Fourth Gospel.[70] The structure of the verse parallels (and is presumably equivalent to) the failure of the darkness to overcome the light (John 1.5) and the failure of "his own" to receive him (John 1.11). On the other side of the Johannine binary, the cognitive activity posited for "his own" is described as "receiving" (λαμβάνειν) him. Λαμβάνειν can also serve double duty in terms of receiving physically, hospitably, on the one hand, and intellectually, on the other. In fact, the definitive feature for this group is its cognitive act: the whole group is "those who receive" and "those who believe." It bears recalling, however, that our probing of classical drama found no divine priming quite so cosmic and abstract; no characters were cast there in such terms as "the darkness" or "the light."

Verse 7 offers another moment in the prologue where the reader might be divinely primed to understand the mind of a character: "He [John] came as a witness to testify to the light, so that all might believe through him (οὗτος ἦλθεν

---

70   Larsen, *Recognizing the Stranger*, 81.

εἰς μαρτυρίαν, ἵνα μαρτυρήσῃ περὶ τοῦ φωτός, ἵνα πάντες πιστεύσωσιν δι᾽ αὐτοῦ)." This can be read either as the divine intention or as John's human motivation. A glimpse into a mind is granted on either reading; the question is whether that mind is God's, John's, or—and this third possibility seems most likely, in light of what we have seen above about the conforming of characters' wills to the divine will—both. An additional reason for seeing John's will in sync with the divine, choosing the third option, is the language used in verse 13 for those who become "children of God." They are "those who are born, not of blood or of the will of the flesh or of the will of man, but of God (οἳ οὐκ ἐξ αἱμάτων οὐδὲ ἐκ θελήματος σαρκὸς οὐδὲ ἐκ θελήματος ἀνδρὸς ἀλλ᾽ ἐκ θεοῦ ἐγεννήθησαν)." Their acts of receiving and believing are not (only) human cognitive acts; they are acts of falling in step with the divine will.

If the narrator in this reading of the Fourth Gospel is analogous to the prologue gods of Greek tragedy, his subsequent activity extends his reach further into the Gospel-as-drama than his theatrical analogues. Gods could and did take active roles in some dramas (e.g., Dionysus in Euripides's *Bacchae*; the God of Moses in Ezekiel's *Exagoge*), but those figures performed a different function than a prologue god like Aphrodite at the beginning of Euripides's *Hippolytus*. The Johannine narrator, like the prologue gods, mediates access to the minds of the characters in the Gospel.[71]

One final twist to consider in our reading of "divine priming" in the Fourth Gospel with the help of our dramatist's lens is that Jesus, the central character in the Gospel, also has access to what is non-perceptible about the human characters around him in the story. We have remarked on this above in connection to the Johannine Jesus's perception of the "true" and "false" desires in those he encounters.

The second technique discussed in chapter 5 for representing the inner lives of tragedy's dramatis personae was "dialogue," conversations between two or more characters without the intrusion of the narrator. Dialogue is a striking feature of the Fourth Gospel, and one of the chief technical features of the Gospel to have led scholars to link it with drama.[72] John's dialogues, like their counterparts in the classical tragic tradition, include cognitive content.

---

71   A partial list of instances where he provides for the audience information about a character's inner experience that would count as a "non-perceptible" in Bal's terminology would include the following passages: 1.18, 37, 39, 40, 47; 2.11, 17, 22, 23, 24–25; 4.1, 27, 41, 45, 47, 50, 53; 5.6; 6.2, 14, 15, 19, 22, 24, 60, 61, 64; 7.5, 15, 31, 32, 40; 8.9, 27, 30; 9.1, 8, 18, 22, 35, 40; 10.6, 42; 11.4, 6, 20, 29, 31, 32, 33, 45; 12.9, 12, 16, 18, 29, 37, 42; 13.1, 3–4, 21, 28; 16.19; 18.4; 19.6, 8, 13, 26, 28, 33; 20.6, 8, 12, 14, 20; 21.7, 21.

72   Connick points to "dialogue" as the means by which "life, character, or a story is told" in the definition he adopts for "drama." C. Milo Connick, "The Dramatic Character of

242   CHAPTER 6

When Mary Magdalene is accosted by a pair of angels in white, sitting where Jesus's body had been, they address her directly and ask her why she is crying (γύναι, τί κλαίεις;) (John 20.13). The deictic language in character speech calls attention to her tears and, by extension, her distress. Tears can signify cognitive states in any genre, but they are especially important in tragedy as a perceptible indicator of an interior state. Unlike the tragedies we looked at in chapter 5, however, the audience of John 20 will have already learned about these tears from the narrator: "Mary stood weeping outside the tomb. As she wept, she bent over to look into the tomb (Μαρία δὲ εἰστήκει πρὸς τῷ μνημείῳ ἔξω κλαίουσα. ὡς οὖν ἔκλαιεν παρέκυψεν εἰς τὸ μνημεῖον)" (John 20.11). Compare this to what, in terms of using tears to signify a cognitive state, is a common device in classical tragedy: Andromache, reflecting on fates decided for her and her son Astyanax, says to him, "My child, you are weeping (ὦ παῖ, δακρύεις). Do you realize your misfortune?" (Euripides, *Tro.* 759). Tragic tears materialize in conversation.

The Johannine angels' question, then, does not supply the reader with new information about Mary's emotional or cognitive state. Weeping happens on several other occasions in John, too, always in narrator speech (cf. John 11.31, 33, 35). By putting weeping in character speech in chapter 21, however, the angels (John 20.13) and Jesus (John 20.15) create an opportunity for Marȳ to speak. Her explanation to the angels and, by extension, to the audience confirms that she misunderstands the tableau before her: "She said to them, 'They have taken away my Lord, and I do not know where they have laid him' (λέγει αὐτοῖς ὅτι ῏Ηραν τὸν κύριόν μου, καὶ οὐκ οἶδα ποῦ ἔθηκαν αὐτόν)" (John 20.13). Structurally, this is comparable to the common device in tragedy where a character says something that the audience understands is based on a misunderstanding (e.g., Pentheus speaking to the disguised Dionysus [Euripides, *Bacch.* 537–608]). If there were any doubts about her misunderstanding, in the next verse the narrator tells the reader explicitly that she turned and "saw Jesus standing there, but she did not know that it was Jesus (θεωρεῖ τὸν Ἰησοῦν ἑστῶτα, καὶ οὐκ ᾔδει ὅτι Ἰησοῦς ἐστιν)" (John 20.14). Jesus asks the same question of her as had the angels, adding an explanatory question τίνα ζητεῖς, using language John's reader has been conditioned to associate with the discourse of desire (cf. John 1.38; 4.23, 27; 5.18;

------

the Fourth Gospel," *JBL* 67 (1948): 159. Domeris notes, "a comparison with the Synoptic versions illustrates John's tendency to introduce dialogue wherever possible," though he does not elaborate. William R. Domeris, "The Johannine Drama," *JTSA* 42 (1983): 31. Brant puts dialogue as a feature of first importance even in the title to her book: *Dialogue and Drama: Elements of Greek Tragedy in the Fourth Gospel.*

GENRE, INNOVATION, AND JOHANNINE CHARACTERIZATION 243

and *passim*). She persists in her misunderstanding, now "thinking that he was the gardener (δοκοῦσα ὅτι ὁ κηπουρός ἐστιν)" (John 20.15), and she asks him for directions to where he may have placed the body. Mary's inner state of misunderstanding, grounded in grief, is brought out in dialogue first with the angels and subsequently with Jesus.

Jesus's dialogue with Mary accomplishes in short compass a variation on a pattern followed by many of the dialogues in the Fourth Gospel. Connick offers this schematization: "(1) someone makes an introductory statement or asks a question; (2) Jesus replies by uttering a profound saying; (3) this saying, often capable of a double interpretation, is misunderstood and its spiritual significance is not discerned; (4) Jesus then corrects the mistake; if a second question shows that he has done so effectively, (5) he then gives further, more detailed instruction on the subject."[73] This schema holds up pretty well, except I would argue that it is rarely clear that Jesus is "effective" in "correct[ing] the mistake." To be sure, he does go on to give further instruction on "the subject" in, for example, chapters 3 (birth ἄνωθεν) and 4 (the place for worship), but in neither case is it clear that his interlocutor has fully grasped the significance of what he says (as indicated in each case by their subsequent action). His conversation with Nicodemus, for example, is launched by Nicodemus's remark, "Rabbi, we know that you are a teacher who has come from God; for no one can do these signs that you do apart from the presence of God" (John 3.2), a remark that a properly primed reader will recognize as being true on a profound level. Jesus takes the opportunity, however, to steer the conversation in such a way as to highlight Nicodemus's failure to understand. The function of the dialogue here, as often in the Gospel, is to contrast the understanding of Jesus with another character's failure to understand. Such contrasts emerge in dialogues in other genres as well (e.g., Plato's Socratic dialogues), but they are a regular and poignant feature of tragedy, made possible (from the audience's perspective) by the operation of discrepant awareness.

What is especially Johannine about the Nicodemus dialogue is its suggestion that Jesus understands what is inside his interlocutor better than the person understands himself. The dialogue ends with Jesus calling into question Nicodemus's status as a "teacher of Israel," a status we now see that Nicodemus took for granted when he greeted Jesus as a "teacher from God" (John 3.2, 10). Jesus, as constructed at the end of chapter 2, knows what is inside a person and needs no one to testify about anything (cf. John 2.23–25). Jesus does not need Nicodemus's validation either as a "teacher" or "from God," and he knows that Nicodemus understands himself to be part of that class. "Are you a teacher of

---

73   Connick, "The Dramatic Character of the Fourth Gospel," 167.

244   CHAPTER 6

Israel," Jesus asks, "and yet you do not know these things?" (John 3.10). At that point the dialogue effectively ends, and, although Jesus continues to speak, Nicodemus is silent and not obviously the intended recipient of what Jesus has to say. The "you" Jesus uses shifts from the singular (John 3.3–10) to the plural (John 3.11–12), effectively panning out from Nicodemus to a general audience in what follows.

We discovered in chapters 4 and 5 above that dialogue works best to reveal the states of mind of a protagonist when that person is in conversation with a bosom companion and confidante, like Polycharmus to Chaereas in *Callirhoe*, or Pylades to Orestes in Euripides's *Iphigenia in Tauris*, or the chorus of Greek slaves to Helen in Euripides's *Helen*. The Fourth Gospel contains several characters we might be tempted to view in this role, such as the beloved disciple, whose "ideal" characteristics have been discussed above. The only conversation between Jesus and the beloved disciple, however, is at table in the presence of the rest of Jesus's disciples, and says little about Jesus's inner experience. The conversation is prompted by Jesus's remark that one of his company will betray him (John 13.21). Peter prompts the beloved disciple to ask who Jesus means, and Jesus obliges by identifying Judas Iscariot (John 13.26). This exchange may be meaningful to an attentive reader, but as it stands the disciples are left baffled. Jesus, handing a piece of bread (cf. John 6.35) to Judas as a token identifying him as the betrayer, says "Do quickly what you are going to do" (John 13.27). The disciples, however, are unable to connect this with what Jesus has just been saying about betrayal: "Now no one at the table knew why he said this to him. Some thought that, because Judas had the common purse, Jesus was telling him, 'Buy what we need for the festival'; or, that he should give something to the poor" (John 13.29). This is as close as John comes to putting the beloved disciple and Jesus in dialogue. The beloved disciple, then, seems a poor candidate for the role of bosom friend who gives the protagonist opportunities to describe his inner states. Jesus has φίλοι in John, but no special friend who stands apart from the larger group; and he speaks more freely with his inner circle, but Jesus has no reason to filter himself in conversation with anyone with whom he dialogues. In this respect, he is more akin to the unfiltered mad characters of Greek tragedy discussed above: Cassandra, not Orestes or Pylades; Medea, not Hippolytus or his manservant.

Monologue is a third technique by which a character's interior experiences can be revealed in drama. Unlike dialogues, monologues can be delivered with or without the presence of other characters. The dialogue with Nicodemus, we saw, gave way to monologue at John 3.11. Something comparable happens in the dialogue later in the same chapter between John and his interlocutors.

GENRE, INNOVATION, AND JOHANNINE CHARACTERIZATION   245

They bring him a report about Jesus baptizing, and the crowds flocking to him, to which John replies, "No one can receive anything except what has been given from heaven. You yourselves are my witnesses that I said ..." (John 3.27–30). John continues speaking with first- and second-person pronouns through verse 30, when, although no indication is given that John has stopped speaking, the text switches to use third-person narration through the end of the chapter. In both cases, the interlocutor fades away and the speaker carries on with a monologue. To these we might add some of Jesus's longer discourses, which, though typically prompted by a short question or remark, are not true dialogues. They are monologues triggered by a question or a remark that end, usually, in division among the listeners (e.g., John 6.52, 60–64; 7.30–31, 40–44; 10.19–21). Both John the Baptist in the first chapters of the Gospel and Jesus in the longer discourses clustered towards the end of the Gospel function in a way comparable to the "messenger" figure in Greek drama, both reporting what they have heard from the Father to those who will listen.

The prayers of Jesus (e.g., in John 17) provide the Fourth Gospel's closest analogue to what later critics would call a soliloquy. These remarks, however, are directed to another character (God) and so may be treated as a unilateral dialogue. In this sense they are not unlike dramatic dialogues between tragedy's protagonists and their trusted companions. As in those cases, there is no concern that what the speaker "really" thinks is being filtered out of the conversation. A relationship of perfect trust exists between God and Jesus to such an extent that, as he says in connection to the raising of Lazarus, "Father, I thank you for having heard me. I knew that you always hear me, but I have said this for the sake of the crowd standing here, so that they may believe that you sent me" (John 11.41b–42). The Johannine Jesus is so in tune with the mind of God that the comment is "externalized" only for the sake of those listening in. Again, this is comparable to some of the conversations shared by bosom companions in drama "for the crowd's sake." To the extent that in Jesus's prayers the Father is an artificial placeholder for the listening partner in dialogue (artificial because he already knows everything Jesus is telling him), those same discourses might well be understood functionally as monologues. As we have seen repeatedly in this chapter, God and Jesus are functionally co-extensive, at least where the will is concerned. What Jesus prays is what God would pray, because Jesus in some significant sense is God.

When Jesus delivers monologues in the Fourth Gospel, they reveal little about his feelings and thought processes. They reveal, rather, that which already is, both about the state of the world and "what is inside" those with whom he interacts. When other characters deliver monologues or participate

246   CHAPTER 6

in a dialogue, however, they do try to describe what is going on inside. John, for example, explains to no one in particular his thought-process for recognizing Jesus:

> Here is the Lamb of God who takes away the sin of the world! ... I myself did not know him; but I came baptizing for this reason, that he might be revealed to Israel.... I saw the Spirit descending like a dove, and it remained on him. I myself did not know him, but the one who sent me to baptize with water said to me, 'He on whom you see the Spirit descend and remain is the one who baptizes with the Holy Spirit.' And I myself have seen and have testified that this is the Son of God.
>
>   John 1.29–34

What is usually and correctly discussed as John's "testimony" can easily be redescribed as a discursive account of how John moved from not-recognizing to recognizing Jesus as the "Lamb of God" and "Son of God." John is not the only character to describe his thoughts out loud. Nicodemus, as we saw above, offers "for no one can do these signs that you do apart from the presence of God" as the criterion by which he "knows" (οἴδαμεν) that Jesus is a teacher from God. The first person plural could indicate that Nicodemus is speaking on behalf of a larger group, possibly the chief priests and the Pharisees with whom he is in dialogue at the end of chapter 7, or it could just as easily be an instance of the "royal we," where the subject is Nicodemus alone. In favor of this latter option is the fact that Nicodemus is presented as acting out of step with the other leaders whenever he appears in the Gospel (cf. John 7.50–52; 19.39). In either case, such claims are routinely turned in the Gospel to reveal what the speaking character does *not* know, in contrast with what Jesus does (see, e.g., John 4.10, 22, 31; 5.39, 42, 45–46; 6.26, 42; 7.28–29; 8.14, 19, 43–47, 55). This pattern is sufficiently marked in the first chapters of the Gospel to allow readers to use it as a hermeneutical key later in the Gospel whenever characters make claims to knowledge, whether or not the claim is explicitly interrogated and broken down by this drama's final epistemic adjudicator.

This hermeneutical key unlocks some interesting possibilities for reading dramatic irony in the "confessions" encountered later in the Gospel (e.g., John 4.19; 6.69; 11.27; 20.28), as well as apparently unproblematized assertions like that of Martha: "Even now I know that God will give you [Jesus] whatever you ask of him" (John 11.22). What she says is true on its face, just as true as Nicodemus's assertion that Jesus is a teacher from God in chapter 3. Just because a statement is true, however, does not in John entail that the speaker grasps its full significance. Nicodemus evidently does not understand what it

GENRE, INNOVATION, AND JOHANNINE CHARACTERIZATION 247

means to be a teacher of Israel, a teacher from God; the Samaritan woman evidently does not understand what she is asking for when she (nevertheless rightly) asks for a drink of Jesus's "living water" (John 4.15; cf. the request of the crowd at 6.34 for bread from heaven); Caiaphas evidently does not understand the profundity of his statement that his associates know nothing and that it is better for one man to die for the people than have the whole people destroyed (John 11.49–50). Johannine scholars have noticed the double entendres, and I have commented on them myself throughout this chapter. More of a challenge, however, are statements characters make to or about Jesus that do not, from the privileged vantage point of the audience, appear to do justice to the full revelation Jesus offers of himself in the Fourth Gospel. When the Samaritan woman recognizes Jesus as a prophet (John 4.19), for example, she is only partly right. When Peter acknowledges that Jesus alone has the "words of eternal life" (ῥήματα ζωῆς αἰωνίου), he will nevertheless go on to demonstrate repeatedly that he does not yet understand (John 6.68; cf. John 13.6; 18.10–11, 17–27; 20.6–10). Similarly, Martha seems to combine true statements about Jesus (John 11.21, 22, 24, and especially 27) with subsequent behavior that illustrates her as-yet imperfect understanding of her assertions. A good example comes when Jesus commands that the stone be removed and Martha objects, "Lord, already there is a stench because he has been dead four days" (John 11.39). The Fourth Gospel conditions readers to suspend endorsement whenever a character other than Jesus claims to know something, even where the contents of that claim are not explicitly called into question in narrative time, since these claims more often than not turn out to be true only in a way that the character does not (yet) understand. Most "recognitions" of Jesus on this reading of the Fourth Gospel turn out to be simulacra or, at best, partial recognitions.

The parenthetical "yet" in the second-to-last sentence of the previous paragraph raises a pair of issues to which both the romances and the dramas have trained our attention: discrepant awareness and delayed recognition. Recognition scenes in drama can be communicated only by means of what characters say and do.[74] Discrepant awareness is a broader cognitive category that includes failures to recognize and can be resolved into what we might call "consistent awareness" when a recognition scene takes place. Such scenes, in the Fourth Gospel, the Greek novels, and classical drama, are often facilitated

---

74   Recall Brant's observation, mentioned in chapter 15 above, that "recognition is a cognitive act and therefore something private. In a narrative, an omniscient narrator can reveal what occurs in a character's head. In a performance piece, recognition must be played out on the dramatic and theatrical axes so that the audience can see or hear the event happen." Brant, *Dialogue and Drama*, 51.

248 CHAPTER 6

by the presence of "signs" or "tokens." John's preference for speaking of σημεῖα ("signs") instead of "miracles" or "wonders" is a site of perennial interest, as is the presence of σημεῖα as "tokens" that facilitate recognition. What is important here is that many of the "recognitions" in John, partial or total (the Gospel is frustratingly coy on this point), play out in character speech, without third-person narration. This is true especially in the case of Thomas (John 20.24–29). The scene in which Mary recognizes Jesus when he speaks her name (John 20.16) has a helping gloss added by the narrator ("supposing him to be the gardener..."), which comments on her cognitive state, but that comment is not strictly necessary to understand the dialogue that starts with Jesus's question, "Woman, why are you weeping?" and concludes with her cry of recognition "Rabbouni!" (John 20.15–16).

5 Conclusion

Conventions for facilitating access to the minds of characters in each of these genres, used as a guide for reading the Fourth Gospel, are useful for highlighting important aspects of characterization that might otherwise go overlooked. By resisting the temptation to limit "the genre" of John to one or another classical, fossilized form identified by a "list of features," we have seen that any of these can be made plausible conversation partners. There is a danger, of course, that the kind of reading advanced here falls afoul of the critique of family resemblance approaches to genre, where "anything can be made to resemble anything." In response, it is worth noting that some of the connections work better than others. One of the most important discoveries of this study was that—at least where conventions of representing cognition are concerned—the biographical connection turns out to be less illuminating for John than the conventions of the novels and classical drama, such as "reactions to encounters with the protagonist," or the "creation of dialogic portraits of tragic misunderstanding and understanding." The final word has yet to be said about John and the mind-representing conventions of genre. To paraphrase the Evangelist, there are many other intergeneric relationships to explore; if every one of them were written down, the world itself could not contain the books that would be written (cf. John 21.25).

Epilogue

Narratives produced in faraway times and places naturally raise questions for modern readers about the extent to which our interpretive horizons are able to meet those of the people who produced and first read those narratives. Nowhere is this more evident than in the assumptions readers bring to texts about the minds of characters, the "paper people" who speak and act in those narratives. Scholars of Johannine characterization, then, are right to wonder about the extent to which the minds they attribute to characters in the Gospel resemble those that would have been imagined by the people who produced and read those narratives in the first century. In the case of the Fourth Gospel, the weight of this interpretive challenge has become increasingly felt in recent scholarly conversations about genre and characterization: Genre, insofar as genres condition the historical production and reception of texts, especially in their function of creating readerly expectations, and so to misapprehend the genre is to start off on the wrong foot; characterization, insofar as historically-sensitive interpretations of characters are bound up with assumptions about psychology and anthropology in the text's social context.

As we have become more aware of the historical contingency of our own ideas of what it means to be human, we have concurrently become more aware of the potential distance between our own senses of what it means to be a person and other (including ancient) possible ways of configuring the self. If we are able to relativize and historicize our own understandings of the human subject, we must also entertain the possibility that ancient people had different ideas about what it meant to be human. Operating as literary historians, then, we would like to be able to bracket our own auto-anthropological and psychological assumptions to engage with those operative in the texts we seek to understand. There is a danger, however, that in our eagerness to articulate difference, we caricature ancient anthropologies as everything we are not. If we think of ourselves as autonomous, dynamic, introspective individuals who control our own destinies, there is a temptation to paint ancient people as collectivist, static, and anti-introspective. Whether or not such views bear up to scrutiny, however, will depend on the extent to which they succeed in explaining the data of the available texts.

Because our primary access to how ancient people understood the mind and its functions is mediated by texts, we are left in the position of having to read those texts carefully for clues. The search does not yield a complete picture, but there is enough to facilitate meaningful conversations. Such inquiries may

© KONINKLIJKE BRILL NV, LEIDEN, 2019 | DOI:10.1163/9789004396043_008

eventually yield grand conclusions about the history of human metacognition, but the more limited task of this project has been to explore genre conventions for representing cognitive phenomena in four particular genres. That is to say, one of the methodological obstacles faced by the historian of real human self-conceptualizations is that literary genres have their own, characteristic ways of representing minds and using them to achieve aims consonant with the functions of the genre. What is a possibly insurmountable obstacle for the historian of ideas, then, is an opportunity to the historian of literature and literary forms. To the extent that it has been possible, I have attempted in this book to attend to patterns of form and presentation of minds in ancient texts, recognizing the significance of social contextual information about what it meant to be a thinking subject, but focusing primarily on the history of textual patterns of representing minds in different generic traditions.

When every genre has its own conventions for representing the minds of its subjects, cognitive literary studies (including especially the cognitive narratology associated with Alan Palmer and Lisa Zunshine) become helpful for framing questions and methodology for studying those genres. The findings of this study have been that the representation of minds in ancient historiography, biography, romance, and tragedy is never an end in itself. Instead, the patterned representations of character interiority point beyond themselves to do genre-determined kinds of work. Individual and collective minds are often theorized to account for the causes of events in historiography, to account for the (un)ethical behavior of imitable figures in biography, to account for the emotions involved in love in the novels, to account for the tragic ironies of classical drama. Those predictable patterns, like any set of genre conventions, are susceptible to interference, to bending, even to breaking. In the course of the study, we have come up with examples both of authors conforming their narratives to the mind-representing conventions of a given genre—especially in the work of Josephus in relation to historiography, of Philo in relation to biography, of *Aseneth* in relation to the Greek novel, and of Ezekiel in relation to classical drama. We have also witnessed some of the ways in which new texts innovate over and against genre traditions.

On any reading of the data collected in this project, the Fourth Gospel is an innovative text. Reading it in conversation with the conventions of these four genres, I have shown in each case that an alignment sheds light on familiar Johannine themes and motifs. No one of these genre relationships, captures the full picture, although some are more illuminating of the Fourth Gospel's cognitive content than others. As we have had opportunity to notice repeatedly in this study, genres—both in antiquity and today—do not operate in isolation from each other. A text like Chariton's *Callirhoe* can make use of

EPILOGUE

cognition-drawing conventions associated with epic, tragedy, comedy, rhetoric, and historiography, in addition to the romance tradition. Accordingly, we should be delighted to find the Fourth Gospel creatively entwined with an intergeneric web of cognition-drawing conventions that includes, but is not limited to, historiography, βίοι, the novel, and drama.

Bibliography

Abbott, H. Porter. "Unreadable Minds and the Captive Reader." *Style* 42 (2008): 448–67.

Africa, Thomas W. *Phylarchus and the Spartan Revolution.* Berkeley: University of California Press, 1961.

Ahearne-Kroll, Patricia D. "'Joseph and Aseneth' and Jewish Identity in Greco-Roman Egypt." PhD diss, The University of Chicago, 2005.

Ahearne-Kroll, Patricia. "Joseph and Aseneth." Pages 2525–88 in *Outside the Bible: Ancient Jewish Writings Related to Scripture.* Edited by Louis H. Feldman, James L. Kugel, and Lawrence H. Schiffman. Vol. 1. 3 vols. Lincoln: University of Nebraska Press, 2013.

Allman, William F. *The Stone Age Present: How Evolution Has Shaped Modern Life: From Sex, Violence, and Languages to Emotions, Morals, and Communities.* New York: Simon & Schuster, 1994.

Anderson, Graham. "The Management of Dialogue in Ancient Fiction." Pages 217–30 in *A Companion to the Ancient Novel.* Edited by Edmund P. Cueva. BCAW. Chichester: Wiley Blackwell, 2014.

Anderson, J. K. *Xenophon.* London: Duckworth, 1974.

Anderson, Paul N., Felix Just, S.J., and Tom Thatcher, eds. *John, Jesus, and History, Volume 1: Critical Appraisals of Critical Views.* SBLSymS 44. Brill: Leiden, 2007.

Anderson, Paul N., Felix Just, S.J., and Tom Thatcher, eds. *John, Jesus, and History, Volume 2: Aspects of Historicity in the Fourth Gospel.* ECL 2. Atlanta: SBL, 2009.

Anderson, Paul N., Felix Just, S.J., and Tom Thatcher, eds. *John, Jesus, and History, Volume 3: Glimpses of Jesus through the Johannine Lens.* ECL 18. Atlanta: SBL, 2016.

Arnson Svarlien, Diane. *Euripides: Alcestis, Medea, Hippolytus.* Indianapolis: Hackett Publishing, 2007.

Ashton, John. *Understanding the Fourth Gospel.* 2nd ed. Oxford: Oxford University Press, 2007.

Attridge, Harold W. "Divine Sovereignty and Human Responsibility in the Fourth Gospel." Pages 183–99 in *Revealed Wisdom: Studies in Apocalyptic in Honour of Christopher Rowland.* Edited by John F. Ashton. AGJU/AJEC 88. Boston: Brill, 2014.

Attridge, Harold W. "Genre Bending in the Fourth Gospel." *JBL* 121 (2002): 3–21.

Attridge, Harold W. "The Gospel of John: Genre Matters?" Pages 27–45 in *The Gospel of John as Genre Mosaic.* Edited by Kasper Bro Larsen. SANt 3. Göttingen: Vandehoeck & Rupprecht, 2015.

Attridge, Harold W. "Historiography." Pages 157–83 in *Jewish Writings of the Second Temple Period: Apocrypha, Pseudepigrapha, Qumran, Sectarian Writings, Philo, Josephus.* Edited by Michael E. Stone. CRINT 2. Assen: Van Gorcum, 1984.

Attridge, Harold W. "Are John's Ethics Apolitical?" *NTS* 62 (2016).

Attridge, Harold W. "The Restless Quest for the Beloved Disciple." *Essays on John and Hebrews.* WUNT 264. Tübingen: Mohr Siebeck, 2010.

Auken, Sune. "Contemporary Genre Studies." Pages 47–66 in *The Gospel of John as Genre Mosaic.* Edited by Kasper Bro Larsen. SANt 3. Göttingen: Vandehoeck & Rupprecht, 2015.

Auken, Sune. "Genre and Interpretation." Pages 154–83 in *Genre and....* Edited by Sune Auken, P. S. Lauridsen, and A. J. Rasmussen. CStG 2. Copenhagen: Ekbátana, 2015.

Bain, David. "Audience Address in Greek Tragedy." *ClQ* 25 (1975): 13–25.

Bakhtin, M. M. "Forms of Time and of the Chronotope in the Novel: Notes toward a Historical Poetics." Pages 84–258 in *The Dialogic Imagination: Four Essays.* Edited by Michael Holquist, Translated by Caryl Emerson and Michael Holquist. UTPSS 1. Austin: University of Texas Press, 1981.

Bal, Mieke. *Narratology: Introduction to the Theory of Narrative.* 3rd ed. Toronto: University of Toronto Press, 2009.

Baragwanath, Emily. *Motivation and Narrative in Herodotus.* OCM. Oxford: Oxford University Press, 2008.

Barker, Andrew. "Aristoxenus." *OCD.* Edited by Simon Hornblower, Antony Spawforth, and Esther Eidinow. 4th ed. Oxford: Oxford University Press, 2012.

Barnes, T. D. "Christians and the Theater: E. Togo Salmon Papers I." Pages 161–80 in *Roman Theater and Society.* Edited by William J. Slater. Ann Arbor: University of Michigan Press, 1996.

Baron, Christopher A. *Timaeus of Tauromenium and Hellenistic Historiography.* Cambridge: Cambridge University Press, 2012.

Barrett, James. *Staged Narrative: Poetics and the Messenger in Greek Tragedy.* JPICL. Berkeley: University of California Press, 2002.

Barthes, Roland. "The Death of the Author." Pages 142–48 in *Image, Music, Text.* Translated by Stephen Heath. New York: Hill and Wang, 1977.

Bauckham, Richard. "The Fourth Gospel as the Testimony of the Beloved Disciple." Pages 120–39 in *The Gospel of John and Christian Theology.* Edited by Richard Bauckham and Carl Mosser. Grand Rapids: Eerdmans, 2008.

Bauckham, Richard. *The Testimony of the Beloved Disciple: Narrative, History, and Theology in the Gospel of John.* Grand Rapids: Baker Academic, 2007.

Bauckham, Richard, ed. *The Gospels for All Christians: Rethinking the Gospel Audiences.* Grand Rapids: Eerdmans, 1998.

Becker, Eve-Marie. *Das Markus-Evangelium im Rahmen antiker Historiographie.* WUNT 194. Tübingen: Mohr Siebeck, 2006.

Becker, Eve-Marie. "Patterns of Early Christian Thinking and Writing of History: Paul—Mark—Acts." Pages 276–313 in *Thinking, Recording, and Writing History in the Ancient World.* Edited by Kurt A. Raaflaub. Chichester: Wiley Blackwell, 2014.

BIBLIOGRAPHY

Bennema, Cornelis. "Christ, the Spirit and the Knowledge of God: A Study in Johannine Epistemology." Pages 107–33 in *The Bible and Epistemology*. Edited by Mary Healy and Robin Parry. Milton Keynes: Paternoster, 2007.

Bennema, Cornelis. *Encountering Jesus: Character Studies in the Gospel of John*. Milton Keynes: Paternoster, 2009.

Bennema, Cornelis. *A Theory of Character in New Testament Narrative*. Minneapolis: Fortress, 2014.

Berger, Peter L., and Thomas Luckmann. *The Social Construction of Reality: A Treatise in the Sociology of Knowledge*. Garden City: Doubleday, 1966.

Bernier, Jonathan. *Aposynagōgos and the Historical Jesus in John: Rethinking the Historicity of the Johannine Expulsion Passages*. BibInt 122. Leiden: Brill, 2013.

Betz, Hans Dieter. *Galatians: A Commentary on Paul's Letter to the Churches in Galatia*. Hermeneia. Philadelphia: Fortress, 1979.

Bigelow, James, and Amy Poremba. "Achilles' Ear? Inferior Human Short-Term and Recognition Memory in the Auditory Modality." *PLoS ONE* 9 (2014).

Bilezikian, Gilbert G. *The Liberated Gospel: A Comparison of the Gospel of Mark and Greek Tragedy*. Grand Rapids: Baker Book House, 1977.

Billault, Alain. "Characterization in the Ancient Novel." Pages 115–30 in *The Novel in the Ancient World*. Edited by Gareth L. Schmeling. MnS 159. Leiden: Brill, 1996.

Blamire, A. *Plutarch: Life of Kimon*. ClaHa 2. London: Institute of Classical Studies, University of London, 1989.

de Boer, Pieter A. H. *Fatherhood and Motherhood in Israelite and Judean Piety*. Leiden: Brill, 1974.

Boersma, Hans. "A New Age Love Story: Worldview and Ethics in the Gospel of John." *CTJ* 38 (2003): 103–119.

Bohak, Gideon. *Joseph and Aseneth and the Jewish Temple in Heliopolis*. EJL 10. Atlanta: Scholars, 1996.

Booth, Wayne C. *The Rhetoric of Fiction*. 2nd ed. Chicago: University of Chicago Press, 1983.

Borgen, Peder. *Bread from Heaven: An Exegetical Study of the Concept of Manna in the Gospel of John and the Writings of Philo*. NovTSup 10. Leiden: Brill, 1965.

Bowen, Clayton R. "The Fourth Gospel as Dramatic Material." *JBL* 49 (1930): 292–305.

Bowersock, G. W. "Suetonius in the Eighteenth Century." Pages 52–65 in *From Gibbon to Auden: Essays on the Classical Tradition*. Oxford: Oxford University Press, 2009.

Bowie, Ewen. "The Chronology of the Earlier Greek Novels since B. E. Perry: Revisions and Precisions." *AN* 2 (2002): 47–63.

Bowie, Ewen. "The Readership of the Greek Novels in the Ancient World." Pages 435–59 in *The Search for the Ancient Novel*. Edited by James Tatum. Baltimore: Johns Hopkins University Press, 1994.

Bowie, Ewen. "Who Read the Ancient Greek Novels?" *The Ancient Novel: Classical Paradigms and Modern Perspectives.* Edited by James Tatum and Gail M. Vernazza. Hanover: Dartmouth College, 1990.

Braginskaya, Nina. "*Joseph and Aseneth* in Greek Literary History: The Case of the 'First Novel.'" Pages 79–105 in *The Ancient Novel and Early Christian and Jewish Narrative: Fictional Intersections.* Edited by Maralia P. Futre Pinheiro, Judith Perkins, and Richard Pervo. ANS. Groningen: Barkhuis, 2012.

Brant, Jo-Ann A. *Dialogue and Drama: Elements of Greek Tragedy in the Fourth Gospel.* Peabody: Hendrickson, 2004.

Brant, Jo-Ann A. "Mimesis and Dramatic Art in Ezekiel." *Ancient Fiction: The Matrix of Early Christian and Jewish Narrative.* Edited by Jo-Ann A. Brant, Charles W. Hedrick, and Chris Shea. SBLSymS 32. Leiden: Brill, 2005.

Braun, Martin. *History and Romance in Graeco-Oriental Literature.* Oxford: Blackwell, 1938.

Bray, Henry Truro. *Essays on God and Man: Or A Philosophical Inquiry Into the Principles of Religion.* St. Louis: Nixon-Jones Printing, 1888.

Brenk, Frederick E. *In Mist Apparelled: Religious Themes in Plutarch's Moralia and Lives.* MnS 48. Leiden: Brill, 1977.

Brethes, Romain. "Pour une typologie du rire dans les romans grecs: topos littéraire, jeu narratologique et nouvelle lecture du monde." *BAGB* 1 (2003): 113–129.

Brooks, E. W., ed. *Joseph and Asenath, the Confession and Prayer of Asenath, Daughter of Pentephres the Priest.* Vol. 7. 8 vols. TED 2. London: Macmillan, 1918.

Brown, Raymond E. *The Gospel According to John I–XII: A New Translation with Introduction and Commentary.* AB 29. Garden City: Doubleday, 1966.

Brown, Raymond E. *The Gospel According to John XIII–XXI: A New Translation with Introduction and Commentary.* AB 29A. Garden City: Doubleday, 1970.

Bullard, Collin Blake. *Jesus and the Thoughts of Many Hearts: Implicit Christology and Jesus' Knowledge in the Gospel of Luke.* LNTS 530. New York: T. & T. Clark, 2015.

Bultmann, Rudolf. *Theology of the New Testament.* 2 vols. London: SCM Press, 1955.

Burchard, Christoph. "Joseph and Aseneth." Pages 177–247 in *OTP.* Edited by James H. Charlesworth. Vol. 2. 2 vols. Garden City: Doubleday, 1983.

Burchard, Christoph. *Joseph und Aseneth kritisch herausgegeben von Christoph Burchard mit Unterstützung von Carsten Burfeind & Uta Barbara Fink.* PVTG 5. Leiden: Brill, 2003.

Burian, Peter. "From Repertoire to Canon." Pages 228–83 in *The Cambridge Companion to Greek Tragedy.* Edited by P. E. Easterling. Cambridge: Cambridge University Press, 1997.

Burke, Seán. *The Death and Return of the Author: Criticism and Subjectivity in Barthes, Foucault and Derrida.* 2nd ed. Edinburgh: Edinburgh University Press, 1998.

BIBLIOGRAPHY

Burke, Seán. *The Ethics of Writing: Authorship and Legacy in Plato and Nietzsche.* Edinburgh: Edinburgh University Press, 2008.

Burridge, Richard A. *Imitating Jesus: An Inclusive Approach to New Testament Ethics.* Grand Rapids: Eerdmans, 2007.

Burridge, Richard A. *What Are the Gospels?: A Comparison with Graeco-Roman Biography.* 2nd ed. Grand Rapids: Eerdmans, 2004.

Butte, George. *I Know That You Know That I Know: Narrating Subjects from Moll Flanders to Marnie.* ThINS. Columbus: Ohio State University Press, 2004.

Butts, James R. "The Progymnasmata of Theon: A New Text with Translation and Commentary." PhD diss, The Claremont Graduate School, 1986.

Calabi, Francesca. "Theatrical Language in Philo's *In Flaccum*." Pages 91–116 in *Italian Studies on Philo of Alexandria.* Edited by Francesca Calabi. SPhAMA 1. Leiden: Brill, 2003.

Cancik, Hubert. "The History of Culture, Religion, and Institutions in Ancient Historiography: Philological Observations Concerning Luke's History." *JBL* 116 (1997): 673–95.

Carter, Warren. *John and Empire: Initial Explorations.* New York: T. & T. Clark, 2008.

Champion, Craige B. *Cultural Politics in Polybius' Histories.* JPICL. Berkeley: University of California Press, 2004.

Chandler, Daniel. "Schema Theory and the Interpretation of Television Programmes," April 1997. http://users.aber.ac.uk/dgc/Documents/short/schematv.html.

Charlesworth, James H., ed. *Old Testament Pseudepigrapha.* 2 vols. Garden City: Doubleday, 1983–85.

Charnwood, G. R. B. *According to Saint John.* Boston: Little, Brown, & Co., 1925.

Chesnutt, Randall D. *From Death to Life: Conversion in Joseph and Aseneth.* JSPSup 16. Sheffield: Sheffield Academic Press, 1995.

Chesnutt, Randall D. "Revelatory Experiences Attributed to Biblical Women in Early Jewish Literature." Pages 107–25 in *"Women like This": New Perspectives on Jewish Women in the Greco-Roman World.* Edited by Amy-Jill Levine. Atlanta: Scholars, 1991.

Chesnutt, Randall D. "The Dead Sea Scrolls and the Meal Formula in *Joseph and Aseneth*: From Qumran Fever to Qumran Light." Pages 397–426 in *The Bible and the Dead Sea Scrolls: The Dead Seas Scrolls and the Qumran Community.* Edited by James H. Charlesworth. Waco: Baylor University Press, 2006.

Chew, Kathryn S. "Achilles Tatius, Sophistic Master of Novelistic Conventions." Pages 62–75 in *A Companion to the Ancient Novel.* Edited by Edmund P. Cueva and Shannon N. Byrne. BCAW. Chichester, West Sussex: Wiley Blackwell, 2014.

Chew, Kathryn S. "Focalization in Xenophon of Ephesos' *Ephesiaka*." Pages 47–60 in *Ancient Fiction and Early Christian Narrative.* Edited by Ronald F. Hock, J. Bradley Chance, and Judith Perkins. SBLSymS 6. Atlanta: Scholars, 1998.

Cohen, Shaye J. D. *The Beginnings of Jewishness: Boundaries, Varieties, Uncertainties.* HCS 31. Berkeley: University of California Press, 1999.

Cohn, Dorrit. *The Distinction of Fiction.* Baltimore: Johns Hopkins University Press, 1999.

Collins, John J. *Between Athens and Jerusalem: Jewish Identity in the Hellenistic Diaspora.* Grand Rapids: Eerdmans, 2000.

Collins, John J. "Joseph and Aseneth: Jewish or Christian?" *JSP* 14 (2005): 97–112.

Collins, John J., and George W. E. Nickelsburg, eds. *Ideal Figures in Ancient Judaism: Profiles and Paradigms.* SCS 12. Chico: Scholars, 1980.

Collins, Raymond F. "Representative Figures." Pages 1–45 in *These Things Have Been Written: Studies on the Fourth Gospel.* Grand Rapids: Eerdmans, 1990.

Collins, Raymond F. "The Representative Figures of the Fourth Gospel. Part I." *DRev* 94 (1976): 26–46.

Collins, Raymond F. "The Representative Figures of the Fourth Gospel. Part II." *DRev* 94 (1976): 118–132.

Connick, C. Milo. "The Dramatic Character of the Fourth Gospel." *JBL* 67 (1948): 159–69.

Conway, Colleen M. "The Production of the Johannine Community: A New Historicist Perspective." *JBL* 121 (2002): 479–95.

Conybeare, F. C., and St. George William Joseph Stock. *A Grammar of Septuagint Greek.* Grand Rapids: Zondervan, 1980.

Cornford, Francis M. *Thucydides Mythistoricus.* London: Edward Arnold, 1907.

Crane, Mary Thomas. *Shakespeare's Brain: Reading with Cognitive Theory.* Princeton: Princeton University Press, 2001.

Cribiore, Raffaella. *Gymnastics of the Mind: Greek Education in Hellenistic and Roman Egypt.* Princeton: Princeton University Press, 2005.

Cueva, Edmund P. *The Myths of Fiction: Studies in the Canonical Greek Novels.* Ann Arbor: University of Michigan Press, 2004.

Culler, Jonathan. "Presupposition and Intertextuality." *MLN* 91 (1976): 1380–96.

Culler, Jonathan. *Structuralist Poetics: Structuralism, Linguistics and the Study of Literature.* London: Routledge, 1975.

Culpepper, R. Alan. *Anatomy of the Fourth Gospel: A Study in Literary Design.* Philadelphia: Fortress, 1983.

Culpepper, R. Alan. *The Gospel and Letters of John.* Nashville: Abingdon, 1998.

Culy, Martin M. *Echoes of Friendship in the Gospel of John.* NTMon 30. Sheffield: Sheffield Phoenix Press, 2010.

Darbo-Peschanski, Catherine. *Le discours du particulier: essai sur l'enquête hérodotéenne.* Paris: Seuil, 1987.

Davidson, James. "The Gaze in Polybius' Histories." *JRS* 81 (1991): 10–24.

Davidson, John. "Theatrical Production." Pages 194–211 in *A Companion to Greek Tragedy.* Edited by Justina Gregory. Oxford: Blackwell, 2005.

de Jonge, Marinus. *Jesus, Stranger from Heaven and Son of God: Jesus Christ and the Christians in Johannine Perspective*. Translated by John E. Steely. SBSt 11. Missoula: Scholars, 1977.

Delcor, Matthias. "Un roman d'amour d'origine thérapeute: Le Livre de Joseph et Asénath." *BLE* 63 (1962): 3–27.

Derow, P. S. "Historical Explanation: Polybius and His Predecessors." Pages 73–90 in *Greek Historiography*. Edited by Simon Hornblower. Oxford: Clarendon, 1994.

Destinon, Justus von. *Die Quellen des Flavius Josephus*. Kiel: Lipsius & Tischer, 1882.

D'Huys, V. "XRHSIMON KAI TERPNON in Polybios' Schlachtschilderungen. Einige literarische Topoi in seiner Darstellung der Schlacht bei Zama (XV 9–16)." Pages 267–88 in *Purposes of History: Studies in Greek Historiography from the 4th to the 2nd Centuries B.C.: Proceedings of the International Colloquium, Leuven, 24–26 May 1988*. Edited by H. Verdin, G. Schepens, and E. De Keyser. StHell 30. Leuven, 1990.

Dibelius, Martin. "Der erste christliche Historiker." Pages 112–25 in *Aus der Arbeit der Universität 1946/47*. Edited by Hans Freiherr von Campenhausen. SUHei 3. Berlin: Springer, 1948.

Dickey, Eleanor. *Ancient Greek Scholarship: A Guide to Finding, Reading, and Understanding Scholia, Commentaries, Lexica, and Grammatical Treatises, from Their Beginnings to the Byzantine Period*. APACRS 7. New York: Oxford University Press, 2007.

Diggle, James, ed. *Theophrastus: Characters*. CCTC 43. Cambridge: Cambridge University Press, 2004.

Dihle, Albrecht. *Studien zur griechischen Biographie*. 2nd ed. Göttingen: Vandenhoeck & Ruprecht, 1970.

Dihle, Albrecht. "The Gospels and Greek Biography." Pages 361–86 in *The Gospel and the Gospels*. Edited by Peter Stuhlmacher. Grand Rapids: Eerdmans, 1991.

Dillon, John. "Philo and Hellenistic Platonism." Pages 223–32 in *Philo of Alexandria and Post-Aristotelian Philosophy*. Edited by Francesca Alesse. SPhA 5. Leiden: Brill, 2008.

Dillon, John. *The Middle Platonists: 80 BC to AD 220*. Rev. ed. Ithaca: Cornell University Press, 1996.

Dindorf, W., ed. *Scholia Graeca in Euripidis Tragoedias*. 4 vols. Oxford: Oxford University Press, 1863.

Dinkler, Michal Beth. "'The Thoughts of Many Hearts Shall Be Revealed': Listening in on Lukan Interior Monologues." *JBL* 134 (2015): 373–99.

Docherty, Susan. "*Joseph and Aseneth*: Rewritten Bible or Narrative Expansion?" *JSJ* 35 (2004): 27–48.

Dodd, C. H. *Historical Tradition in the Fourth Gospel*. Cambridge: Cambridge University Press, 1963.

Dodds, Eric Robertson, ed. *Euripides: Bacchae*. 2nd ed. Oxford: Clarendon, 1986.

Domeris, William R. "The Johannine Drama." *JTSA* 42 (1983): 29–35.

Doody, Margaret A. "The Representation of Consciousness in the Ancient Novel." Pages 35–45 in *Remapping the Rise of the European Novel*. Edited by J. Mander. Oxford: Voltaire Foundation, 2007.

Doran, Madeleine. "'Discrepant Awareness' in Shakespeare's Comedies." *MPh* 60 (1962): 51–55.

Dormeyer, Detlev. *Das Markusevangelium als Idealbiographie von Jesus Christus, dem Nazarener*. SBB 43. Stuttgart: Verlag Katholisches Bibelwerk, 1999.

Dox, Donnalee. *The Idea of the Theater in Latin Christian Thought: Augustine to the Fourteenth Century*. Ann Arbor: University of Michigan Press, 2004.

Dubrow, Heather. *Genre*. London: Methuen, 1982.

Duff, Tim. *Plutarch's Lives: Exploring Virtue and Vice*. Oxford: Clarendon, 1999.

Duke, Paul D. *Irony in the Fourth Gospel*. Atlanta: John Knox Press, 1985.

Dunderberg, Ismo. *The Beloved Disciple in Conflict?: Revisiting the Gospels of John and Thomas*. Oxford: Oxford University Press, 2006.

Easterling, P. E. "From Repertoire to Canon." Pages 211–27 in *The Cambridge Companion to Greek Tragedy*. Edited by P. E. Easterling. Cambridge: Cambridge University Press, 1997.

Eckstein, Arthur M. "Polybius, Phylarchus, and Historiographical Criticism." *CP* 108 (2013): 314–38.

Egan, Kieran. "Thucydides, Tragedian." Pages 63–92 in *The Writing of History: Literary Form and Historical Understanding*. Edited by Robert H. Canary and Henry Kozicki. Madison: University of Wisconsin Press, 1978.

Ehrman, Bart D. *Forgery and Counterforgery: The Use of Literary Deceit in Early Christian Polemics*. Oxford: Oxford University Press, 2013.

Elliott, Scott S. *Reconfiguring Mark's Jesus: Narrative Criticism after Poststructuralism*. BMW 41. Sheffield: Sheffield Phoenix Press, 2011.

Else, Gerald Frank. *The Structure and Date of Book 10 of Plato's Republic*. Heidelberg: Carl Winter, 1972.

Estes, Douglas. *The Temporal Mechanics of the Fourth Gospel: A Theory of Hermeneutical Relativity in the Gospel of John*. BibInt 92. Leiden: Brill, 2008.

Evans, Katherine G. "Alexander the Alabarch: Roman and Jew." Pages 576–94 in *Society of Biblical Literature 1995 Seminar Papers*. Edited by Eugene H. Lowering. SBLSP 34. Atlanta: Scholars, 1995.

Farrell, Joseph. "Classical Genre in Theory and Practice." *NLitHist* 34 (2003): 383–408.

Fauconnier, Gilles, and Mark Turner. *The Way We Think: Conceptual Blending and the Mind's Hidden Complexities*. New York: BasicBooks, 2003.

Feldman, Louis H. *Josephus: Judean Antiquities, Books 1–4*. Edited by Steve Mason. FJTC 3. Leiden: Brill, 1999.

Feldman, Louis H. "Josephus' Portrait of Moses." *JQR* 82 (1992): 285–328.

Feldman, Louis H. *Josephus's Interpretation of the Bible*. HCS 27. Berkeley: University of California Press, 1998.

Feldman, Louis H. *Philo's Portrayal of Moses in the Context of Ancient Judaism*. CJA 15. Notre Dame: University of Notre Dame Press, 2007.

Feldman, Louis H. "The Influence of the Greek Tragedians on Josephus." Pages 413–43 in *Judaism and Hellenism Reconsidered*. JSJS 107. Leiden: Brill, 2006.

Feldman, Louis H., James L. Kugel, and Lawrence H. Schiffman, eds. *Outside the Bible: Ancient Jewish Writings Related to Scripture*. Vol. 3. 3 vols. Lincoln: University of Nebraska Press, 2013.

Fenn, Richard K. *The Death of Herod: An Essay in the Sociology of Religion*. Cambridge: Cambridge University Press, 1992.

Fink, Uta Barbara. *Joseph und Aseneth: Revision des griechischen Textes und Edition der zweiten lateinischen Übersetzung*. PVTG 5. Berlin: De Gruyter, 2008.

Finley, John H., Jr. "Euripides and Thucydides." *HSCP* 49 (1938): 23–68.

Flower, Michael A. *Theopompus of Chios: History and Rhetoric in the Fourth Century BC*. Oxford: Oxford University Press, 1994.

Fludernik, Monika. *Towards a "Natural" Narratology*. London: Routledge, 1996.

Fornara, Charles W. *The Nature of History in Ancient Greece and Rome*. Berkeley: University of California Press, 1983.

Fortescue, Michael. "Thoughts about Thought." *CogLin* 12 (2001): 15–45.

Foster, Edith, and Donald Lateiner, eds. *Thucydides and Herodotus*. Oxford: Oxford University Press, 2012.

Fowler, Alastair. *Kinds of Literature: An Introduction to the Theory of Genres and Modes*. Cambridge: Harvard University Press, 1982.

Fowler, Alastair. "The Life and Death of Literary Forms." *NLitHist* 2 (1971): 199–216.

Frey, Jörg, Clare K. Rothschild, and Jens Schröter, eds. *Die Apostelgeschichte im Kontext antiker und frühchristlicher Historiographie*. BZNW 162. Berlin: de Gruyter, 2009.

Frickenschmidt, Dirk. *Evangelium als Biographie: die vier Evangelien im Rahmen antiker Erzählkunst*. TANZ 22. Tübingen: Francke, 1997.

Fromentin, Valérie, and Sophie Gotteland. "Thucydides' Ancient Reputation." Pages 13–25 in *A Handbook to the Reception of Thucydides*. Edited by Christine Lee and Neville Morley. Oxford: John Wiley & Sons, 2015.

Frye, Northrop. *Anatomy of Criticism; Four Essays*. Princeton: Princeton University Press, 1957.

Furnish, Victor Paul. *The Love Command in the New Testament*. NTL. London: SCM Press, 1973.

Fusillo, Massimo. "The Conflict of Emotions: A Topos in the Greek Erotic Novel." Pages 60–82 in *Oxford Readings in the Greek Novel*. Edited by Simon Swain. Oxford: Oxford University Press, 1999.

Fusillo, Massimo. *Il romanzo greco: polifonia ed eros*. Venice: Marsilio Editori, 1989.

Gallarte, Israel Muñoz. "Hérodote et Plutarque: à propos de la rencontre entre Solon et Crésus, roi de Lydie." *Ploutarchos* 8 (2011): 117–32.

Geiger, Joseph. *Cornelius Nepos and Ancient Political Biography.* Hist.E 47. Stuttgart: Steiner Verlag Wiesbaden, 1985.

Geljon, Albert C. *Philonic Exegesis in Gregory of Nyssa's De vita Moysis.* BJS 333. Providence: Brown Judaic Studies, 2002.

Genette, Gérard. *Narrative Discourse: An Essay in Method.* Ithaca: Cornell University Press, 1980.

Gibson, Craig A. *Libanius's Progymnasmata: Model Exercises in Greek Prose Composition and Rhetoric.* WGRW 27. Atlanta: SBL, 2008.

Gill, Christopher. *Personality in Greek Epic, Tragedy, and Philosophy: The Self in Dialogue.* Oxford: Clarendon, 1996.

Gill, Christopher. *The Structured Self in Hellenistic and Roman Thought.* New York: Oxford University Press, 2006.

Goddard, Cliff. "Thinking across Languages and Cultures: Six Dimensions of Variation." *CogLin* 14 (2003): 109–140.

Goldhill, Simon. *Reading Greek Tragedy.* Cambridge: Cambridge University Press, 1986.

Goodenough, Erwin R. "Philo's Exposition of the Law and His De vita Mosis." *HTR* 26 (1933): 109–25.

Goold, G. P. "Introduction." *Chariton: Callirhoe.* LCL 481. Cambridge: Harvard University Press, 1995.

Grant, Michael. *Herod the Great.* New York: American Heritage Press, 1971.

Graverini, Luca. "From the Epic to The Novelistic Hero." Pages 288–299 in *A Companion to the Ancient Novel.* Edited by Edmund P. Cueva. BCAW. Chichester, West Sussex: Wiley Blackwell, 2014.

Gregory, Justina, ed. *A Companion to Greek Tragedy.* BCAW. Oxford: Blackwell, 2005.

Grene, David, and Richmond Alexander Lattimore, eds. *Euripides.* 3 vols. CGT. Chicago: University of Chicago Press, 1959.

Grethlein, Jonas. "Social Minds and Narrative Time: Collective Experience in Thucydides and Heliodorus." *Narrative* 23 (2015): 123–39.

Habicht, Christian. "Introduction." *Polybius: The Histories, Books I and II.* Edited by F. W. Walbank and Christian Habicht. LCL 128. Cambridge: Harvard University Press, 2010.

Hadas, Moses, ed. *The Third and Fourth Books of Maccabees.* JAL. New York: Harper, 1953.

Hadas-Lebel, Mireille. "Les Juifs et le théâtre dans l'antiquité." *CJu* 14 (2003): 14–17.

Hadavas, Constantine T. "The Structure, Form, and Meaning of Plutarch's 'Life of Solon.'" PhD diss, University of North Carolina at Chapel Hill, 1995.

Hägerland, Tobias. "John's Gospel: A Two-Level Drama?" *JSNT* 25 (2003): 309–22.

Hägg, Tomas. *Narrative Technique in Ancient Greek Romances: Studies of Chariton, Xenophon Ephesius, and Achilles Tatius.* Stockholm: Svenska institutet i Athen and Almqvist & Wiksells Boktryckeri Aktiebolag, 1971.

Hägg, Tomas. *The Art of Biography in Antiquity.* Cambridge: Cambridge University Press, 2012.

Hägg, Tomas. *The Novel in Antiquity.* Rev. ed. University of California Press, 1991.

Hakola, Raimo. *Identity Matters: John, the Jews, and Jewishness.* NovTSup 118. Leiden: Brill, 2005.

Hamilton, Richard. "Announced Entrances in Greek Tragedy." *HSCP* 82 (1978): 63–82.

Hammond, N. G. L., and F. W. Walbank. *A History of Macedonia: 336–167 BC.* Vol. 1. 3 vols. Oxford: Clarendon, 1972.

Hardison, O. B., ed. *Aristotle's Poetics: A Translation and Commentary for Students of Literature.* Translated by Leon Golden. Tallahassee: University Presses of Florida, 1981.

Harris, Elizabeth. *Prologue and Gospel: The Theology of the Fourth Evangelist.* JSNTSup 107. Sheffield: Sheffield Academic Press, 1994.

Harris, William V. *Restraining Rage: The Ideology of Anger Control in Classical Antiquity.* Cambridge: Harvard University Press, 2009.

Hayes, D. A. *John and His Writings.* New York: The Methodist Book Concern, 1917.

Hays, Richard B. *The Moral Vision of the New Testament: Community, Cross, New Creation: A Contemporary Introduction to New Testament Ethics.* San Francisco: HarperSanFrancisco, 1996.

Heath, Malcolm. *The Poetics of Greek Tragedy.* Stanford: Stanford University Press, 1987.

Helmbold, W. C., and Edward N. O'Neil. *Plutarch's Quotations.* PhMon 19. Baltimore: American Philological Association, 1959.

Henten, Jan Willem van. "Constructing Herod as a Tyrant: Assessing Josephus' Parallel Passages." *Flavius Josephus: Interpretation and History.* Edited by Jack Pastor, Pnina Stern, and Menahem Mor. JSJS 146. Leiden: Brill, 2011.

Henten, Jan Willem van. *Josephus: Judean Antiquities, Book 15.* Edited by Steve Mason. FJTC 7b. Leiden: Brill, 2014.

Herman, David. "Scripts, Sequences, and Stories: Elements of a Postclassical Narratology." *PMLA* 112 (1997): 1046–1059.

Hirsch, E. D. *The Aims of Interpretation.* Chicago: University of Chicago Press, 1976.

Hirsch, E. D. *Validity in Interpretation.* New Haven: Yale University Press, 1967.

Hitchcock, F. R. M. "Is the Fourth Gospel a Drama?" *Theol.* 7 (1923): 307–17.

Hitchcock, F. R. M. "The Dramatic Development of the Fourth Gospel." *Exp.* 4 (1907): 266–79.

Hock, Ronald F. *The Chreia and Ancient Rhetoric: Commentaries on Aphthonius's Progymnasmata.* WGRW 31. Atlanta: SBL, 2012.

Hock, Ronald F. "The Rhetoric of Romance." Pages 445–66 in *Handbook of Classical Rhetoric in the Hellenistic Period: 330 BC–AD 400*. Edited by Stanley E. Porter. Boston: Brill, 2001.

Holladay, Carl R., ed. *Fragments from Hellenistic Jewish Authors. Volume II: Poets*. SBLTT 30. Atlanta: Scholars, 1989.

Holzberg, Niklas. *The Ancient Novel: An Introduction*. London: Routledge, 1995.

Houlden, J. L. *Ethics and the New Testament*. New York: Oxford University Press, 1977.

Huizinga, Johan. "A Definition of the Concept of History." Pages 1–10 in *Philosophy and History: Essays Presented to Ernst Cassirer*. Oxford: Clarendon, 1936.

Humphrey, Edith McEwan. *Joseph and Aseneth*. GApPs. Sheffield: Sheffield Academic Press, 2000.

Hunt, Steven A., D. Francois Tolmie, and Ruben Zimmermann, eds. *Character Studies in the Fourth Gospel*. WUNT 314. Tübingen: Mohr Siebeck, 2013.

Hylen, Susan. *Imperfect Believers: Ambiguous Characters in the Gospel of John*. Louisville: Westminster John Knox, 2009.

Ingarden, Roman. "The Functions of Language in the Theater." Pages 377–96 in *The Literary Work of Art: An Investigation on the Borderlines of Ontology, Logic, and Theory of Literature*. Translated by George G. Grabowicz. Evanston: Northwestern University Press, 1973.

Iser, Wolfgang. *The Act of Reading: A Theory of Aesthetic Response*. Baltimore: Johns Hopkins University Press, 1978.

Iser, Wolfgang. *The Implied Reader: Patterns of Communication in Prose Fiction from Bunyan to Beckett*. Baltimore: Johns Hopkins University Press, 1978.

Jacobson, Howard. "Ezekiel's *Exagoge*, One Play or Four?" *GRBS* 43 (2003): 391–96.

Jacobson, Howard. *The Exagoge of Ezekiel*. Cambridge: Cambridge University Press, 1983.

Jacobson, Howard. "The Identity and Role of Chum in Ezekiel's 'Exagoge.'" *HUSLA* 9 (1981): 139–46.

Jauss, Hans Robert. "Theory of Genres and Medieval Literature." Pages 76–109 in *Toward an Aesthetic of Reception*. Translated by Timothy Bahti. THLit 2. Minneapolis: University of Minnesota Press, 1982.

Jochum, K. P. S. *Discrepant Awareness: Studies in English Renaissance Drama*. NSAA 13. Frankfurt am Main: Lang, 1979.

Johnson, William A. *Readers and Reading Culture in the High Roman Empire: A Study of Elite Communities*. CCSoc. New York: Oxford University Press, 2010.

Jülicher, Adolf. *An Introduction to the New Testament*. New York: G. P. Putnam's Sons, 1904.

Kanagaraj, Jey J. "The Implied Ethics of the Fourth Gospel: A Reinterpretation of the Decalogue." *TynBul* 52 (2001): 33–60.

Käsemann, Ernst. *The Testament of Jesus: A Study of the Gospel of John in the Light of Chapter 17*. Translated by Gerhard Krodel. Philadelphia: Fortress, 1968.

BIBLIOGRAPHY 265

Kasher, Aryeh. *King Herod: A Persecuted Persecutor: A Case Study in Psychohistory and Psychobiography*. Translated by Karen Gold. SJ 36. Berlin: De Gruyter, 2007.

Keener, Craig S. "Studies in the Knowledge of God in the Fourth Gospel in Light of Its Historical Context." M.Div Thesis, Assemblies of God Theological Seminary, 1986.

Keener, Craig S. *The Gospel of John: A Commentary*. 2 vols. Peabody: Hendrickson, 2003.

Kennedy, George A. *Aristotle: On Rhetoric: A Theory of Civic Discourse*. New York: Oxford University Press, 1991.

Kennedy, George A. *Invention And Method: Two Rhetorical Treatises from the Hermogenic Corpus*. WGRW 15. Atlanta: SBL, 2005.

Kennedy, George A. *Progymnasmata: Greek Textbooks of Prose Composition and Rhetoric*. WGRW 10. Atlanta: SBL, 2003.

Kennedy, George A, ed. *The Cambridge History of Literary Criticism: Volume 1: Classical Criticism*. Cambridge: Cambridge University Press, 1989.

Kilpatrick, G. D. "Living Issues in Biblical Scholarship: The Last Supper." *ExpTim* 64 (1952): 4–8.

Kim, Lawrence Young. *Homer between History and Fiction in Imperial Greek Literature*. GCRW. Cambridge: Cambridge University Press, 2010.

Knobl, Ranja. "Biographical Representations of Euripides. Some Examples of Their Development from Classical Antiquity to Byzantium." PhD diss, Durham University, 2008.

Koester, Craig R. "Rethinking the Ethics of John: A Review Article." *JSNT* 36 (2013): 85–98.

Kohn, Thomas D. "The Tragedies of Ezekiel." *GRBS* 43 (2002): 5–12.

Kok, Kobus. "As the Father Has Sent Me, I Send You: Towards a Missional-Incarnational Ethos in John 4." Pages 168–96 in *Moral Language in the New Testament: The Interrelatedness of Language and Ethics in Early Christian Writings*. Edited by Ruben Zimmermann, J. G. van der Watt, and Susanne Luther. WUNT 2/296. Tübingen: Mohr Siebeck, 2010.

König, Jason. "Body and Text." Pages 127–44 in *The Cambridge Companion to the Greek and Roman Novel*. Edited by Tim Whitmarsh. Cambridge: Cambridge University Press, 2008.

Konstan, David. *Sexual Symmetry: Love in the Ancient Novel and Related Genres*. Princeton: Princeton University Press, 1994.

Konstan, David. *The Emotions of the Ancient Greeks: Studies in Aristotle and Classical Literature*. RCLec. Toronto: University of Toronto Press, 2006.

Kooten, George H. van. "The 'True Light Which Enlightens Everyone' (John 1:9): John, Genesis, The Platonic Notion of the 'True, Noetic Light', and the Allegory of the Cave in Plato's Republic." Pages 149–94 in *The Creation of Heaven and*

Earth: Re-Interpretations of Genesis in the Context of Judaism, Ancient Philosophy, Christianity, and Modern Physics. Edited by George H. van Kooten. Leiden: Brill, 2005.

Kraemer, Ross Shepard. *When Aseneth Met Joseph: A Late Antique Tale of the Biblical Patriarch and His Egyptian Wife, Reconsidered.* New York: Oxford University Press, 1998.

Kristeva, Julia. "Word, Dialogue and Novel." Pages 35–61 in *The Kristeva Reader.* Edited by Toril Moi. Oxford: Basil Blackwell, 1986.

Lacy, Phillip de. "Biography and Tragedy in Plutarch." *AJP* 73 (1952): 159–71.

Lagache, Daniel. *La jalousie amoureuse; psychologie descriptive et psychanalyse. Vol. 2: La jalousie vécue.* Paris: Presses universitaires de France, 1947.

Landau, Tamar. *Out-Heroding Herod: Josephus, Rhetoric, and the Herod Narratives.* AGJU/AJEC 63. Leiden: Brill, 2006.

Lanfranchi, Pierluigi. *L'Exagoge d'Ezechiel le Tragique: Introduction, texte, traduction et commentaire.* SVTP 21. Leiden: Brill, 2006.

Lang, Mabel L. "Participial Motivation in Thucydides." *Mn.* 48 (1995): 48–65.

Laqueur, Richard. *Der jüdische Historiker Flavius Josephus; ein biographischer Versuch auf neuer quellenkritischer Grundlage.* 2nd ed. Darmstadt: Wissenschaftliche Buchgesellschaft, 1970.

Larsen, Kasper Bro. "Narrative Docetism: Christology and Storytelling in the Gospel of John." *The Gospel of John and Christian Theology.* Edited by Richard Bauckham and Carl Mosser. Grand Rapids: Eerdmans, 2008.

Larsen, Kasper Bro. "The Recognition Scenes and Epistemological Reciprocity in the Fourth Gospel." Pages 341–56 in *The Gospel of John as Genre Mosaic.* Edited by Kasper Bro Larsen. SANt 3. Göttingen: Vandehoeck & Rupprecht, 2015.

Larsen, Kasper Bro. *Recognizing the Stranger: Recognition Scenes in the Gospel of John.* BibInt 93. Leiden: Brill, 2008.

Larsen, Kasper Bro, ed. *The Gospel of John as Genre Mosaic.* SANt 3. Göttingen: Vandehoeck & Rupprecht, 2015.

Last, Richard. "The Social Relationships of Gospel Writers: New Insights from Inscriptions Commending Greek Historiographers." *JSNT* 37 (2015): 223–52.

Lateiner, Donald. *The Historical Method of Herodotus.* Toronto: University of Toronto Press, 1989.

Lausberg, Heinrich. *Handbook of Literary Rhetoric: A Foundation for Literary Study.* Edited by David E. Orton and R. Dean Anderson. Boston: Brill, 1998.

Lee, Christine, and Neville Morley, eds. *A Handbook to the Reception of Thucydides.* Oxford: John Wiley & Sons, 2015.

Legras, Bernard. "La sanction du plagiat littéraire en droit grec et hellénistique." Pages 443–61 in *Symposion 1999: vorträge zur griechischen und hellenistischen*

Rechtsgeschichte. Edited by Gerhard Thür and F. Javier Fernández Nieto. Pazo de Mariñàn: La Coruña, 2003.

Leo, Friedrich. *Die griechisch-römische Biographie nach ihrer litterarischen Form*. Leipzig: Teubner, 1901.

Lincoln, Andrew T. *Truth on Trial: The Lawsuit Motif in the Fourth Gospel*. Peabody: Hendrickson, 2000.

Longley, Georgina. "Thucydides, Polybius, and Human Nature." Pages 68–84 in *Imperialism, Cultural Politics, and Polybius*. Edited by Christopher Smith and Liv Mariah Yarrow. Oxford: Oxford University Press, 2012.

Lovibond, Sabina. "Plato's Theory of Mind." *Psychology*. Edited by Stephen Everson. Companions to Ancient Thought 2. Cambridge: Cambridge University Press, 1991.

Lowe, Malcolm. "Who Were the IOUDAIOI?" *NovT* 18 (1976): 101–30.

Luce, T. James. *The Greek Historians*. London: Routledge, 1997.

MacAlister, Suzanne. *Dreams and Suicides: The Greek Novel from Antiquity to the Byzantine Empire*. New York: Routledge, 1996.

MacDonald, Dennis Ronald. *Christianizing Homer: The Odyssey, Plato, and the Acts of Andrew*. New York: Oxford University Press, 1994.

MacDonald, Dennis Ronald. *Does the New Testament Imitate Homer?: Four Cases from the Acts of the Apostles*. New Haven: Yale University Press, 2003.

MacDonald, Dennis R. *The Dionysian Gospel: The Fourth Gospel and Euripides*. Minneapolis: Fortress, 2017.

MacDonald, Dennis Ronald. *The Homeric Epics and the Gospel of Mark*. New Haven: Yale University Press, 2000.

MacDonald, Dennis Ronald. *Mythologizing Jesus: From Jewish Teacher to Epic Hero*. Lanham: Rowman & Littlefield, 2015.

MacDonald, Dennis Ronald. *Luke and Vergil: Imitations of Classical Greek Literature*. NTGL 2. Lanham: Rowman & Littlefield, 2015.

MacDonald, Dennis Ronald, ed. *Mimesis and Intertextuality in Antiquity and Christianity*. SAC. Harrisburg: Trinity Press International, 2001.

Macgregor, G. H. C. *The Gospel of John*. London: Hodder and Stoughton, 1928.

MacRae, G. W. "Theology and Irony in the Fourth Gospel." Pages 103–13 in *The Gospel of John as Literature: An Anthology of Twentieth-Century Perspectives*. Edited by Mark W. G. Stibbe. NTTS 17. Leiden: Brill, 1993.

Malherbe, Abraham J. *Moral Exhortation: A Greco-Roman Sourcebook*. LEC 4. Philadelphia: Westminster, 1989.

Malina, Bruce J. *Timothy: Paul's Closest Associate*. PSNBSF. Collegeville: Liturgical, 2008.

Mañas, Mónica Durán. "Hérodote et Plutarque: l'histoire d'Arion." *Ploutarchos* 8 (2011): 67–79.

Mansfeld, Jaap. *Prolegomena: Questions to Be Settled before the Study of an Author or a Text*. PhAnt 61. Leiden: Brill, 1994.

Marguerat, Daniel. *The First Christian Historian: Writing the "Acts of the Apostles."* SNTSMS 121. Cambridge: Cambridge University Press, 2002.

Marincola, John, ed. *Authority and Tradition in Ancient Historiography*. Cambridge: Cambridge University Press, 1997.

Marincola, John, ed. *A Companion to Greek and Roman Historiography*. BCAW. Oxford: Blackwell, 2007.

Marincola, John, ed. *Greek and Roman Historiography*. ORCS. Oxford: Oxford University Press, 2011.

Marincola, John, "Polybius, Phylarchus, and 'Tragic History': A Reconsideration." Pages 73–90 in *Polybius and His World: Essays in Memory of F. W. Walbank*. Edited by Bruce Gibson and Thomas Harrison. Oxford: Oxford University Press, 2013.

Marrou, Henri Irénée. *A History of Education in Antiquity*. Translated by George Lamb. New York: Sheed and Ward, 1956.

Marshak, Adam Kolman. *The Many Faces of Herod the Great*. Grand Rapids: Eerdmans, 2015.

Martyn, J. Louis. *History and Theology in the Fourth Gospel*. 3rd ed. NTL. Louisville: Westminster John Knox, 2003.

Mastronarde, Donald J. *The Art of Euripides: Dramatic Technique and Social Context*. Cambridge: Cambridge University Press, 2010.

Matera, Frank J. *New Testament Ethics: The Legacies of Jesus and Paul*. Louisville: Westminster John Knox Press, 1996.

McCarthy, E. Doyle. "The Emotions: Senses of the Modern Self." *ÖZS* 27 (2002): 30–49.

McCarthy, E. Doyle. "The Social Construction of Emotions: New Directions from Culture Theory." *SPEm* 2 (1994): 267–79.

McGing, Brian C. *Polybius' Histories*. OACL. New York: Oxford University Press, 2010.

Meeks, Wayne A. "'Am I a Jew?'—Johannine Christianity and Judaism." Pages 163–86 in *Christianity, Judaism and Other Greco-Roman Cults: Studies for Morton Smith at 60*. Edited by Jacob Neusner. Vol. 1. 4 vols. SJLA 12. Leiden: Brill, 1975.

Meeks, Wayne A. "The Ethics of the Fourth Evangelist." Pages 317–26 in *Exploring the Gospel of John: In Honor of D. Moody Smith*. Edited by R. Alan Culpepper and Carl Clifton Black. Louisville: Westminster John Knox, 1996.

Meeks, Wayne A. "The Man from Heaven in Johannine Sectarianism." *JBL* 91 (1972): 44–72.

Miller, Carolyn R. "Genre as Social Action." *QJSp* 70 (1984): 151–67.

Miller, William Ian. *The Anatomy of Disgust*. Cambridge: Harvard University Press, 1997.

Mirhady, David C., and Yun Lee Too. *Isocrates I*. OCG 4. University of Texas Press, 2000.

Molinié, Georges. *Chariton: Le roman de Chairéas et Callirhoé*. Budé. Paris: Belles lettres, 1979.

Momigliano, Arnaldo. *The Development of Greek Biography*. Expanded ed. Cambridge: Harvard University Press, 1993.

Montiglio, Silvia. *Love and Providence: Recognition in the Ancient Novel*. Oxford: Oxford University Press, 2013.

Moore, Stephen D., and Yvonne Sherwood. *The Invention of the Biblical Scholar: A Critical Manifesto*. Minneapolis: Fortress, 2011.

Morales, Helen. "Challenging Some Orthodoxies: The Politics of Genre and the Ancient Greek Novel." Pages 1–12 in *Fiction on the Fringe: Novelistic Writing in the Post-Classical Age*. Edited by Grammatiki A. Karla. MnS 310. Leiden: Brill, 2009.

Morales, Helen. "The History of Sexuality." Pages 39–55 in *The Cambridge Companion to the Greek and Roman Novel*. Edited by Tim Whitmarsh. Cambridge: Cambridge University Press, 2008.

Morgan, John R. "Make-Believe and Make Believe: The Fictionality of the Greek Novels." Pages 175–229 in *Lies and Fiction in the Ancient World*. Edited by Christopher Gill and T. P. Wiseman. Austin: University of Texas Press, 1993.

Morgan, John R. "Nymphs, Neighbours and Narrators: A Narratological Approach to Longus." *Mn.* (2003): 171–190.

Morgan, John R., and Meriel Jones, eds. *Philosophical Presences in the Ancient Novel*. ANS 10. Eelde: Barkhuis, 2007.

Morgan, John R., and Richard Stoneman, eds. *Greek Fiction: The Greek Novel in Context*. London: Routledge, 1994.

Morgan, Teresa. *Literate Education in the Hellenistic and Roman Worlds*. CCSt. Cambridge: Cambridge University Press, 1998.

Mossman, J. M. "Tragedy and Epic in Plutarch's Alexander." Pages 209–28 in *Essays on Plutarch's Lives*. Edited by Barbara Scardigli. Oxford: Clarendon, 1995.

Mroczek, Eva. *The Literary Imagination in Jewish Antiquity*. Oxford: Oxford University Press, 2016.

Müller, Karl, ed. *Fragmenta Historicorum Graecorum*. Vol. 3. 5 vols. Paris: A. F. Didot, 1849.

Myers, Alicia D. *Characterizing Jesus: A Rhetorical Analysis on the Fourth Gospel's Use of Scripture in Its Presentation of Jesus*. LNTS 458. London: T. & T. Clark, 2012.

Najman, Hindy. "The Idea of Biblical Genre: From Discourse to Constellation." Pages 307–21 in *Prayer and Poetry in the Dead Sea Scrolls and Related Literature: Essays in Honor of Eileen Schuller on the Occasion of Her 65th Birthday*. Edited by Jeremy Penner, Ken M. Penner, and Cecilia Wassen. STDJ 98. Leiden: Brill, 2012.

Nässelqvist, Dan. *Public Reading in Early Christianity: Lectors, Manuscripts, and Sound in the Oral Delivery of John 1–4*. NovTSup 163. Leiden: Brill, 2016.

Nässelqvist, Dan. "Translating the Aural Gospel: The Use of Sound Analysis in Performance-Oriented Translation." *Translating Scripture for Sound and Performance: New Directions in Biblical Studies*. Edited by James A. Maxey and Ernst R. Wendland. BPCrit 6. Eugene: Cascade Books, 2012.

Newsom, Carol A. "Spying out the Land: A Report from Genology." Pages 437–50 in *Seeking Out the Wisdom of the Ancients: Essays Offered to Honor Michael V. Fox on the Occasion of His Sixty-Fifth Birthday*. Edited by Ronald L. Troxel, Kelvin G. Friebel, and Dennis Robert Magary. Winona Lake: Eisenbrauns, 2005.

Nicholson, Godfrey C. *Death as Departure: The Johannine Descent-Ascent Schema.* SBLDS 63. Chico: Scholars, 1983.

Nickelsburg, George W. E. "Good and Bad Leaders." Pages 49–65 in *Ideal Figures in Ancient Judaism: Profiles and Paradigms*. Edited by John Joseph Collins and George W. E. Nickelsburg. SCS 12. Chico: Scholars, 1980.

Nickelsburg, George W. E. *Jewish Literature between the Bible and the Mishnah: A Historical and Literary Introduction*. 2nd ed. Minneapolis: Fortress, 2005.

Nicolai, Roberto. "Thucydides Continued." Pages 691–719 in *Brill's Companion to Thucydides*. Edited by Antonios Rengakos and Antonis Tsakmakis. BCCS. Leiden: Brill, 2006.

Nielsen, J. T. "The Lamb of God: The Cognitive Structure of a Johannine Metaphor." Pages 217–56 in *Imagery in the Gospel of John: Terms, Forms, Themes, and Theology of John*. Edited by Jörg Frey, J. G. van der Watt, and Ruben Zimmermann. WUNT 200. Tübingen: Mohr Siebeck, 2006.

Nikiprowetzky, Valentin. *Le commentaire de l'écriture chez Philon d'Alexandrie: son caractère et sa portée, observations philologiques*. ALGHJ 11. Leiden: Brill, 1977.

Nissen, Johannes. "Community and Ethics in the Gospel of John." Pages 194–212 in *New Readings in John: Literary and Theological Perspectives: Essays from the Scandinavian Conference on the Fourth Gospel in Århus 1997*. Edited by Johannes Nissen and Sigfred Pedersen. Sheffield: Sheffield Academic Press, 1999.

Norton-Piliavsky, Jonathan. *Contours in the Text: Textual Variation in the Writings of Paul, Josephus and the Yaḥad*. LNTS 430. London: T. & T. Clark, 2011.

Nünlist, René. *The Ancient Critic at Work: Terms and Concepts of Literary Criticism in Greek Scholia*. Cambridge: Cambridge University Press, 2009.

Nünlist, René. "The Homeric Scholia on Focalization." *Mn.* 56 (2003): 61–71.

Palmer, Alan. *Fictional Minds*. FN. Lincoln: University of Nebraska Press, 2004.

Palmer, Alan. *Social Minds in the Novel*. TIN. Columbus: Ohio State University Press, 2010.

Paré, Anthony, Doreen Starke-Meyerring, and Lynn McAlpine. "The Dissertation as Multi-Genre: Many Readers, Many Readings." Pages 179–93 in *Genre in a Changing World*. Edited by Charles Bazerman, Adair Bonini, and Débora de Carvalho Figueiredo. Fort Collins: Parlor, 2009.

BIBLIOGRAPHY

Parsenios, George L. *Departure and Consolation: The Johannine Farewell Discourses in Light of Greco-Roman Literature*. NovTSup 117. Leiden: Brill, 2005.

Parsenios, George L. "'No Longer in the World' (John 17:11): The Transformation of the Tragic in the Fourth Gospel." *HTR* 98 (2005): 1–21.

Parsenios, George L. *Rhetoric and Drama in the Johannine Lawsuit Motif.* WUNT 258. Tübingen: Mohr Siebeck, 2010.

Parsenios, George L. "The Silent Spaces between Narrative and Drama." Pages 85–97 in *The Gospel of John as Genre Mosaic*. Edited by Kasper Bro Larsen. SANt 3. Göttingen: Vandehoeck & Rupprecht, 2015.

Payen, Pascal. "Plutarch the Antiquarian." Pages 235–48 in *A Companion to Plutarch*. Edited by Mark Beck. BCAW. Oxford: Blackwell, 2014.

Pearson, Lionel. "Prophasis and Aitia." *TAPA* 83 (1952): 205–23.

Pearson, Lionel. "Thucydides as Reporter and Critic." *TAPA* 78 (1947): 37–60.

Pédech, Paul. *La méthode historique de Polybe*. CEA. Paris: Société d'édition "Les Belles Lettres," 1964.

Pelling, Christopher. "Plutarch and Roman Politics." Pages 159–87 in *Past Perspectives: Studies in Greek and Roman Historical Writing: Papers Presented at a Conference in Leeds, 6–8 April 1983*. Edited by I. S. Moxon, J. D. Smart, and A. J. Woodman. Cambridge: Cambridge University Press, 1986.

Pelling, Christopher. "Plutarch's Adaptation of His Source-Material." Pages 91–115 in *Plutarch and History: Eighteen Studies*. Swansea: Classical Press of Wales, 2002.

Pelling, Christopher. "Synkrisis in Plutarch's Lives." Pages 83–96 in *Miscelanea Plutarchea*. Edited by Frederick E. Brenk. Ferrara: Giornale filologico ferrarese, 1986.

Pelling, Christopher. "Thucydides' Speeches." Pages 176–90 in *Thucydides*. Edited by Jeffrey S. Rusten. Oxford: Oxford University Press, 2009.

Pelling, Christopher. "Truth and Fiction in Plutarch's Lives." Pages 143–70 in *Plutarch and History: Eighteen Studies*. Swansea: Classical Press of Wales, 2002.

Peppard, Michael. *The Son of God in the Roman World: Divine Sonship in Its Social and Political Context*. New York: Oxford University Press, 2011.

Perowne, Stewart. *The Life and Times of Herod the Great*. London: Hodder and Stoughton, 1957.

Pervo, Richard I. "The Ancient Novel Becomes Christian." Pages 685–718 in *The Novel in the Ancient World*. Edited by Gareth L. Schmeling. MnS 159. Leiden: Brill, 1996.

Pervo, Richard I. "Joseph and Aseneth and the Greek Novel." Pages 171–81 in *1976 SBL Seminar Papers*. Edited by G. W. MacRae. Missoula: Scholars, 1976.

Pervo, Richard I. *Profit With Delight: The Literary Genre of the Acts of the Apostles*. Minneapolis: Fortress, 1987.

Philonenko, Marc. *Joseph et Aséneth: Introduction, texte critique, traduction et notes*. StPb 13. Leiden: Brill, 1968.

Pinheiro, Maralia P. Futre, Judith Perkins, and Richard Pervo, eds. *The Ancient Novel and Early Christian and Jewish Narrative: Fictional Intersections*. ANS 16. Groningen: Barkhuis, 2012.

Pitts, Andrew. "The Genre of the Third Gospel and Greco-Roman Historiography: A Reconsideration." Atlanta, 2015.

Pitts, Andrew. "Greco-Roman Historiography and Luke's Use of Scripture." PhD diss, McMaster Divinity School, 2014.

Poe, Joe Park. "Word and Deed: On 'Stage-Directions' in Greek Tragedy." *Mn.* 56 (2003): 420–48.

Praeder, Susan Marie. "Luke-Acts and the Ancient Novel." Pages 269–92 in *1981 SBL Seminar Papers*. Missoula: Scholars, 1981.

Quast, Kevin. *Peter and the Beloved Disciple: Figures for a Community in Crisis*. JSNTSup 32. Sheffield: JSOT Press, 1989.

Rabinowitz, Nancy Sorkin. *Greek Tragedy*. BICW. Malden: Blackwell, 2008.

du Rand, J. A. "The Characterization of Jesus as Depicted in the Narrative of the Fourth Gospel." *Neot* 19 (1985): 18–36.

Reardon, B. P., ed. *Chariton Aphrodisiensis: de Callirhoe narrationes amatoriae*. BSGRT. Monachii: Saur, 2004.

Reardon, B. P., ed. *Collected Ancient Greek Novels*. 2nd ed. Berkeley: University of California Press, 2008.

Reardon, B. P., ed. *The Form of Greek Romance*. Princeton: Princeton University Press, 1991.

Reardon, B. P. "Theme, Structure, and Narrative in Chariton." Pages 1–27 in *Later Greek Literature*. Edited by John J. Winkler and Gordon Willis Williams. YCS 27. Cambridge: Cambridge University Press, 1982.

Reinhartz, Adele. *Befriending the Beloved Disciple: A Jewish Reading of the Gospel of John*. New York: Continuum, 2001.

Reinhartz, Adele. "Judaism in the Gospel of John." *Int* 63 (2009): 382–93.

Repath, Ian. "Emotional Conflict and Platonic Psychology in the Greek Novel." Pages 53–84 in *Philosophical Presences in the Ancient Novel*. Edited by J. R. Morgan and Meriel Jones. ANS 10. Eelde: Barkhuis, 2007.

Richardson, Peter. *Herod: King of the Jews and Friend of the Romans*. SPNT. Columbia: University of South Carolina Press, 1996.

Riggan, William. *Pícaros, Madmen, Naïfs, and Clowns: The Unreliable First-Person Narrator*. Norman: University of Oklahoma Press, 1981.

Robinson, James McConkey. *The Problem of History in Mark*. SBT 21. London: SCM Press, 1957.

Robinson, T. M. *Plato's Psychology*. Toronto: University of Toronto Press, 1970.

Rogkotis, Zacharias. "Thucydides and Herodotus: Aspects of Their Intertextual Relationship." Pages 57–86 in *Brill's Companion to Thucydides*. Edited by Antonios Rengakos and Antonis Tsakmakis. BCCS. Leiden: Brill, 2006.

Rohde, Erwin. *Der griechische Roman und seine Vorläufer*. 3rd ed. Leipzig: Breitkopf & Härtel, 1914.

Roisman, Hanna M. "The Veiled Hippolytus and Phaedra." *Hermes* 127 (1999): 397–409.

de Romilly, Jacqueline. "Plutarch and Thucydides or the Free Use of Quotations." *Phoenix* 42 (1988): 22–34.

Rood, Tim. "Thucydides and His Predecessors." *Histos* 2 (1998): 230–67.

Rosenmeyer, Thomas G. "Ancient Literary Genres: A Mirage?" *YCGL* 34 (1985): 74–84.

Rowland, Christopher. *The Open Heaven: A Study of Apocalyptic in Judaism and Early Christianity*. New York: Crossroad, 1982.

Royse, James R. "The Works of Philo." Pages 32–64 in *The Cambridge Companion to Philo*. Edited by Adam Kamesar. Cambridge: Cambridge University Press, 2009.

Rozik, Eli. "The Functions of Language in Theatre." *ThResInt* 18 (1993): 104–14.

Ruffatto, Kristine J. "Polemics with Enochic Traditions in the Exagoge of Ezekiel the Tragedian." *JSP* 15 (2006): 195–210.

Ruiz-Montero, C. *La estructura de la novela griega*. Salamanca: Ediciones Universidad de Salamanca, 1988.

Russell, D. A., and Michael Winterbottom, eds. *Classical Literary Criticism*. Rev. ed. OWC. Oxford: Oxford University Press, 1998.

Russell, D. A. *Plutarch*. 2nd ed. Bristol: Bristol Classical, 2001.

Ryan, Marie-Laure. "Fiction, Non-Factuals, and the Principle of Minimal Departure." *Poetics* 9 (1980): 403–22.

Ryan, Marie-Laure. *Possible Worlds, Artificial Intelligence, and Narrative Theory*. Bloomington: Indiana University Press, 1991.

Sacks, Kenneth. *Polybius on the Writing of History*. UCPCS 24. Berkeley: University of California Press, 1981.

Sanders, Jack T. *Ethics in the New Testament: Change and Development*. Philadelphia: Fortress, 1975.

Sandmel, Samuel. *Herod: Profile of a Tyrant*. Philadelphia: Lippincott, 1967.

Sansone, David. *Greek Drama and the Invention of Rhetoric*. Chichester: Wiley Blackwell, 2012.

Schadewaldt, Wolfgang. *Monolog und Selbstgespräch; Untersuchungen zur Formgeschichte der griechischen Tragödie*. NPU 2. Berlin: Weidmann, 1926.

Schalit, Abraham. *König Herodes: der Mann und sein Werk*. 2nd ed. SJ 4. Berlin: De Gruyter, 2001.

Schenkeveld, Dirk M. "The Lexicon of the Narrator and His Characters: Some Aspects of Syntax and Choice of Words in Chariton's Chaereas and Callirhoe." *GCNov* 4 (1993): 17–30.

Schettino, Maria Teresa. "The Use of Historical Sources." Pages 417–36 in *A Companion to Plutarch*. Edited by Mark Beck, Translated by Pia Bertucci. BCAW. Oxford: Blackwell, 2014.

Schmeling, Gareth L., ed. *The Novel in the Ancient World*. MnS 159. Leiden: Brill, 1996.

Schmid, Wilhelm. "Chariton." Pages 2168–71 in *PRE*. Neue bearbeitung. III 2. Stuttgart: J. B. Metzler, 1899.

Schorn, Stefan. *Satyros aus Kallatis: Sammlung der Fragmente mit Kommentar*. Basel: Schwabe, 2004.

Schrage, Wolfgang. *The Ethics of the New Testament*. Translated by David Edward Green. Philadelphia: Fortress, 1988.

Schürer, Emil. *The History of the Jewish People in the Age of Jesus Christ (175 BC–AD 135)*. Edited by Géza Vermès, Fergus Millar, Matthew Black, and Martin Goodman. Vol. 3.1. 3 vols. Edinburgh: T. & T. Clark, 1986.

Schwartz, Daniel R. "On Abraham Schalit, Herod, Josephus, the Holocaust, Horst R. Moehring, and the Study of Ancient Jewish History." *JH* 2 (1987): 9–28.

Schwartz, Daniel R. "Philo: His Family and His Times." Pages 9–31 in *The Cambridge Companion to Philo*. Edited by Adam Kamesar. Cambridge: Cambridge University Press, 2009.

Scourfield, J. H. D. "Anger and Gender in Chariton's *Chaereas and Callirhoe*." *Ancient Anger: Perspectives from Homer to Galen*. Edited by Susanna Braund and Glenn W. Most. YCS 32. Cambridge: Cambridge University Press, 2004.

Shapiro, Susan O. "Herodotus and Solon." *ClA* 15 (1996): 348–64.

Shuler, Philip L. *A Genre for the Gospels: The Biographical Character of Matthew*. Philadelphia: Fortress, 1982.

Shutt, R. J. H. *Studies in Josephus*. London: SPCK, 1961.

Sievers, Joseph. "Herod, Josephus, and Laqueur: A Reconsideration." Pages 83–112 in *Herod and Augustus: Papers Presented at the IJS Conference, 21st–23rd June 2005*. Edited by David M. Jacobson and Nikos Kokkinos. Leiden: Brill, 2009.

Sinding, Michael. "After Definitions: Genre, Categories, and Cognitive Science." *Genre* 35 (2002): 181–219.

Skinner, Christopher W., ed. *Characters and Characterization in the Gospel of John*. LNTS 461. London: Bloomsbury, 2013.

Smith, Christopher, and Liv Mariah Yarrow, eds. *Imperialism, Cultural Politics, and Polybius*. Oxford: Oxford University Press, 2012.

Smith, D. Moody. "Ethics and the Interpretation of the Fourth Gospel." Pages 109–22 in *Word, Theology, and Community in John*. Edited by John Painter, R. Alan Culpepper, and Fernando F. Segovia. St. Louis: Chalice Press, 2002.

Smith, D. Moody. *Johannine Christianity: Essays on Its Setting, Sources, and Theology*. Edinburgh: T. & T. Clark, 2006.

Smith, James K. A. "Staging the Incarnation: Revisioning Augustine's Critique of Theatre." *LitTh* 15 (2001): 123–39.

Smith, Justin Marc. *Why Bíos?: On the Relationship between Gospel Genre and Implied Audience*. LNTS 518. London: Bloomsbury, 2015.

BIBLIOGRAPHY

Smith, Tyler. "Characterization in John 4 and the Prototypical Type-Scene as a Generic Concept." Pages 233–47 in *The Gospel of John as Genre Mosaic*. Edited by Kasper Bro Larsen. SANt 3. Göttingen: Vandehoeck & Rupprecht, 2015.

Sommerstein, Alan H. *Greek Drama and Dramatists*. New York: Routledge, 2002.

Sommerstein, Alan H., and Catherine Atherton, eds. *Education in Greek Fiction*. NCLS 4. Bari: Levante, 1997.

Sommerstein, Alan H., and Isabelle C. Torrance. "The Tongue and the Mind: Responses to Euripides, Hippolytus 612." Pages 289–94 in *Oaths and Swearing in Ancient Greece*. BzAlt 307. Berlin: de Gruyter, 2014.

Sparks, H. F. D., ed. *The Apocryphal Old Testament*. Oxford: Clarendon, 1985.

Stadter, Philip A. *A Commentary on Plutarch's Pericles*. Chapel Hill: University of North Carolina Press, 1989.

Stadter, Philip A. "Introduction." Pages viii–xxvi in *Plutarch: Greek Lives*. OWC. Oxford: Oxford University Press, 1998.

Stadter, Philip A. "Plutarch and Rome." Pages 13–31 in *A Companion to Plutarch*. Edited by Mark Beck. BCAW. Oxford: Blackwell, 2014.

Stadter, Philip A. "Thucydides as 'Reader' of Herodotus." Pages 39–66 in *Thucydides and Herodotus*. Edited by Edith Foster and Donald Lateiner. Oxford: Oxford University Press, 2012.

Stadter, Philip A., and L. Van der Stockt, eds. *Sage and Emperor: Plutarch, Greek Intellectuals, and Roman Power in the Time of Trajan (98–117 AD)*. SyFLL A29. Leuven: Leuven University Press, 2002.

Stanton, Graham. *Jesus of Nazareth in New Testament Preaching*. SNTSMS 27. London: Cambridge University Press, 1974.

Stark, Isolde. "Zur Erzählperspektive im griechischen Liebesroman." *Ph.* 128 (1984): 256–270.

Stephens, Susan A. "'Popularity' of the Ancient Novel." *The Ancient Novel: Classical Paradigms and Modern Perspectives*. Edited by James Tatum and Gail M. Vernazza. Hanover: Dartmouth College, 1990.

Stephens, Susan A. "Who Read the Ancient Novels?" Pages 405–18 in *The Search for the Ancient Novel*. Edited by James Tatum. Baltimore: Johns Hopkins University Press, 1994.

Stephens, Susan A., and John J. Winkler, eds. *Ancient Greek Novels: The Fragments: Introduction, Text, Translation, and Commentary*. Princeton: Princeton University Press, 1995.

Sterling, Gregory E. *Historiography and Self-Definition: Josephos, Luke-Acts, and Apologetic Historiography*. NovTSup 64. Leiden: Brill, 1992.

Sterling, Gregory E. "'Prolific in Expression and Broad in Thought': International References to Philo's Allegorical Commentary and Exposition of the Law." *ERFC* 40 (2012): 55–76.

Sterling, Gregory E. "The Jewish Appropriation of Hellenistic Historiography." Pages 231–43 in *Greek and Roman Historiography*. Edited by John Marincola. ORCS. Oxford: Oxford University Press, 2011.

Stibbe, Mark W. G., ed. *John as Storyteller: Narrative Criticism and the Fourth Gospel*. Cambridge: Cambridge University Press, 1992.

Stibbe, Mark W. G., ed. *John's Gospel*. NTRea. London: Routledge, 1994.

Storey, Ian Christopher, and Arlene Allan. *A Guide to Ancient Greek Drama*. 2nd ed. BGCL. Chichester: Wiley Blackwell, 2014.

Stovell, Beth M. *Mapping Metaphorical Discourse in the Fourth Gospel: John's Eternal King*. LingBS 5. Leiden: Brill, 2012.

Strachan, R. H. *The Fourth Evangelist: Dramatist or Historian?* New York: George H. Doran Co., 1925.

Swain, Simon. *Hellenism and Empire: Language, Classicism, and Power in the Greek World, AD 50–250*. Oxford: Clarendon, 1996.

Swales, John M. *Genre Analysis: English in Academic and Research Settings*. Cambridge: Cambridge University Press, 1990.

Talbert, Charles H. *What Is a Gospel?: The Genre of the Canonical Gospels*. Philadelphia: Fortress, 1977.

Tam, Josaphat Chi-Chiu. *Apprehension of Jesus in the Gospel of John*. WUNT 2/399. Tübingen: Mohr Siebeck, 2015.

Teets, Sarah Christine. "ΧΑΡΙΖΟΜΕΝΟΣ ΗΡΩΔΗΙ: Josephus' Nicolaus of Damascus in the Judaean Antiquities." *Histos* 7 (2013): 88–127.

Temmerman, Koen de. *Crafting Characters: Heroes and Heroines in the Ancient Greek Novel*. Oxford: Oxford University Press, 2014.

Termini, Christina. "Philo's Thought within the Context of Middle Judaism." Pages 95–123 in *The Cambridge Companion to Philo*. Edited by Adam Kamesar. Cambridge: Cambridge University Press, 2009.

Thackeray, H. St. J. *Josephus, the Man and the Historian*. New York: Ktav, 1968.

Thatcher, Tom. *Why John Wrote a Gospel: Jesus, Memory, History*. Louisville: Westminster John Knox, 2006.

Thompson, Marianne Meye. *The Humanity of Jesus in the Fourth Gospel*. Philadelphia: Fortress, 1988.

Thompson, Marianne Meye. "The 'Spiritual Gospel': How John the Theologian Writes History." Pages 103–7 in *John, Jesus, and History*. Edited by Paul N. Anderson, Felix Just, S.J., and Tom Thatcher. ECL 2. Atlanta: SBL, 2009.

Thornton, John. "Oratory in Polybius' Histories." Pages 21–42 in *Hellenistic Oratory: Continuity and Change*. Edited by Christos Kremmydas and Kathryn Tempest. Oxford: Oxford University Press, 2013.

Toher, Mark. "Nicolaus and Herod in the 'Antiquitates Judaicae.'" *HSCP* 101 (2003): 427–47.

Tolbert, Mary Ann. *Sowing the Gospel: Mark's World in Literary-Historical Perspective*. Minneapolis: Fortress, 1989.

Tsakmakis, Antonis. "Leaders, Crowds, and the Power of the Image: Political Communication in Thucydides." Pages 161–87 in *Brill's Companion to Thucydides*. Edited by Antonios Rengakos and Antonis Tsakmakis. BCCS. Leiden: Brill, 2006.

Van der Stockt, Luc. "Plutarch in Plutarch: The Problem of the Hypomnemata." Pages 331–40 in *La biblioteca di Plutarco : atti del IX Convegno plutarcheo, Pavia, 13–15 giugno 2002*. Edited by Italo Gallo. Collectanea 23. Napoli: M. D'Auria, 2004.

Van der Stockt, Luc. "A Plutarchan Hypomnema on Self-Love." *AJP* 120 (1999): 575–99.

Van Seters, John. *In Search of History: Historiography in the Ancient World and the Origins of Biblical History*. Winona Lake: Eisenbrauns, 1997.

Vanhoozer, Kevin J. *Faith Speaking Understanding: Performing the Drama of Doctrine*. Westminster John Knox Press, 2014.

Vermes, Géza. *The True Herod*. London: Bloomsbury, 2014.

Veyne, Paul. *Did the Greeks Believe in Their Myths?: An Essay on the Constitutive Imagination*. Translated by Paula Wissing. Chicago: University of Chicago Press, 1988.

Vines, Michael E. *The Problem of Markan Genre: The Gospel of Mark and the Jewish Novel*. AcBib 3. Leiden: Brill, 2002.

Von Wahlde, Urban C. "The Jews in the Gospel of John: Fifteen Years of Research (1983–1998)." *ETL* 76 (2000): 30–55.

Von Wahlde, Urban C. "The Johannine 'Jews': A Critical Survey." *NTS* 28 (1982): 33–60.

Votaw, Clyde Weber. "The Gospels and Contemporary Biographies." *AmJT* 19 (1915): 45–73.

Votaw, Clyde Weber. "The Gospels and Contemporary Biographies: Concluded." *AmJT* 19 (1915): 217–49.

Votaw, Clyde Weber. *The Gospels and Contemporary Biographies in the Greco-Roman World*. Philadelphia: Fortress, 1970.

Wagner, Ellen, ed. *Essays on Plato's Psychology*. New York: Lexington Books, 2001.

Walbank, F. W. *A Historical Commentary on Polybius*. Vol. 1. 3 vols. Oxford: Clarendon, 1957.

Walbank, F. W. "History and Tragedy." *Hist.* 9 (1960): 216–34.

Walbank, F. W. *Polybius*. SCLec 42. Berkeley: University of California Press, 1972.

Walbank, F. W. "Polybius' Perception of the One and the Many." Pages 212–30 in *Polybius, Rome, and the Hellenistic World: Essays and Reflections*. Cambridge: Cambridge University Press, 2002.

Walbank, F. W. "Profit or Amusement: Some Thoughts on the Motives of Hellenistic Historians." Pages 231–41 in *Polybius, Rome, and the Hellenistic World: Essays and Reflections*. Cambridge: Cambridge University Press, 2002.

Warren, Meredith J. C. *My Flesh Is Meat Indeed: A Nonsacramental Reading of John 6:51–58*. Minneapolis: Fortress, 2015.

Waterfield, Robin. *Euripides: Orestes and Other Plays*. OWC. Oxford: Oxford University Press, 2001.

Waterfield, Robin. *Plutarch: Greek Lives*. OWC. Oxford: Oxford University Press, 1998.

van der Watt, J. G. "The Gospel of John's Perception of Ethical Behaviour." *Skriflig* 45 (2011): 431–447.

van der Watt, J. G., and Ruben Zimmermann, eds. *Rethinking the Ethics of John: "Implicit Ethics" in the Johannine Writings*. WUNT 291. Tübingen: Mohr Siebeck, 2012.

van der Watt, Jan G. "Ethics through the Power of Language: Some Explorations in the Gospel according to John." Pages 139–67 in *Moral Language in the New Testament: The Interrelatedness of Language and Ethics in Early Christian Writings*. Edited by Ruben Zimmermann, J. G. van der Watt, and Susanne Luther. WUNT 2/296. Tübingen: Mohr Siebeck, 2010.

Wehrli, Fritz. *Die Schule des Aristoteles: Aristoxenus*. Vol. 2. 10 vols. 2nd ed. Basel: Schwabe, 1967.

Wellek, René, and Austin Warren. *Theory of Literature*. 3rd ed. Harmondsworth: Penguin, Pelican, 1982.

West, S. "Joseph and Asenath: A Neglected Greek Romance." *ClQ* 24 (1974): 70–81.

Westermann, Claus. *Gospel of John in the Light of the Old Testament*. Translated by Siegfried S. Schatzmann. Peabody: Hendrickson, 1998.

Whitmarsh, Tim. "Introduction." Pages 1–14 in *The Cambridge Companion to the Greek and Roman Novel*. Edited by Tim Whitmarsh. Cambridge: Cambridge University Press, 2008.

Whitmarsh, Tim. *Narrative and Identity in the Ancient Greek Novel: Returning Romance*. GCRW. Cambridge: Cambridge University Press, 2011.

Wieneke, Joseph. "Ezechielis Iudaei poetae Alexandrini fabulae quae inscribitur Exagoge : fragmenta." Diss, Münster: Monasterii Westfalorum, Aschendorff, 1931.

Wills, Lawrence M., ed. *Ancient Jewish Novels: An Anthology*. Oxford: Oxford University Press, 2002.

Wills, Lawrence M., *The Jewish Novel in the Ancient World*. MyPo. Eugene: Wipf and Stock, 2015.

Wills, Lawrence M., *The Quest of the Historical Gospel: Mark, John, and the Origins of the Gospel Genre*. London: Routledge, 1997.

Winston, David. "Sage and Super-Sage in Philo of Alexandria." Pages 815–24 in *Pomegranates and Golden Bells: Studies in Biblical, Jewish and Near Easter Ritual, Law and Literature in Honor of Jacob Milgrom*. Edited by D. P. Wright, D. N. Freedman, and A. Hurvitz. Winona Lake: Eisenbrauns, 1995.

Woodhead, A. G. "Thucydides' Portrait of Cleon." *Mn.* 13 (1960): 289–317.

BIBLIOGRAPHY

Wright, Benjamin G. "Joining the Club: A Suggestion about Genre in Early Jewish Texts." *DSD* 17 (2010): 289–314.

Wycherley, R. E. "Aristophanes and Euripides." *GR* 15 (1946): 98–107.

Yarbro Collins, Adela. "Genre and the Gospels." *JR* 75 (1995): 239–46.

Yarbro Collins, Adela. *Mark: A Commentary.* Hermeneia. Minneapolis: Fortress, 2007.

Yarbro Collins, Adela. "Mark and His Readers: The Son of God among Greeks and Romans." *HTR* 93 (2000): 85–100.

Ziegler, Konrat. "Polybios." *PW*, 1952.

Zunshine, Lisa. *Strange Concepts and the Stories They Make Possible: Cognition, Culture, Narrative.* Baltimore: Johns Hopkins University Press, 2008.

Zunshine, Lisa. "Theory of Mind and Experimental Representations of Fictional Consciousness." *Narrative* 11 (2003): 270–91.

Zunshine, Lisa. *Why We Read Fiction: Theory of Mind and the Novel.* TIN. Columbus: Ohio State University Press, 2006.

Index of Ancient Texts

1. Hebrew Bible / Old Testament / LXX

Genesis

37–50	154
41.46	154
41.50–52	154
46.20	154
24.3–4	157
24.37–38	157
27.46–28.1	157

Exodus 57, 62

1	200
1–14	57
1–15	198
1.15	57
2.3–5	198
2.4	199
2.9–10	205
2.11–12	200
2.11–15	109, 200
2.14	59
2.15–22	112
3.6	59, 108, 109
3.11	108
3.13	108, 109
4.1	109
4.3	59
4.10	59
4.14	109
4.14–16	59
7.8–13	110
7–12	54
10.29	57
11.8	60
11.10	57
12.36	109
12.37	57
12.43–9	198
14.4	60
14.5–15.21	198
14.28	201
15.7	60
16.2–3	58
16.20	60

20.21	111
32.10–12	60
32.19	60

Leviticus

10.16	60
24.10–12	113

Numbers

11.1	60
11.10	60
11.33	60
14.34	60
16.15	60
16.22	60
25.4	60
31.14	60
32.14	60

Deuteronomy

1.37	60
4.21	60
6.15	60
9.8	60
9.10–20	60
11.17	60
13.18	60
29.19	60
29.22–23 LXX	60
29.27 LXX	60
32.19	60
33.10	60

Daniel

11.27	216

2 Maccabees

2.24	32

Tobit

4.12–13	157

2. New Testament

Matthew

5.43–44	220
8.21	141

INDEX OF ANCIENT TEXTS

Mark

3.31–35	223
10.29	223
7.11–12	223
10.19	223

Luke

2.48	223
9.59	141
4.29	216
6.32–36	220
14.26	223

John

1–6	239
1.1	236, 239
1.1–18	172
1.2	239
1.4	239
1.5	235, 239, 240
1.6	209, 239
1.8–9	240
1.9–13	210
1.9	239
1.10	239
1.11–12	239
1.11	239, 240
1.12	239
1.13	239
1.14	235, 236, 239
1.15	239
1.17–18	210
1.17	239
1.18	228, 235, 239, 241
1.19–21	176
1.29–34	246
1.35–42	228
1.37	241
1.38	242
1.39	241
1.40	241
1.43–51	228
1.47	241
1.49	209
2.1–11	210
2.1–5	228
2.6–8	228
2.6	223

2.11	241
2.14–22	209
2.17	241
2.22	241
2.23–25	217, 243
2.23	241
2.24–25	241
3	210, 243, 246
3.2	218, 240, 243
3.3–10	244
3.10	243, 244
3.11–12	244
3.11	244
3.16	237
3.19	231, 235
3.27–30	244
3.29	230, 232
3.31–36	176
3.35	231
4	243
4.1–3	209
4.1	241
4.10	246
4.15	247
4.19	246, 247
4.22	246
4.23	242
4.27	241, 242
4.29	235
4.31	246
4.34	211
4.41	241
4.45	241
4.46–54	210
4.47	241
4.50	241
4.53	241
5.1–15	210
5.6	241
5.7	218
5.9–16	223
5.17	211
5.18	242
5.19	211
5.20	211, 231
5.21	211
5.22	211

INDEX OF ANCIENT TEXTS

John (cont.)

5.23	211
5.25–26	211
5.27	211
5.30	211, 212
5.39	246
5.41	236
5.42	246
5.45–46	246
6.1–15	210
6.2	241
6.14	241
6.15	209, 241
6.16–21	210
6.17	240
6.19	241
6.22	241
6.24	241
6.26	246
6.34	247
6.35	244
6.37–40	212, 215
6.38	213
6.41	211
6.42	246
6.51–58	119
6.52	211, 245
6.60–64	245
6.60	241
6.61	241
6.64	217, 241
6.68	247
6.69	246
7–12	239
7–8	217
7	216
7.5	241
7.15	241
7.19	216
7.20	217
7.23	223
7.28–29	246
7.30–31	245
7.31	241
7.32	216, 241
7.40–44	245
7.40	241
7.43–44	216

7.50–52	246
7.50–51	237
7.51	235
8.9	241
8.12	235
8.14	246
8.19	246
8.21	235
8.27	241
8.30	241
8.34	235
8.37	216
8.40	216, 236
8.43–47	246
8.44	215
8.48	217
8.50	176
8.55	246
8.59	216
9.1–41	210
9.1	241
9.2	217
9.3	217
9.4	211
9.8	241
9.11	235
9.14–16	223
9.16	218, 235
9.18	241
9.22	236, 241
9.24	218, 235
9.25	218
9.27b–28	218
9.31	218, 222
9.34	235
9.35	241
9.39–41	234
9.40	241
9.41	235
9.45–54	210
10.1–16	233
10.6	241
10.17–18	211
10.17	231
10.19–21	245
10.33	236
10.39	216
10.42	241

INDEX OF ANCIENT TEXTS

11.1–57	210
11.3	231
11.4	241
11.5	231
11.6	241
11.11	230
11.20	241
11.21	247
11.22	213, 246, 247
11.24	247
11.27	246, 247
11.29	241
11.31	241, 242
11.32	241
11.33	241, 242
11.35	242
11.36	231
11.39–44	213
11.39	247
11.41b–42	245
11.43–44	211
11.45	241
11.47	209
11.47–50	235
11.49–50	247
11.50	218, 235
12.9–19	209
12.9	241
12.12	241
12.13–15	209
12.16	241
12.18	241
12.25	231
12.27	212
12.29	241
12.35	235, 240
12.37	241
12.42	236, 241
12.43	231
12.46	240
13–17	239
13.1	231, 241
13.3–4	241
13.6	247
13.13–15	224
13.21	241, 244
13.23	225, 231
13.26	244
13.27	244

13.28	241
13.29	244
13.30	240
13.34	224, 232
13.36	214
14.13	214
14.15–31	232
14.21	232
14.26	209
14.30–31	176
14.31	176
15.7	213
15.9–10	232
15.12	232
15.13	224, 232
15.14	230
15.17	232
15.19	231
15.22	235
15.26	209
16.2	236
16.7	209
16.8–9	235
16.19	217, 241
16.23–24	213, 215
16.27	231
17	213, 245
17.4	211
17.5	213, 215, 236
17.23	232
17.24	215, 232
17.26	232
18–19	173
18.4	241
18.5	216
18.10–11	247
18.17–27	247
18.17	236
18.30	229
18.31	229
18.33–19.22	209
18.38–39	229
19	223
19.1–6	229
19.6	241
19.7	229
19.8	229, 241
19.12	216, 229, 230

INDEX OF ANCIENT TEXTS

John (cont.)

19.13	241
19.25	173
19.26	225, 231, 241
19.26–27	223, 225–26
19.28	241
19.31	223
19.33	241
19.38	237
19.38–40	237
19.39	240, 246
20.1	240
20.2	231
20.6–10	247
20.6	241
20.8	241
20.11	242
20.12	241
20.13	242
20.14	241, 242
20.15–16	248
20.15	242, 243
20.16	248
20.20	225, 241
20.24–29	234, 248
20.28	246
20.31	169, 213, 237
21	213
21.3	240
21.7	225, 231, 241
21.15–17	231, 233
21.18–19	225
21.18	213
21.19	214
21.20	225
21.21	241
21.24	225, 235
21.25	248

Acts of the Apostles	116
17.28	179
26.14	179

1 Corinthians

15.33	179

Galatians

1.4	216

2 Thessalonians

2.8–12	216

Titus

1.12–13	150
1.12	179

1 John

4.8	220

3. Other Ancient Jewish and Christian Sources

1 Clement

37.4	179

1 Enoch

100.5	216

1QM

XIII, 14–18	216

4 Ezra

6.27–28	216

Acts of Peter

35–40	214

Artapanus	28, 32
(apud Eusebius, *Praep. ev.* 9.27.18)	
	200

Aseneth

1.1	155
1.3–6	158
1.3	158
1.6–7	163
1.7–9	158
2.1	158
3.3	163, 164
3.5	164
4.1	163, 164
4.2	164
4.7	158
4.8	164
4.9	163, 164
4.10	163
6.1–2	159
6.1	158, 162, 164, 228

INDEX OF ANCIENT TEXTS

6.3–4	160	23.7	158
7.2	157	23.9–10	164
7.3	163	23.9	165
7.8	159, 163	23.10	165
7.15	163	24.1	164
8.8	163, 164	24.7–8	162
9.1	164	24.11	164
10.1	164	24.19	164
10.4	232	25.6	161
10.6–7	162	26.8	164
10.8	162	27.11–28.1	162
10.13	159	28.7	164
11.2	159	28.15	161
11.3	159	28.16–17	237
11.10	164	28.17	164
11.15	159		
11.17–19	159	**Augustine**	167, 179
12.1–13.15	159		
12.5	158	**Clement of Alexandria**	
13.13	162	*Stromata*	
14.3–17.10	160	1.25.155	196
14.10	164	(apud Eusebius, *Hist. eccl.* 6.14.5–6)	
15.11	163		30, 186
16.2	164		
16.9	159	**Demetrius**	28, 32
16.11	159		
16.12	159, 160	**Eupolemus**	28, 32
16.14	159, 160		
17.9	161	**Eusebius**	40, 195–96
17.10	159	*Ecclesiastical History*	
18.1	159	2.25	214
18.3	164	6.14	30
18.4	162		
18.7	162	*Preparation for the Gospel*	
18.9–10	163	9.27	200
18.10	163, 164	9.28	196
18.11	163, 164	9.436	166, 196
19.1–11	161	29.4–16	196
19.4	163, 164		
19.5–7	160	**Ezekiel the Tragedian**	
19.10	161	*Exagoge*	
20.7	162, 163, 164	7–8	203
21.2	164	16	198
21.4	163, 164	18	199
22.7	164	21–22	203
22.8	164	32–35	205
22.13	158	36–39	205
23.7–8	159	42–45	200
		47	205

INDEX OF ANCIENT TEXTS

Exagoge (cont.)

50	205
51–53	205
54	205
55–56	205
58	197
66–67	197, 206
68–89	204
68–82	200
90–95	203
99	204
102	204
149–51	206
156–60	198
193–242	198, 201
202–4	201
205–13	201–2
214–19	202
220	202
222	202
224–31	202
232–36	202
238–41	202
241–42	202
243–69	197
243–48	202

Flavius Josephus
Against Apion

1.54	55
2.181	224

Jewish Antiquities

1–12	55
1.1	54
1.5	55
1.8	54
1.13	54
1.14–15	55
1.15	54
1.16	54
1.18–24	54
2–4	58, 61
2.205–7	200
2.205	56
2.206	57
2.219	60
2.239	60
2.240	58

2.267	60
2.268	59
2.270	59
2.274	59
2.275	59
2.2776	59
2.293	54, 60
2.294–313	54
2.296	61
2.310	60, 61
2.321	58
2.322	61
2.323	61
2.324	58
2.327	61
2.333	61
2.334	58
2.336	60
2.342	59, 61
2.348	61
3.11	58
3.12	60
3.13–14	60
3.21	60
3.33–38	60
3.33	60
3.45	58
3.98	58
3.150	61
3.306	58
3.310	60
3.315–16	60
3.321	60
4.9	60
4.63	60
4.89	58
4.141–44	60
4.167	58
4.168	61
4.169	60
4.317	61
4.326–31	56
4.326	60
13–17	55
14–17	62, 65
14.8	65
14.9	65
14.22	65

INDEX OF ANCIENT TEXTS

14.25	65
14.28	66
14.156–17.200	64
14.165–67	68
14.172–75	68
15.127–147	68
15.194	68
15.211–12	115
15.271	68
15.303	68
15.305–16	62
15.328	68
15.330	68
15.382–387	68
16.7	66
16.31–57	68
16.66	66
16.71	67
16.73	67
16.75	67
16.76	67
16.78	67
16.84	67
16.90–99	68
16.105–20	68
16.209–16	68
16.339–50	68
16.375–76	68
16.379–83	68
17.96–120	68
18.259–60	102

Jewish War

1.1–2	58
1.3	32
1.201–673	64
1.373–79	68
1.429–30	62
1.630–6	68
5.184–237	68

Gregory of Nyssa
De vita Moysis 105

Jubilees

20.4	157
22.20	157
30.7–16	157
46	200

Philo of Alexandria
On Rewards and Punishments

52–54	107
53	104, 107, 113

On the Life of Abraham

1.2	105

On the Life of Joseph

1.1	104–5

On the Life of Moses

1.1	77
1.2	108
1.3	108
1.10	110
1.13–14	110
1.20	108
1.24	108
1.25	108
1.26	111
1.27	108
1.28–30	109
1.34–39	109
1.36	109
1.40	112
1.43–44	200
1.44	109
1.51–57	112
1.51	112
1.74	108
1.77	112
1.83	109
1.84	109
1.88	109
1.141	109
1.142	109
1.146	112
1.160–1	113
1.301–3	114
2.2	106
2.25–44	106
2.28	108
2.45–57	106
2.66	113
2.142	113
2.161	113
2.170	113
2.196	114
2.260	113

288 INDEX OF ANCIENT TEXTS

On the Virtues

52	104, 107

Ps.Philo
Liber antiquitatum biblicarum — 32

Tertullian — 167, 179

4. Greek and Roman Sources

Achilles Tatius

Leucippe and Clitophon	119, 126, 134, 145, 234
1.4	132
1.6	132
2.29	126, 132
3.5	150
3.11	132
3.15	149
5.7–18	149
5.7	149
5.11	142
5.17–18	142
5.13	132
5.27	142
6.6–7	132
6.19	132
7.4	132, 149

Aelius Theon

Progymnasmata	25
6	25
16	28
60	24, 25
115	25
116	25, 140

Aeschylus

Agamemnon	185, 197

Choephori	
523–50	204

Eumenides — 197

Persae	197
181–210	204

Alexander Polyhistor
Peri Ioudaiōn

apud Eusebius, *Praep. ev.* 9.28	196
apud Eusebius, *Praep. ev.* 9.436d	166
apud Eusebius, *Praep. ev.* 29.4–16	196

Appian of Alexandria

Roman History	53

Aristophanes — 187
Frogs	
1471	189

Aristotle

Poetics	
1447b–1448a	22
1448a	22
1448b	22
1449a	17
1449b	17
1450a–1450b	16
1450b	16, 18, 19, 21
1450b–1451a	178
1453b	18
1455a	16, 23
1456a	18, 24
1456b–1459a	24
1459b	21
1460b	186
1461a	17

Rhetoric	20–21
1378a	129
1379a–1380a	129
1379a	129
1403a	18
1404b	23
1408a–b	24
1410b35–36	15
1416a	189

Nicomachean Ethics	127–28
1105b	128

Arrian

Anabasis	52, 53, 93

INDEX OF ANCIENT TEXTS

Epicteti dissertationes	107	1.8.1–4	145
		1.8.3–4	159
Artapanus	28, 32	1.11.2	138
apud Eusebius,		1.14.1	137
Praep. ev. 9.27.18	200	1.14.6–10	145
		2.2.3–4	136
Caesar		2.3.6	137, 150, 160, 228
Bellum gallicum	53	2.4.1	131, 138
		2.4.4	131
Cassius Dio		2.4.5	137
Roman History	53	2.5.7	138
		2.5.8–9	138
Chariton		2.5.11	182
Callirhoe		2.6.2	138
1.1.1	131, 133, 136	2.6.4	137
1.1.2	137, 139	2.6.5	139
1.1.3	137, 146	2.7.4	132
1.1.4	137, 139	2.8.1	139
1.1.6	146	2.9.2	143
1.1.7–9	132	2.10.7	150, 152, 229
1.1.7	131, 146, 159, 228	2.11.1	143
1.1.8	146, 151	2.11.4	143
1.1.9	151	3.2.6	138, 140
1.1.11–12	151	3.2.15	137
1.1.13–15	162	3.3.1	150
1.1.14	138, 146	3.3.6	137
1.1.15–16	147	3.3.11	150
1.1.15	147	3.3.16	140
1.1.16	137, 151	3.3.17–18	150
1.2.1–6	144	3.4.1	129
1.2.6	151, 152	3.4.7–14	148
1.4.11–12	152	3.4.13	140
1.3.2	152	3.4.14	182
1.5.1	147, 149	3.5.5–6	141
1.5.2	150	3.5.5	141
1.7.1–3	142	3.6.5	152
1.8.1–4	145	3.8.1	152
1.8.1	151	3.9.1	145
1.8.3–4	147, 159	3.9.2	146
1.9.4	149	3.9.3	140–1
1.9.6	139	3.9.4	137, 141
1.10.1–8	142, 144	3.9.5–3.10.3	150
1.11.2–3	144	3.10.3	130
1.11.6–7	136	4.1.9	228
1.1.15	132	4.2.1–3	232
1.1.16	132	4.5.4–5	140
1.3.6	138, 139	4.4.5	137
1.4.2	136, 140	4.5.9	127
1.4.12–1.5.1	145		

INDEX OF ANCIENT TEXTS

Callirhoe (cont.)

4.5.10	129
4.6.7	131
4.7.5	137
5.2.6	140
5.3.2–9	160
5.9.1	228
5.10.10	150
6.2.2	136
6.2.8–9	232
6.3.5	136, 137
6.3.8	138
6.4.5	137
6.4.7	137
6.4.10	140, 141, 152
6.5.2	136
6.5.7–8	139
6.5.10	140, 149
6.6.8	138
6.6.10	140
6.7.12	152
7.1.7–8	150
7.2.5	140
8.1.3	137
8.1.7–10	148
8.1.4	123
8.1.8	148
8.4.13–14	136
8.5.8	129, 134
8.7.1–8.8.11	134

Cicero
In Verrem

2.64.155	239

De inventione rhetorica	23
De oratore	23

De legibus

1.5	32

Orator ad M. Brutum

204	39

Damascius
Life of Isidore 71

Demetrius
On Style 19, 23

Dio Chrysostom	33
Diodorus Siculus	93

Library of History

9.2.1	95

Dionysius of Halicarnassus,
Roman Antiquities

1.8.2	35
1.8.3	28
5.56.1	35

Euripides

Alcestis	176, 184
Bacchae	173–74, 177, 180, 207
644	203
671–801	181
Children of Hercules	184

Daughters of Troy

36–38	181
39–40	181
42	182
98–152	185
348	185
359–60	185
408	185
759	242
1239	184

Electra	180–81, 184
114–15	179
341–44	203
945–46	192
Helen	199, 244
179	184
31–67	199

Hippolytus

5–10	190
8–11	188
8	190
10–13	191
14–15	188
25–30	190
26–42	188

INDEX OF ANCIENT TEXTS

26–27	188
28	188, 194
38–40	188
38–39	188
43–45	239
43	188, 190
46–50	192
58–113	193
73–74	180
88–120	193, 195
88–105	194
103	193
305–10	190
309–52	193
364–65	187
390–402	193
391	193
433–81	194
450–55	190
473–76	190
517–18	189
520	191
570	189
589–95	191
605–15	192
612	189
633–34	190
640	190
695–701	194
725–30	190
727–30	193
855	190
875–98	195
887–90	195
935–80	190
955–60	191
1003–11	190
1008–10	191
1010–12	191
1013–14	192
1014–24	192
1024–31	192
1032–35	192
1090–91	189
1090	191
1098–101	189
1146	190
1157–1254	201

1164	195
1192–93	190
1251–54	190
1260	194
1286–1341	195
1317–23	190
1331	190
1398	190
1405	190
1406–14	194
1406	194
1413	190
1415	193
1416–21	193
1417	190
Hippolytus Veiled	198–99
Ion	204–5
11–13	183
42–50	183
246	182
1609–13	181
Iphigeneia at Tauris	184, 199, 244
5–6	184
6–56	199
28–30	184
42–62	184
54–55	184
1433–77	204
482–787	192
498	184
Medea	
24–33	181
409–19	185, 186
516–19	17, 182
1004	203
1012	181
1021–80	186
Orestes	180, 184, 203–4
34–37	180
43–45	181
60	181
128–32	185
202–7	181
1573	203

INDEX OF ANCIENT TEXTS

Heliodorus
Aethiopica   134, 135, 144, 145, 149, 156
  2.1   150
  3.3.8   138
  3.6–8   150
  4.6.1   138
  6.9.4   138

Herodotus
Histories   28, 32–38, 42, 51, 52, 75,
              77, 87–88, 92–102
  1.1–2   40
  1.1   34, 37
  1.29   95
  1.30.13–14   97
  1.31   97
  1.32   98–99, 99–199
  1.33   100
  1.34   96
  1.53   96
  1.73–79   96
  2.112–120   33
  2.118   34
  2.119   34
  2.120   35
  8.11.3   38
  8.94   87

Homer   15, 17, 19, 33, 37, 88, 131,
       137, 141, 143, 146, 177–78,
       198–99, 228

Iliad   33
  4   19
  6.62   19–20
  8.164   20
  10.199   11
  14.187   11
  22.82–83   141

Odyssey   33, 119, 177, 191

Horace
Ars poetica   16, 86
  189–90   168

Isocrates   39, 75
Evagoras   78
  1.39   79

  1.44   76
  1.48–49   79
  1.5   79
  1.8   75
  1.66   79

Peace
  8.101   239

Julian
"Letter to a Priest"
  301b–c   122   122

Life of Aesop   77, 117, 118, 119

Livy   40
Ab urbe condita
  21   53

Longus
Daphnis and Chloe   124, 143, 155–56

Lucian   93
How to Write History   38, 77
  8   48
  13   48
  27   44
  34   51
  51   41
  59   39

Nicolaus of Damascus   11, 52, 55, 57,
                 62–63, 65, 68

Philostratus   33, 117

Plato   15–16
Apology   76

Ion   15

Laws
  879e   59

Phaedrus   22
  246a   22

Republic   15, 23, 112
  2.378   16

INDEX OF ANCIENT TEXTS

2.380	16
5.473	106
6	83
10	22
10.599	15

Theaetetus
154b	189

Timaeus 23

Plutarch
Aemilius Paullus
1	74

Alexander 78, 85, 112
1.1–2	80, 81, 82, 222

Aratus 46, 80

Aristides
1	92
10.7–9	91

Artaxerxes 80

Cimon 85, 93
2	85
2.4–5	86
5	80
10.4–5	92
12.5–6	92
13.4–5	92
16.9–10	92

Comp. Aristoph. et Men.
853d	115

Comp. Sol. Publ.
1.1	80

Demosthenes
11.7	80
22	91
31	88

Lycurgus 94
27.3–4	89

Nicias 83
1	80, 88, 89
1.5	83, 84

On Freedom from Anger
456f	99

On the Divine Vengeance
550d	84

On the Malice of Herodotus 39, 87102
855b	87
855e	87
856d	87
858d–f	93
868a	87

Otho 80

Pericles 93
1.4	83, 90
2	84
2.2	83, 90
3.2–4	79
7	59
10.7	91

Philopoemen 79

Phocion
4.2	91

Publicola 80, 102

Solon 71, 77, 92–102, 107, 221–22
1	92
2.3	100
3.2	100
5.2	100
6	115
14.3–6	100
20.1	100
21.3	101
25.5	101
27	85
27.1	94
27.2–3	95
27.3	95, 96
27.4	97
27.5–6	98
27.6–7	99
27.9	100
28.4	93
29.1	101
29.3	101

INDEX OF ANCIENT TEXTS

Sulla

2.1	79

Themistocles — 46

22.2	86
32.3	90
32.4	46

Virtues of Women

243c–d	84
243d	85

Philostratus
Vita Apollonii — 33, 117

Polybius, *Histories*

1.3–4	41
1.4.1–2	41
1.12.6	42
2.14.16	41
2.17.6	41
2.56	45
2.56.6	46
2.56.9	46
2.56.10	46
2.56.11	48
2.56.13	48
2.58.11–12	47
2.58.12	41, 45, 47
2.59.3	41
3.6	68
3.6.1	49
3.6.5	49
3.6.7	49
3.6.12–14	49
3.9.6	50
3.10.3	50
3.10.6	50
3.90	44
5.33.2	41
5.53	43
5.106	51
7.1.1	50
7.1.3	50
7.66.2–3	70
12.25a.5	43
12.25i.5	43
22.18.1–11	50
22.18.6	49

29.12	41
36.1.7	43
38.4.8	42
60.3	43

Porphyry
Life of Plotinus — 106, 107

Ps.Callisthenes
Life of Alexander — 115, 117, 121

Ps.Hecataeus
On the Jews — 32

Ps.Hermogenes
On Forceful Speaking

7.1–2	23

Ps.Longinus — 19

Quintilian
Education of the Orator — 23

Rhetoric for Alexander — 23

Rhetoric for Herennius — 23

Sallust
Bellum catilinae — 53

Bellum jugurthinum — 53

Satyrus of Callatis
Life of Euripides — 28, 167

Secundus the Silent
Philosopher — 77, 118

Sophocles — 179, 186, 197
Antigone — 171

Electra

417–23	204

Oedipus rex — 176, 177

924–1085	18

Trachiniae — 176

Strabo — 33

INDEX OF ANCIENT TEXTS

Theophrastus
Characters 25

Theopompus 39, 45, 58, 92
Philippica 38, 75

Thucydides 28, 32, 33, 35–44, 51, 52, 68, 87–90

History of the Peloponnesian War
1.22 37, 42, 44, 48
1.23 42, 68
1.73 38
1.76 38
1.86 38
1.88 38
1.90 38
1.91 38

2.39 89
3.31 42

Xenophon 38, 42
Agesilaus 74, 75

Cyropaedia 75, 76, 115, 117

Hellenica 38

Memorabilia 28, 75, 78

Xenophon Ephesius
Ephesiaca 117, 122, 136, 141, 157
1.1.4 158
4.2 132
4.2.1–2 149
4.5.1–3 149
4.5.2 149

Index of Modern Authors

Abbott, H. P.   12n31
Africa, T. W.   45n59
Ahearne-Kroll, P. D.   120n21, 154n101, 154n102, 155n108, 156n113, 157n118, 161n128, 163n130
Allan, A.   198n100
Allman, W. F.   12n29
Anderson, G.   143n83
Anderson, J. K.   74n8
Anderson, P. N.   30n5
Arnson Svarlien, D.   186n73
Ashton, J.   209n3, 210n7, 216n20, 221n36
Attridge, H. W.   5n2, 6n7, 32n12, 176n35, 177, 210n8, 211n10, 213n14, 225n46
Auken, S.   5n1, 7n12, 56n89, 208n1

Bain, D.   185n72
Bakhtin, M. M.   118
Bal, M.   12n30, 134–35, 217, 241n71
Baragwanath, E.   33n16, 102n87
Barker, A.   76n15
Barnes, T. D.   167n3, 178n47
Baron, C. A.   43n52
Barrett, J.   201n110
Barthes, R.   10n20
Bauckham, R.   30, 31, 226n51
Becker, E.-M.   31n9, 39n35, 53n81, 73n5
Bennema, C.   13n33, 14n34
Berger, P. L.   8n16
Bernier, J.   236n63
Betz, H. D.   24n68
Bigelow, J.   10n24
Bilezikian, G. G.   168n7
Billault, A.   154n101
Blamire, A.   92
de Boer, Pieter A.   223n41
Boersma, H.   218n26
Bohak, G.   157n116
Booth, Wayne C.   149n94
Borgen, P.   27n77
Bowen, C. R.   169, 171
Bowersock, G. W.   77n18
Bowie, E.   120n22, 121n24, 122n26, 133n57, 146n89
Braginskaya, N.   155n106

Brant, J-A. A.   174–75, 179n48, 198n101, 201n111, 238n66, 242n72, 247n74
Braun, M.   156n109
Bray, H. T.   30n6
Brenk, F. E.   74n8
Brethes, R.   133n58
Brown, R. E.   29, 172, 210n6, 223n40, 231n59
Brown, S.   219n26
Bullard, C. B.   217n23
Bultmann, R.   72, 171, 224
Burchard, C.   154n102, 156n110, 161n128
Burke, S.   10n20
Burridge, R. A.   5n3, 8n13, 72n3, 73–75, 76n14, 79n25, 105, 219–21
Butte, G.   5n4, 12n31
Butts, R. R.   25n70

Calabi, F.   179n49
Cancik, H.   31n9
Carter, W.   230n56
Champion, C. B.   51n76
Chandler, D.   27n78
Charnwood, G. R. B.   169n12
Chesnutt, R. D.   155n103, 157n117, 157n119, 158n121, 159n124
Chew, K. A.   124n30, 132n53, 136n63
Cohen, S. J. D.   211n9
Cohn, D.   48n69
Collins, J. J.   153n99, 196n95, 198n100, 198n101, 225n48
Collins, R.   226
Connick, C. M.   169–71, 241n72, 243
Conway, C. M.   169n10
Conybeare, F. C.   57n91
Cornford, F. M.   36n22
Crane, M. T.   9n18
Cribiore, R.   24n64
Cueva, E. P.   123n28
Culler, J.   8n15, 10, 73n6
Culpepper, R. A.   13–14, 171n16, 173, 177, 238n65
Culy, M. M.   230n58

D'Huys, V.   41n41
Darbo-Peschanski, C.   33n14

INDEX OF MODERN AUTHORS

Davidson, James   46n61
Davidson, John   182n61
Delcor, M.   158n121
Derow, P. S.   42n46
Destinon, J. von   63n107
Dibelius, M.   31n9
Dickey, E.   19n48
Dihle, A.   52n78, 75, 76n13, 78n19
Dillon, J.   99n81, 104n95
Dinkler, M. B.   81n33, 217n23
Docherty, S.   155n103
Dodd, C. H.   29
Dodds, E. R.   181n55
Domeris, W. R.   171–72, 242n72
Doody, M. A.   142n81
Doran, M.   195n91
Dormeyer, D.   75
Dox, D.   167n4
du Rand, J. A.   14n33
Dubrow, H.   73n6
Duff, T.   71n2, 81–82, 221n38
Duke, P. D.   218n25
Dunderberg, I.   225n48

Easterling, P. E.   179n48
Eckstein, A. M.   45n59
Egan, K.   36n22
Ehrman, B. D.   88n50
Elliott, S. S.   116n5
Else, G. F.   22n58
Estes, D.   209n4
Evans, K. G.   103n90

Farrell, J.   6n7, 26, 39n35, 86n46
Fauconnier, F.   12n31
Feldman, L.   52n79, 59n99, 63n108, 108n105, 112, 179n49
Fenn, R. K.   64n110
Fink, U. B.   159n123
Finley, J. H., Jr.   179n49
Flower, M. A.   39n36, 39n38
Fludernik, M.   124n32
Fornara, C. W.   37n27, 38n32
Fortescue, M.   6n5
Fowler, A.   6–7, 73n6
Frickenschmidt, D.   75
Fromentin, V.   36n22
Frye, N.   73n6
Furnish, V. P.   221n37
Fusillo, M.   126n35, 136n63, 158n122

Gallarte, I. M.   92n61, 93n63, 94n65, 100n83
Geiger, J.   78n20
Geljon, A. C.   105–6
Genette, G.   134–35, 189
Gibson, C. A.   24n65
Gill, C.   143n84
Goddard, C.   6n5
Goldhill, S.   131n49, 198n100
Goodenough, E. R.   104n93, 105, 106n102
Goold, G. P.   116n4, 120n23
Gotteland, S.   36n22
Grant, M.   64n109
Graverina, L.   146n89
Grethlein, J.   9n18, 38n30, 44n54, 48n69

Habicht, C.   50
Hadas-Lebel, M.   201n110
Hadavas, C. T.   92n61
Hägerland, T.   168n6
Hägg, T.   71n2, 76n13, 76n15, 117, 123n26, 123n27, 123n28, 124n30, 136n63, 139n72, 141n79, 149n95, 158n122, 233n60
Hakola, R.   211n9
Hamilton, R.   180n54
Hammond, N. G. L.   50n73
Harris, E.   172n20
Harris, W. V.   138n67, 208n2
Hayes, D. A.   169n12
Hays, R. B.   219n26
Heath, M.   131n49
Helmbold, W. C.   88n51
Henten, J. W. van   63n107
Herman, D.   12n31
Hirsch, E. D.   73n6
Hitchcock, F. R. M.   168–69, 171, 173, 177
Hock, R. F.   24n65, 124n30, 144n85
Holzberg, N.   124n30
Houlden, J. L.   219n26
Humphrey, E. M.   159n124
Hylen, S.   13n33

Ingarden, R.   175
Iser, W.   10n21

Jacobson, H.   179n50, 196n94, 196n95, 196n96, 197, 198n100, 198n101, 199–200, 203n113, 204, 205n116, 206n117
Jauss, H. R.   5n1
Jochum, K. P. S.   195n91
Johnson, W. A.   10n23

de Jonge, M. 209n5
Jülicher, A. 169n12

Käsemann, E. 209n5, 211–12
Kasher, A. 64n110
Keener, C. S. 14n34, 30–31, 213n15, 214n17, 216n21, 217n24, 223, 225–26, 234n61, 239n67, 239n69
Kennedy, G. A. 15n35, 20n54, 21n56, 23n60, 24n64, 24n65, 24n66, 25n69, 25n71
Kilpatrick, G. D. 157n119,
Kim, L. Y. 33n15, 37n24
Knobl, R. 187n75
Koester, C. R. 218n26
Kohn, T. D. 196n94
König, J. 132n54, 132n55
Konstan, D. 122n26, 126n35, 126n36, 127n38, 130n46, 131n50, 141n78, 150n96
Kooten, G. H. van 26n77
Kraemer, R. S. 153, 155n103, 155n107, 160n126
Kristeva, J. 8n14

Lacy, P. de 179n49
Lagache, D. 126n36
Landau, T. 63n108, 68n115
Lanfranchi, P. 196n92, 196n95, 200n108, 201n110
Lang, M. L. 37n28, 37n29
Laqueur, R. 63n107
Larsen, K. B. 8n17, 119, 131n50, 161, 177, 227n54, 240
Last, R. 31n9
Lateiner, D. 33n14
Lausberg, H. 24n67, 41n45
Legras, B. 88n50
Leo, F. 76–77
Lincoln, A. T. 27n77, 176
Longley, G. 36n21, 43n50
Lovibond, S. 23n59
Lowe, M. 211n9
Luce, T. J. 33n13

MacAlister, S. 141n78
Macdonald, D. R. 174, 178n46
MacGregor, G. H. C. 169n12
MacRae, G. W. 218n25
Malina, B. J. 81n33
Mañas, M. D. 88n50
Mansfeld, J. 105, 106n102

Marguerat, D. 31n9
Marincola, J. 45n56, 47, 53n81, 58n94
Marrou, H. I. 24n64
Marshak, A. K. 64n109
Martyn, J. L. 167n6, 172–73, 209n4, 216n20, 236n63
Mastronarde, D. J. 181n58, 183n64
Matera, F. J. 219n26
McAlpine, L. 56n89
McCarthy, E. D. 125n33, 125n34
McGing, B. C. 36n21, 40n40, 41n43, 42n48, 44n53
Meeks, W. A. 209n5, 216n21, 218n26, 220n32, 221n36, 225n45
Miller, C. R. 173n23
Miller, W. I. 127n36
Mirhady, D. C. 79n23
Molinié, G. 146n89
Momigliano, A. 7, 52n78, 71n1, 77n16, 78, 79n22, 79n27, 80n28
Montiglio, S. 124n31, 160
Moore, S. D. 11n25
Morales, H. 121n23, 141n80
Morgan, J. R. 115n1, 133n58, 157n114
Morgan, T. 24n64
Mossman, J. M. 179n49
Mroczek, E. 56n88, 155n104
Myers, A. D. 14n33, 25n68

Najman, H. 27n79
Nässelqvist, D. 10n23
Newsom, C. A. 7n12, 27n78, 31n10
Nicholson, G. C. 209n5
Nickelsburg, G. W. E. 52n79, 157n115, 225n48
Nicolai, R. 38n33
Nielsen, J. T. 8n17
Nikiprowetzky, V. 105n97
Nissen, J. 218n26
Norton-Piliavsky, J. 55n86
Nünlist, R. 11n28, 17n41, 20n49, 23n63, 93n64

O'Neil, E. 88n51

Palmer, A. 5, 12n31, 124n32, 250
Paré, A. 56n89
Parsenios, G. 27n77, 170n14, 175–77, 177n43, 179n48, 209n4, 238n65, 239n68

INDEX OF MODERN AUTHORS

Payen, P.   95n68
Pearson, L.   37, 49n71
Pédech, P.   40n39, 41n43, 48n71
Pelling, C.   37n25, 38n32, 78n20, 78n21, 87n47, 89n52, 90n55, 94n67, 97n75, 221n38
Peppard, M.   230n56
Perowne, S.   63n109
Pervo, R.   116n5
Philonenko, M.   155n105
Pitts, A.   31n9, 73n5
Poe, J. P.   180n52
Poremba, A.   10n24
Praeder, S. M.   116n5

Quast, K.   226n53

Rabinowitz, N. S.   198n100
Reardon, B. P.   116n4, 117n6, 122n26, 123n27, 123n29, 124n30, 133n57, 144, 147n90, 159n125
Reinhartz, A.   211n9, 221n36
Repath, I.   120n23
Richardson, P.   64n109
Riggan, W.   149n94
Robinson, J. M.   30n5
Robinson, T. M.   23n59
Rogkotis, Z.   36n23, 37n28
Rohde, E.   120n22, 133n57
Roisman, H. M.   198n102
de Romilly, J.   90n55
Rood, T.   37n23
Rosenmeyer, T. G.   22n58
Rowland, C.   216n19
Royse, J. R.   103n92, 105n98
Rozik, E.   175
Ruffatto, K. J.   200
Ruiz-Montero, C.   136n63
Russell, D. A.   15n36, 16n37, 81n32, 91n58, 94n67
Ryan, M.-L.   13

Sacks, K.   40n39
Sanders, J. T.   219n26
Sandmel, S.   64n109
Schadewaldt, W.   185n70
Schalit, A.   63
Schenkeveld, D. M.   126n35
Schettino, M. T.   94n67

Schmid, W.   133n57
Schmidt, K. L.   72
Schorn, S.   166n1
Schrage, W.   219n26
Schürer, E.   198n100
Schwartz, D. R.   63n108, 63n109, 103n89
Scourfield, J. H. D.   137n67, 139n72
Shapiro, S. O.   97n72
Sherwood, Y.   11n25
Shuler, P. L.   72n3
Shutt, R. J. H.   53n82, 65n111
Sievers, J.   62n106
Sinding, M.   27n78
Skinner, C. W.   14n33, 219n26, 226n51, 226n52
Smith, D. M.   218n26, 225n45
Smith, J. K. A.   167n4
Smith, T.   27n78
Sommerstein, A. H.   156n114, 180n51, 189n80, 198n100
Stadter, P. A.   36n23, 37n26, 78n19, 80n30, 81n32, 87n47, 91n59
Stanton, G.   72n3, 73n5
Stark, I.   136n63
Starke-Meyerring, D.   56n89
Stephens, S. A.   121n24, 121n25
Sterling, G. E   31n9, 32n12, 105n98, 105n100, 107
Stibbe, M. W. G.   171n16, 173–74, 177, 178n44
Stock, St. G. W. J.   57n91
Storey, I. C.   198n100
Stovell, B. M   209n3
Strachan, R. H.   169n12
Swain, S.   78n19
Swales, J. M.   7n12

Talbert, C. H.   72–73, 77
Tam, J. C.-C.   8n17, 14n34
Teets, S. C.   57n92, 62n106
Temmerman, K. de   124n30, 133n58
Termini, C.   104n94
Thackeray, H. St. J.   36n21, 63n108
Thatcher, T.   9n19
Thompson, M. M.   30, 212n12
Thornton, J.   41n45
Toher, M.   62n106, 62n107
Tolbert, Mary A.   116n5, 117–18
Too, Y. L.   79n23
Torrance, I. C.   189n80

INDEX OF MODERN AUTHORS

Tsakmakis, A. 38n33, 43n50
Turner, M. 11n27, 12n31

Van der Stockt, L. 89n52
van der Watt, J. G. 219n26
Van Seters, J. 29n2
Vanhoozer, K. J. 167n4
Vermes, G. 64n109
Veyne, P. 36n22
Vines, M. E. 118, 156n111
Von Wahlde, U. C. 211n9
Votaw, C. W. 72n4

Walbank, F. W. 36n21, 41n41, 41n43, 44n54, 45n57, 47n65, 50n73, 179n49
Warren, A. 73n6
Warren, M. J. C. 119, 227n54
Wehrli, F. 76n15

Wellek, R. 73n6
West, S. 155n105
Westermann, C. 239n67
Whitmarsh, T. 117n7, 120n23
Wieneke, J. 198n101
Wills, L. 115n1, 117–18, 154n100, 156n109, 156n111, 158n121
Winston, D. 111n107
Winterbottom, M. 16n36, 16n37
Woodhead, A. G. 37
Wright, Benjamin G. 27n78, 31n10
Wycherley, R. E. 187n75

Yarbro Collins, A. 8n13, 31n9, 74, 230n56

Ziegler, K. 47n65
Zunshine, L. 5–6, 11n26, 12n29, 12n31, 250

Index of Subjects

anger   21, 48, 50, 59–61, 98–99, 113, 115, 124,
   126–30, 137–39, 161–62, 164–65, 190,
   194, 208
antagonism,
   among writers   33, 36–37, 40–41, 43, 45,
     47–48, 53, 65, 90
   and the Fourth Gospel   175, 221, 223, 227,
     239–40
   divine–human   100, 119, 137, 206, 227
audience   2, 15, 182–88
   and aurality   10, 175
   emotions of   20–23, 41, 46, 48, 90, 115, 182
   of the Fourth Gospel   26, 176
   see also readers
authorial intent   1, 9–10, 19, 26, 54–57, 90

beauty   121, 124, 131, 135–37, 156, 161
   and emotion   132, 163–64
   as productive of desire   136, 158
beloved disciple, the   173, 223–26, 244

causes (αἰτίαι)   29, 34–39, 68–69
   and beginnings   48–49, 51
   and pretexts   42, 48–51, 68–70
character (ethical)   16–19, 21, 74, 77–78, 80,
   114
   and attributed motives   85, 92
   changeable or fixed   192–94
characters (dramatis personae)   16–17
   and genre   5
   antagonists   60, 123, 133, 152–53
   character speech   135, 160, 242, 248
   companion type   150, 184, 232, 244–45
   gods as characters   182, 204
   protagonists   2–4, 93, 109, 112, 123, 132–33,
     142, 153, 160, 189, 221, 244
   psychologizing of   39, 43, 64, 72, 83, 88,
     95, 124
chastity ordeals   141–42, 233–34
clairvoyance   217
cognitive narratology   4, 5–14, 37–38, 122,
   250

deixis   124, 180–82, 203, 242
deliberation   123–24, 141–45, 229

desire (ἐπιθυμία)   70, 127–29, 136–38, 138,
   141–42, 144, 175, 188, 192, 205–6, 210–17,
   234–35
dialogue   76, 143, 145, 169, 179, 184, 188,
   228–29, 235, 238, 241–46
discrepant awareness   67, 144, 150, 187–88,
   190, 195, 206–7, 238, 247
disposition   20, 50–51, 59, 61, 66–67, 83, 122,
   128, 139–40, 152, 158, 188, 193–94, 225
divine priming   183, 188, 210, 238, 240–41
   and epistemic superiority   195, 203, 238,
     247
dreams   163, 184, 192, 197, 204

emotion, passions (πάθη)   91–92, 115, 124–32,
   141, 145, 158, 163–65, 190, 194, 228–29
   and motivation   190
   and trauma   131–2, 228
   management of   16, 111–12
   proxies for   125, 130, 132, 162–63, 242
encomium   75, 78–80

Farewell Discourses   176, 213, 215, 224
fear   38, 59–60, 108–9, 161, 189–90, 199,
   205–6, 229–30
focalization   93, 134–36, 147, 149–50, 189,
   201, 217
   and point of view   134
Fourth Gospel
   and characterization   13–14
   genre of   5, 26
   unity of   168–71

gender   48, 131, 137–42, 152, 160, 227
genre
   and constellations of texts   27
   and family resemblance   6–7
   conventions   1–8, 31–40, 75–92, 120–32,
     179–86, and *passim*
   sets/ecologies   7, 75, 179
Gospels, genre of   8, 71–73
grief   130, 150, 164, 181, 189–90, 194, 232–33

Herod   62–69

INDEX OF SUBJECTS

individuals 10, 37–38, 44
   and groups 50–52
interiority 81–85, 110, 122, 143, 189, 195,
   242–44
investigation (ἱστορία) 28, 33–36, 51

John, Gospel of (*see* Fourth Gospel)
joy 120, 127, 129–30, 163–64, 215, 232

love (ἀγάπη, ἔρως, φιλία) 127–28, 130–31,
   228, 230–33
   at first sight 131, 156–57

madness 180, 184–85
   and unfiltered speech 244
memory 10, 144
messenger
   figure 188, 190, 197–98, 245
   speech 59, 197, 201–2
mimesis 106
   ethical imitation 74, 76–77, 80, 83, 90,
     111–14, 211, 214, 219–31
mimesis of action 16–17, 21–22, 80
mind 6 and *passim*
misunderstanding, misperception, mistake
   8, 96, 124, 135, 146–53, 162–63, 182–83,
   234–37, 242–43
monologue 25, 68, 135, 143, 145, 185–86, 197,
   244–46
Moses 54, 57–62, 102–14, 196–207, 224, 239

narrative
   cognitive dimension of 14, 68, 96, 98, 100
narrator 3, 135
   narrator speech 38, 67, 135–36, 152, 238,
     242
   omniscient 3, 134–36, 146, 175, 182,
     201–3, 237
   unreliable 3, 135, 149

participles as conveyers of cognitive states
   67, 125, 130
performance criticism 175
peripeteia 18, 47–48, 201–2
piety 107–14, 150, 193, 222–26
pity 21, 46, 48, 128–30, 141, 164, 183, 229, 233
plagiarism 88

plot 2–3, 16, 119, 121, 173, 175, 177, 183, 204–5,
   233, 240
progymnasmata 24–25, 28, 140

questions 183–84

reader response criticism 11
readers 4, 10–12
   effects on the mind of 46–47, 108
   epistemic advantage of 144–45, 149, 210,
     240
   expectations of 24–25, 45, 247
   moral formation of 71, 77, 90, 111, 222,
     226
recognition (ἀναγνώρισις) 18, 115, 117, 124,
     145–51, 160–63, 175, 177, 203, 205,
     227–28, 240, 247–48
   and nobility 160–61
   gradual 145–48, 195, 228
   of circumstance 145, 148–49, 162, 188
   partial 161, 247–48
   see also tokens
   type–scene 119
   vertical 160
represented thought 1, 3–5, 145
   and motivation 101, 136
   and dilemma, struggle 164

Scheintod 147–49
self–control 96, 131, 137–38, 164, 228
self, the 81, 85, 123, 125, 143, 249
sententiae
   and character types 138, 140–41
Solon 77, 85, 92–102, 221, 224
speech
   direct 68, 123, 135, 143, 172, 180
   filtered 182–85, 192, 206, 244
   in character (ἠθοποιία, προσωποποιία) 25
   indirect 122, 143, 184
   internal 142–44, 158–60
Stoicism
   and the emotions 16, 126
   Stoic sage 111

theory of mind 5, 11–12, 20–22, 34–35, 46,
     53, 59, 81, 88–93, 101, 142, 151–52, 163,
     180, 190–91, 194, 203–4

INDEX OF SUBJECTS

virtue   79, 82–85, 90, 95, 98–101, 107–14, 192,
   222
   and vice   74–76, 102, 107, 109–10, 128
vividness (ἐναργεία)   11, 15, 23, 41

what is fitting, appropriate, (τὸ πρέπον,
   οἰκεῖος)   15, 20, 23–25, 33, 42–43, 94, 140,
   222
will (τὸ θέλημα)   61, 70, 210–15, (*see also*
   desire)